THE JEKYLL ISLAND CHRONICLES

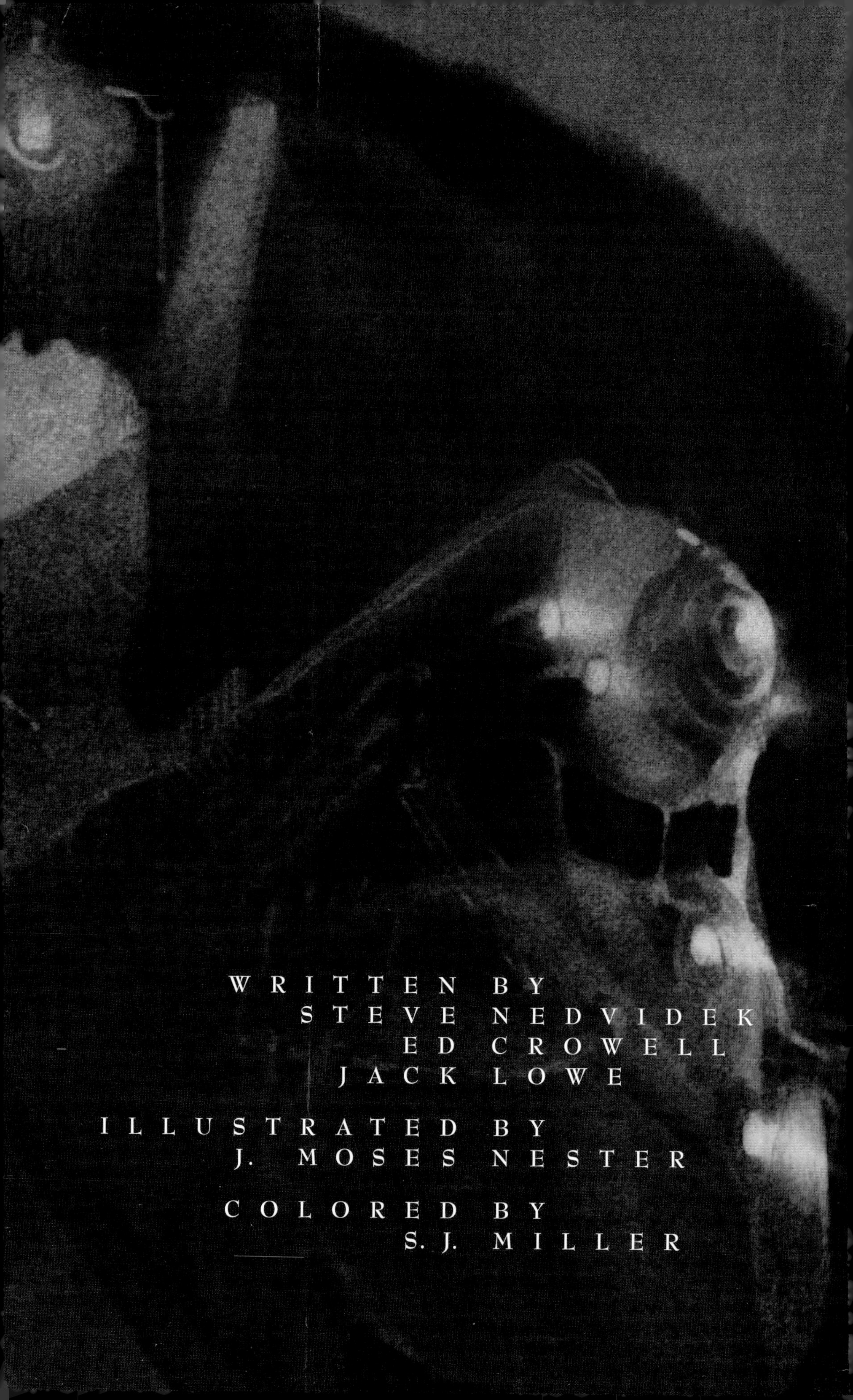

WRITTEN BY
STEVE NEDVIDEK
ED CROWELL
JACK LOWE

ILLUSTRATED BY
J. MOSES NESTER

COLORED BY
S. J. MILLER

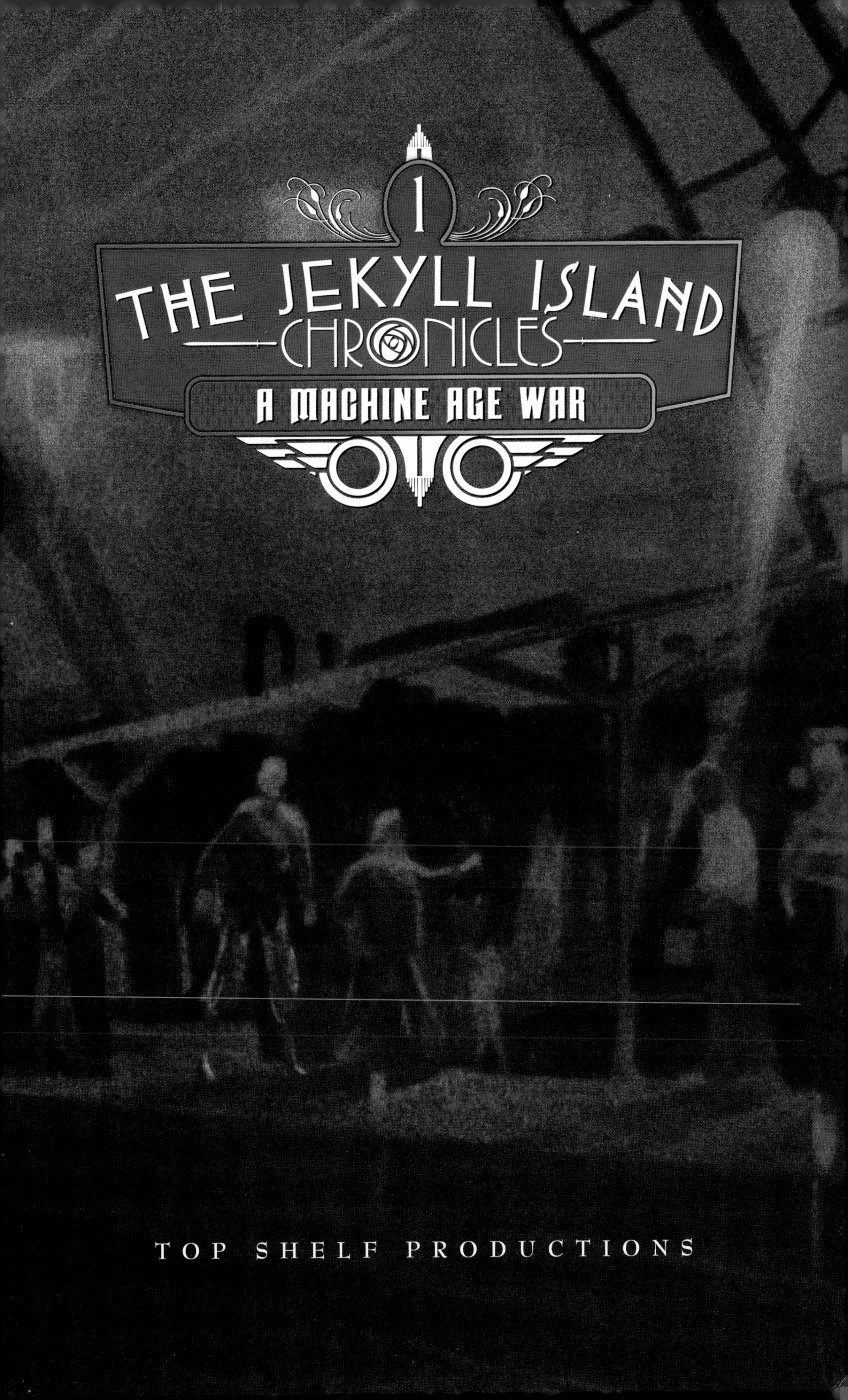

1

THE JEKYLL ISLAND CHRONICLES

A MACHINE AGE WAR

TOP SHELF PRODUCTIONS

The Jekyll Island Chronicles (Book One): A Machine Age War © 2016
Steve Nedvidek, Ed Crowell, and Jack Lowe.

Published by Top Shelf Productions, PO Box 1282, Marietta, GA 30061-1282,
USA. Top Shelf Productions is an imprint of IDW Publishing, a division of Idea
and Design Works, LLC. Offices: 2765 Truxtun Road, San Diego, CA 92106. Top
Shelf Productions®, the Top Shelf logo, Idea and Design Works®, and the IDW logo
are registered trademarks of Idea and Design Works, LLC. All Rights Reserved.
With the exception of small excerpts of artwork used for review purposes, none of
the contents of this publication may be reprinted without the permission of IDW
Publishing. IDW Publishing does not read or accept unsolicited submissions of
ideas, stories, or artwork.

Editor-in-Chief: Chris Staros.

Edited by Chris Staros with Zac Boone.
Colored by S.J. Miller
Designed by J. Moses Nester & Chris Ross.

Visit our online catalog at www.topshelfcomix.com.

Printed in Korea.

ISBN 978-1-60309-388-0

20   19   18   17   6   5   4   3   2

"To my wife, Sue, and my children, Michael, Emily, and Alex, for putting up
with this mid-life crisis with extreme joy, encouragement, and patience.
To my father, Anthony Nedvidek, who taught me how to dream. To Ed and
Jack, for all their work and dedication throughout this amazing journey.
And to God, who has blessed my life with imagination and art and has been
lovingly opening doors along the way."
—Steve Nedvidek

"To my wife, Cynthia, and our children, Kayla and Thomas, for their love
and for serving as inspiration, critics, and muses. To my co-authors, Steve
and Jack, for friendships that preceded—and survived—working together!
You are all gifts from God in my life."
—Ed Crowell

"To my wife, Dawn, and children, Olivia, Adam, and Mary, for their
unfailing love and enthusiastic encouragement. To my co-authors, Steve
and Ed, for their amazing creativity and collaboration, and for friendships
that reflect God's love for me."
—Jack Lowe

To United States Veterans. The authors hope this work in some small
way acknowledges the sacrifice of those who have defended our nation
and its people in WWI and all wars—thank you.

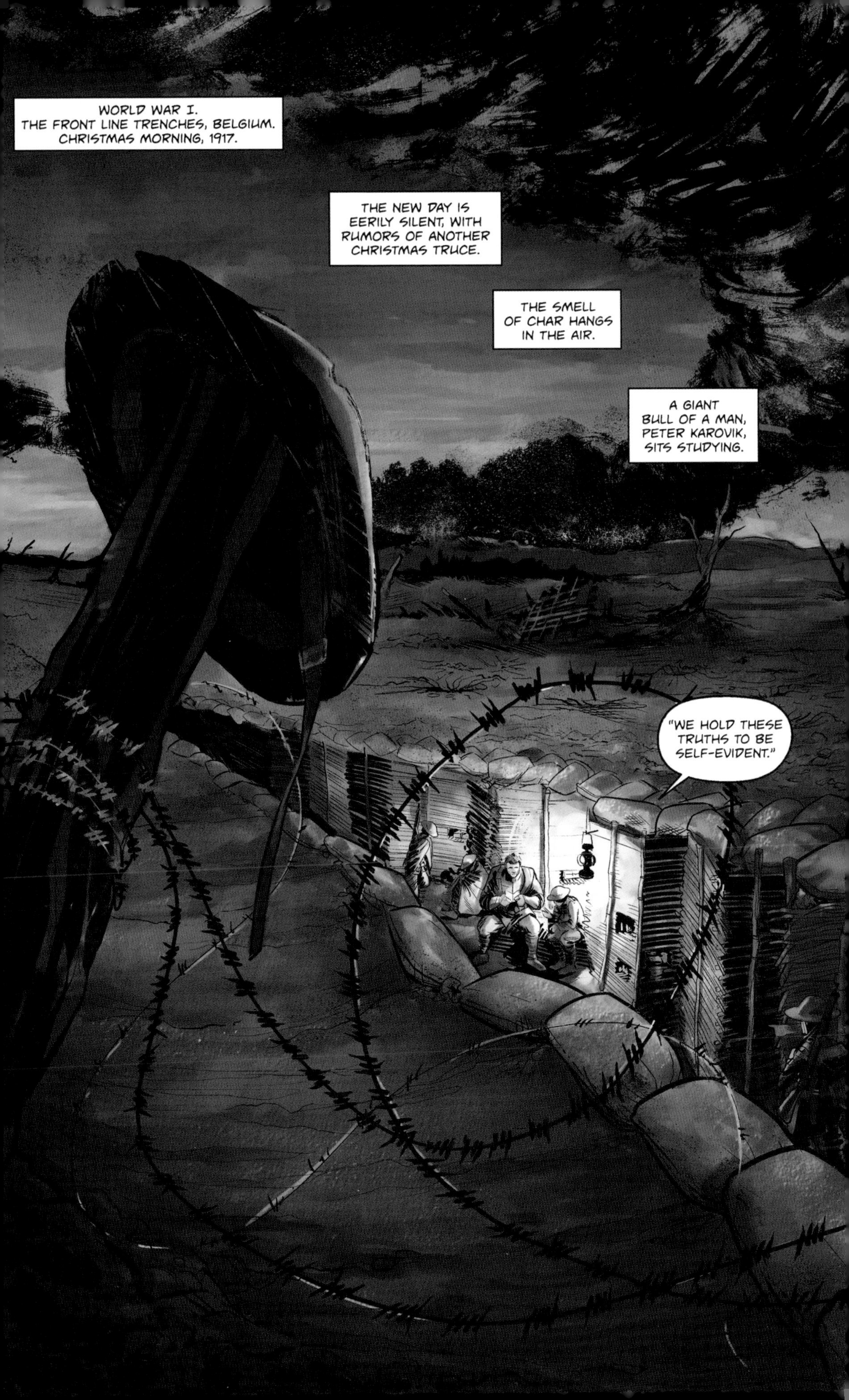
WORLD WAR I.
THE FRONT LINE TRENCHES, BELGIUM.
CHRISTMAS MORNING, 1917.
THE NEW DAY IS EERILY SILENT, WITH RUMORS OF ANOTHER CHRISTMAS TRUCE.
THE SMELL OF CHAR HANGS IN THE AIR.
A GIANT BULL OF A MAN, PETER KAROVIK, SITS STUDYING.
"WE HOLD THESE TRUTHS TO BE SELF-EVIDENT."

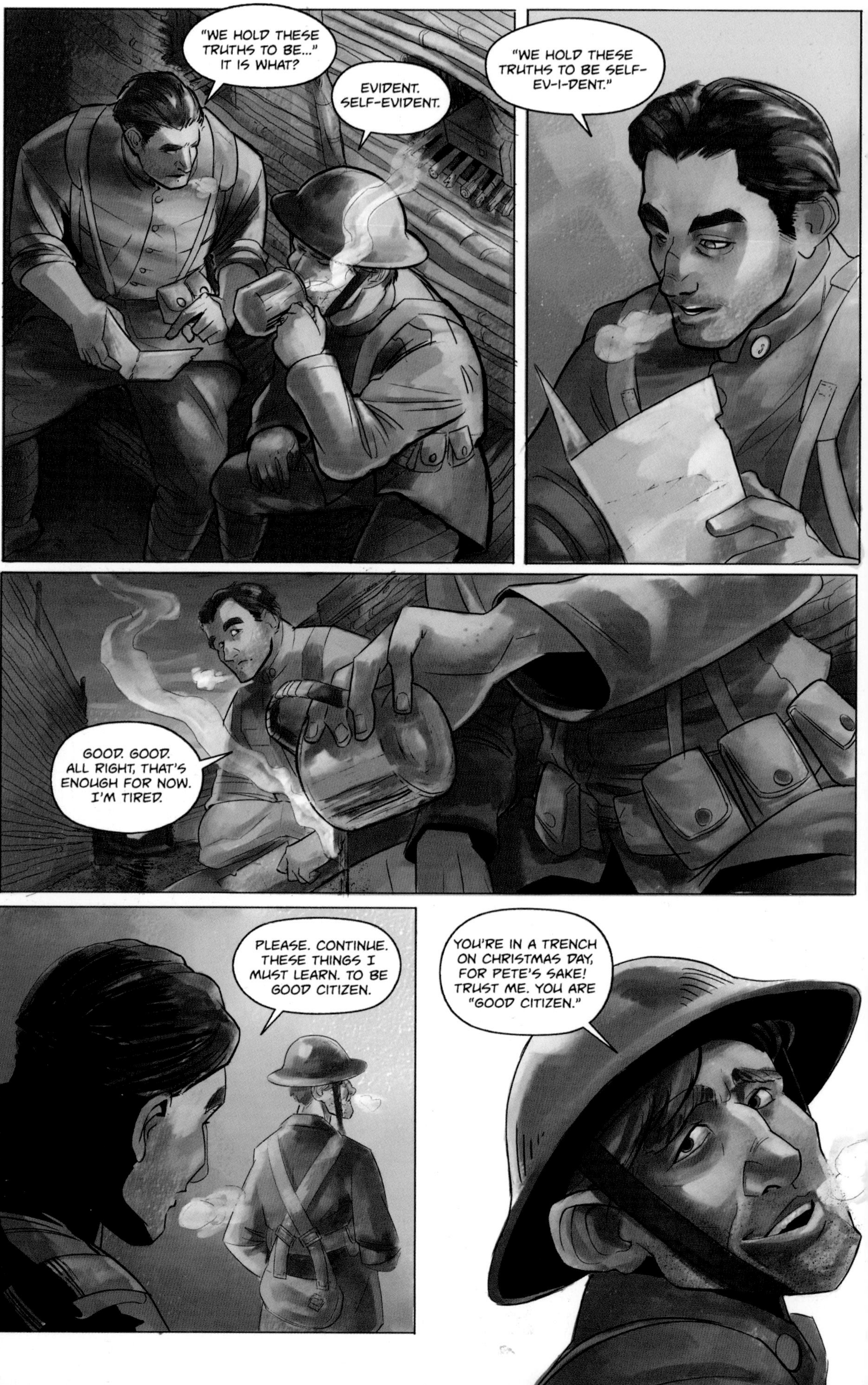
"WE HOLD THESE TRUTHS TO BE..." IT IS WHAT?
EVIDENT. SELF-EVIDENT.
"WE HOLD THESE TRUTHS TO BE SELF-EV-I-DENT."
GOOD. GOOD. ALL RIGHT, THAT'S ENOUGH FOR NOW. I'M TIRED.
PLEASE. CONTINUE. THESE THINGS I MUST LEARN. TO BE GOOD CITIZEN.
YOU'RE IN A TRENCH ON CHRISTMAS DAY, FOR PETE'S SAKE! TRUST ME. YOU ARE "GOOD CITIZEN."

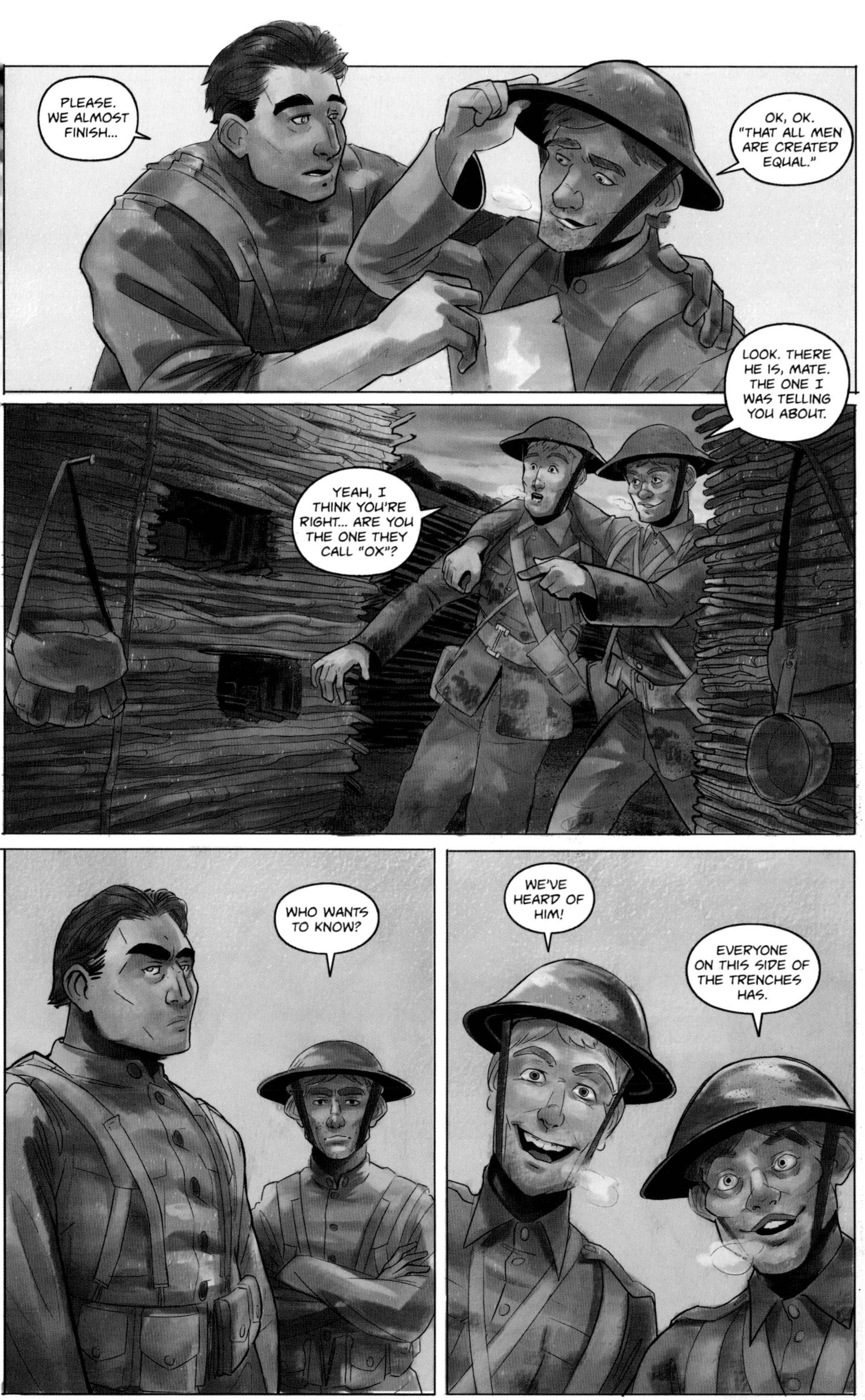
PLEASE. WE ALMOST FINISH...
OK, OK. "THAT ALL MEN ARE CREATED EQUAL."
LOOK. THERE HE IS, MATE. THE ONE I WAS TELLING YOU ABOUT.
YEAH, I THINK YOU'RE RIGHT... ARE YOU THE ONE THEY CALL "OX"?
WHO WANTS TO KNOW?
WE'VE HEARD OF HIM!
EVERYONE ON THIS SIDE OF THE TRENCHES HAS.

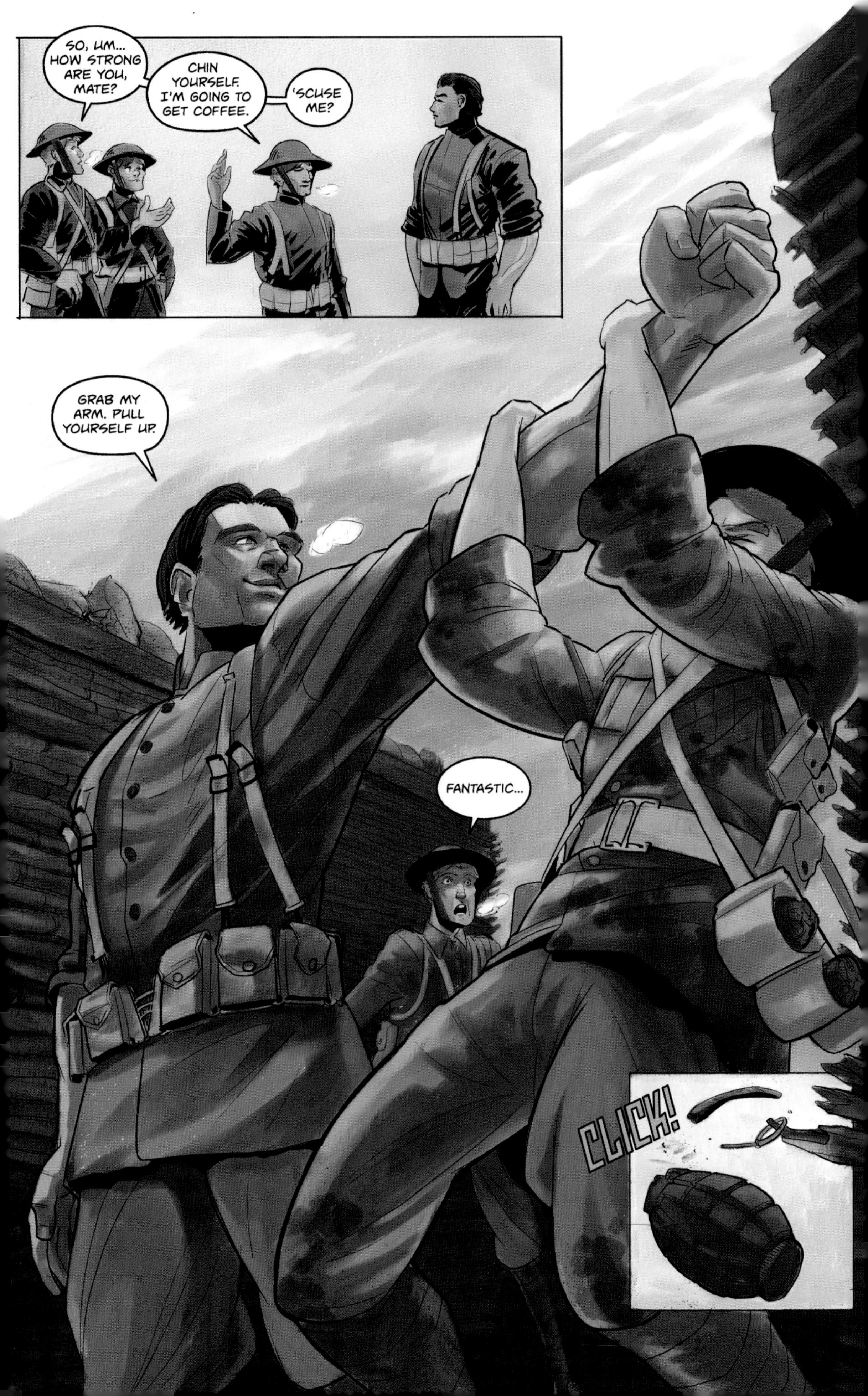
SO, UM... HOW STRONG ARE YOU, MATE?
CHIN YOURSELF. I'M GOING TO GET COFFEE.
'SCUSE ME?
GRAB MY ARM. PULL YOURSELF UP.
FANTASTIC...
CLICK!

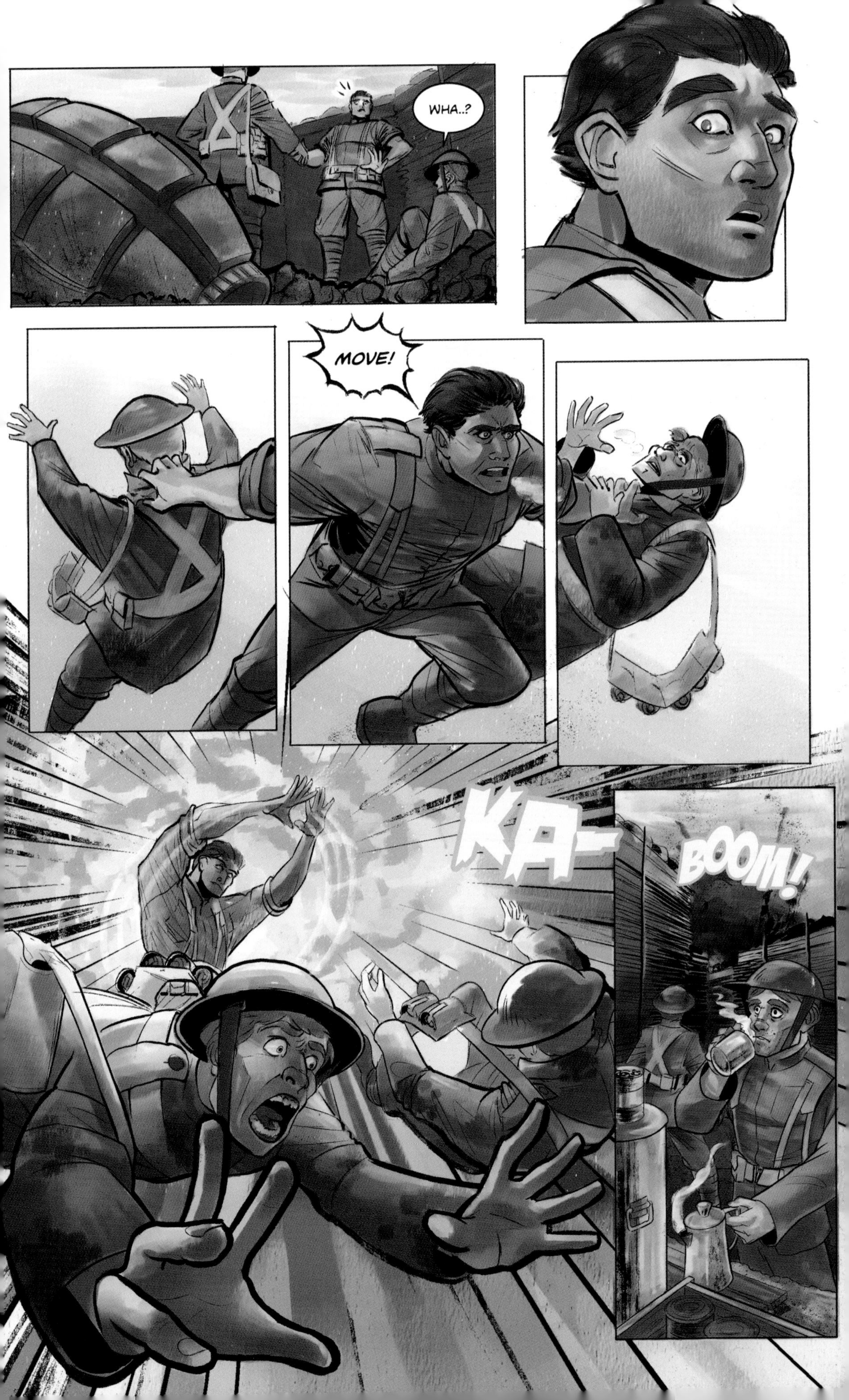
WHA..?
MOVE!
KA-
BOOM!

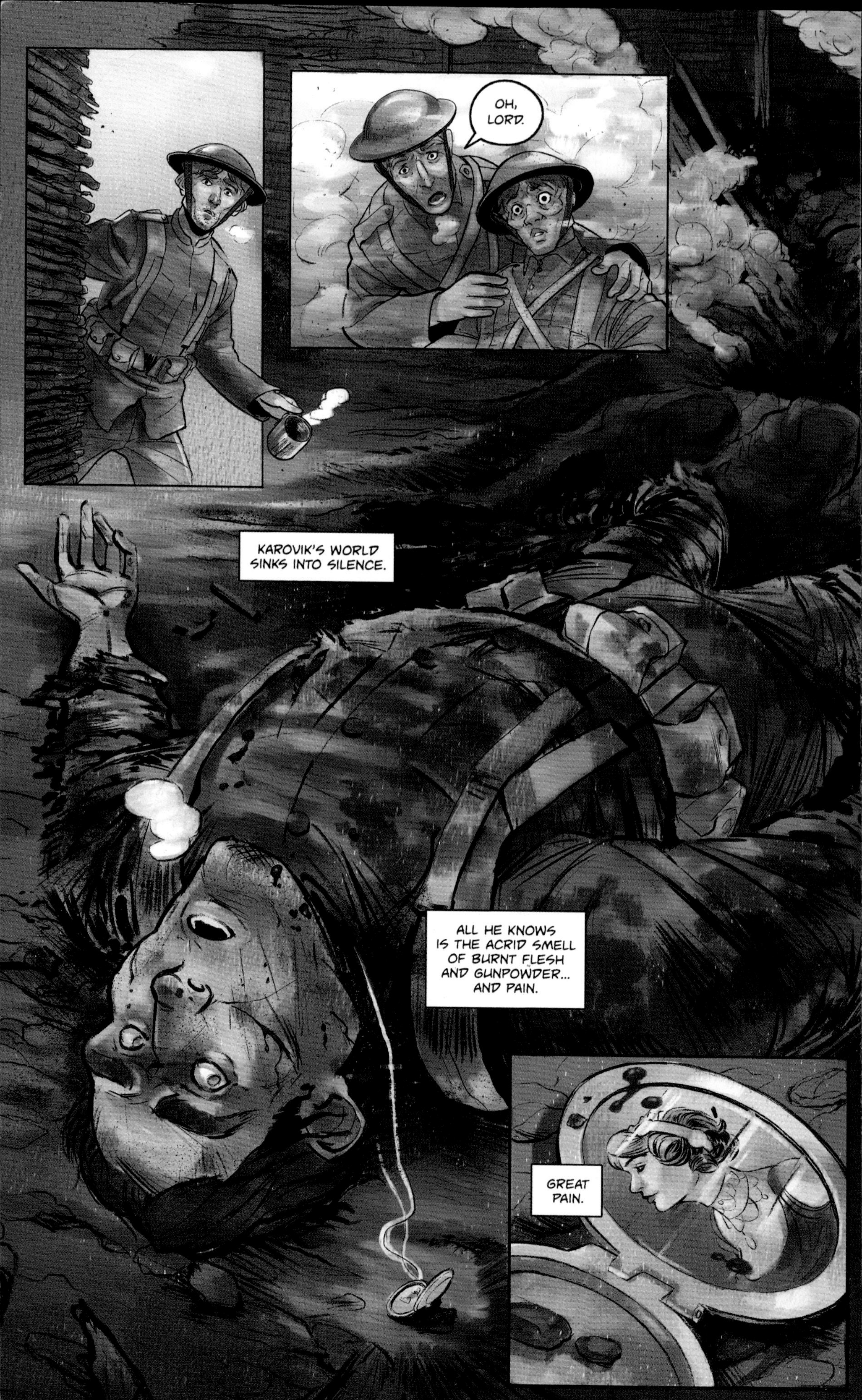
OH, LORD.
KAROVIK'S WORLD SINKS INTO SILENCE.
ALL HE KNOWS IS THE ACRID SMELL OF BURNT FLESH AND GUNPOWDER... AND PAIN.
GREAT PAIN.

THE DAILY ARGUS

ONDAY, NOVEMBER 11, 1918 — LAST EDITION — PRICE: FIVE CENTS

PEACE!

ARMISTICE IS SIGNED!

Official Announcement Made of Agreement Bringing Hostilities to a Clos

CONQUERED ENEMY YIELDS TO TERMS OF MARSHAL FOCH

"This is not a peace. It is an armistice for twenty years."

Washington, Nov. 11 -- (Flash.)
The armistice has been signed.
Timed 2:55 a.m.

Lorem ipsum dolor sit amet, consectetur adipiscing elit. Sed nec mauris pulvinar, ultricies turpis eget, lobortis mauris. Morbi finibus aliquam turpis, vitae hendrerit lectus ultrices vel. Duis maximus erat eget nisl varius, quis consequat mauris molestie. Phasellus fermentum, purus eget interdum tempor, enim arcu placerat augue, a viverra velit orci lacus. Etiam fringilla lacus a quam scelerisque, non euismod velit egestas. Nunc facilisis leo eget enim commodo, non rutrum urna. Nunc sit amet, efficitur tincidunt massa rhoncus sit amet. Vestibulum pharetra felis sodales sollicitudin. In pulvinar bibendum arcu scelerisque. Cras a dui. Sed vel massa pulvinar, efficitur sapien eget, bibendum mauris. Morbi finibus aliquam turpis, vitae hendrerit lectus ultrices vel. Duis maximus erat eget nisl varius, quis consequat.

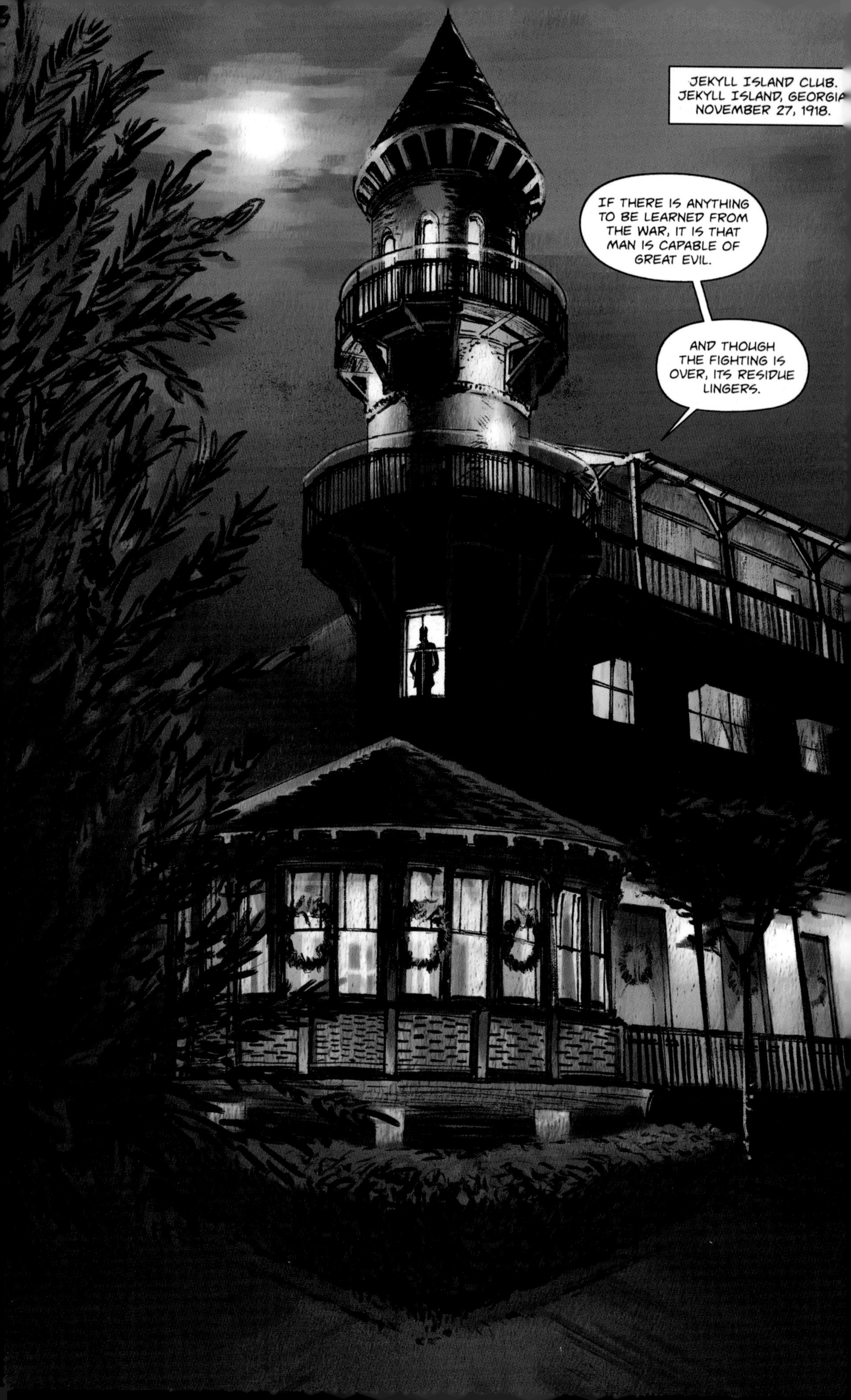
JEKYLL ISLAND CLUB.
JEKYLL ISLAND, GEORGIA
NOVEMBER 27, 1918.
IF THERE IS ANYTHING TO BE LEARNED FROM THE WAR, IT IS THAT MAN IS CAPABLE OF GREAT EVIL.
AND THOUGH THE FIGHTING IS OVER, ITS RESIDUE LINGERS.

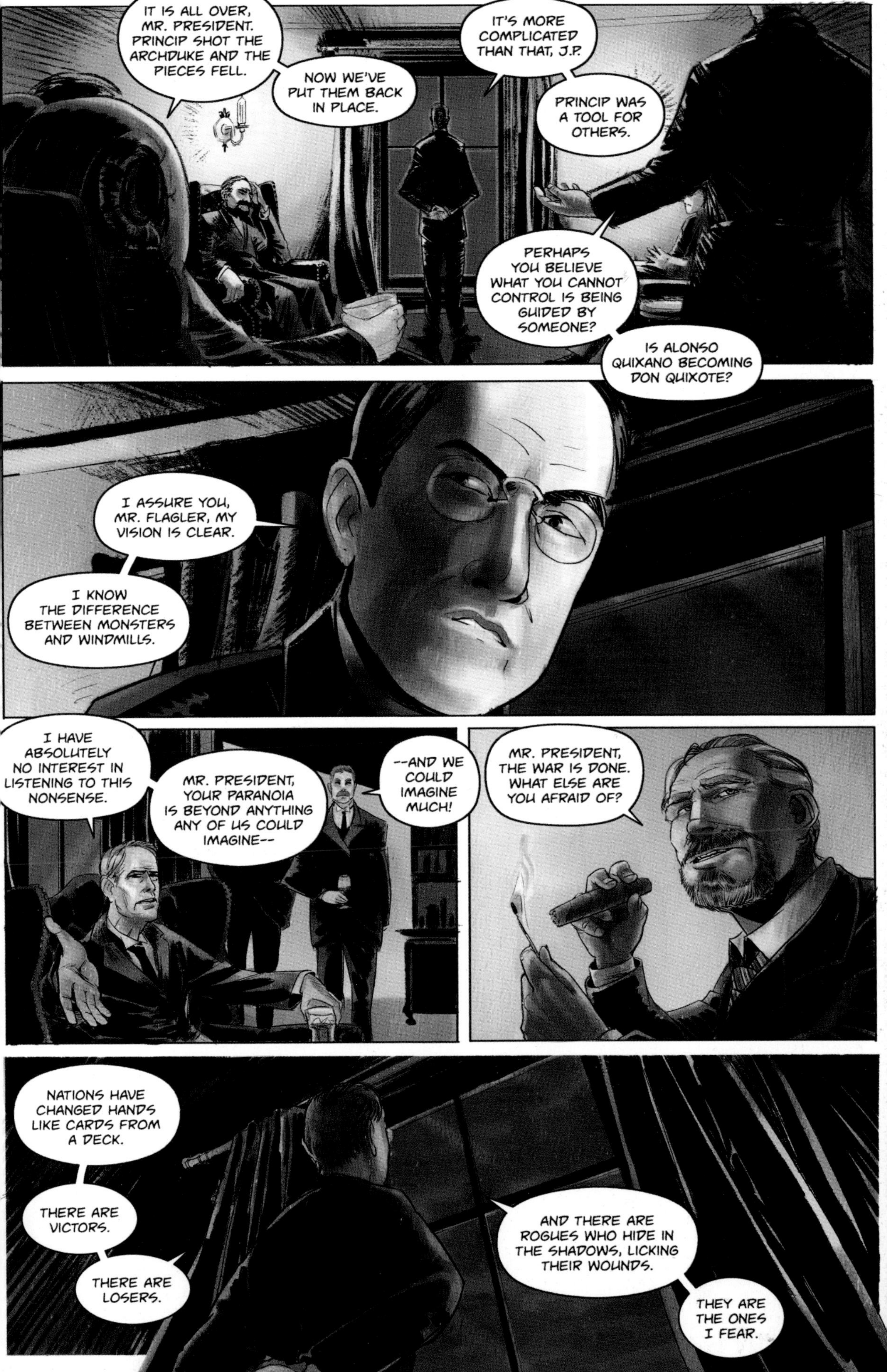
IT IS ALL OVER, MR. PRESIDENT. PRINCIP SHOT THE ARCHDUKE AND THE PIECES FELL.
NOW WE'VE PUT THEM BACK IN PLACE.
IT'S MORE COMPLICATED THAN THAT, J.P.
PRINCIP WAS A TOOL FOR OTHERS.
PERHAPS YOU BELIEVE WHAT YOU CANNOT CONTROL IS BEING GUIDED BY SOMEONE?
IS ALONSO QUIXANO BECOMING DON QUIXOTE?
I ASSURE YOU, MR. FLAGLER, MY VISION IS CLEAR.
I KNOW THE DIFFERENCE BETWEEN MONSTERS AND WINDMILLS.
I HAVE ABSOLUTELY NO INTEREST IN LISTENING TO THIS NONSENSE.
MR. PRESIDENT, YOUR PARANOIA IS BEYOND ANYTHING ANY OF US COULD IMAGINE--
--AND WE COULD IMAGINE MUCH!
MR. PRESIDENT, THE WAR IS DONE. WHAT ELSE ARE YOU AFRAID OF?
NATIONS HAVE CHANGED HANDS LIKE CARDS FROM A DECK.
THERE ARE VICTORS.
THERE ARE LOSERS.
AND THERE ARE ROGUES WHO HIDE IN THE SHADOWS, LICKING THEIR WOUNDS.
THEY ARE THE ONES I FEAR.

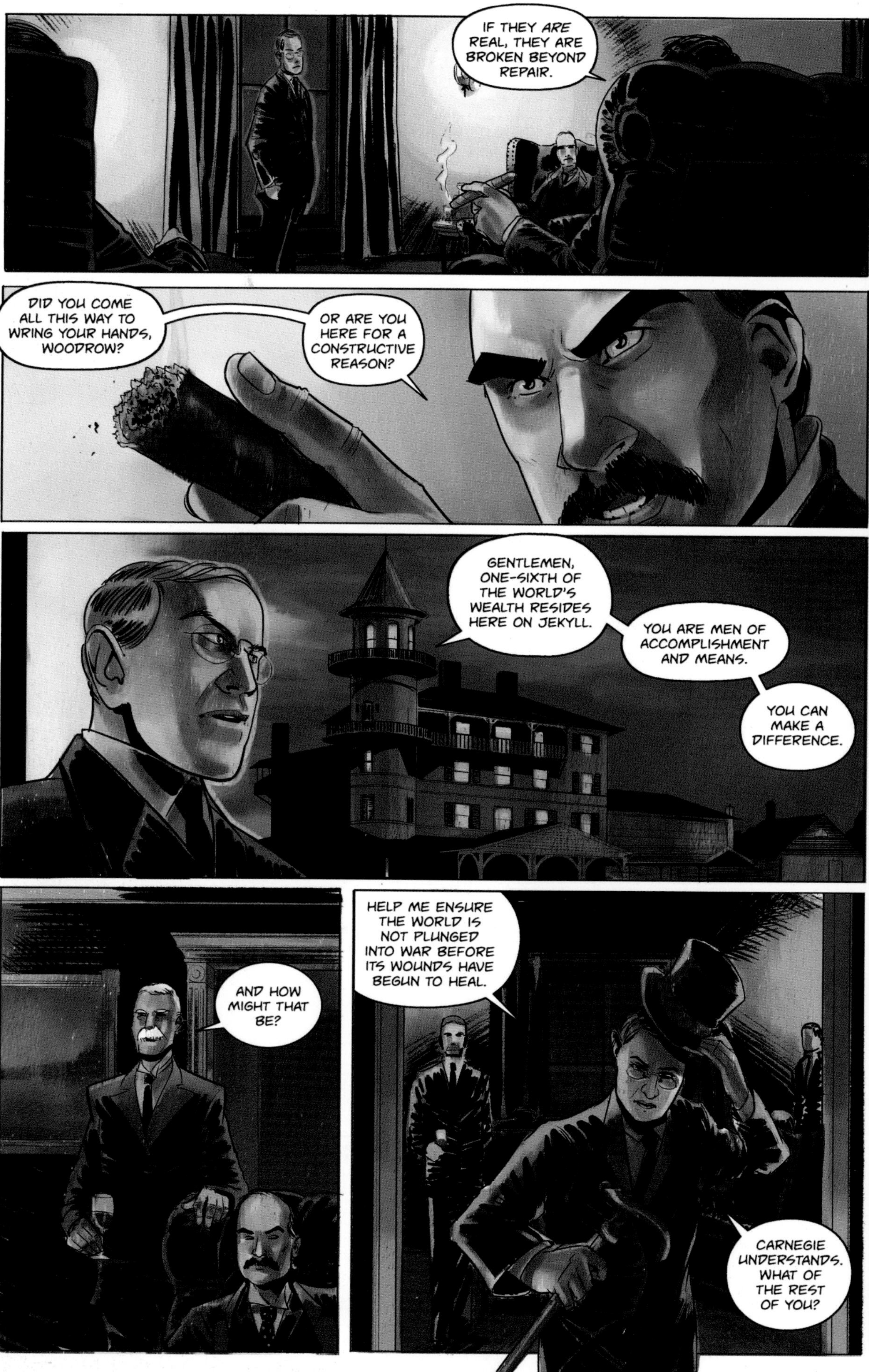
IF THEY *ARE* REAL, THEY ARE BROKEN BEYOND REPAIR.
DID YOU COME ALL THIS WAY TO WRING YOUR HANDS, WOODROW?
OR ARE YOU HERE FOR A CONSTRUCTIVE REASON?
GENTLEMEN, ONE-SIXTH OF THE WORLD'S WEALTH RESIDES HERE ON JEKYLL.
YOU ARE MEN OF ACCOMPLISHMENT AND MEANS.
YOU CAN MAKE A DIFFERENCE.
AND HOW MIGHT THAT BE?
HELP ME ENSURE THE WORLD IS NOT PLUNGED INTO WAR BEFORE ITS WOUNDS HAVE BEGUN TO HEAL.
CARNEGIE UNDERSTANDS. WHAT OF THE REST OF YOU?

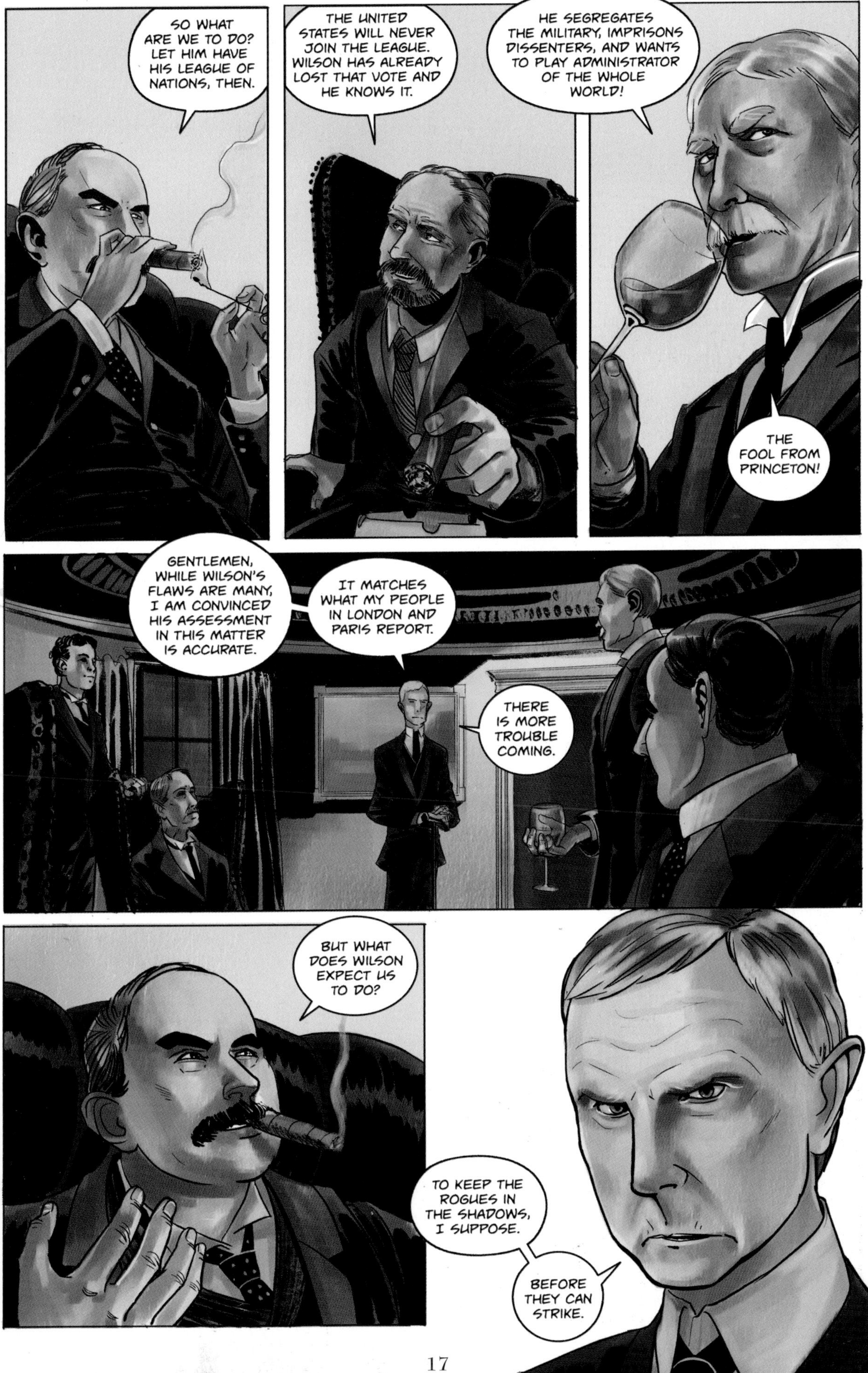
SO WHAT ARE WE TO DO? LET HIM HAVE HIS LEAGUE OF NATIONS, THEN.
THE UNITED STATES WILL NEVER JOIN THE LEAGUE. WILSON HAS ALREADY LOST THAT VOTE AND HE KNOWS IT.
HE SEGREGATES THE MILITARY, IMPRISONS DISSENTERS, AND WANTS TO PLAY ADMINISTRATOR OF THE WHOLE WORLD!
THE FOOL FROM PRINCETON!
GENTLEMEN, WHILE WILSON'S FLAWS ARE MANY, I AM CONVINCED HIS ASSESSMENT IN THIS MATTER IS ACCURATE.
IT MATCHES WHAT MY PEOPLE IN LONDON AND PARIS REPORT.
THERE IS MORE TROUBLE COMING.
BUT WHAT DOES WILSON EXPECT US TO DO?
TO KEEP THE ROGUES IN THE SHADOWS, I SUPPOSE.
BEFORE THEY CAN STRIKE.

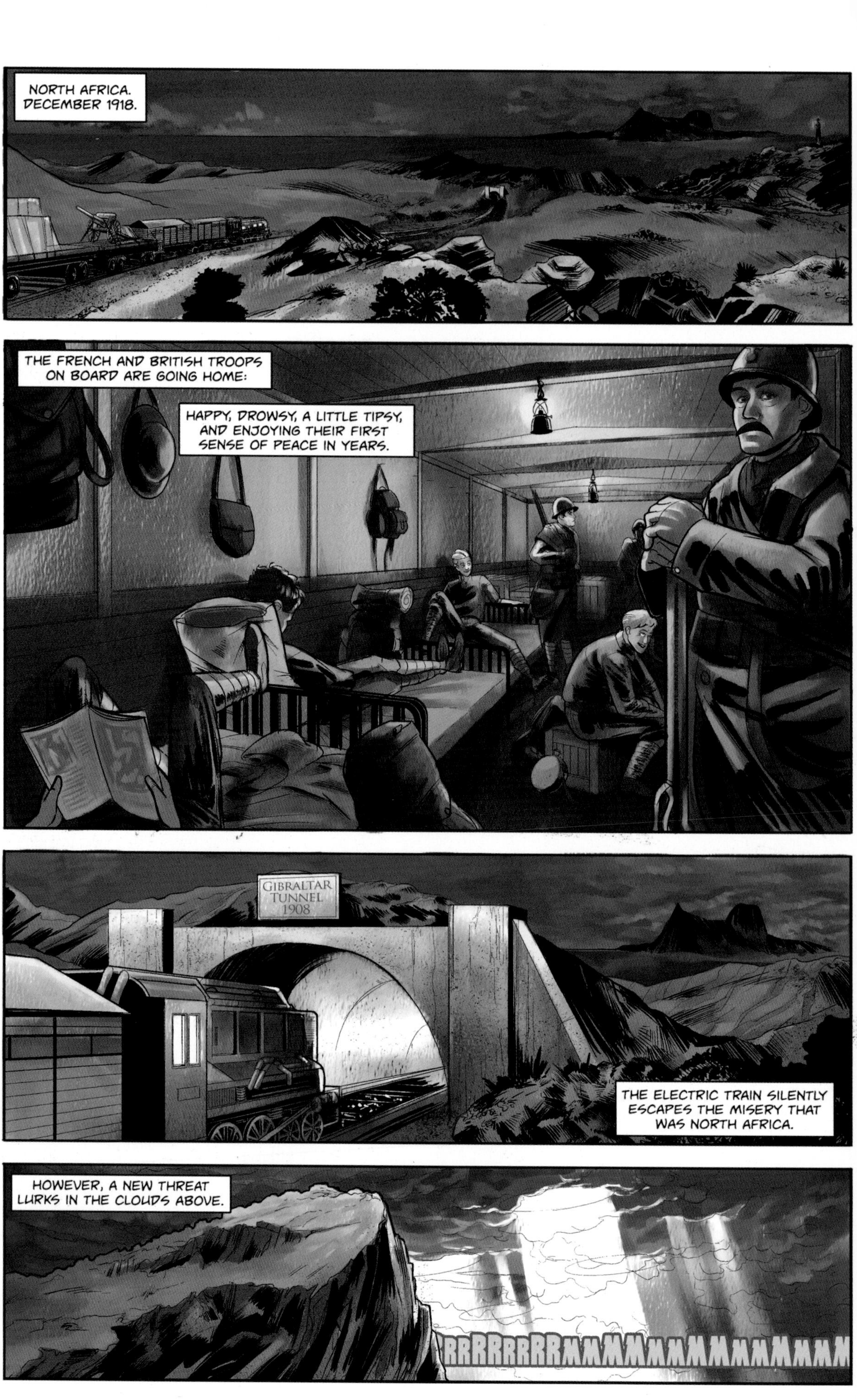
NORTH AFRICA.
DECEMBER 1918.
THE FRENCH AND BRITISH TROOPS ON BOARD ARE GOING HOME:
HAPPY, DROWSY, A LITTLE TIPSY, AND ENJOYING THEIR FIRST SENSE OF PEACE IN YEARS.
GIBRALTAR TUNNEL 1908
THE ELECTRIC TRAIN SILENTLY ESCAPES THE MISERY THAT WAS NORTH AFRICA.
HOWEVER, A NEW THREAT LURKS IN THE CLOUDS ABOVE.
RRRRRRRRMMMMMMMMMMMMMMMMM

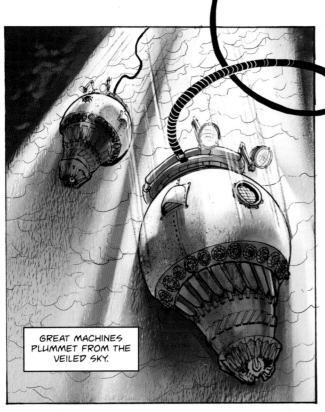

DOWN THEY SINK...

SPLASH!

GREAT MACHINES PLUMMET FROM THE VEILED SKY.

...TEETH SPINNING AND GRINDING...

...SEEKING THE TUNNEL BENEATH THE SEA.

WHHHIIRRRRR

PAK!

CRUNCH!

SECURE THE CABLE TO THE MIDDLE RAIL!

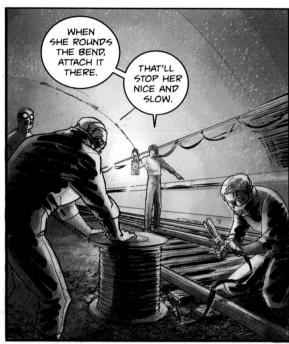

WHEN SHE ROUNDS THE BEND, ATTACH IT THERE.

THAT'LL STOP HER NICE AND SLOW.

LOOK! THE DRILL!

SHE'LL JUMP THE TRACKS!

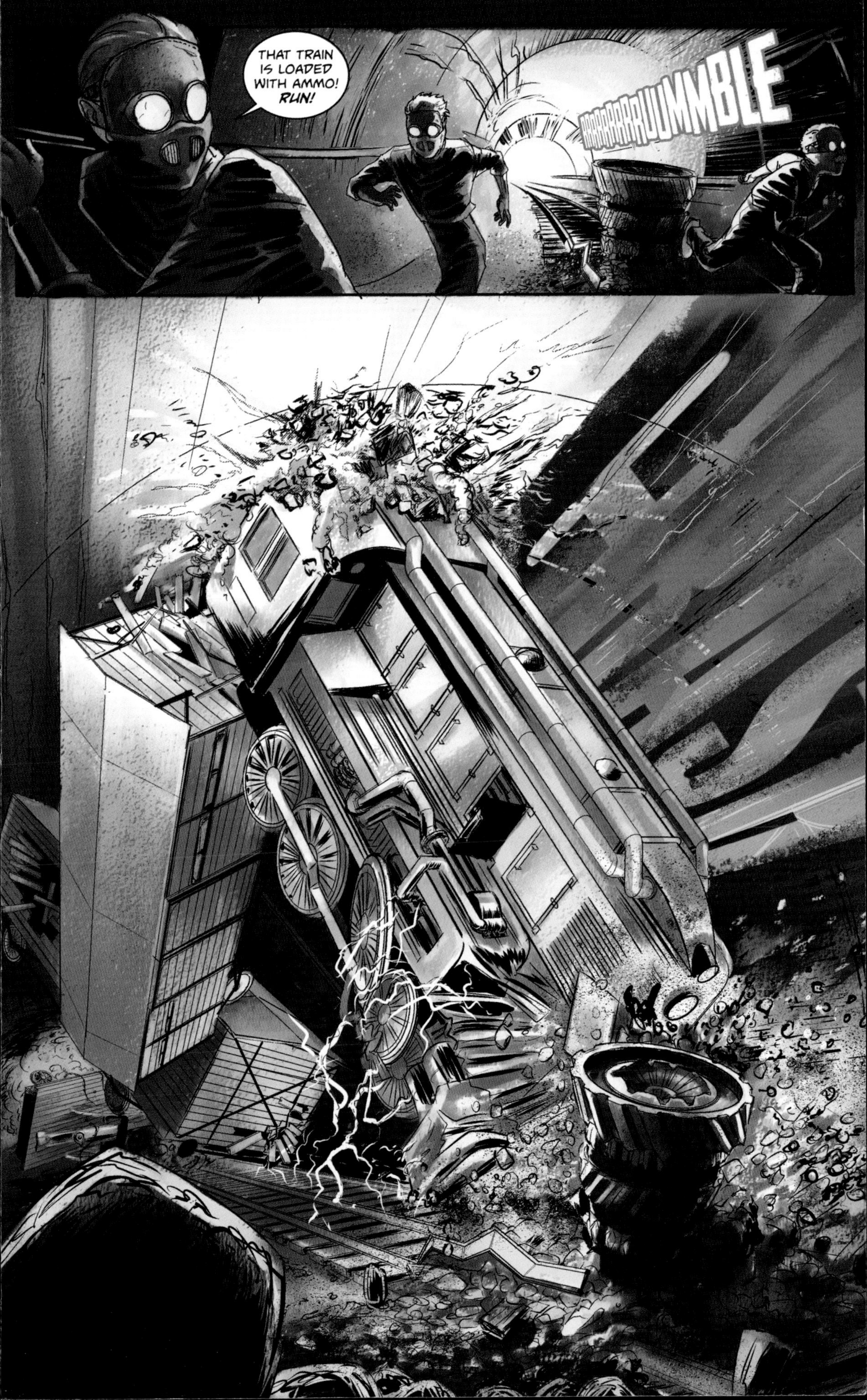
THAT TRAIN IS LOADED WITH AMMO! RUN!
RRRRRRRRRUUMMBLE

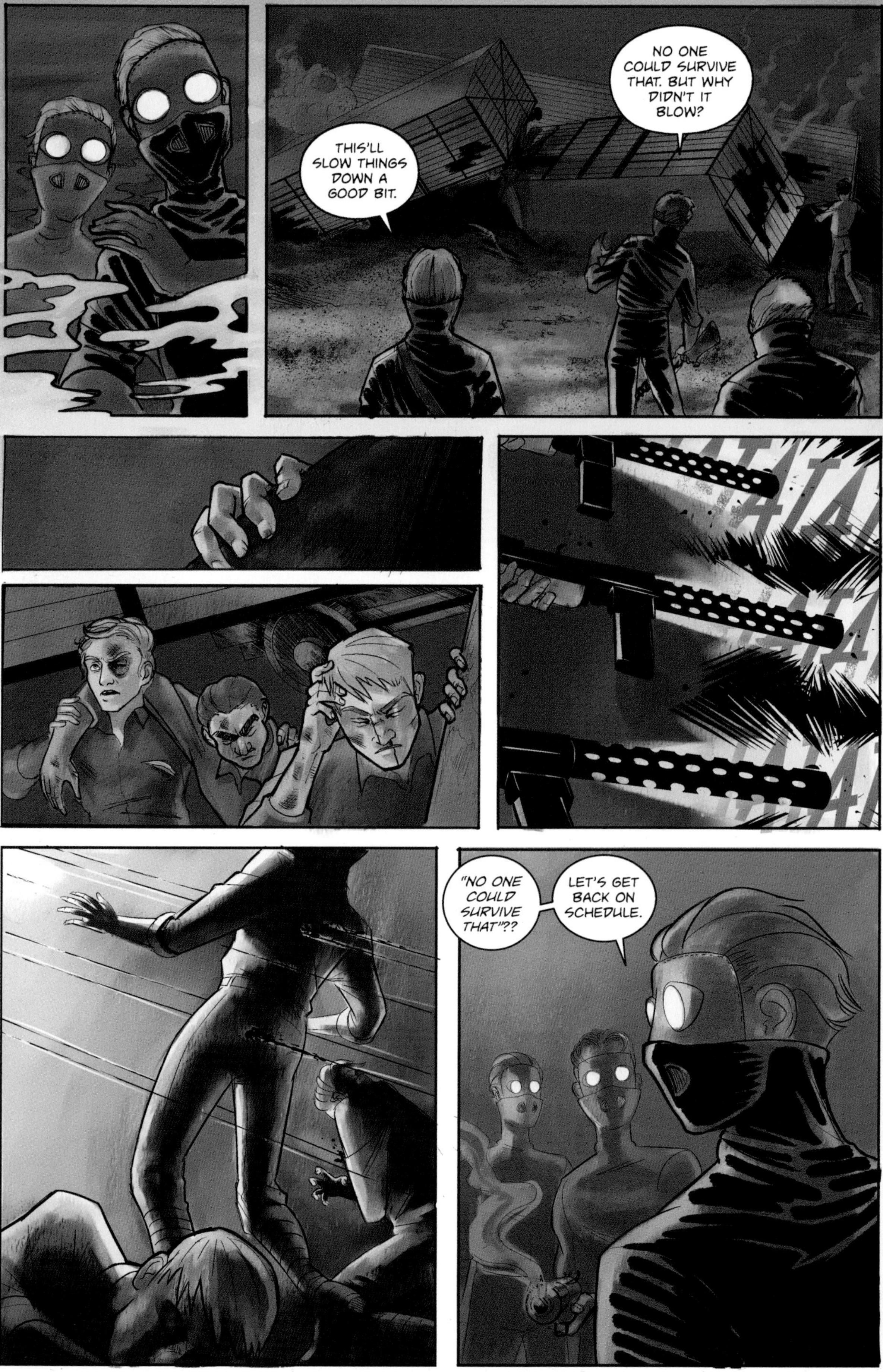
THIS'LL SLOW THINGS DOWN A GOOD BIT.
NO ONE COULD SURVIVE THAT. BUT WHY DIDN'T IT BLOW?
"NO ONE COULD SURVIVE THAT"??
LET'S GET BACK ON SCHEDULE.

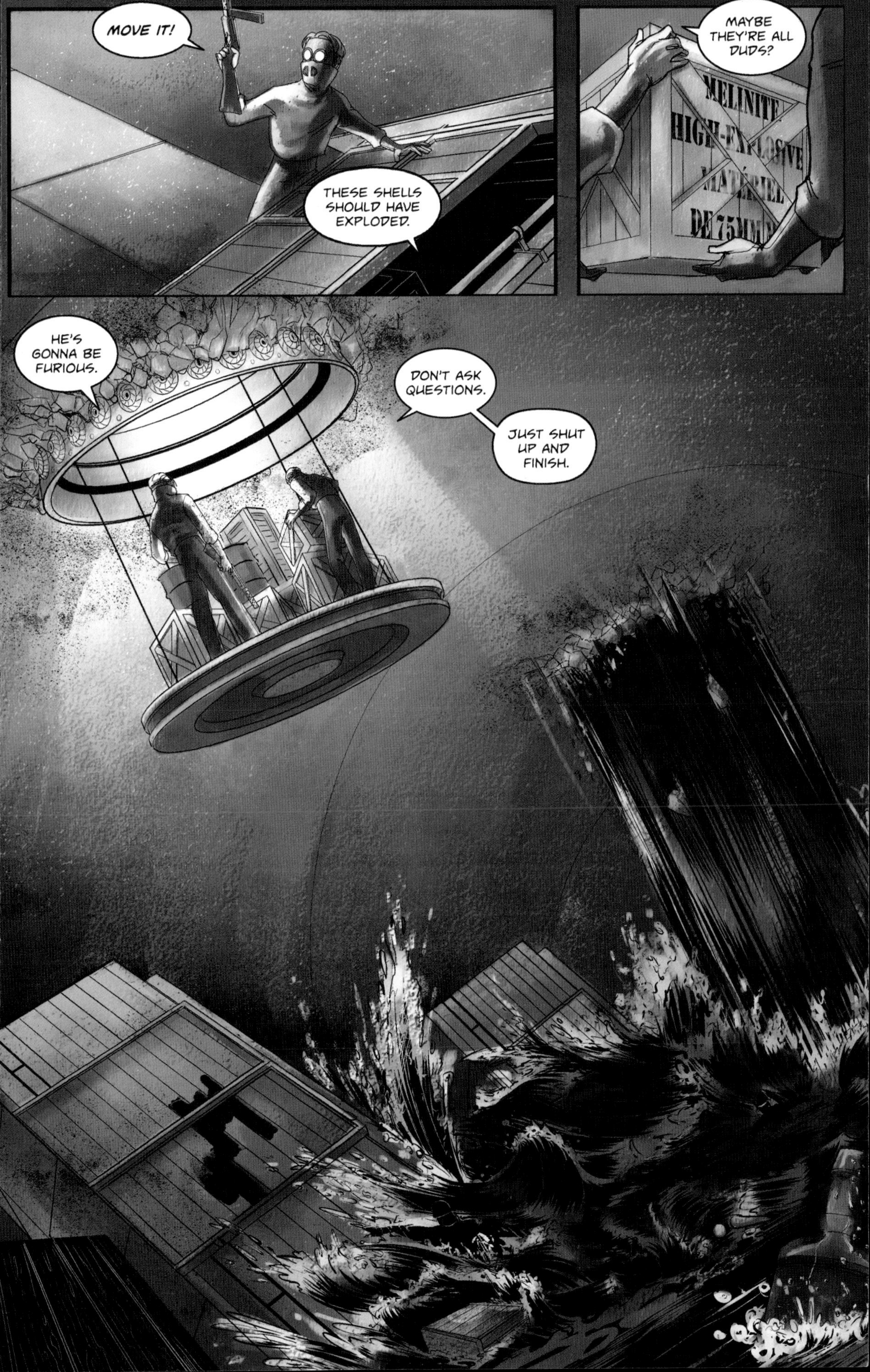
MOVE IT!
THESE SHELLS SHOULD HAVE EXPLODED.
MAYBE THEY'RE ALL DUDS?
MELINITE HIGH-EXPLOSIVE MATÉRIEL DE 75MM
HE'S GONNA BE FURIOUS.
DON'T ASK QUESTIONS.
JUST SHUT UP AND FINISH.

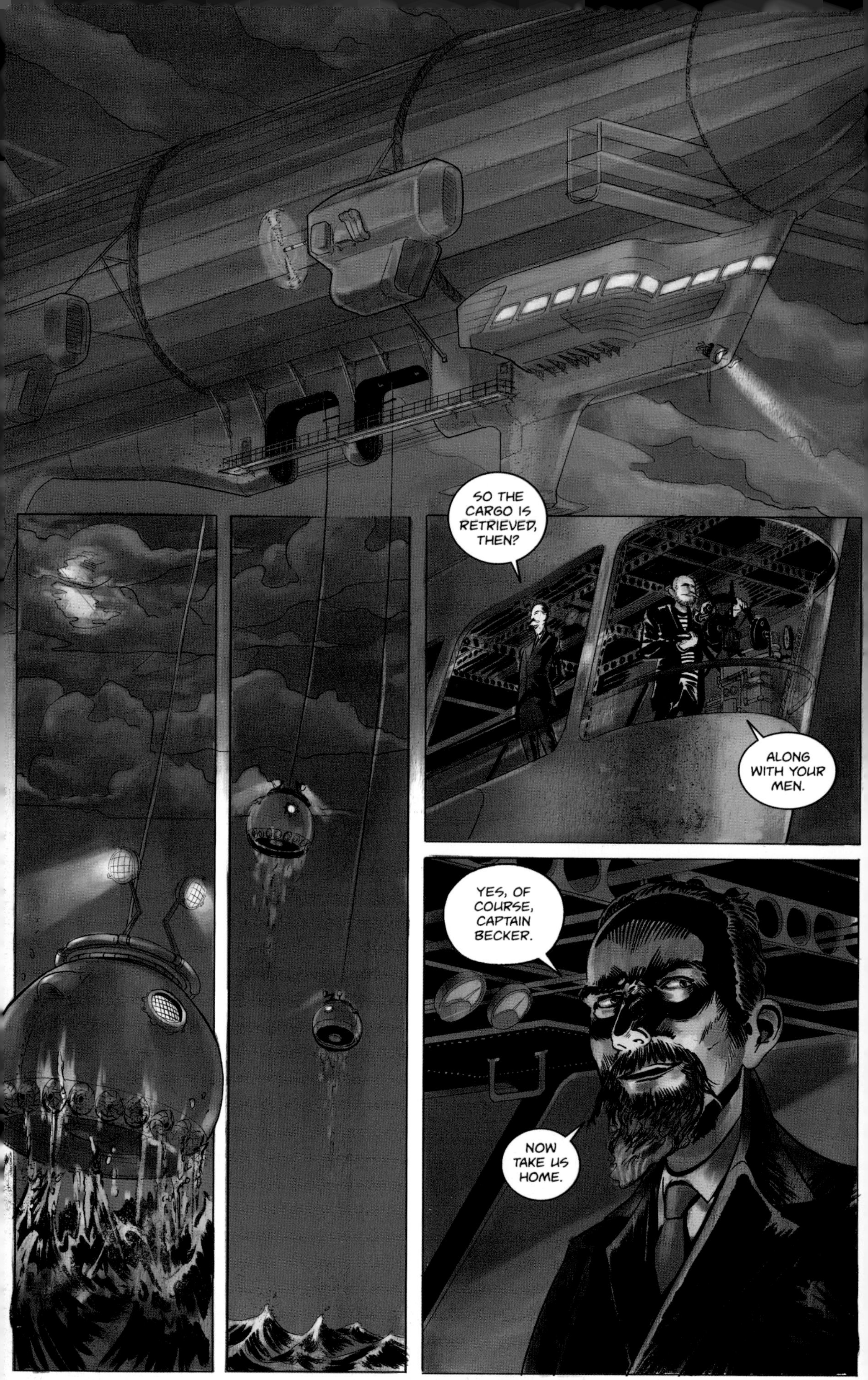
SO THE CARGO IS RETRIEVED, THEN?
ALONG WITH YOUR MEN.
YES, OF COURSE, CAPTAIN BECKER.
NOW TAKE US HOME.

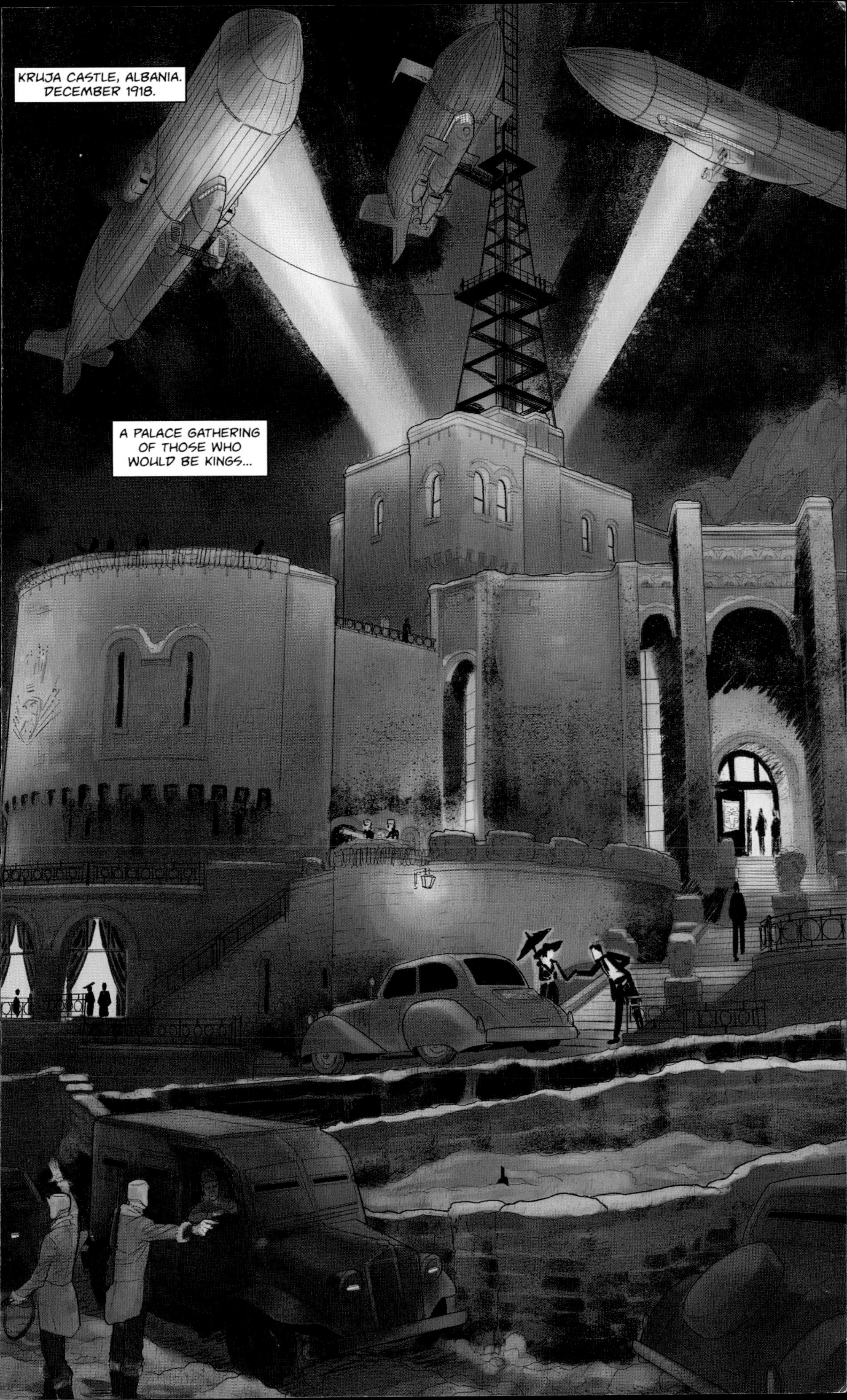
KRUJA CASTLE, ALBANIA. DECEMBER 1918.
A PALACE GATHERING OF THOSE WHO WOULD BE KINGS...

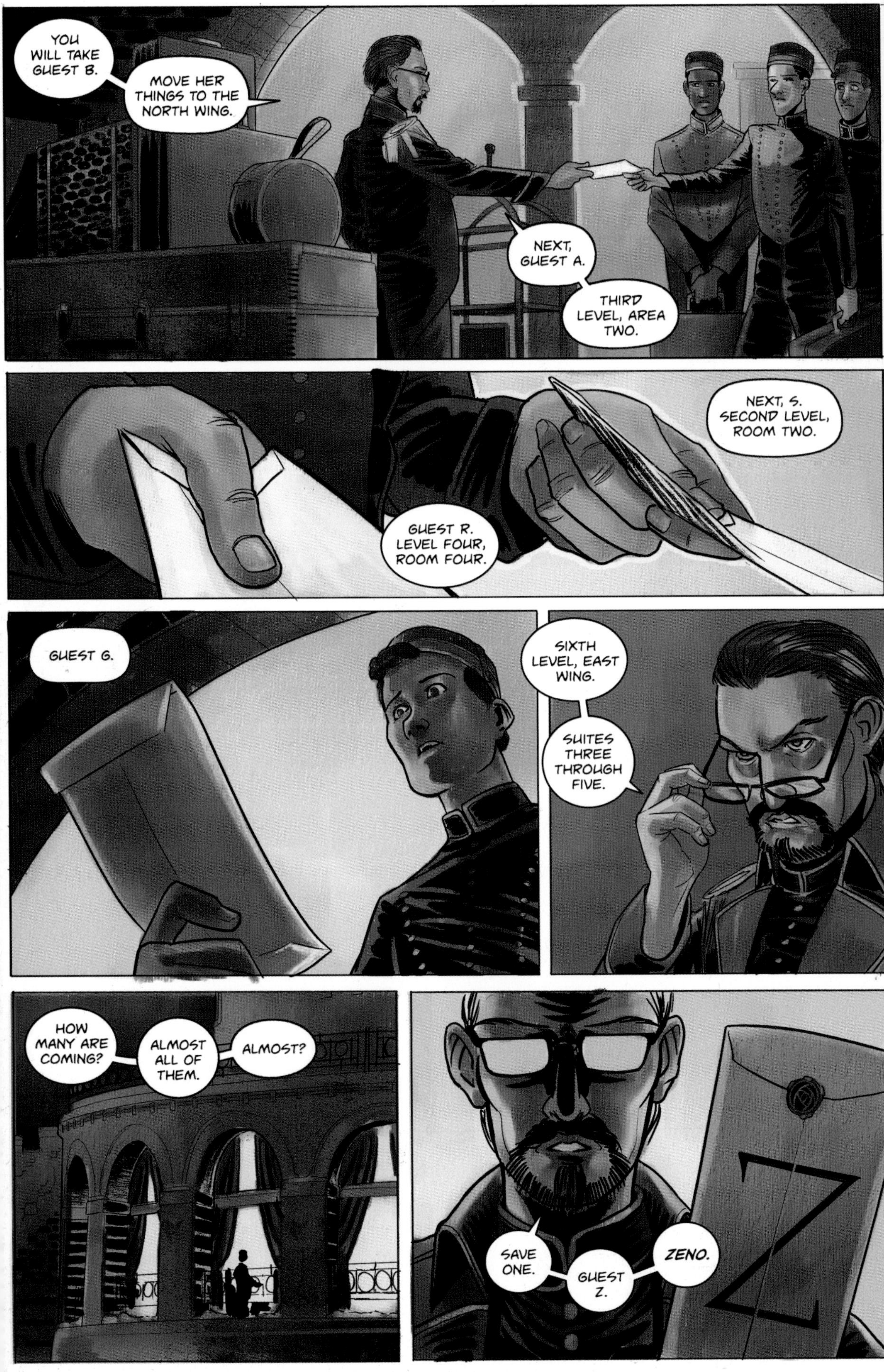
YOU WILL TAKE GUEST B.
MOVE HER THINGS TO THE NORTH WING.
NEXT, GUEST A.
THIRD LEVEL, AREA TWO.
NEXT, S. SECOND LEVEL, ROOM TWO.
GUEST R. LEVEL FOUR, ROOM FOUR.
GUEST G.
SIXTH LEVEL, EAST WING.
SUITES THREE THROUGH FIVE.
HOW MANY ARE COMING?
ALMOST ALL OF THEM.
ALMOST?
SAVE ONE.
GUEST Z.
ZENO.

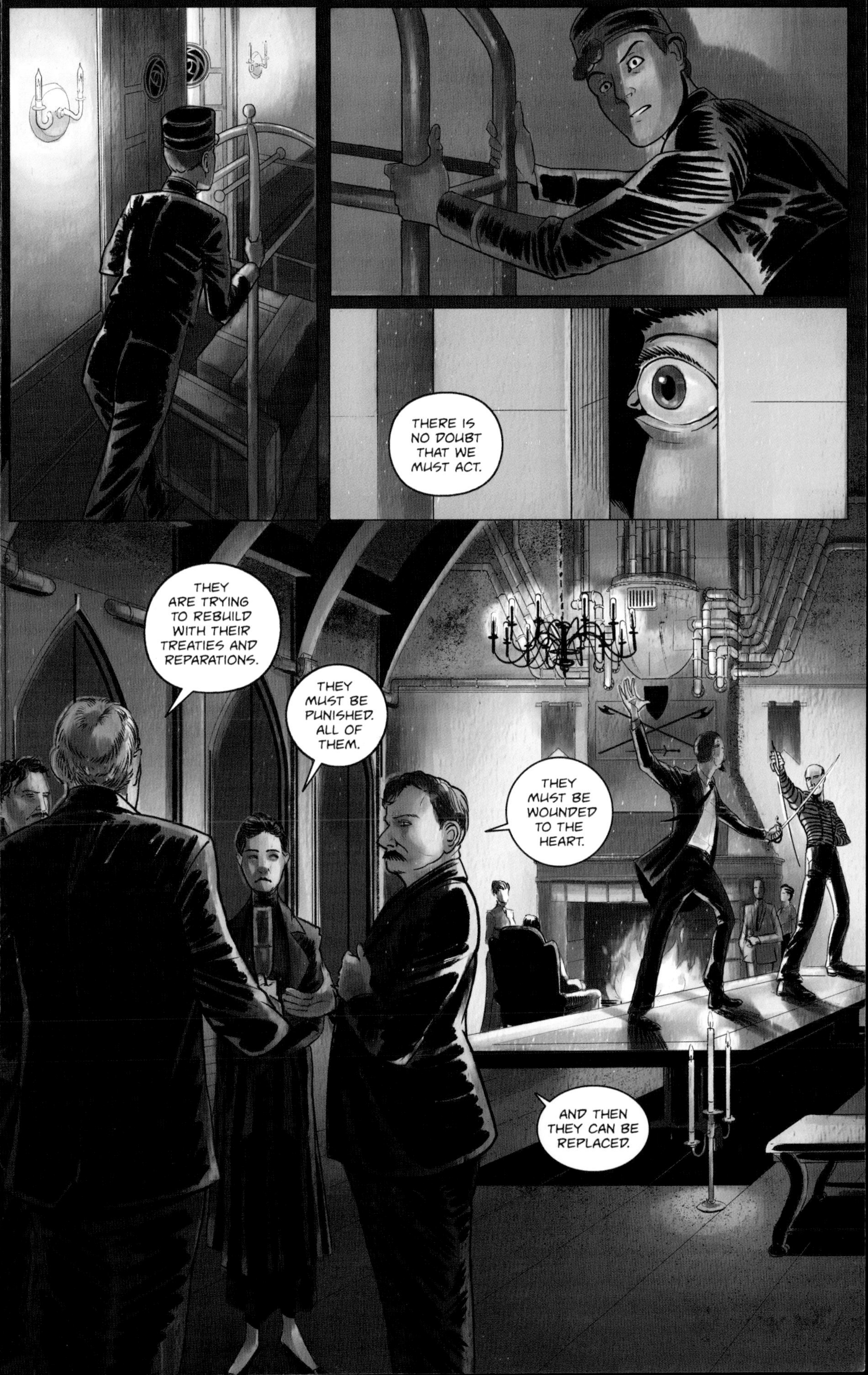
THERE IS NO DOUBT THAT WE MUST ACT.
THEY ARE TRYING TO REBUILD WITH THEIR TREATIES AND REPARATIONS.
THEY MUST BE PUNISHED. ALL OF THEM.
THEY MUST BE WOUNDED TO THE HEART.
AND THEN THEY CAN BE REPLACED.

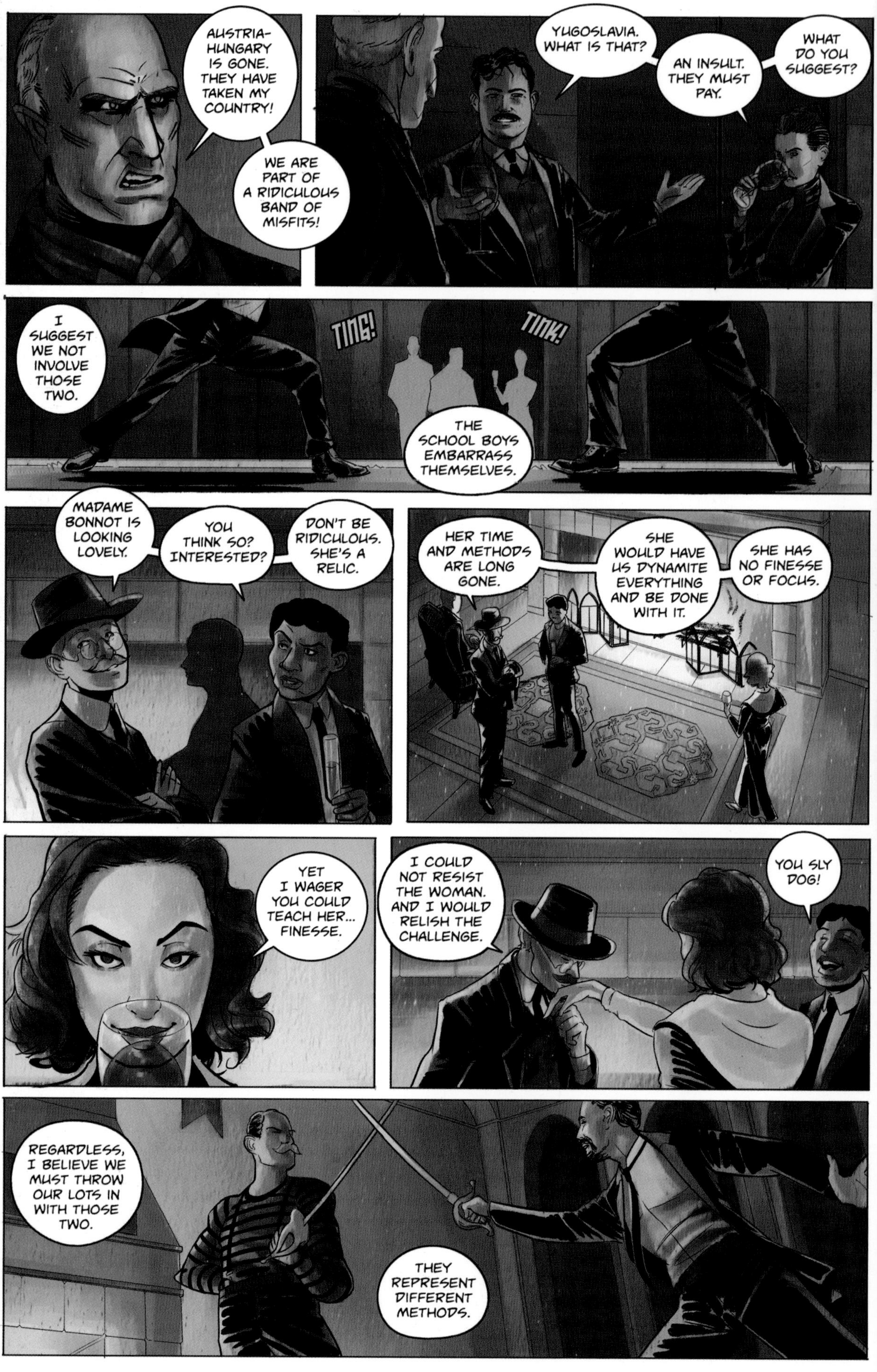
AUSTRIA-HUNGARY IS GONE. THEY HAVE TAKEN MY COUNTRY!
WE ARE PART OF A RIDICULOUS BAND OF MISFITS!
YUGOSLAVIA. WHAT IS THAT?
AN INSULT. THEY MUST PAY.
WHAT DO YOU SUGGEST?
I SUGGEST WE NOT INVOLVE THOSE TWO.
TING!
TINK!
THE SCHOOL BOYS EMBARRASS THEMSELVES.
MADAME BONNOT IS LOOKING LOVELY.
YOU THINK SO? INTERESTED?
DON'T BE RIDICULOUS. SHE'S A RELIC.
HER TIME AND METHODS ARE LONG GONE.
SHE WOULD HAVE US DYNAMITE EVERYTHING AND BE DONE WITH IT.
SHE HAS NO FINESSE OR FOCUS.
YET I WAGER YOU COULD TEACH HER... FINESSE.
I COULD NOT RESIST THE WOMAN. AND I WOULD RELISH THE CHALLENGE.
YOU SLY DOG!
REGARDLESS, I BELIEVE WE MUST THROW OUR LOTS IN WITH THOSE TWO.
THEY REPRESENT DIFFERENT METHODS.

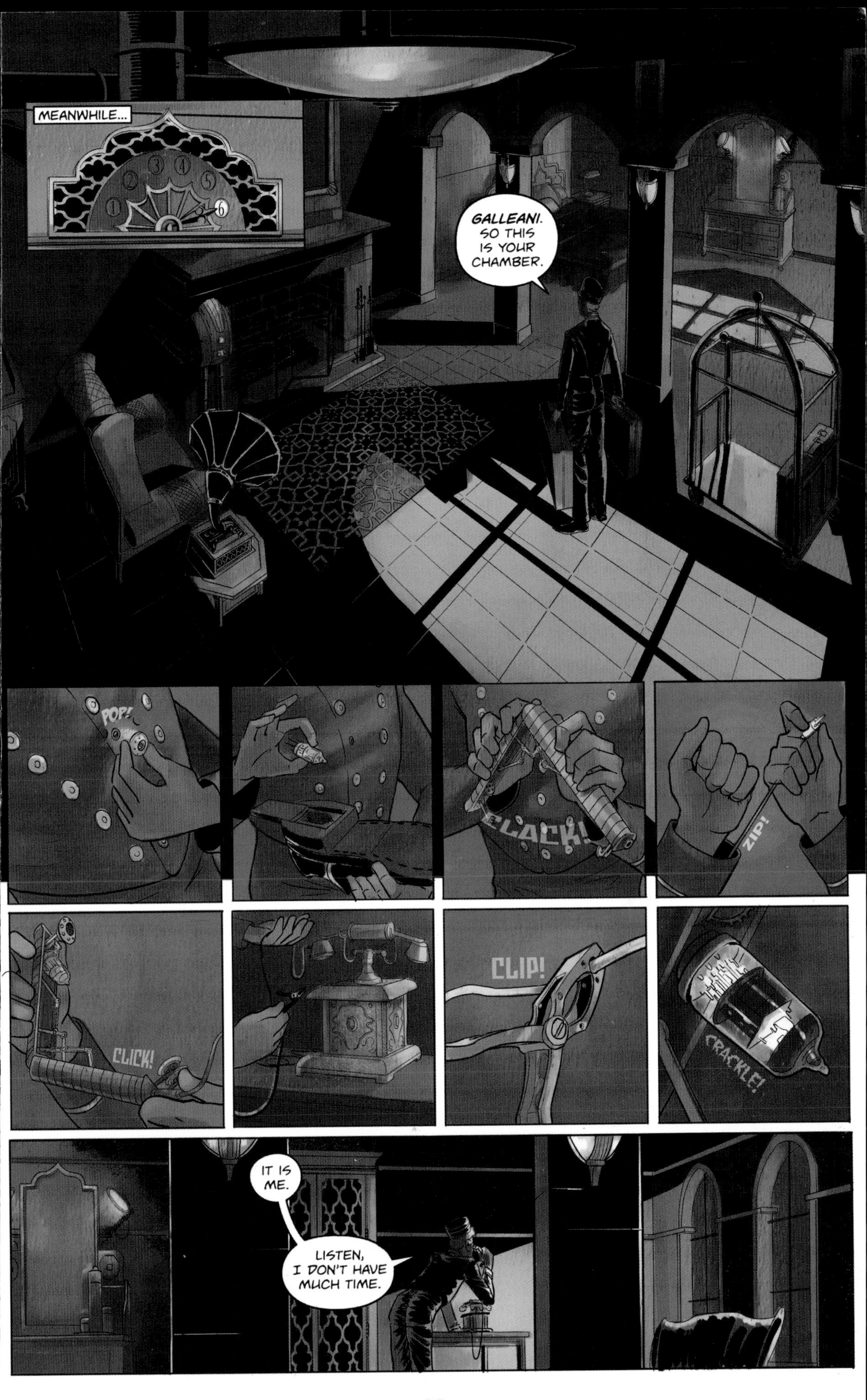
MEANWHILE...
GALLEANI. SO THIS IS YOUR CHAMBER.
POP!
CLACK!
ZIP!
CLICK!
CLIP!
CRACKLE!
IT IS ME.
LISTEN, I DON'T HAVE MUCH TIME.

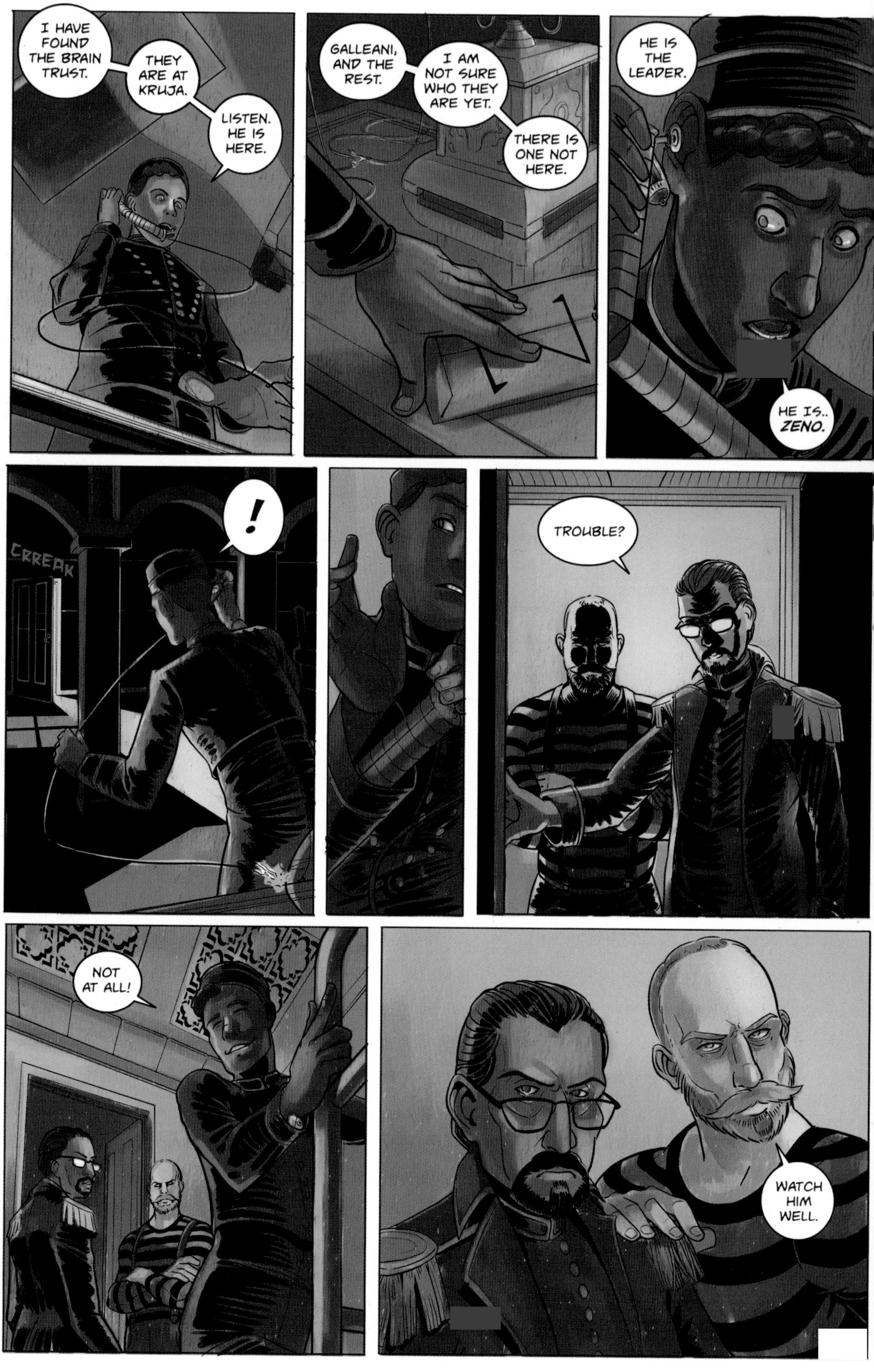
I HAVE FOUND THE BRAIN TRUST.
THEY ARE AT KRUJA.
LISTEN. HE IS HERE.
GALLEANI, AND THE REST.
I AM NOT SURE WHO THEY ARE YET.
THERE IS ONE NOT HERE.
HE IS THE LEADER.
HE IS.. ZENO.
CRREAK
!
TROUBLE?
NOT AT ALL!
WATCH HIM WELL.

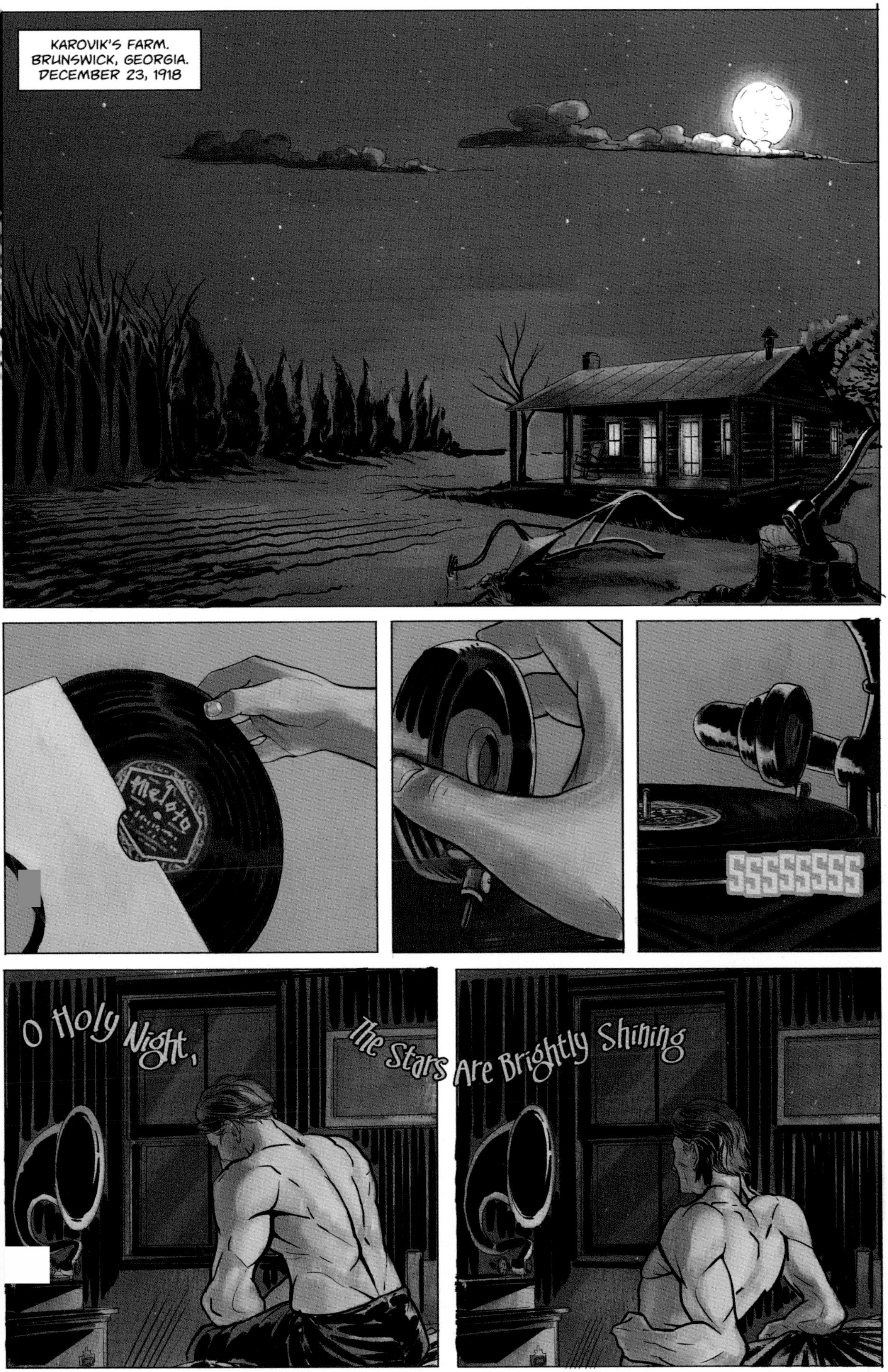

KAROVIK'S FARM.
BRUNSWICK, GEORGIA.
DECEMBER 23, 1918
SSSSSSSS
O Holy Night,
The Stars Are Brightly Shining

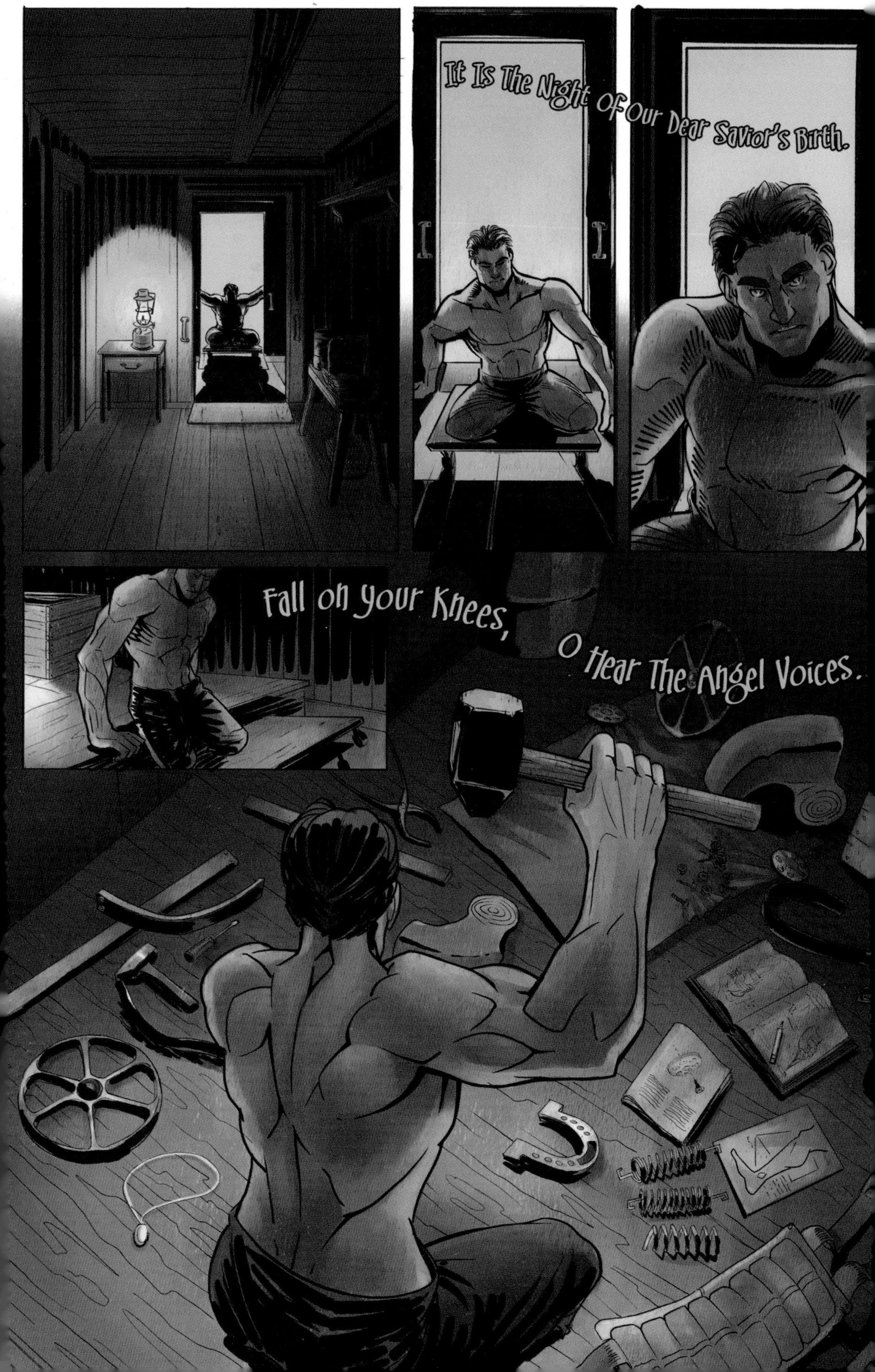

It Is The Night Of Our Dear Savior's Birth.
Fall on your Knees,
O Hear The Angel Voices.

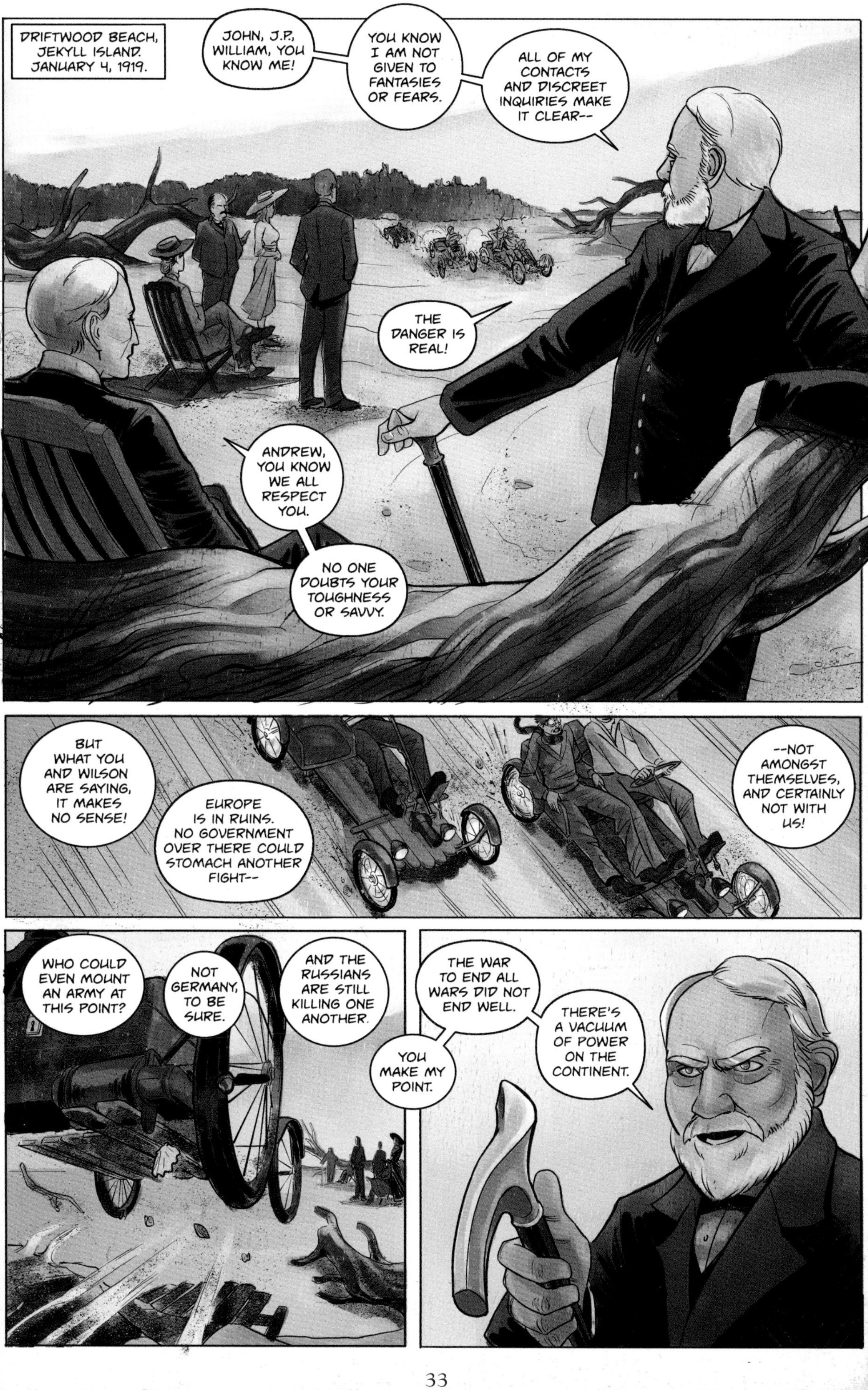
DRIFTWOOD BEACH, JEKYLL ISLAND. JANUARY 4, 1919.
JOHN, J.P., WILLIAM, YOU KNOW ME!
YOU KNOW I AM NOT GIVEN TO FANTASIES OR FEARS.
ALL OF MY CONTACTS AND DISCREET INQUIRIES MAKE IT CLEAR--
THE DANGER IS REAL!
ANDREW, YOU KNOW WE ALL RESPECT YOU.
NO ONE DOUBTS YOUR TOUGHNESS OR SAVVY.
BUT WHAT YOU AND WILSON ARE SAYING, IT MAKES NO SENSE!
EUROPE IS IN RUINS. NO GOVERNMENT OVER THERE COULD STOMACH ANOTHER FIGHT--
--NOT AMONGST THEMSELVES, AND CERTAINLY NOT WITH US!
WHO COULD EVEN MOUNT AN ARMY AT THIS POINT?
NOT GERMANY, TO BE SURE.
AND THE RUSSIANS ARE STILL KILLING ONE ANOTHER.
THE WAR TO END ALL WARS DID NOT END WELL.
YOU MAKE MY POINT.
THERE'S A VACUUM OF POWER ON THE CONTINENT.

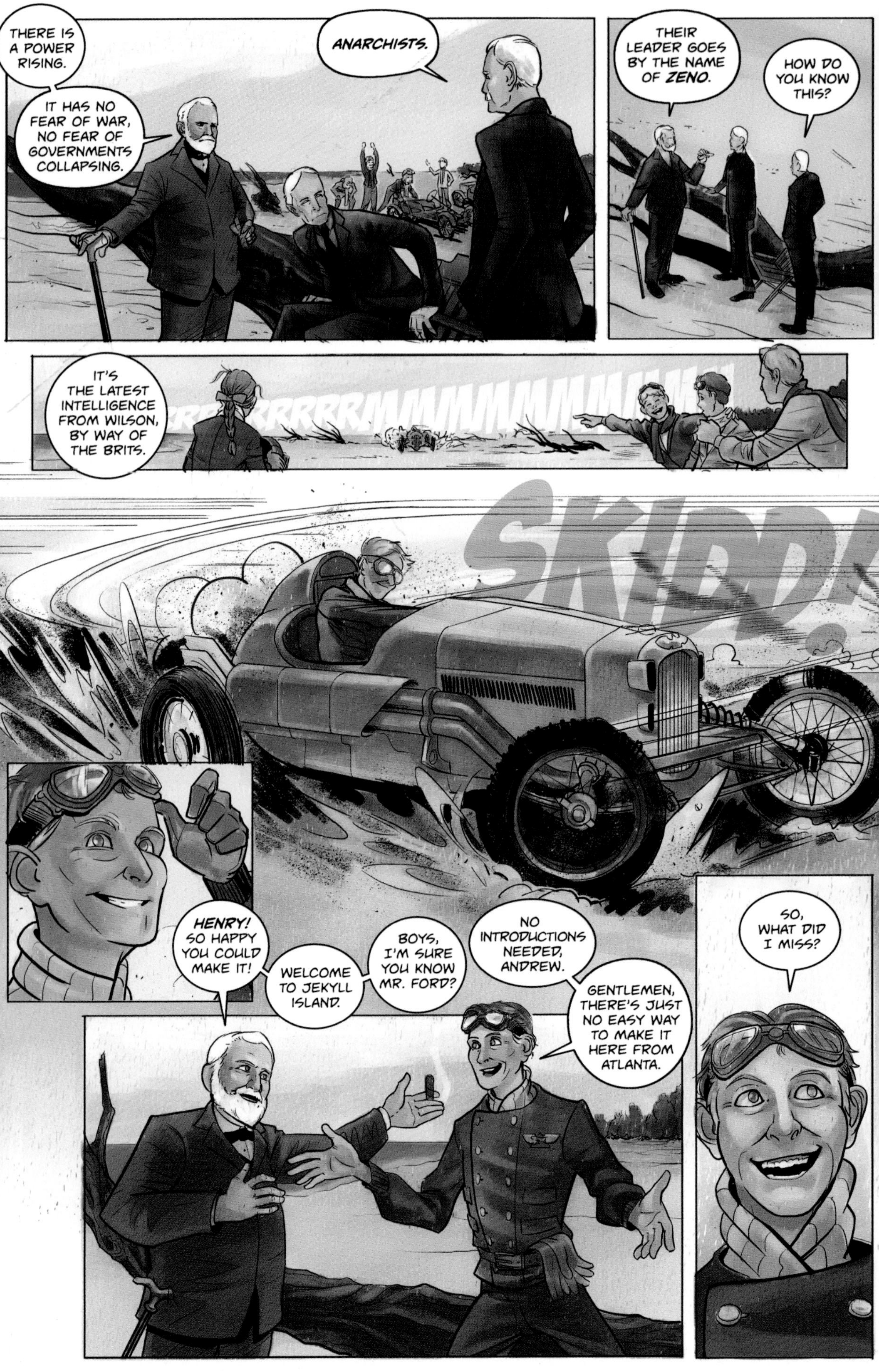
THERE IS A POWER RISING.
IT HAS NO FEAR OF WAR, NO FEAR OF GOVERNMENTS COLLAPSING.
ANARCHISTS.
THEIR LEADER GOES BY THE NAME OF ZENO.
HOW DO YOU KNOW THIS?
IT'S THE LATEST INTELLIGENCE FROM WILSON, BY WAY OF THE BRITS.
SKIDD!
HENRY! SO HAPPY YOU COULD MAKE IT!
WELCOME TO JEKYLL ISLAND.
BOYS, I'M SURE YOU KNOW MR. FORD?
NO INTRODUCTIONS NEEDED, ANDREW.
GENTLEMEN, THERE'S JUST NO EASY WAY TO MAKE IT HERE FROM ATLANTA.
SO, WHAT DID I MISS?

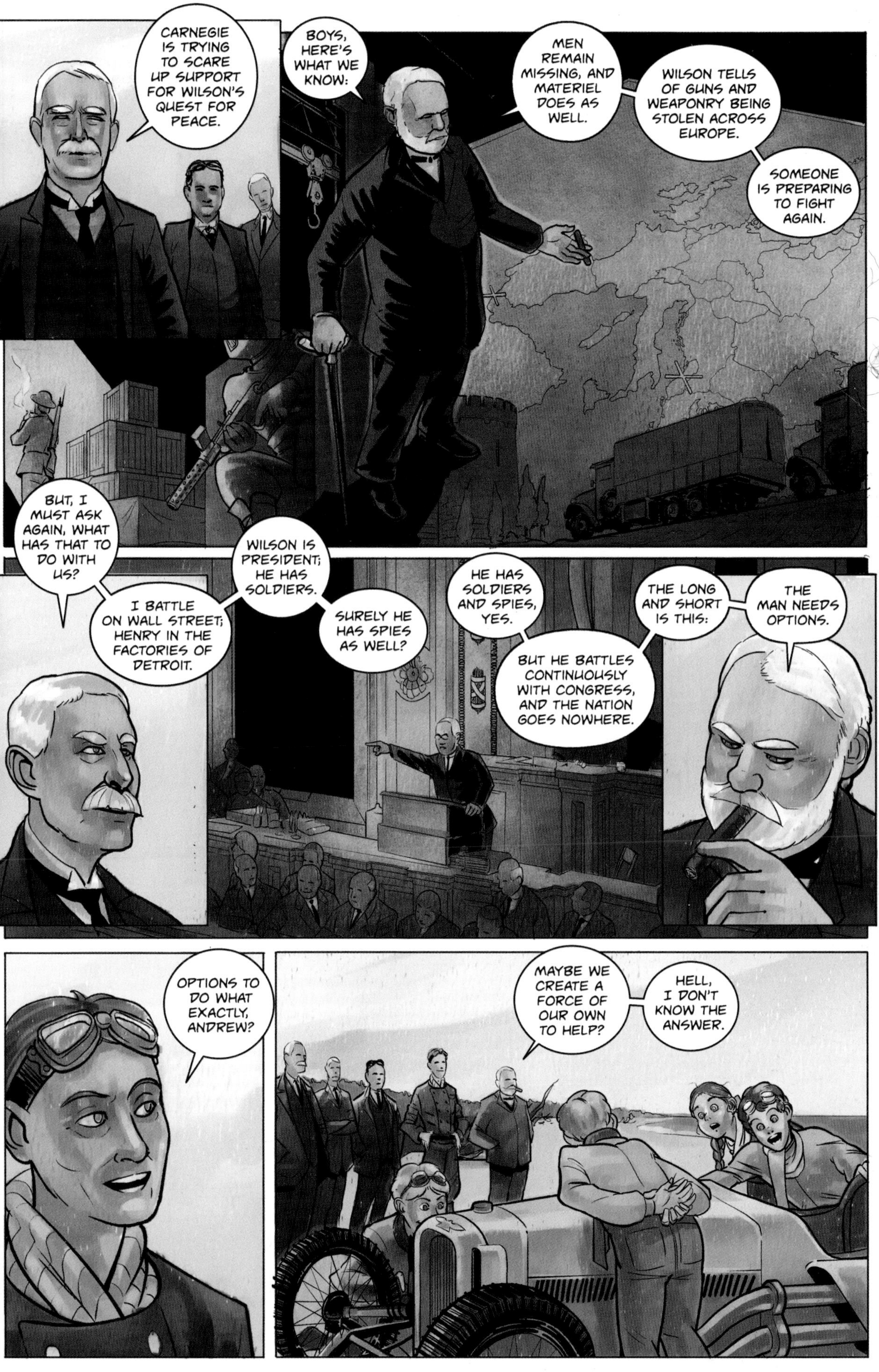
CARNEGIE IS TRYING TO SCARE UP SUPPORT FOR WILSON'S QUEST FOR PEACE.
BOYS, HERE'S WHAT WE KNOW:
MEN REMAIN MISSING, AND MATERIEL DOES AS WELL.
WILSON TELLS OF GUNS AND WEAPONRY BEING STOLEN ACROSS EUROPE.
SOMEONE IS PREPARING TO FIGHT AGAIN.
BUT, I MUST ASK AGAIN, WHAT HAS THAT TO DO WITH US?
I BATTLE ON WALL STREET; HENRY IN THE FACTORIES OF DETROIT.
WILSON IS PRESIDENT; HE HAS SOLDIERS.
SURELY HE HAS SPIES AS WELL?
HE HAS SOLDIERS AND SPIES, YES.
BUT HE BATTLES CONTINUOUSLY WITH CONGRESS, AND THE NATION GOES NOWHERE.
THE LONG AND SHORT IS THIS:
THE MAN NEEDS OPTIONS.
OPTIONS TO DO WHAT EXACTLY, ANDREW?
MAYBE WE CREATE A FORCE OF OUR OWN TO HELP?
HELL, I DON'T KNOW THE ANSWER.

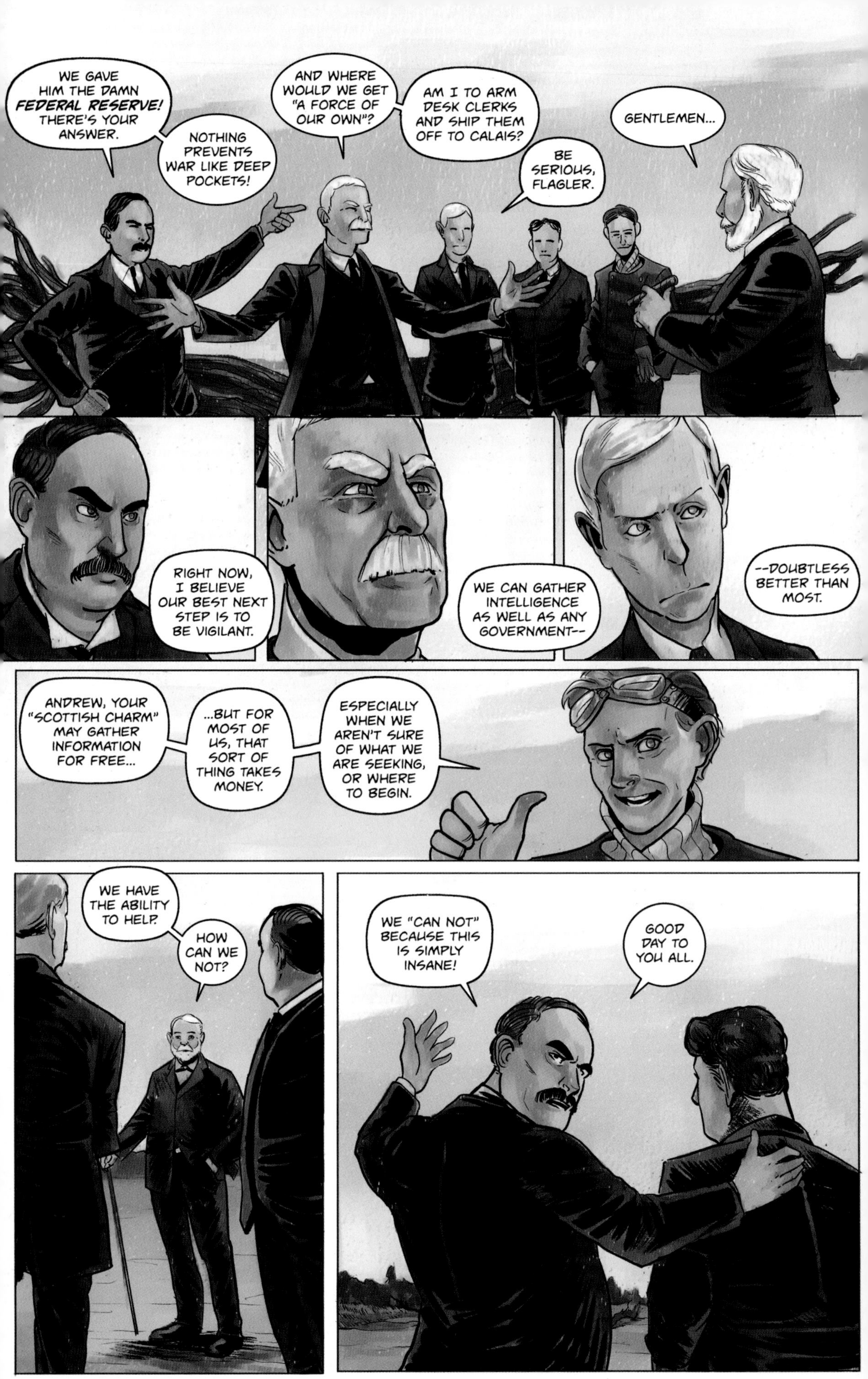
WE GAVE HIM THE DAMN ***FEDERAL RESERVE!*** THERE'S YOUR ANSWER.
NOTHING PREVENTS WAR LIKE DEEP POCKETS!
AND WHERE WOULD WE GET "A FORCE OF OUR OWN"?
AM I TO ARM DESK CLERKS AND SHIP THEM OFF TO CALAIS?
BE SERIOUS, FLAGLER.
GENTLEMEN...
RIGHT NOW, I BELIEVE OUR BEST NEXT STEP IS TO BE VIGILANT.
WE CAN GATHER INTELLIGENCE AS WELL AS ANY GOVERNMENT--
--DOUBTLESS BETTER THAN MOST.
ANDREW, YOUR "SCOTTISH CHARM" MAY GATHER INFORMATION FOR FREE...
...BUT FOR MOST OF US, THAT SORT OF THING TAKES MONEY.
ESPECIALLY WHEN WE AREN'T SURE OF WHAT WE ARE SEEKING, OR WHERE TO BEGIN.
WE HAVE THE ABILITY TO HELP.
HOW CAN WE NOT?
WE "CAN NOT" BECAUSE THIS IS SIMPLY INSANE!
GOOD DAY TO YOU ALL.

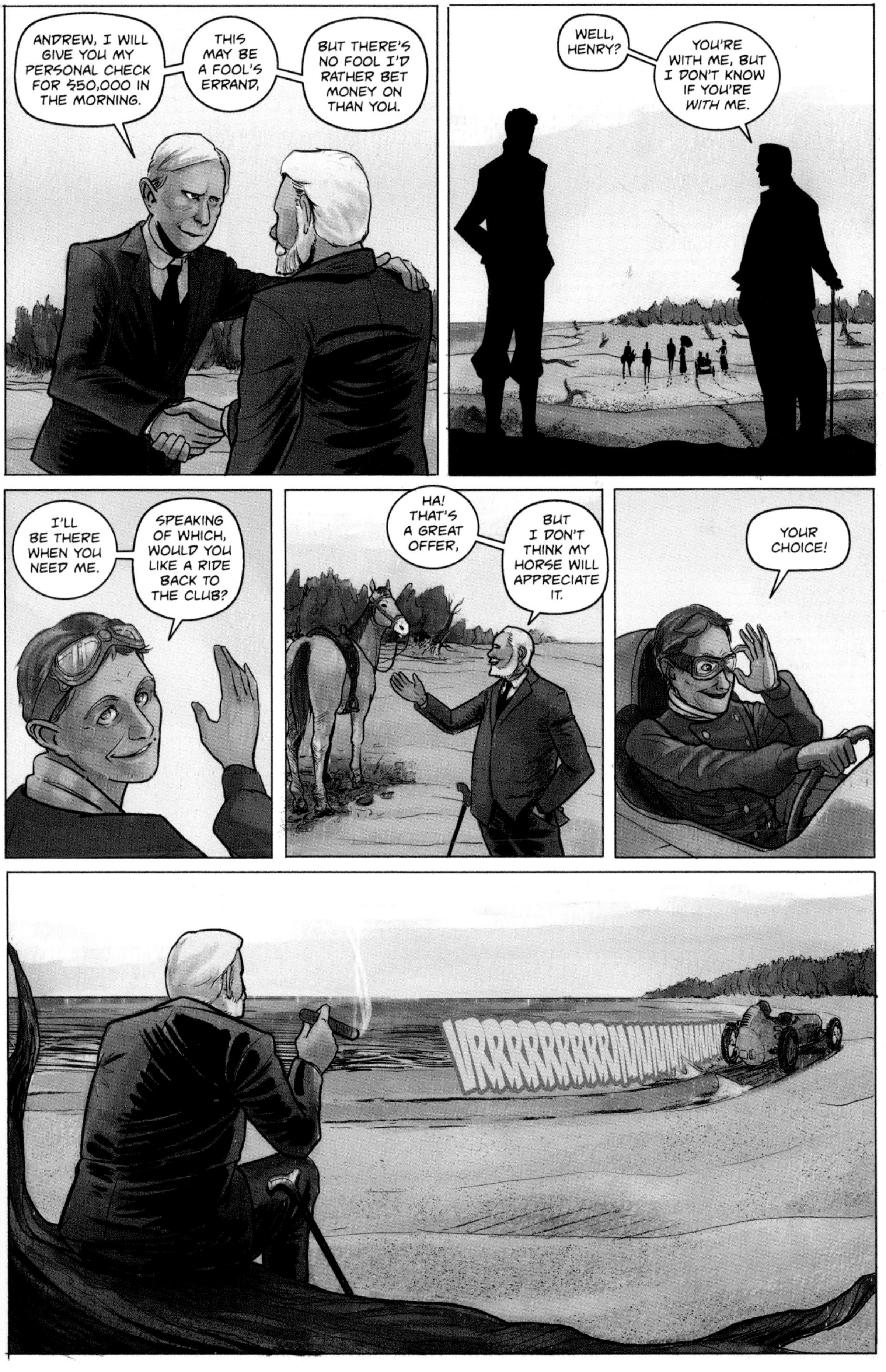
ANDREW, I WILL GIVE YOU MY PERSONAL CHECK FOR $50,000 IN THE MORNING.
THIS MAY BE A FOOL'S ERRAND,
BUT THERE'S NO FOOL I'D RATHER BET MONEY ON THAN YOU.
WELL, HENRY?
YOU'RE WITH ME, BUT I DON'T KNOW IF YOU'RE *WITH ME.*
I'LL BE THERE WHEN YOU NEED ME.
SPEAKING OF WHICH, WOULD YOU LIKE A RIDE BACK TO THE CLUB?
HA! THAT'S A GREAT OFFER,
BUT I DON'T THINK MY HORSE WILL APPRECIATE IT.
YOUR CHOICE!
VRRRRRRRRRMMMMMMMMMMM

Tuesday, March 11, 1919. V.1 No.34, Five Cents. Alvin Lourdes, Publisher

THE WORLD GAZETTE TIMES
GATHERING IN VERSAILLES

Springtime in Paris

A time for love, a time for art, and finally, a time for peace. Delegates from around the world gather at Versailles to come to terms with Germany following the armistice and the end of the Great War. Poland, Czechoslovakia, and France all stand to be winners in the rush for land. Germany's army will likely be reduced significantly as their economy teeters on the brink of chaos, so delegates continue to come and go in the beautiful French countryside, while the push and pull for power continues as the world recovers from the war to end all wars...

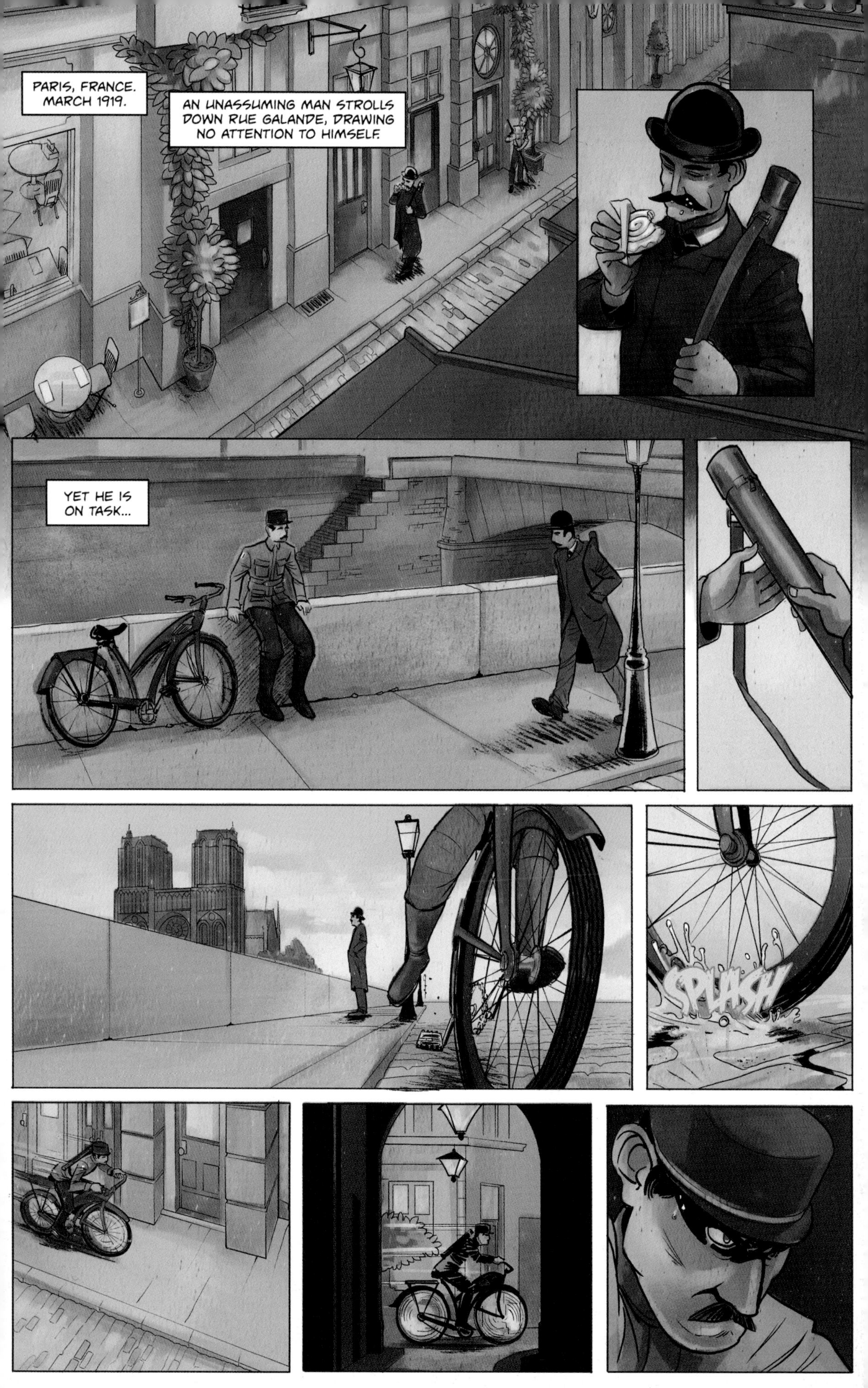
PARIS, FRANCE.
MARCH 1919.
AN UNASSUMING MAN STROLLS DOWN RUE GALANDE, DRAWING NO ATTENTION TO HIMSELF.
YET HE IS ON TASK...
SPLASH

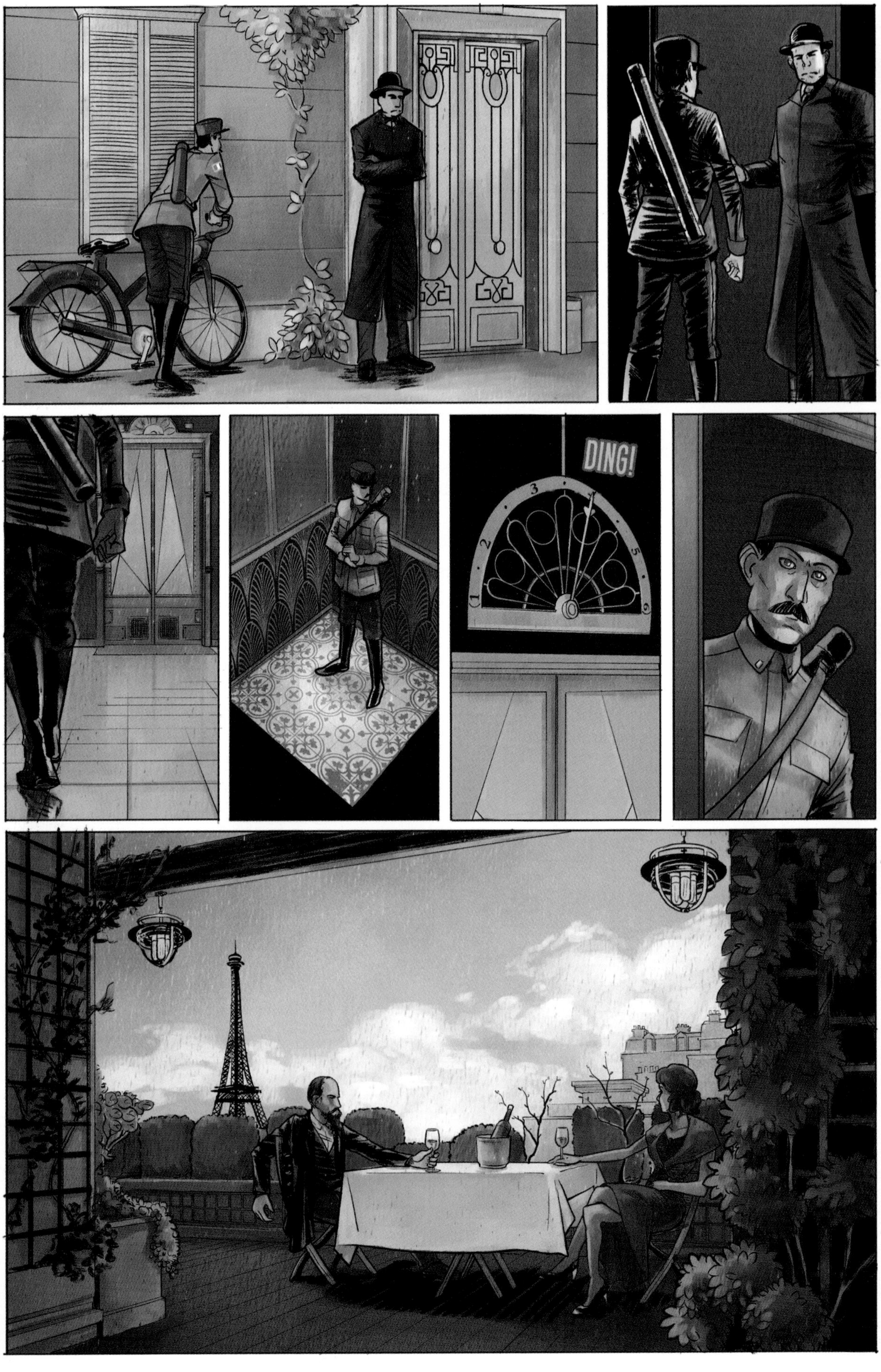
DING!

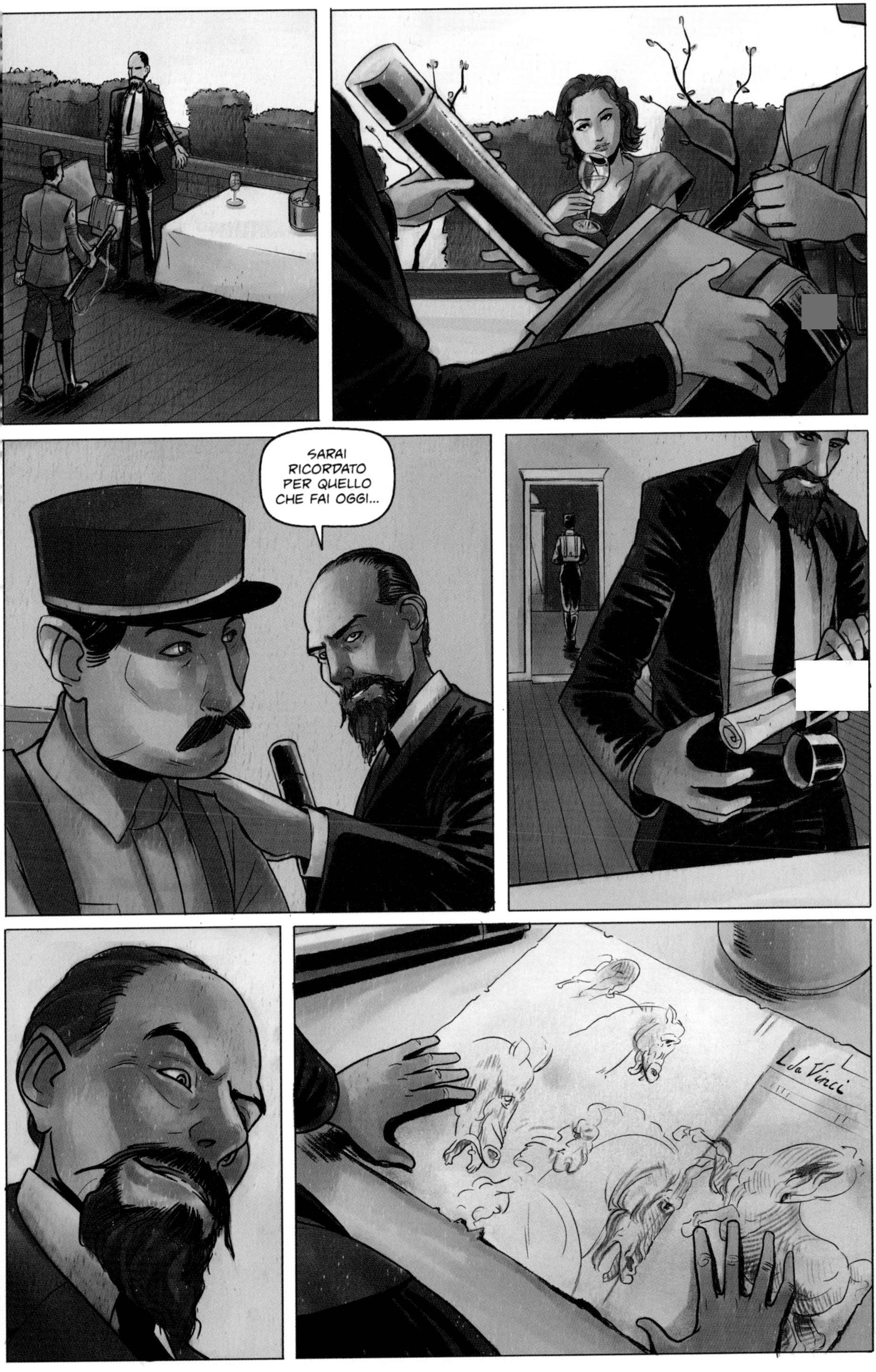
SARAI RICORDATO PER QUELLO CHE FAI OGGI...
L da Vinci

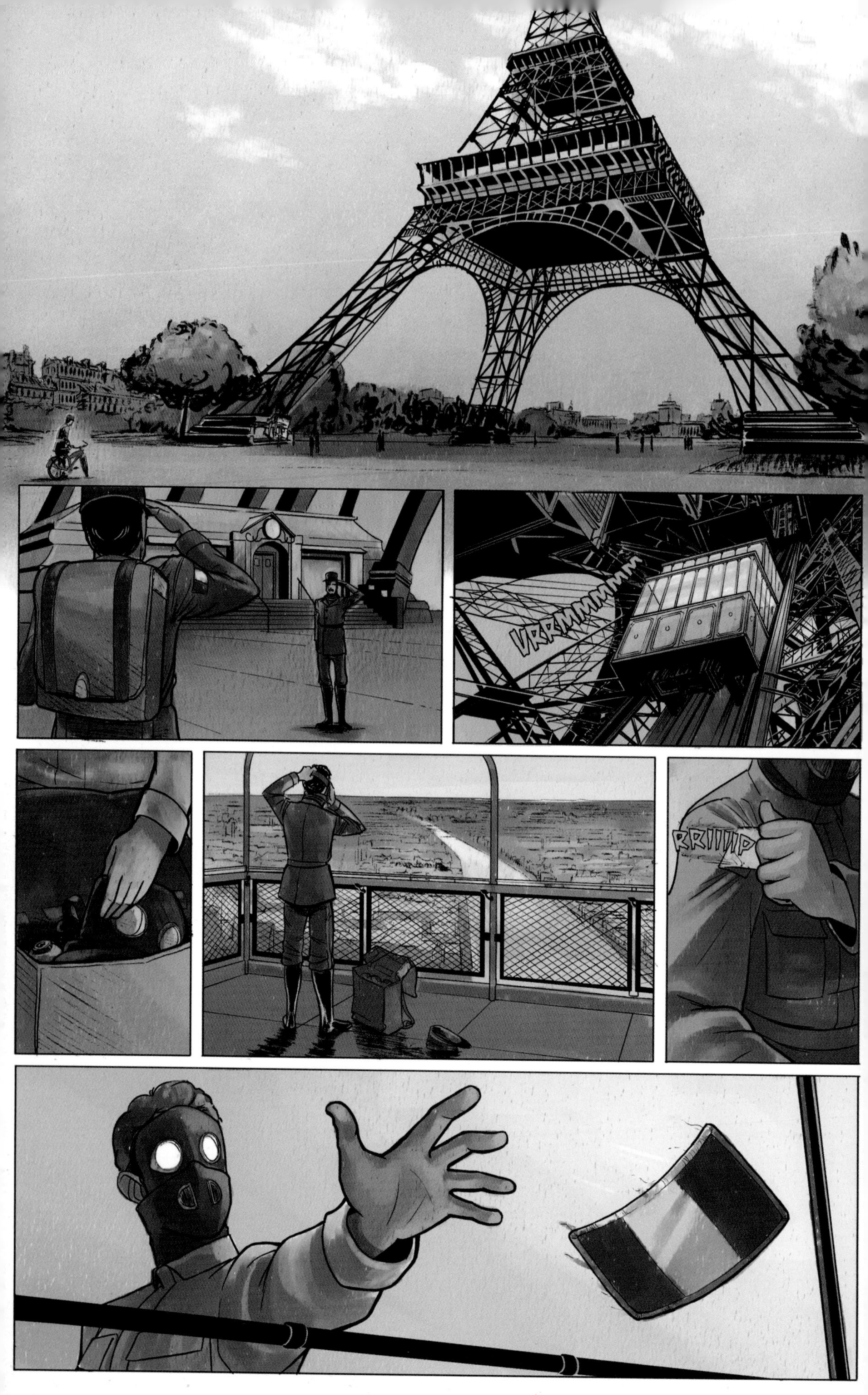
VRRMMMMMMM
RRIIIIP

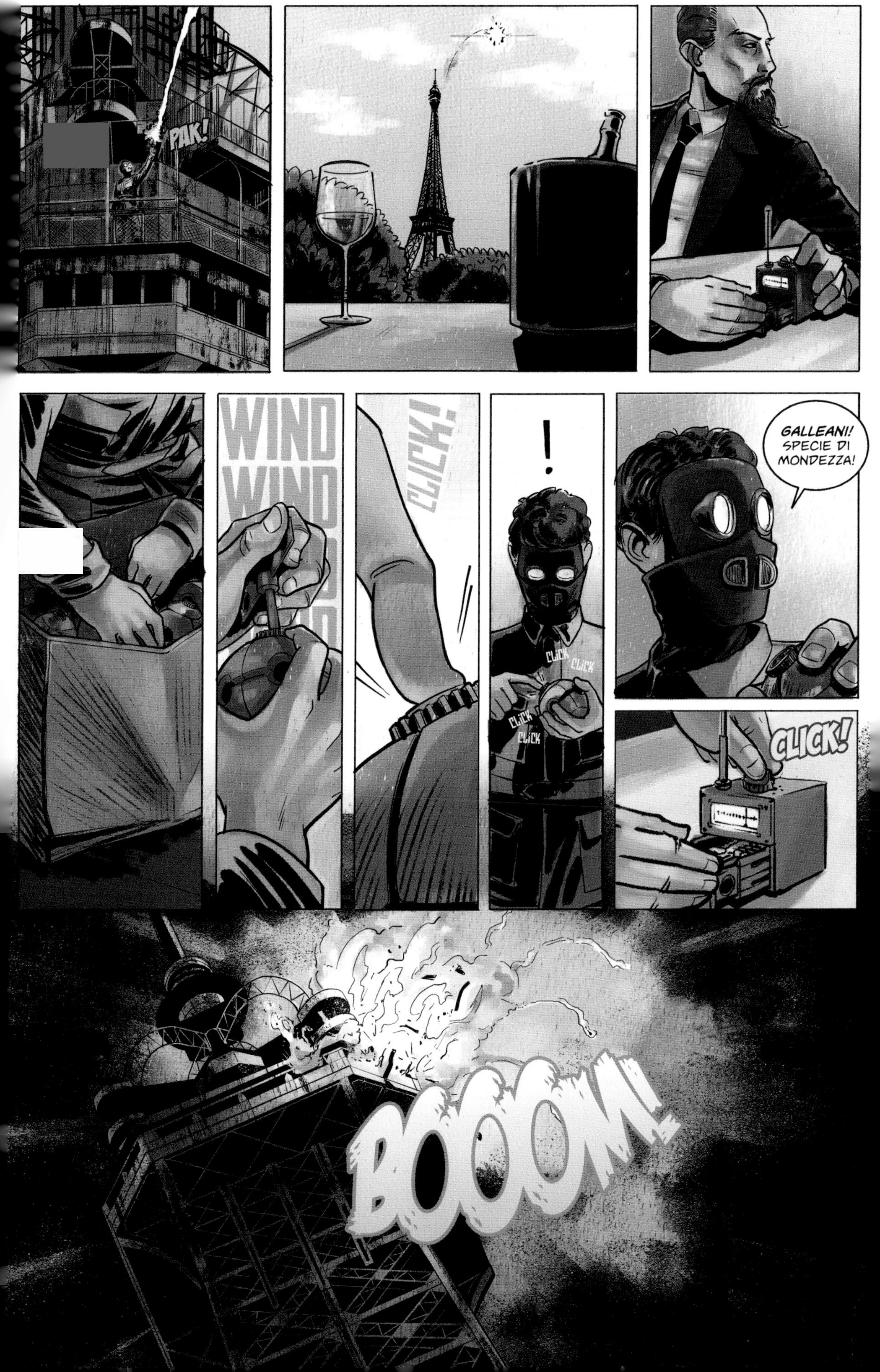
PAK!
WIND
WIND
CLICK!
!
CLICK
CLICK
CLICK
CLICK
GALLEANI! SPECIE DI MONDEZZA!
CLICK!
BOOOM!

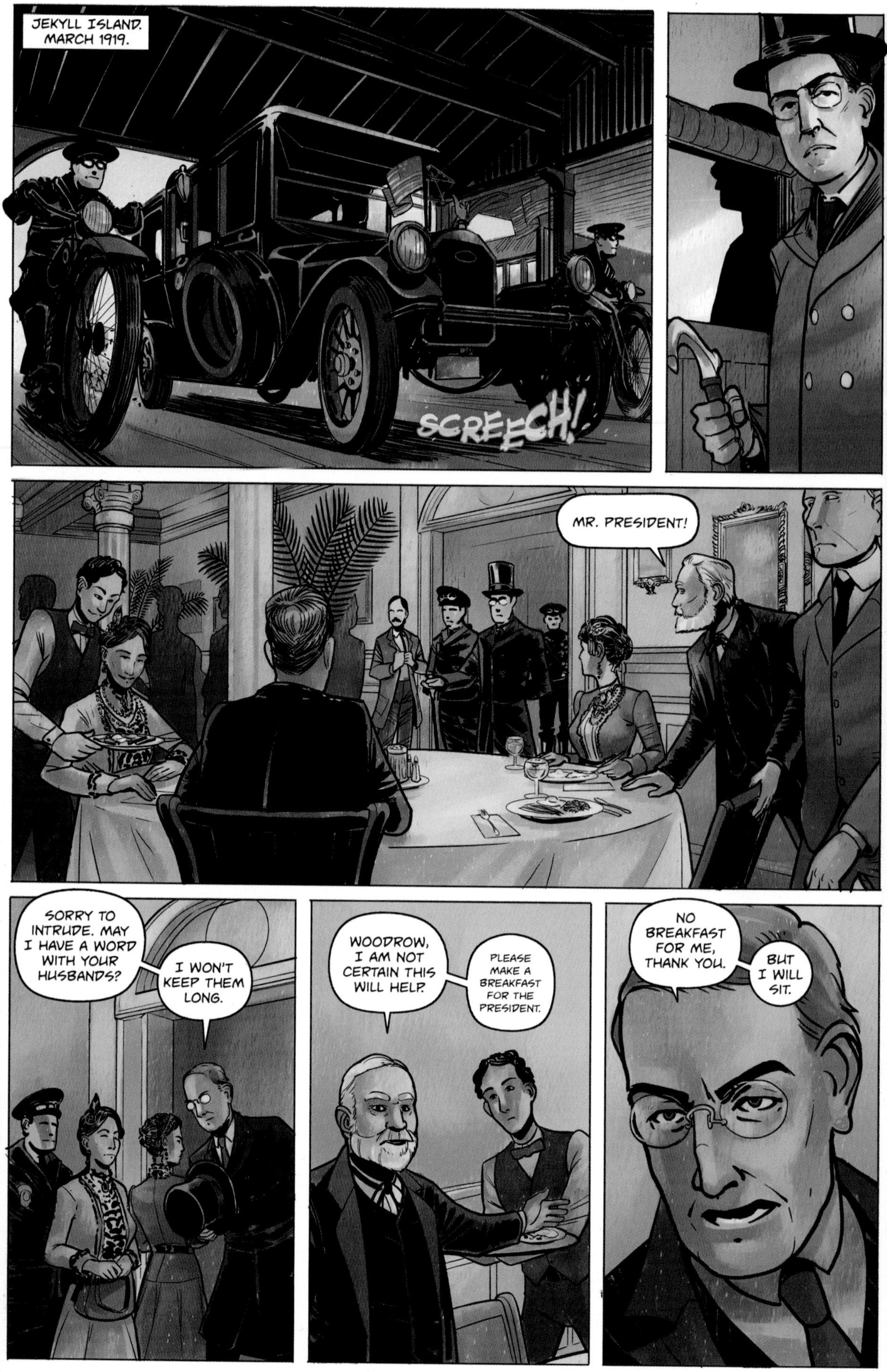
JEKYLL ISLAND. MARCH 1919.
SCREECH!
MR. PRESIDENT!
SORRY TO INTRUDE. MAY I HAVE A WORD WITH YOUR HUSBANDS?
I WON'T KEEP THEM LONG.
WOODROW, I AM NOT CERTAIN THIS WILL HELP.
PLEASE MAKE A BREAKFAST FOR THE PRESIDENT.
NO BREAKFAST FOR ME, THANK YOU.
BUT I WILL SIT.

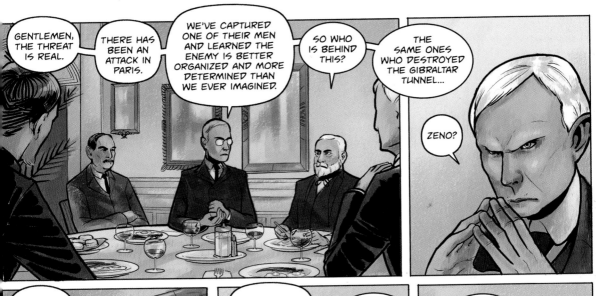

GENTLEMEN, THE THREAT IS REAL.

THERE HAS BEEN AN ATTACK IN PARIS.

WE'VE CAPTURED ONE OF THEIR MEN AND LEARNED THE ENEMY IS BETTER ORGANIZED AND MORE DETERMINED THAN WE EVER IMAGINED.

SO WHO IS BEHIND THIS?

THE SAME ONES WHO DESTROYED THE GIBRALTAR TUNNEL...

ZENO?

WHEN THE CARGO WAS STOLEN IN GIBRALTAR,

I CAME HERE ON YOUR BEHALF AND ASKED FOR AID.

YES, BUT...

WE COMMITTED TO OFFER OUR FINANCIAL RESOURCES.

WE ARE SADDENED BY THE ATTACK ON FRANCE, BUT WHAT WOULD YOU HAVE US DO?

THESE ARE NOT MERE ANARCHISTS!

ZENO KNOWS WHAT HE'S DOING!

SLAM!

SO HE'S AN ORGANIZED ANARCHIST?

HE HAS RESOURCES, TOO--FINANCIAL AND OTHERWISE.

HIS DESIRE IS TO DESTROY ALL OF US,

CREATE CHAOS, AND RE-ESTABLISH HIS FOOTING.

NO! HE HAS FOLLOWERS! AND HE WORKS ON ALL FRONTS!

BUT JUST ONE MAN?

TO HIM, EVERY PERSON ON THE PLANET IS A POTENTIAL WEAPON!

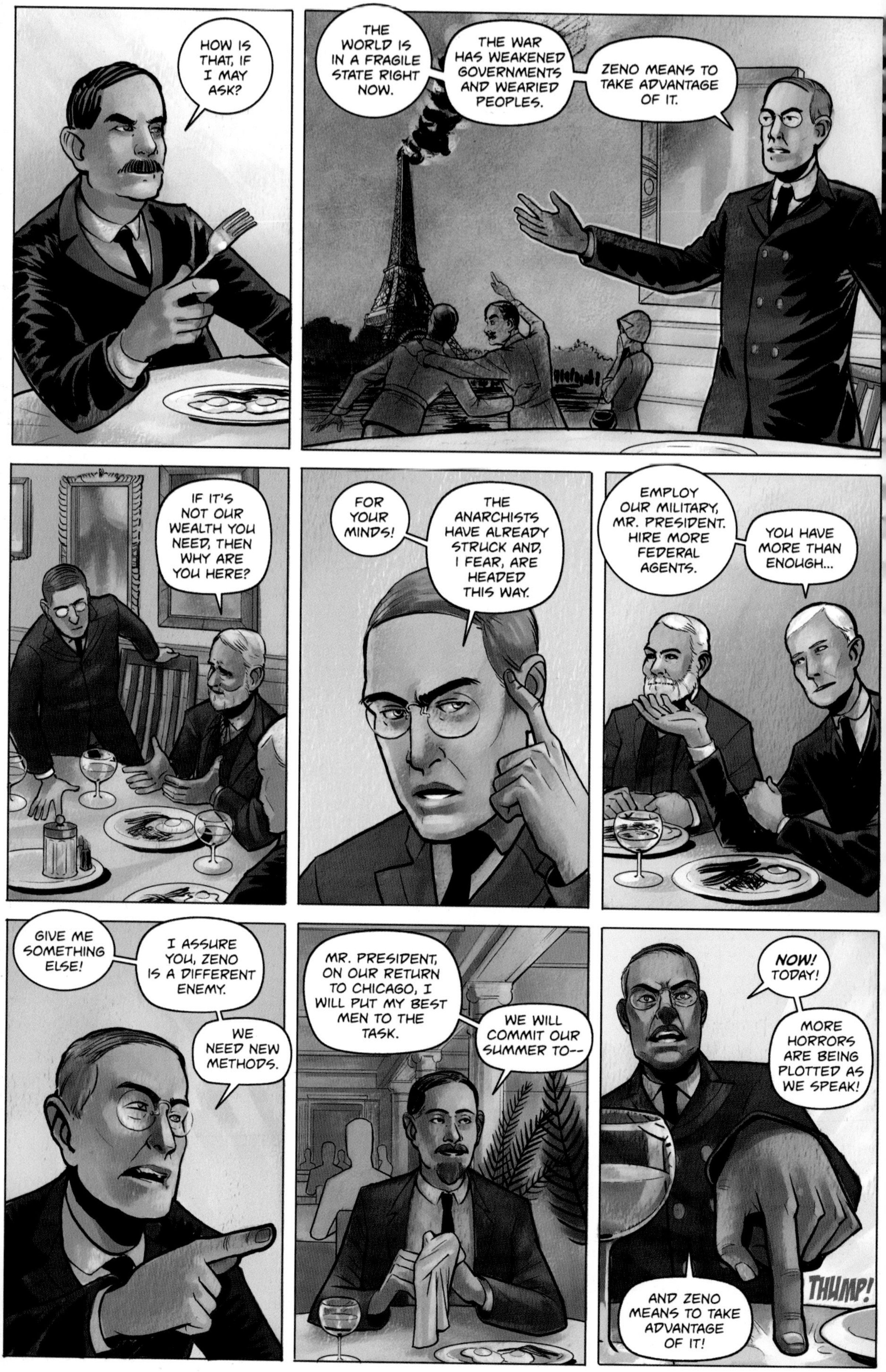
HOW IS THAT, IF I MAY ASK?
THE WORLD IS IN A FRAGILE STATE RIGHT NOW.
THE WAR HAS WEAKENED GOVERNMENTS AND WEARIED PEOPLES.
ZENO MEANS TO TAKE ADVANTAGE OF IT.
IF IT'S NOT OUR WEALTH YOU NEED, THEN WHY ARE YOU HERE?
FOR YOUR MINDS!
THE ANARCHISTS HAVE ALREADY STRUCK AND, I FEAR, ARE HEADED THIS WAY.
EMPLOY OUR MILITARY, MR. PRESIDENT. HIRE MORE FEDERAL AGENTS.
YOU HAVE MORE THAN ENOUGH...
GIVE ME SOMETHING ELSE!
I ASSURE YOU, ZENO IS A DIFFERENT ENEMY.
WE NEED NEW METHODS.
MR. PRESIDENT, ON OUR RETURN TO CHICAGO, I WILL PUT MY BEST MEN TO THE TASK.
WE WILL COMMIT OUR SUMMER TO--
NOW! TODAY!
MORE HORRORS ARE BEING PLOTTED AS WE SPEAK!
THUMP!
AND ZENO MEANS TO TAKE ADVANTAGE OF IT!

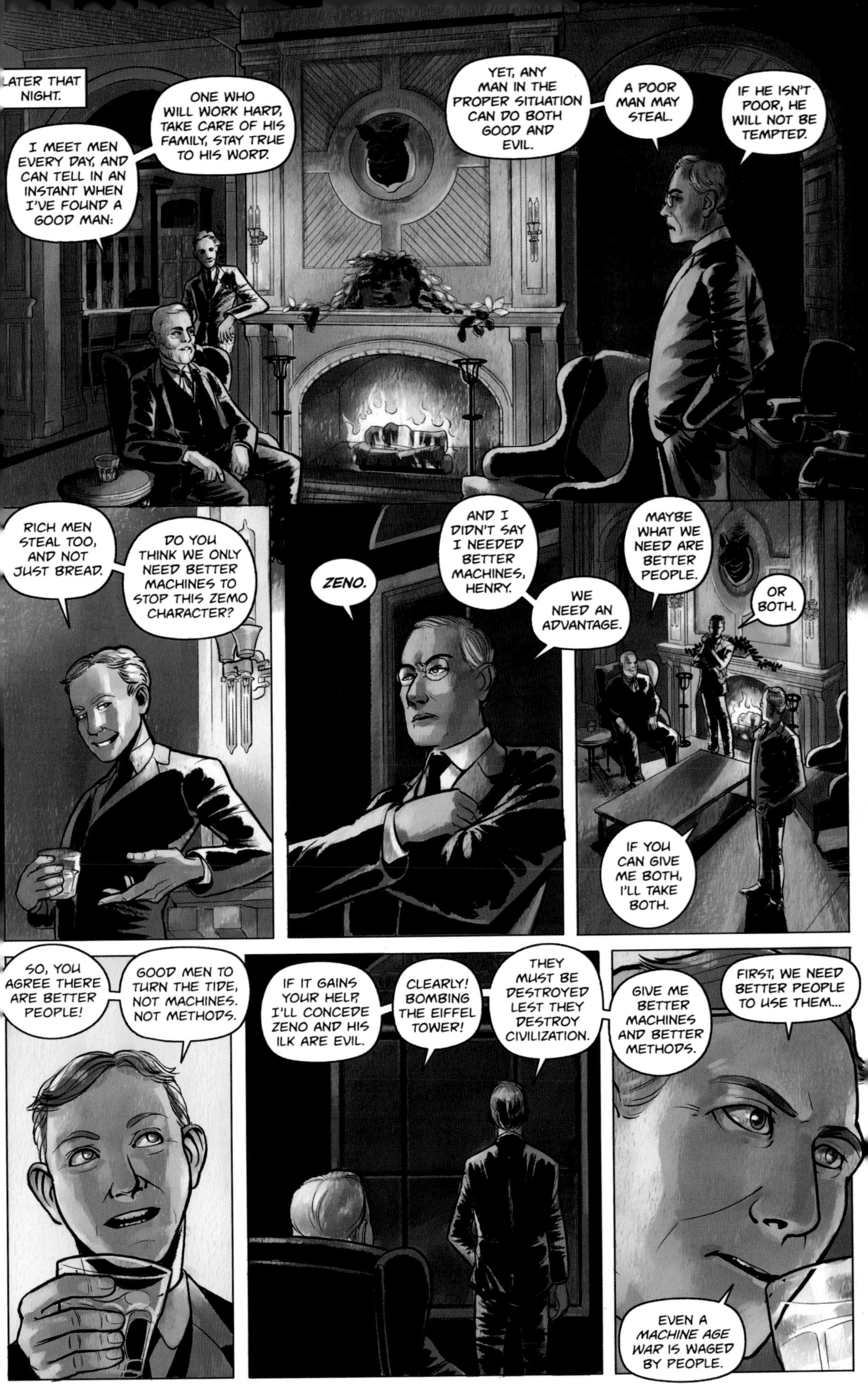
LATER THAT NIGHT.
I MEET MEN EVERY DAY, AND CAN TELL IN AN INSTANT WHEN I'VE FOUND A GOOD MAN:
ONE WHO WILL WORK HARD, TAKE CARE OF HIS FAMILY, STAY TRUE TO HIS WORD.
YET, ANY MAN IN THE PROPER SITUATION CAN DO BOTH GOOD AND EVIL.
A POOR MAN MAY STEAL.
IF HE ISN'T POOR, HE WILL NOT BE TEMPTED.
RICH MEN STEAL TOO, AND NOT JUST BREAD.
DO YOU THINK WE ONLY NEED BETTER MACHINES TO STOP THIS ZEMO CHARACTER?
ZENO.
AND I DIDN'T SAY I NEEDED BETTER MACHINES, HENRY.
WE NEED AN ADVANTAGE.
MAYBE WHAT WE NEED ARE BETTER PEOPLE.
OR BOTH.
IF YOU CAN GIVE ME BOTH, I'LL TAKE BOTH.
SO, YOU AGREE THERE ARE BETTER PEOPLE!
GOOD MEN TO TURN THE TIDE, NOT MACHINES. NOT METHODS.
IF IT GAINS YOUR HELP, I'LL CONCEDE ZENO AND HIS ILK ARE EVIL.
CLEARLY! BOMBING THE EIFFEL TOWER!
THEY MUST BE DESTROYED LEST THEY DESTROY CIVILIZATION.
GIVE ME BETTER MACHINES AND BETTER METHODS.
FIRST, WE NEED BETTER PEOPLE TO USE THEM...
EVEN A MACHINE AGE WAR IS WAGED BY PEOPLE.

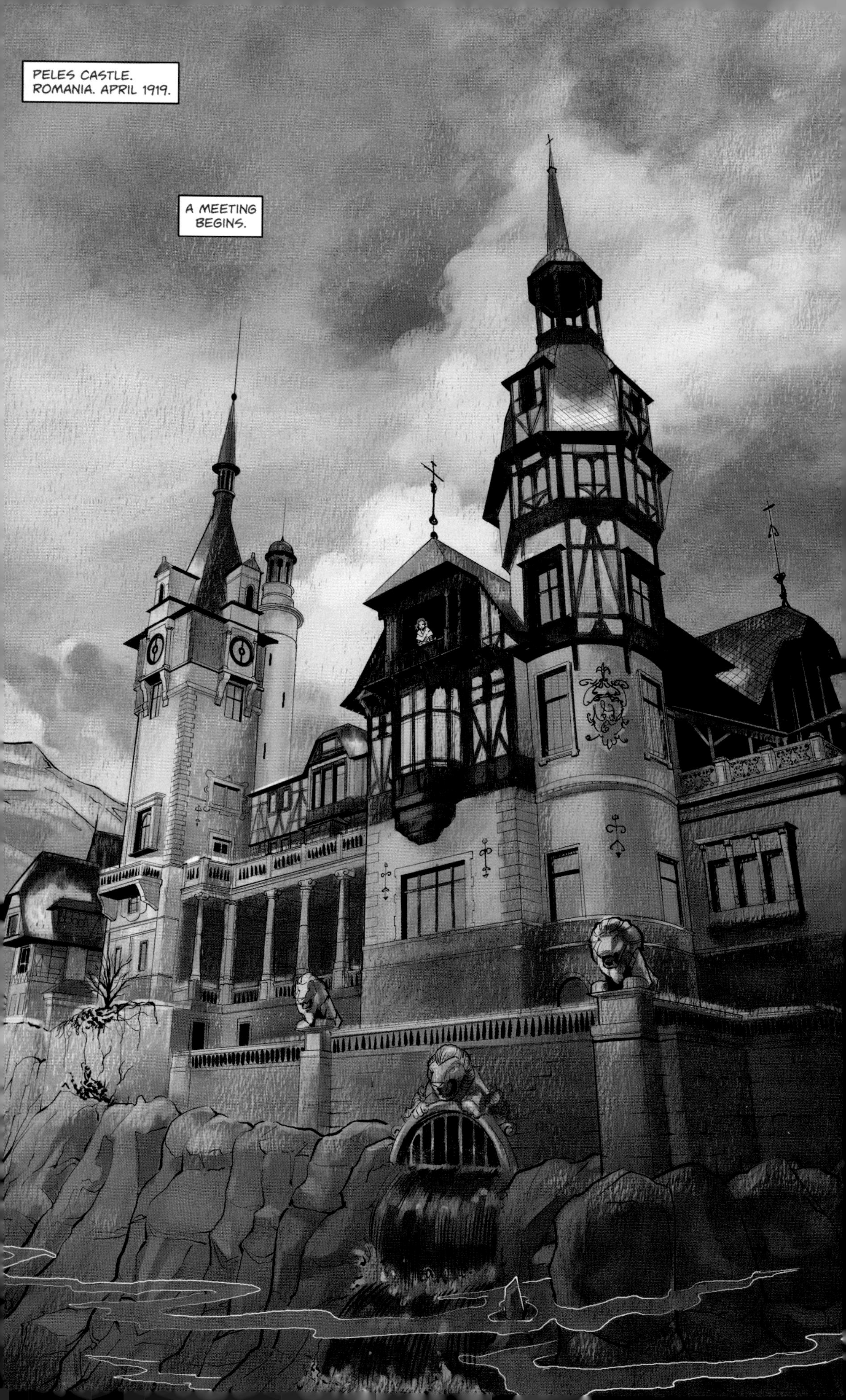
PELES CASTLE. ROMANIA. APRIL 1919.
A MEETING BEGINS.

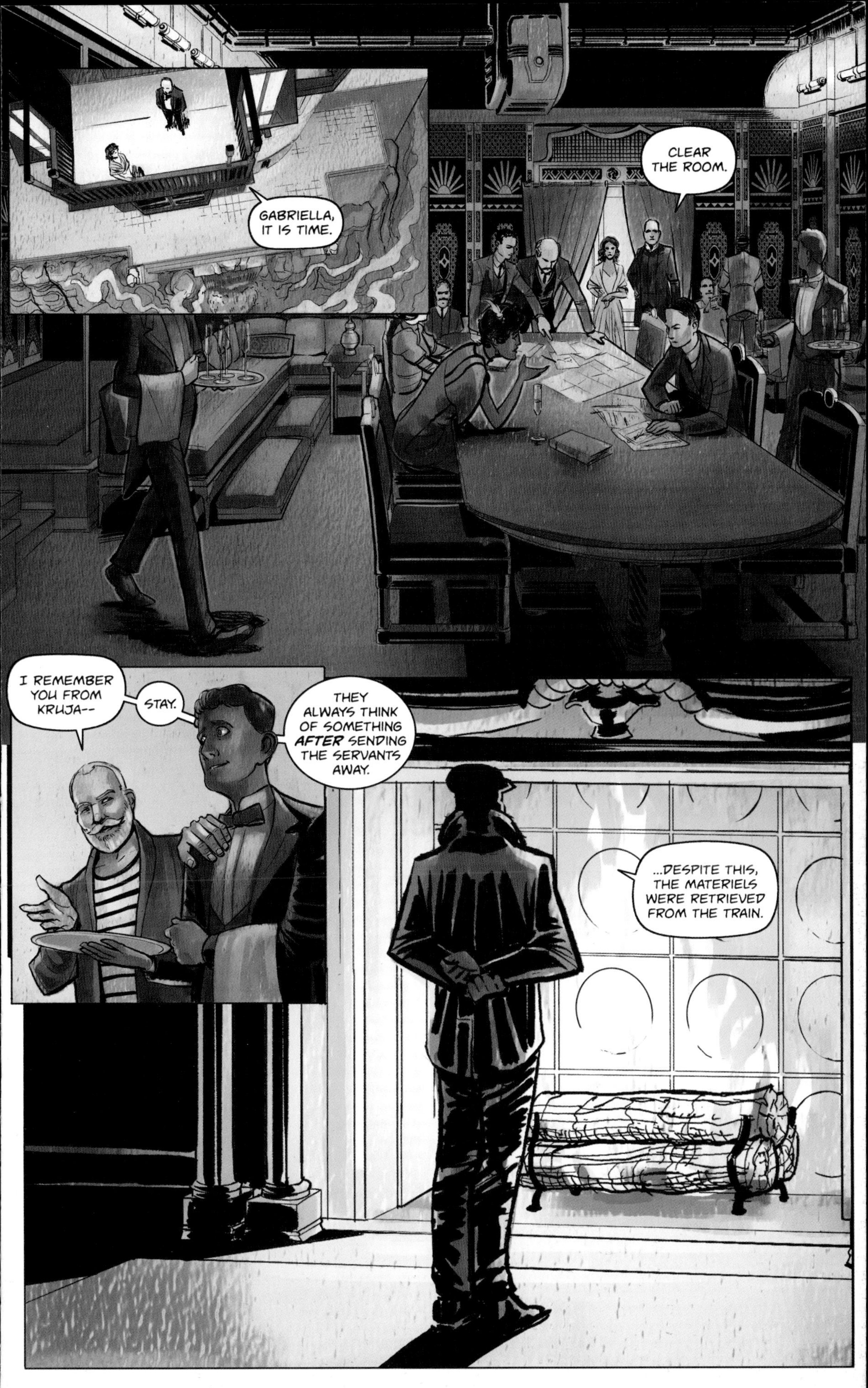
GABRIELLA, IT IS TIME.
CLEAR THE ROOM.
I REMEMBER YOU FROM KRUJA--
STAY.
THEY ALWAYS THINK OF SOMETHING *AFTER* SENDING THE SERVANTS AWAY.
...DESPITE THIS, THE MATERIELS WERE RETRIEVED FROM THE TRAIN.

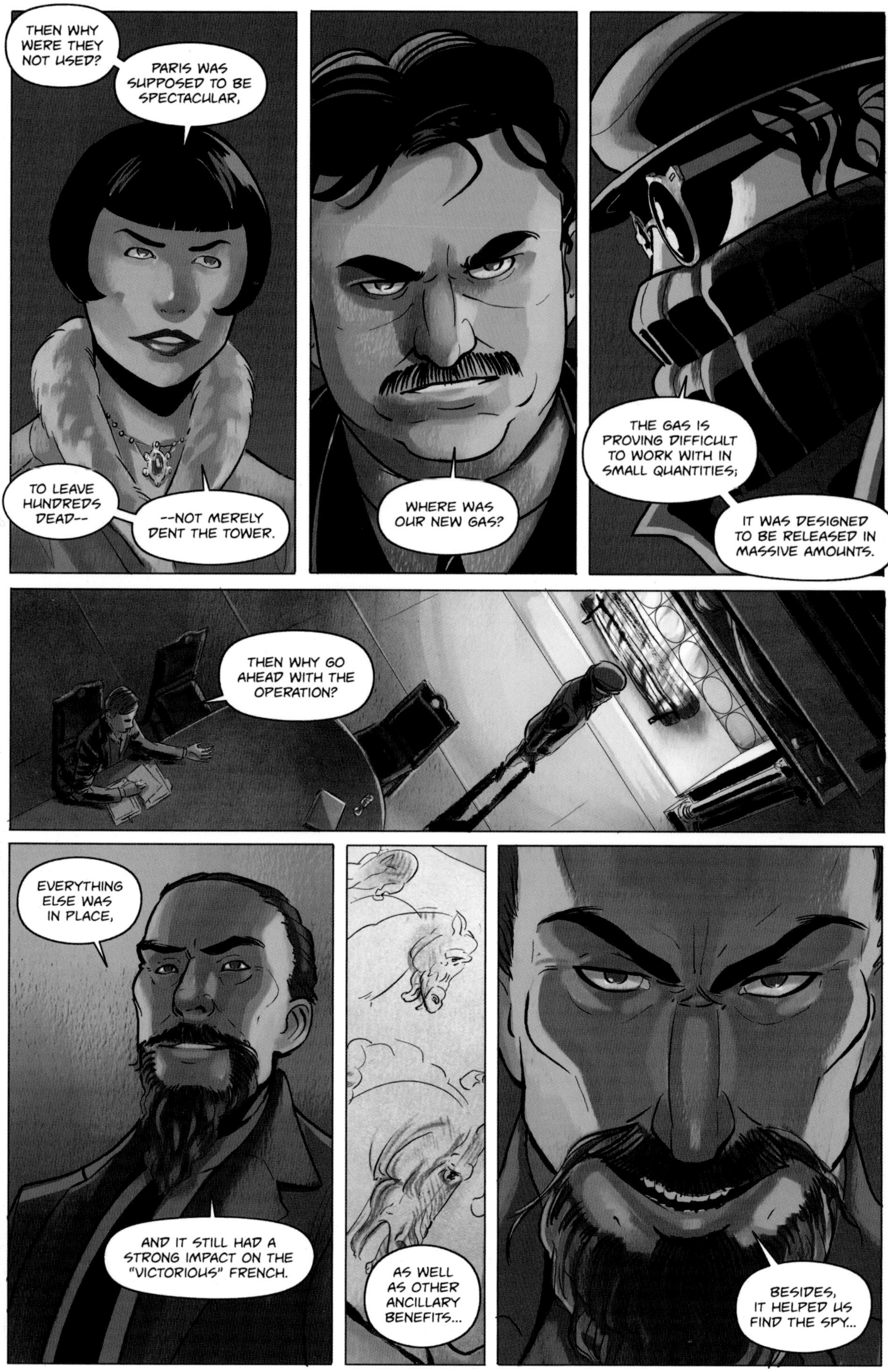
THEN WHY WERE THEY NOT USED?
PARIS WAS SUPPOSED TO BE SPECTACULAR,
TO LEAVE HUNDREDS DEAD--
--NOT MERELY DENT THE TOWER.
WHERE WAS OUR NEW GAS?
THE GAS IS PROVING DIFFICULT TO WORK WITH IN SMALL QUANTITIES;
IT WAS DESIGNED TO BE RELEASED IN MASSIVE AMOUNTS.
THEN WHY GO AHEAD WITH THE OPERATION?
EVERYTHING ELSE WAS IN PLACE,
AND IT STILL HAD A STRONG IMPACT ON THE "VICTORIOUS" FRENCH.
AS WELL AS OTHER ANCILLARY BENEFITS...
BESIDES, IT HELPED US FIND THE SPY...

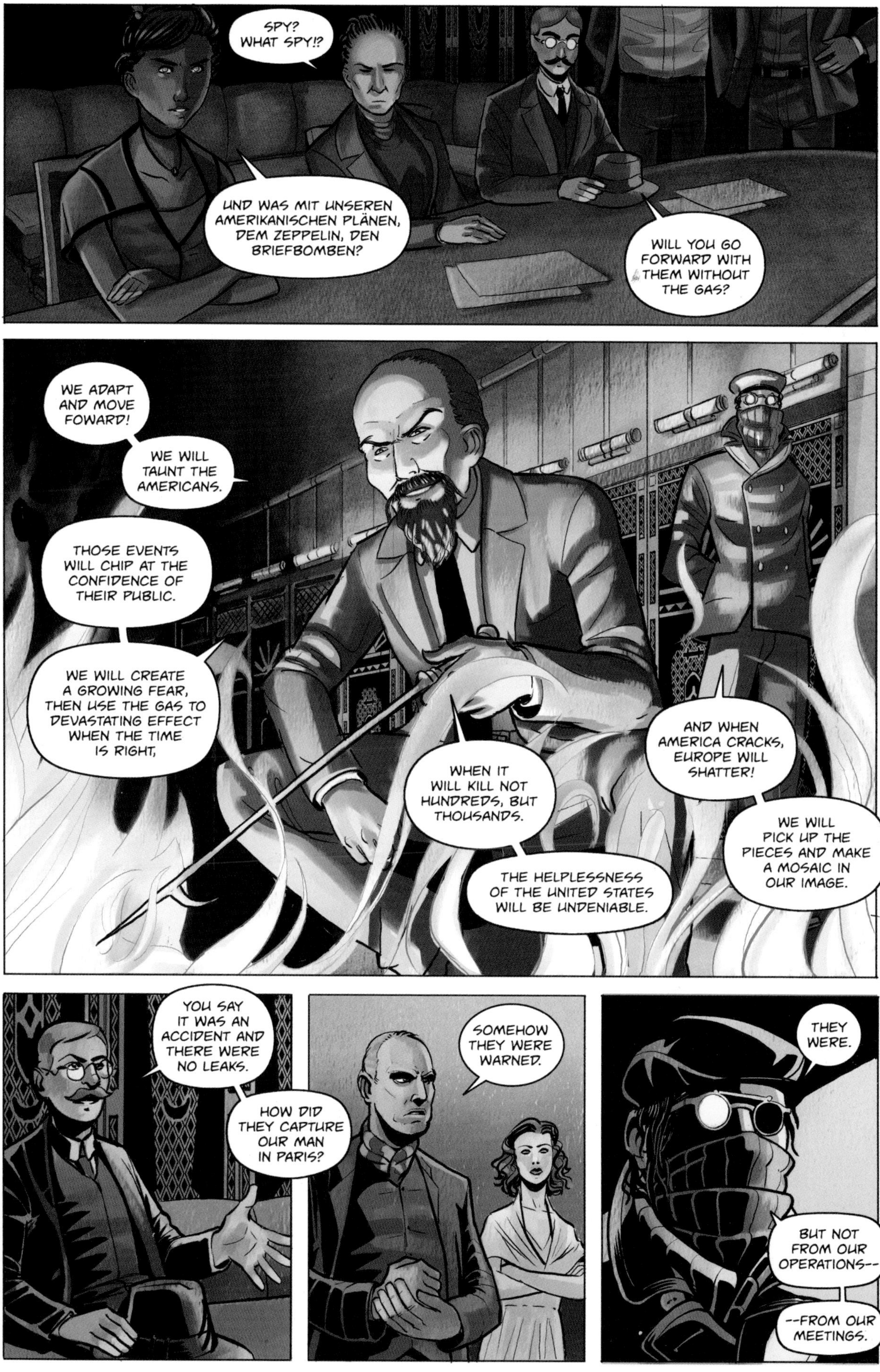
SPY? WHAT SPY!?
UND WAS MIT UNSEREN AMERIKANISCHEN PLÄNEN, DEM ZEPPELIN, DEN BRIEFBOMBEN?
WILL YOU GO FORWARD WITH THEM WITHOUT THE GAS?
WE ADAPT AND MOVE FOWARD!
WE WILL TAUNT THE AMERICANS.
THOSE EVENTS WILL CHIP AT THE CONFIDENCE OF THEIR PUBLIC.
WE WILL CREATE A GROWING FEAR, THEN USE THE GAS TO DEVASTATING EFFECT WHEN THE TIME IS RIGHT,
WHEN IT WILL KILL NOT HUNDREDS, BUT THOUSANDS.
THE HELPLESSNESS OF THE UNITED STATES WILL BE UNDENIABLE.
AND WHEN AMERICA CRACKS, EUROPE WILL SHATTER!
WE WILL PICK UP THE PIECES AND MAKE A MOSAIC IN OUR IMAGE.
YOU SAY IT WAS AN ACCIDENT AND THERE WERE NO LEAKS.
HOW DID THEY CAPTURE OUR MAN IN PARIS?
SOMEHOW THEY WERE WARNED.
THEY WERE.
BUT NOT FROM OUR OPERATIONS--
--FROM OUR MEETINGS.

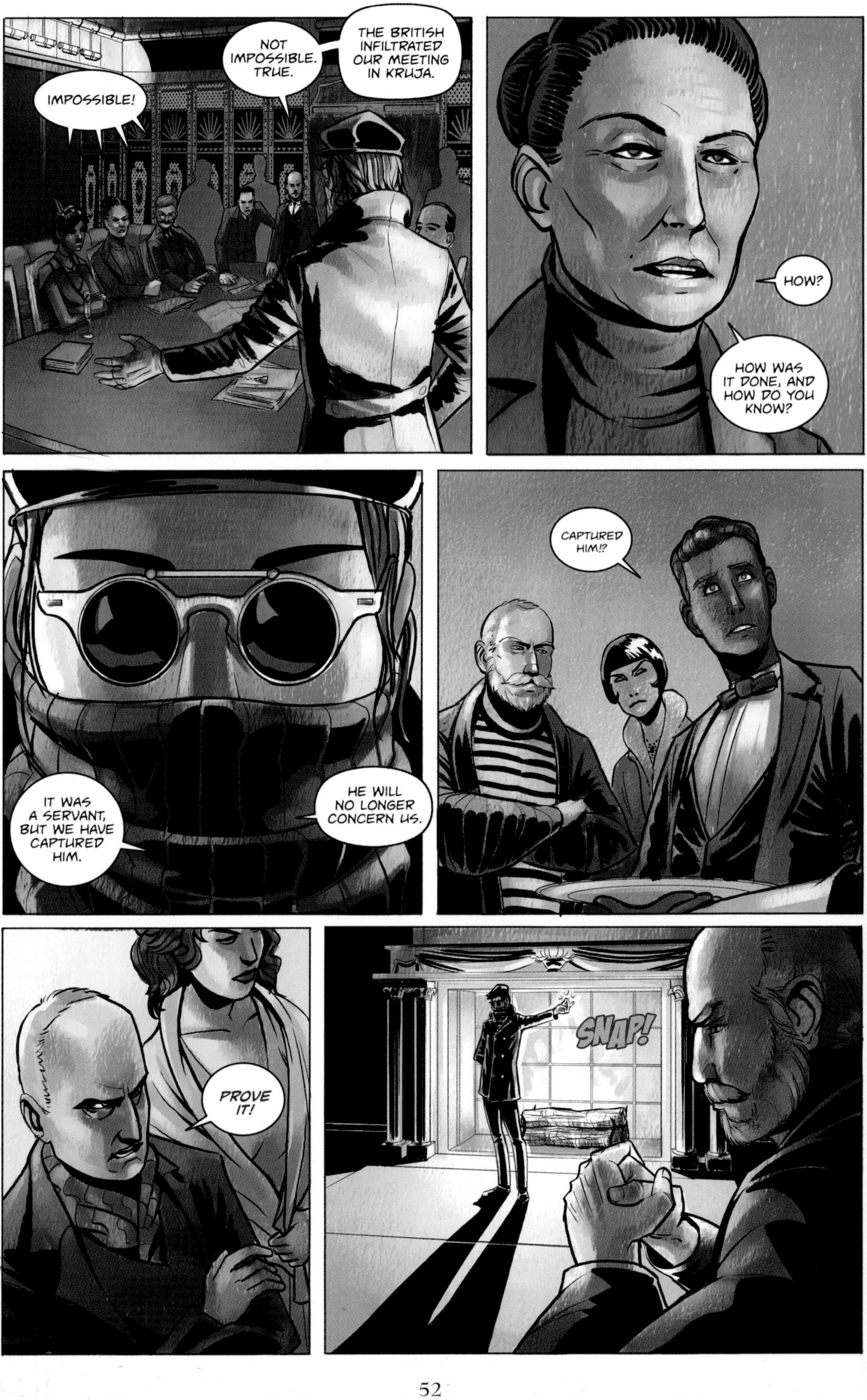
IMPOSSIBLE!
NOT IMPOSSIBLE. TRUE.
THE BRITISH INFILTRATED OUR MEETING IN KRUJA.
HOW?
HOW WAS IT DONE, AND HOW DO YOU KNOW?
IT WAS A SERVANT, BUT WE HAVE CAPTURED HIM.
HE WILL NO LONGER CONCERN US.
CAPTURED HIM!?
PROVE IT!
SNAP!

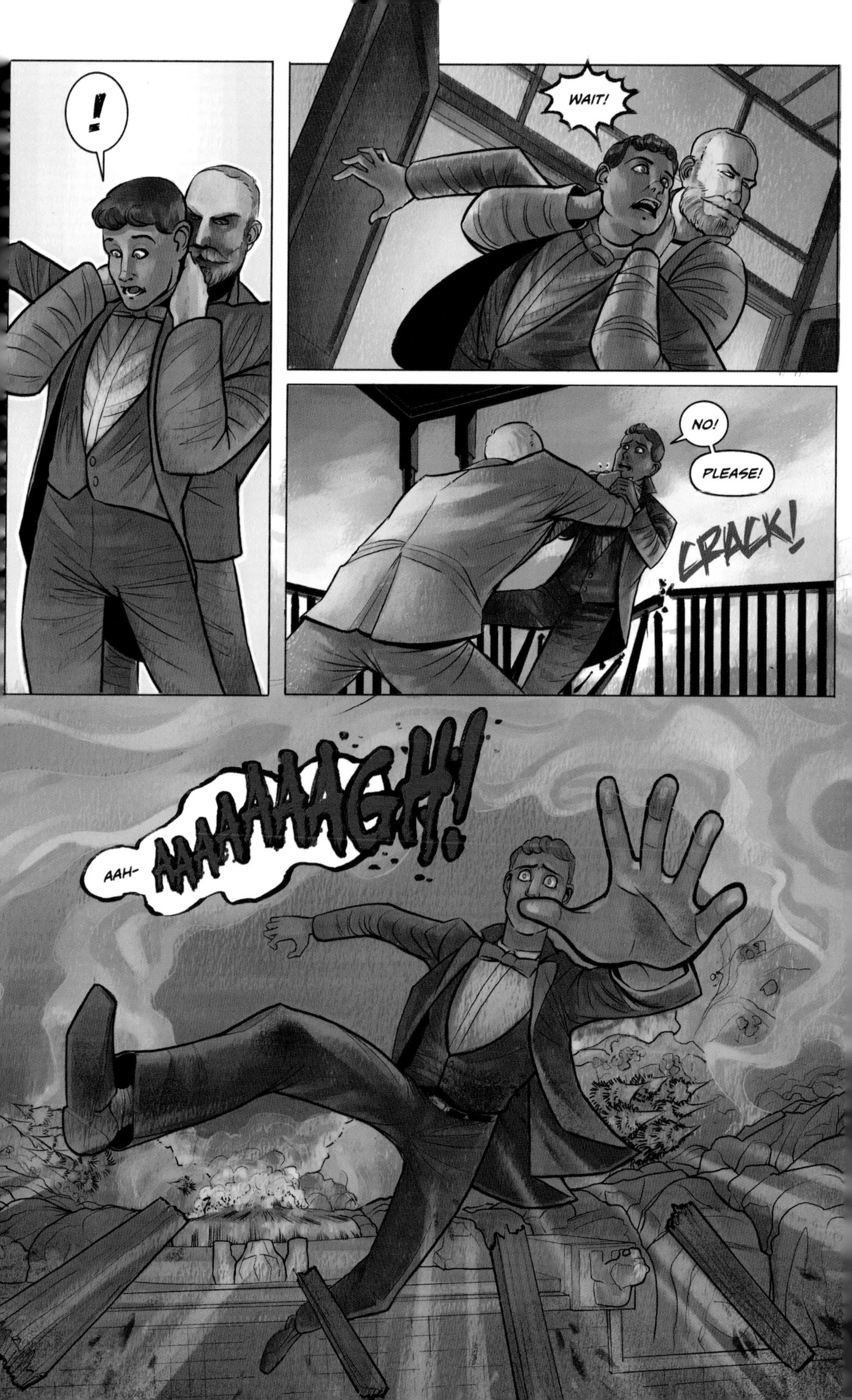
!
WAIT!
NO!
PLEASE!
CRACK!
AAH-
AAAAAAAGH!

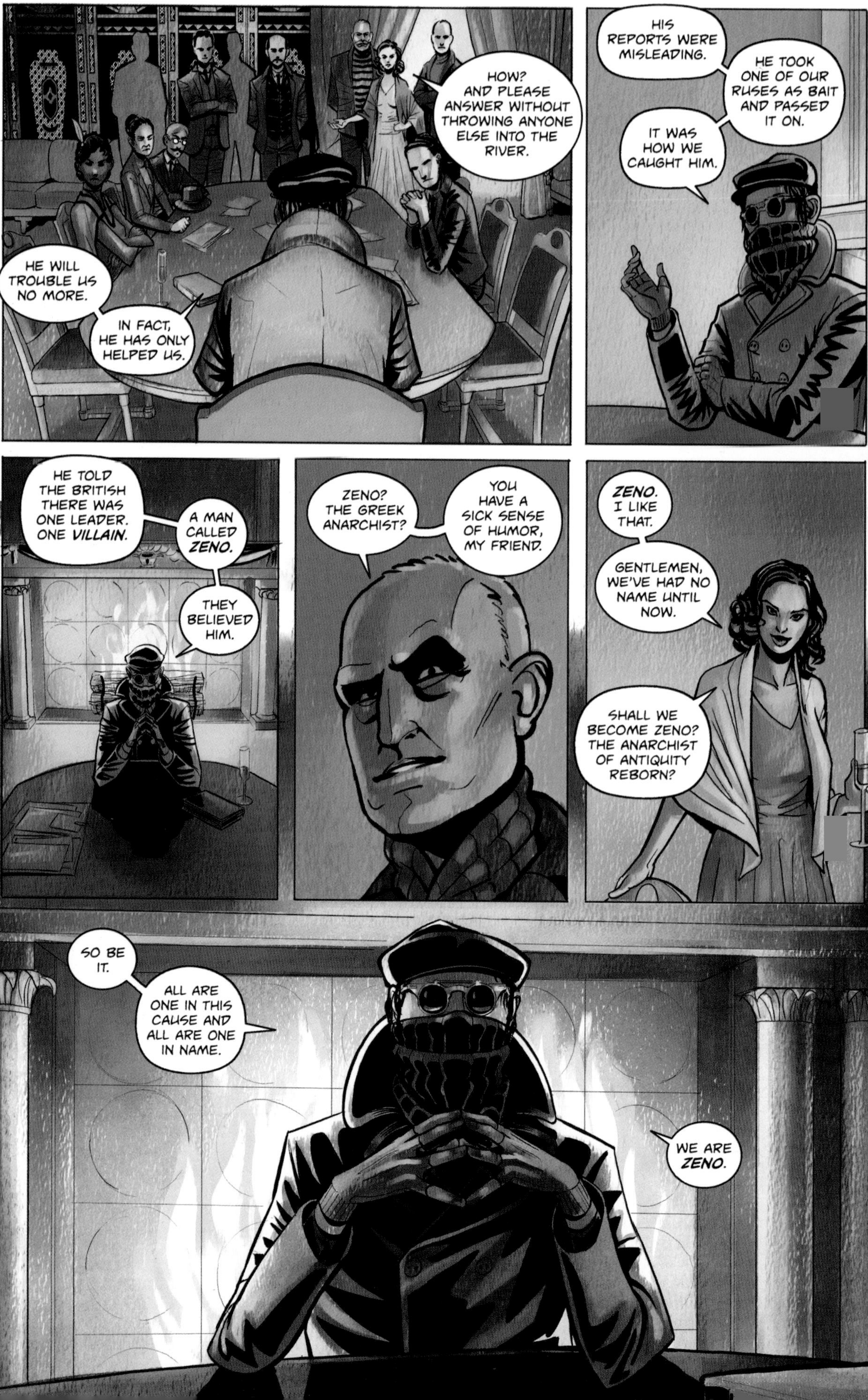
HOW? AND PLEASE ANSWER WITHOUT THROWING ANYONE ELSE INTO THE RIVER.
HE WILL TROUBLE US NO MORE.
IN FACT, HE HAS ONLY HELPED US.
HIS REPORTS WERE MISLEADING.
HE TOOK ONE OF OUR RUSES AS BAIT AND PASSED IT ON.
IT WAS HOW WE CAUGHT HIM.
HE TOLD THE BRITISH THERE WAS ONE LEADER. ONE *VILLAIN*.
A MAN CALLED *ZENO.*
THEY BELIEVED HIM.
ZENO? THE GREEK ANARCHIST?
YOU HAVE A SICK SENSE OF HUMOR, MY FRIEND.
ZENO. I LIKE THAT.
GENTLEMEN, WE'VE HAD NO NAME UNTIL NOW.
SHALL WE BECOME ZENO? THE ANARCHIST OF ANTIQUITY REBORN?
SO BE IT.
ALL ARE ONE IN THIS CAUSE AND ALL ARE ONE IN NAME.
WE ARE *ZENO*.

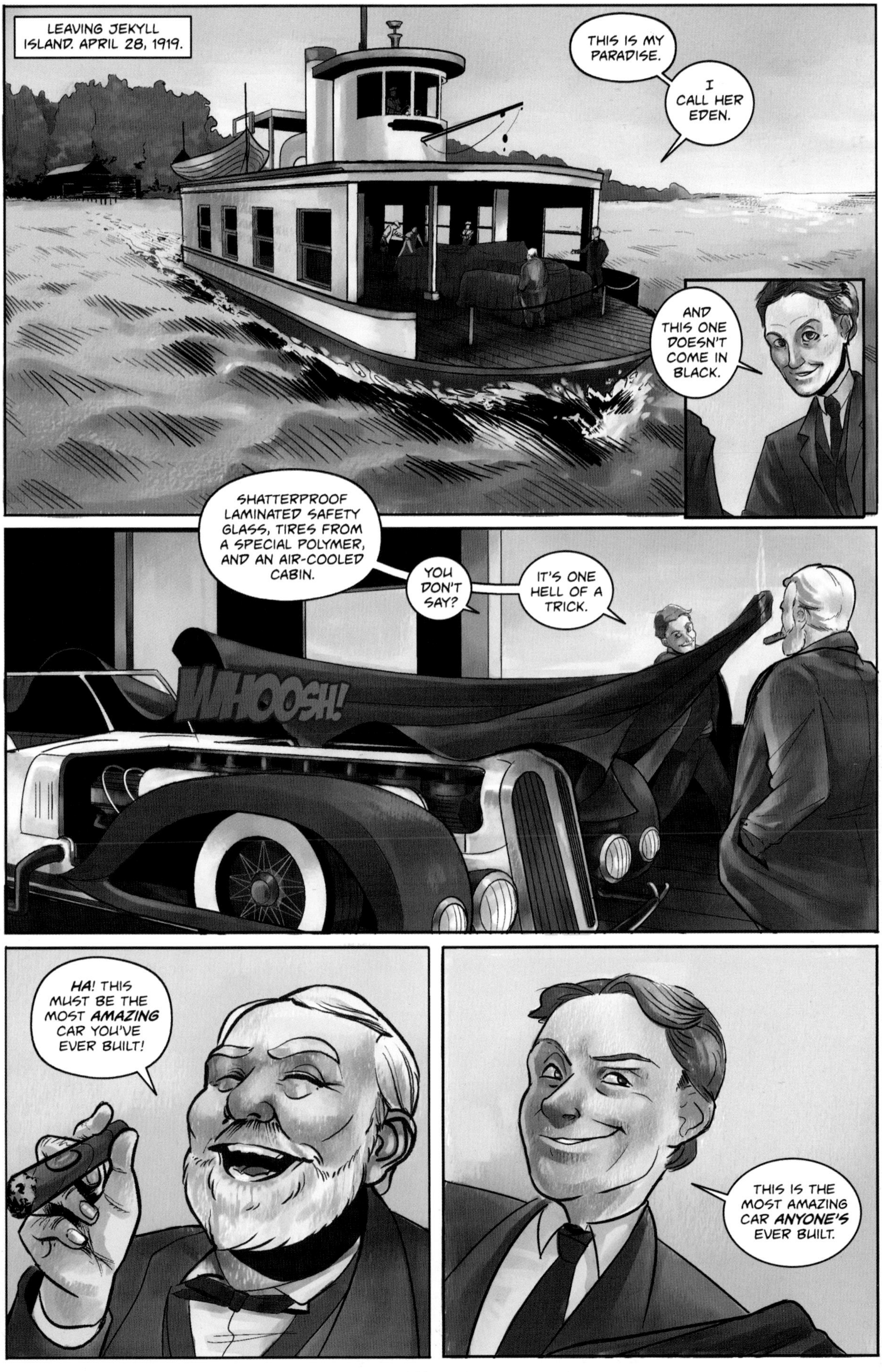
LEAVING JEKYLL ISLAND. APRIL 28, 1919.
THIS IS MY PARADISE.
I CALL HER EDEN.
AND THIS ONE DOESN'T COME IN BLACK.
SHATTERPROOF LAMINATED SAFETY GLASS, TIRES FROM A SPECIAL POLYMER, AND AN AIR-COOLED CABIN.
YOU DON'T SAY?
IT'S ONE HELL OF A TRICK.
WHOOSH!
HA! THIS MUST BE THE MOST AMAZING CAR YOU'VE EVER BUILT!
THIS IS THE MOST AMAZING CAR ANYONE'S EVER BUILT.

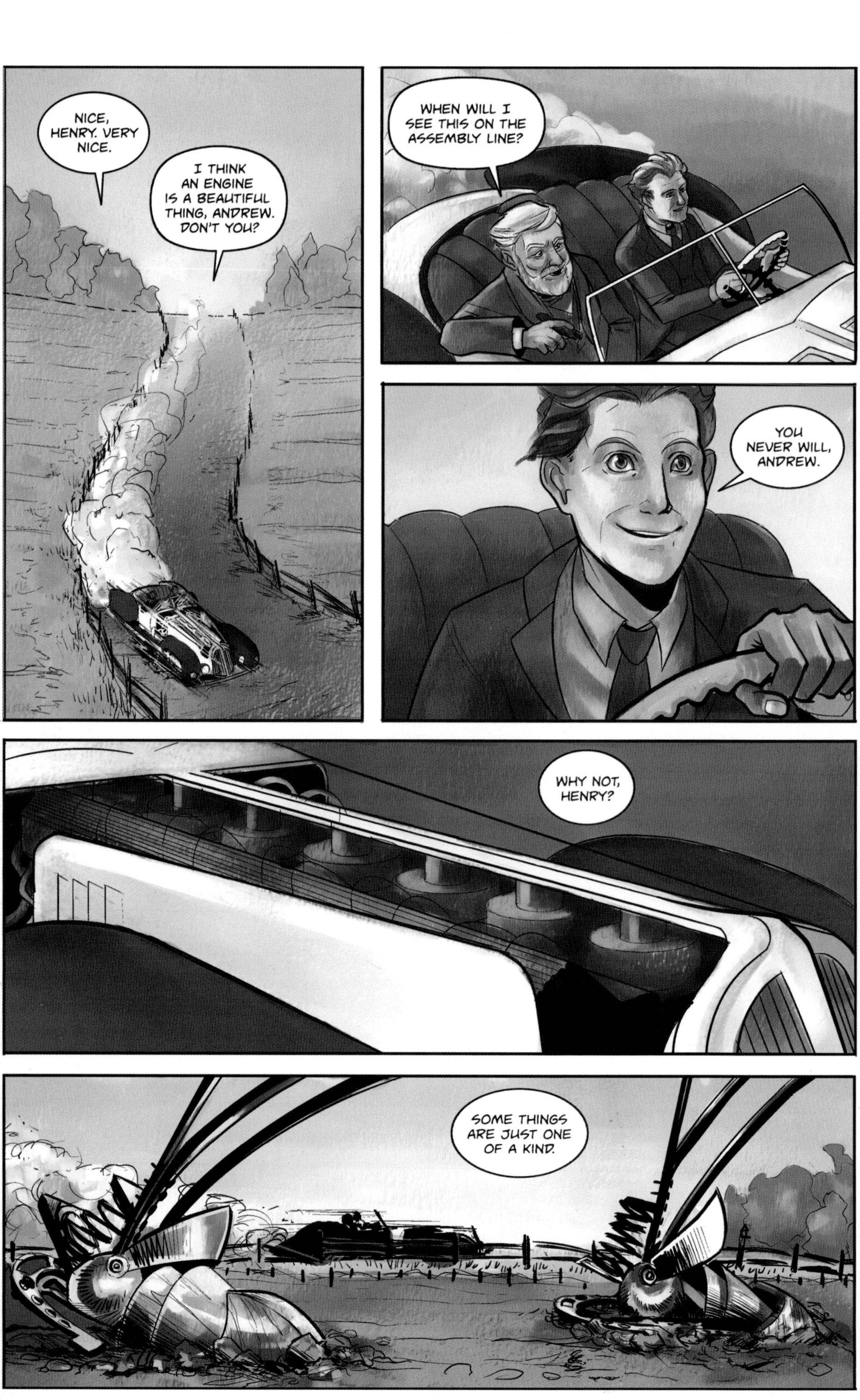
NICE, HENRY. VERY NICE.
I THINK AN ENGINE IS A BEAUTIFUL THING, ANDREW. DON'T YOU?
WHEN WILL I SEE THIS ON THE ASSEMBLY LINE?
YOU NEVER WILL, ANDREW.
WHY NOT, HENRY?
SOME THINGS ARE JUST ONE OF A KIND.

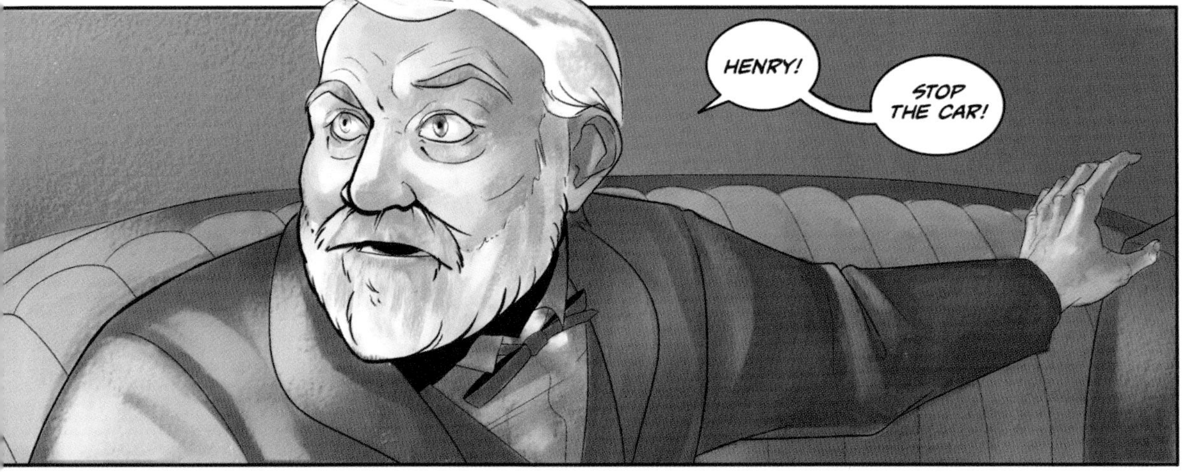
HENRY!
STOP THE CAR!

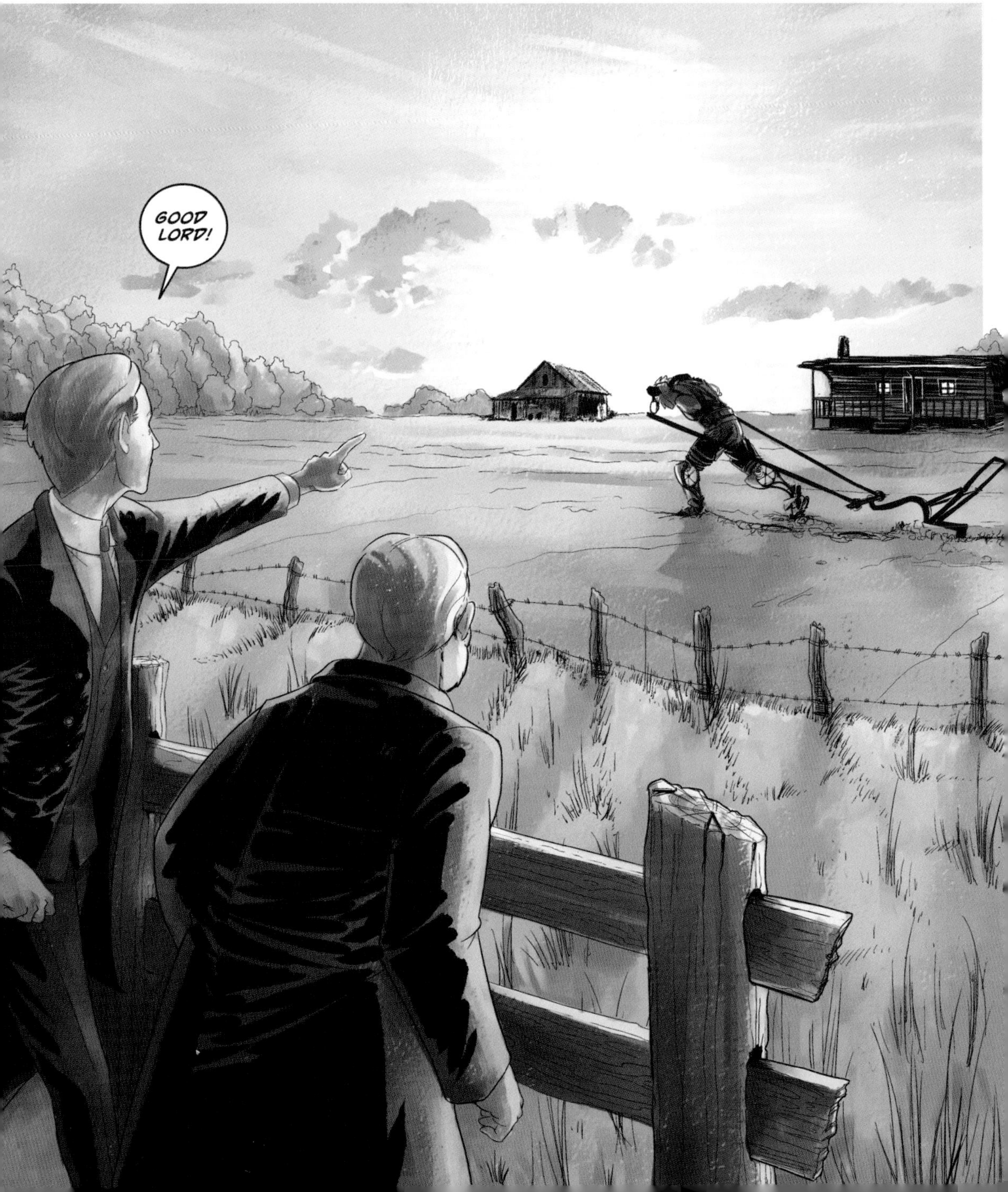
GOOD LORD!

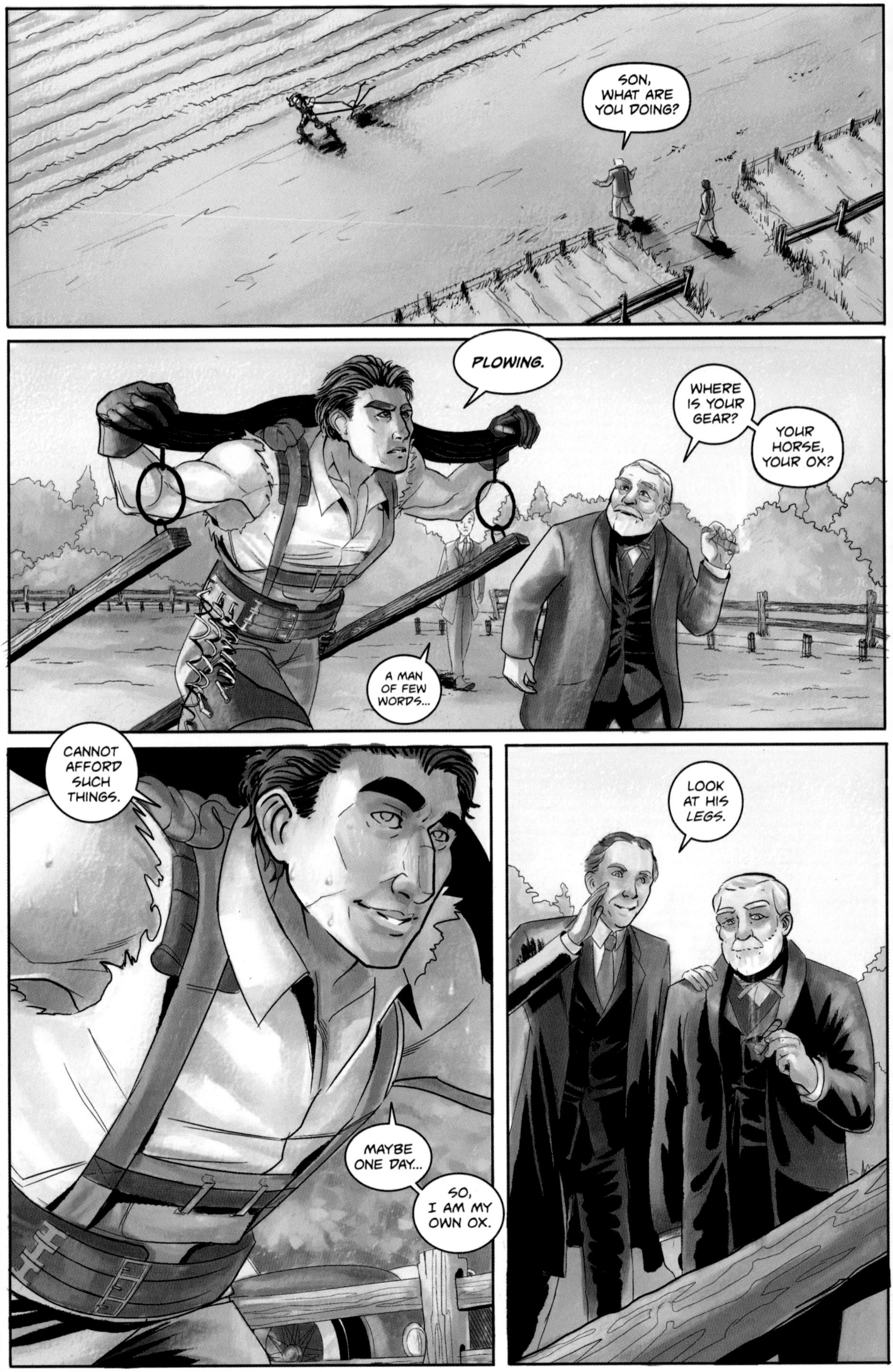
SON, WHAT ARE YOU DOING?
PLOWING.
WHERE IS YOUR GEAR?
YOUR HORSE, YOUR OX?
A MAN OF FEW WORDS...
CANNOT AFFORD SUCH THINGS.
MAYBE ONE DAY...
SO, I AM MY OWN OX.
LOOK AT HIS LEGS.

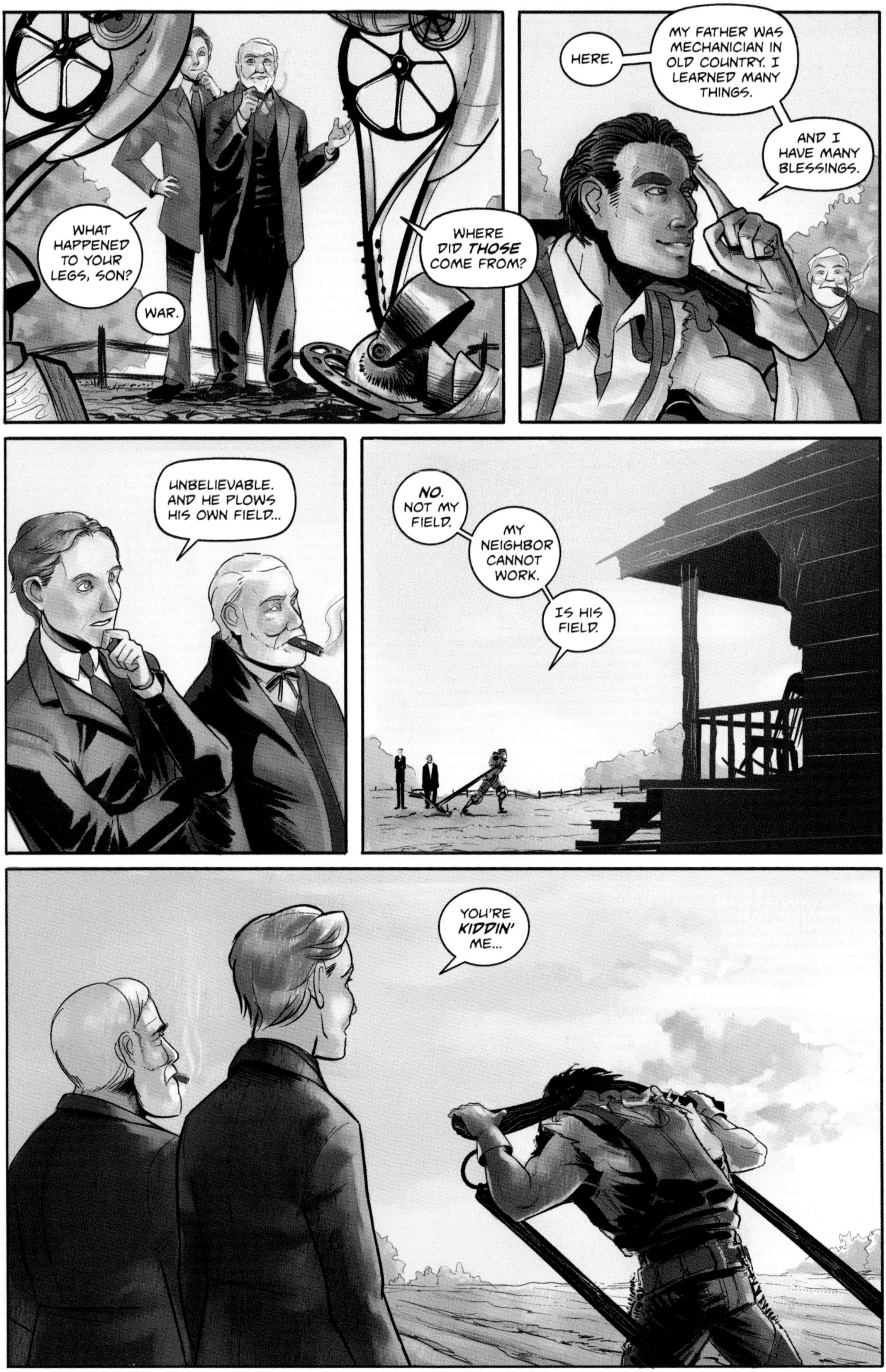
WHAT HAPPENED TO YOUR LEGS, SON?
WAR.
WHERE DID *THOSE* COME FROM?
HERE.
MY FATHER WAS MECHANICIAN IN OLD COUNTRY. I LEARNED MANY THINGS.
AND I HAVE MANY BLESSINGS.
UNBELIEVABLE. AND HE PLOWS HIS OWN FIELD...
NO. NOT MY FIELD.
MY NEIGHBOR CANNOT WORK.
IS HIS FIELD.
YOU'RE *KIDDIN'* ME...

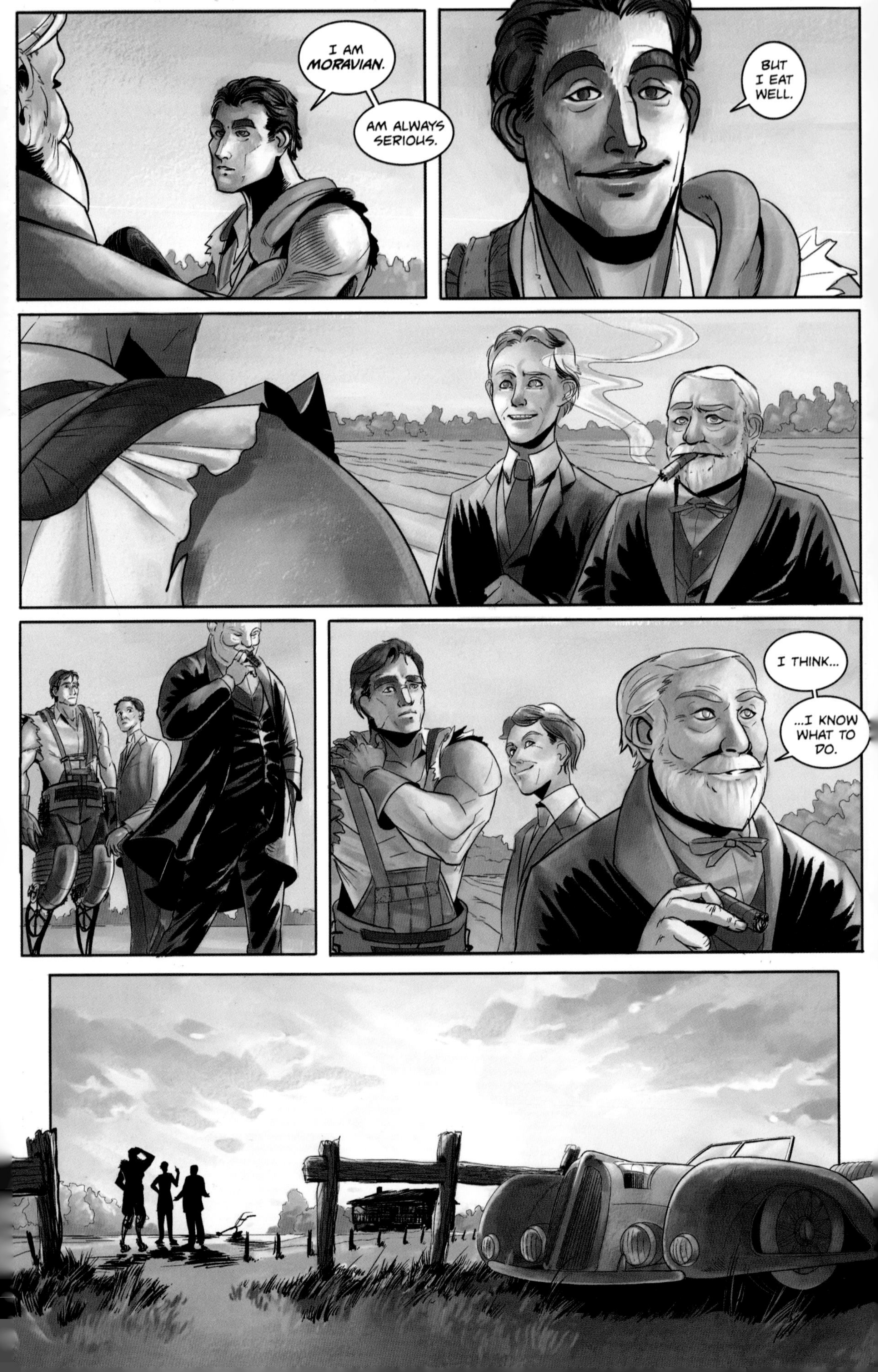
I AM MORAVIAN.
AM ALWAYS SERIOUS.
BUT I EAT WELL.
I THINK...
...I KNOW WHAT TO DO.

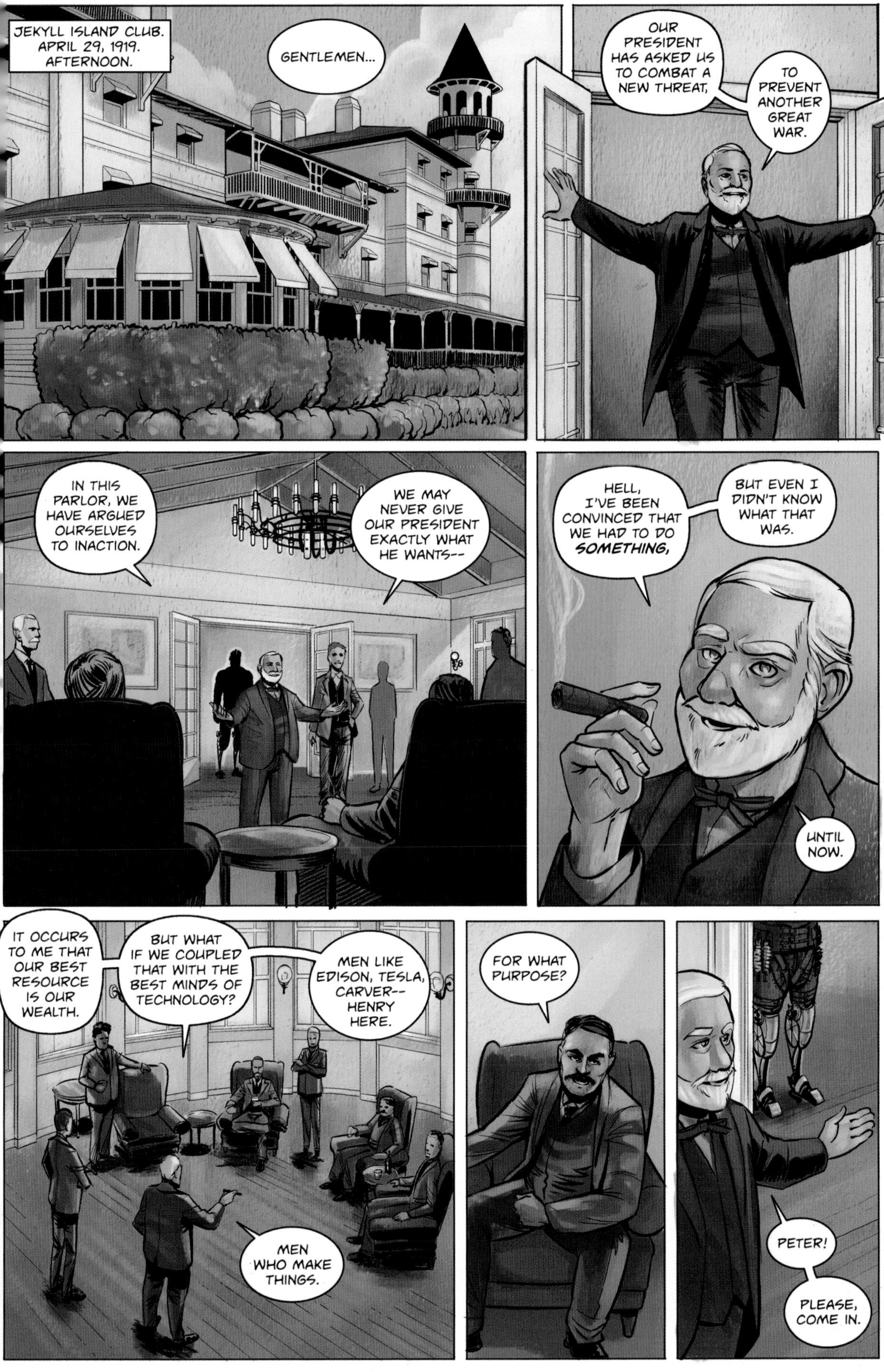
JEKYLL ISLAND CLUB. APRIL 29, 1919. AFTERNOON.
GENTLEMEN...
OUR PRESIDENT HAS ASKED US TO COMBAT A NEW THREAT,
TO PREVENT ANOTHER GREAT WAR.
IN THIS PARLOR, WE HAVE ARGUED OURSELVES TO INACTION.
WE MAY NEVER GIVE OUR PRESIDENT EXACTLY WHAT HE WANTS--
HELL, I'VE BEEN CONVINCED THAT WE HAD TO DO *SOMETHING,*
BUT EVEN I DIDN'T KNOW WHAT THAT WAS.
UNTIL NOW.
IT OCCURS TO ME THAT OUR BEST RESOURCE IS OUR WEALTH.
BUT WHAT IF WE COUPLED THAT WITH THE BEST MINDS OF TECHNOLOGY?
MEN LIKE EDISON, TESLA, CARVER-- HENRY HERE.
MEN WHO MAKE THINGS.
FOR WHAT PURPOSE?
PETER!
PLEASE, COME IN.

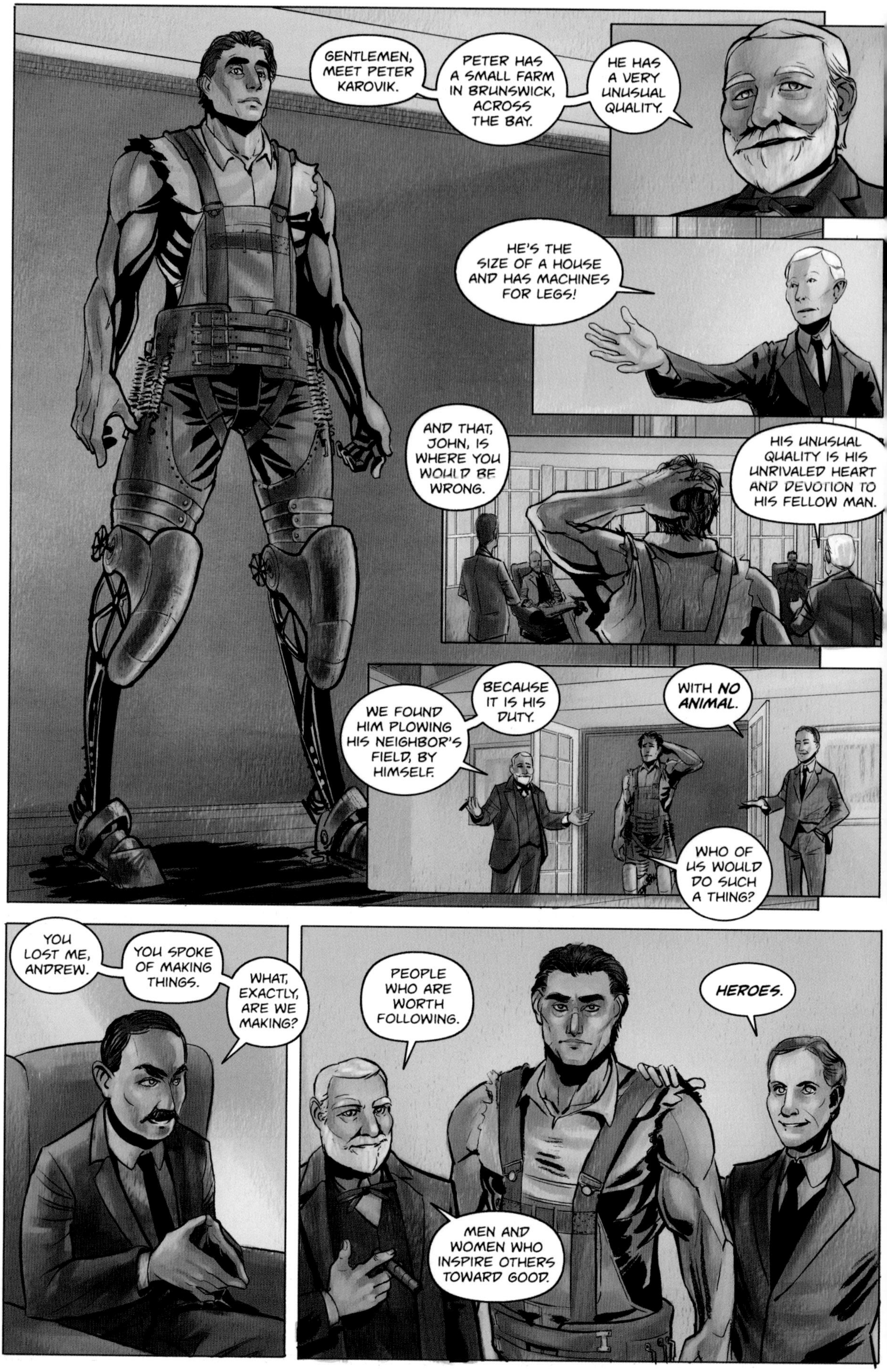
GENTLEMEN, MEET PETER KAROVIK.
PETER HAS A SMALL FARM IN BRUNSWICK, ACROSS THE BAY.
HE HAS A VERY UNUSUAL QUALITY.
HE'S THE SIZE OF A HOUSE AND HAS MACHINES FOR LEGS!
AND THAT, JOHN, IS WHERE YOU WOULD BE WRONG.
HIS UNUSUAL QUALITY IS HIS UNRIVALED HEART AND DEVOTION TO HIS FELLOW MAN.
WE FOUND HIM PLOWING HIS NEIGHBOR'S FIELD, BY HIMSELF.
BECAUSE IT IS HIS DUTY.
WITH ***NO ANIMAL***.
WHO OF US WOULD DO SUCH A THING?
YOU LOST ME, ANDREW.
YOU SPOKE OF MAKING THINGS.
WHAT, EXACTLY, ARE WE MAKING?
PEOPLE WHO ARE WORTH FOLLOWING.
HEROES.
MEN AND WOMEN WHO INSPIRE OTHERS TOWARD GOOD.

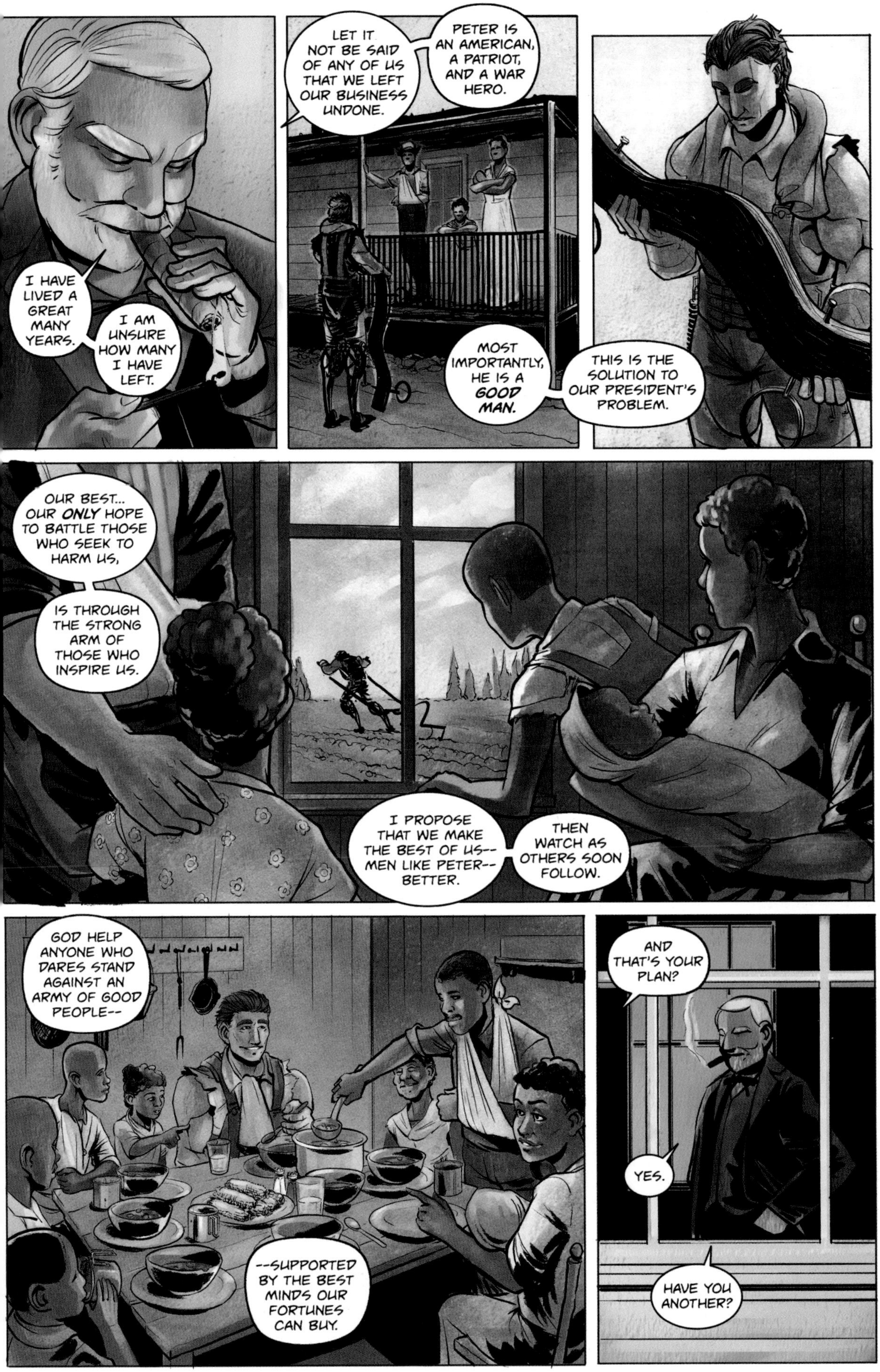
I HAVE LIVED A GREAT MANY YEARS.
I AM UNSURE HOW MANY I HAVE LEFT.
LET IT NOT BE SAID OF ANY OF US THAT WE LEFT OUR BUSINESS UNDONE.
PETER IS AN AMERICAN, A PATRIOT, AND A WAR HERO.
MOST IMPORTANTLY, HE IS A *GOOD MAN.*
THIS IS THE SOLUTION TO OUR PRESIDENT'S PROBLEM.
OUR BEST... OUR *ONLY* HOPE TO BATTLE THOSE WHO SEEK TO HARM US,
IS THROUGH THE STRONG ARM OF THOSE WHO INSPIRE US.
I PROPOSE THAT WE MAKE THE BEST OF US-- MEN LIKE PETER-- BETTER.
THEN WATCH AS OTHERS SOON FOLLOW.
GOD HELP ANYONE WHO DARES STAND AGAINST AN ARMY OF GOOD PEOPLE--
--SUPPORTED BY THE BEST MINDS OUR FORTUNES CAN BUY.
AND THAT'S YOUR PLAN?
YES.
HAVE YOU ANOTHER?

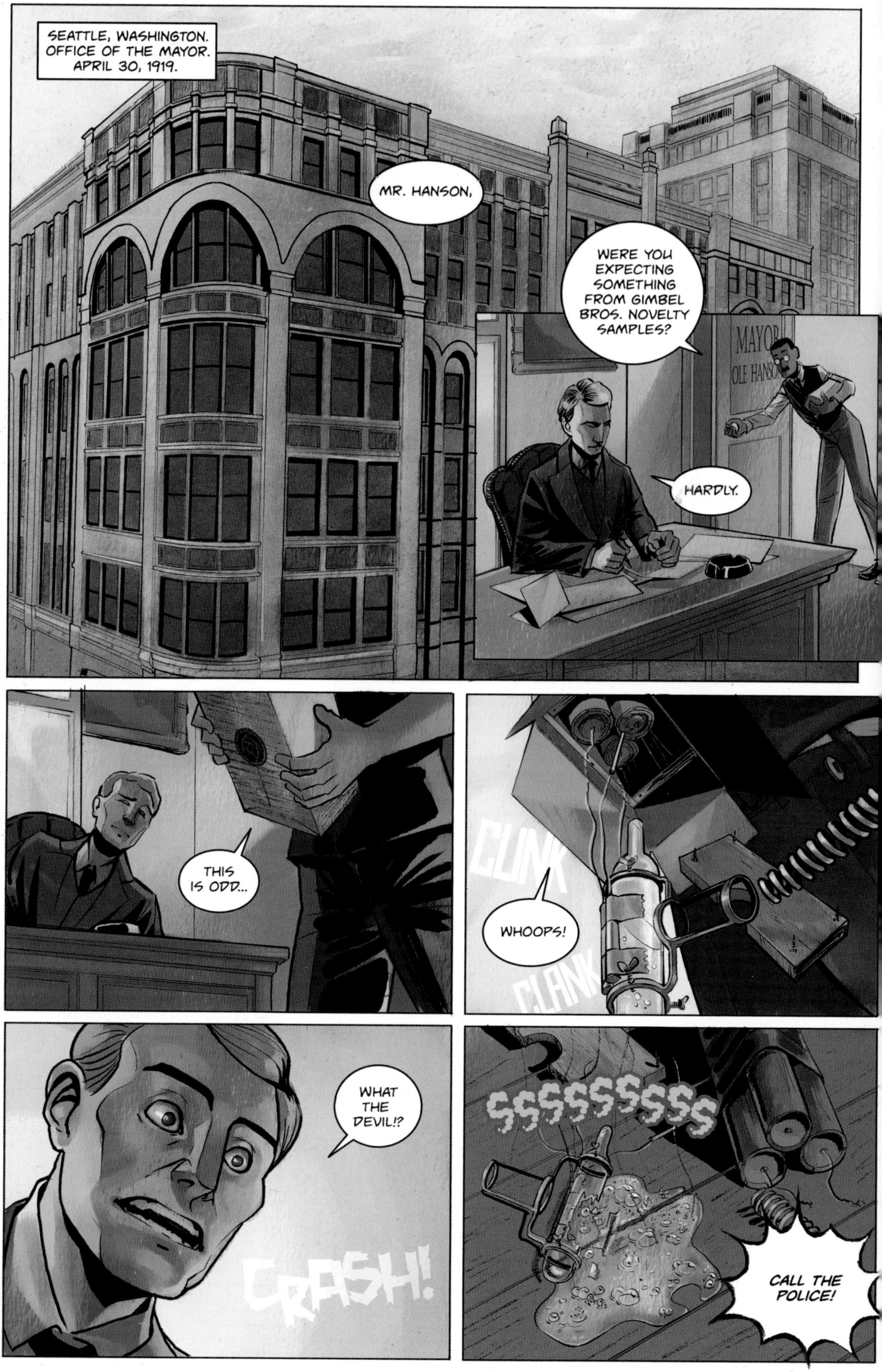
SEATTLE, WASHINGTON. OFFICE OF THE MAYOR. APRIL 30, 1919.
MR. HANSON,
WERE YOU EXPECTING SOMETHING FROM GIMBEL BROS. NOVELTY SAMPLES?
MAYOR OLE HANSON
HARDLY.
THIS IS ODD...
CLINK
WHOOPS!
CLANK
WHAT THE DEVIL!?
CRASH!
SSSSSSSSSS
CALL THE POLICE!

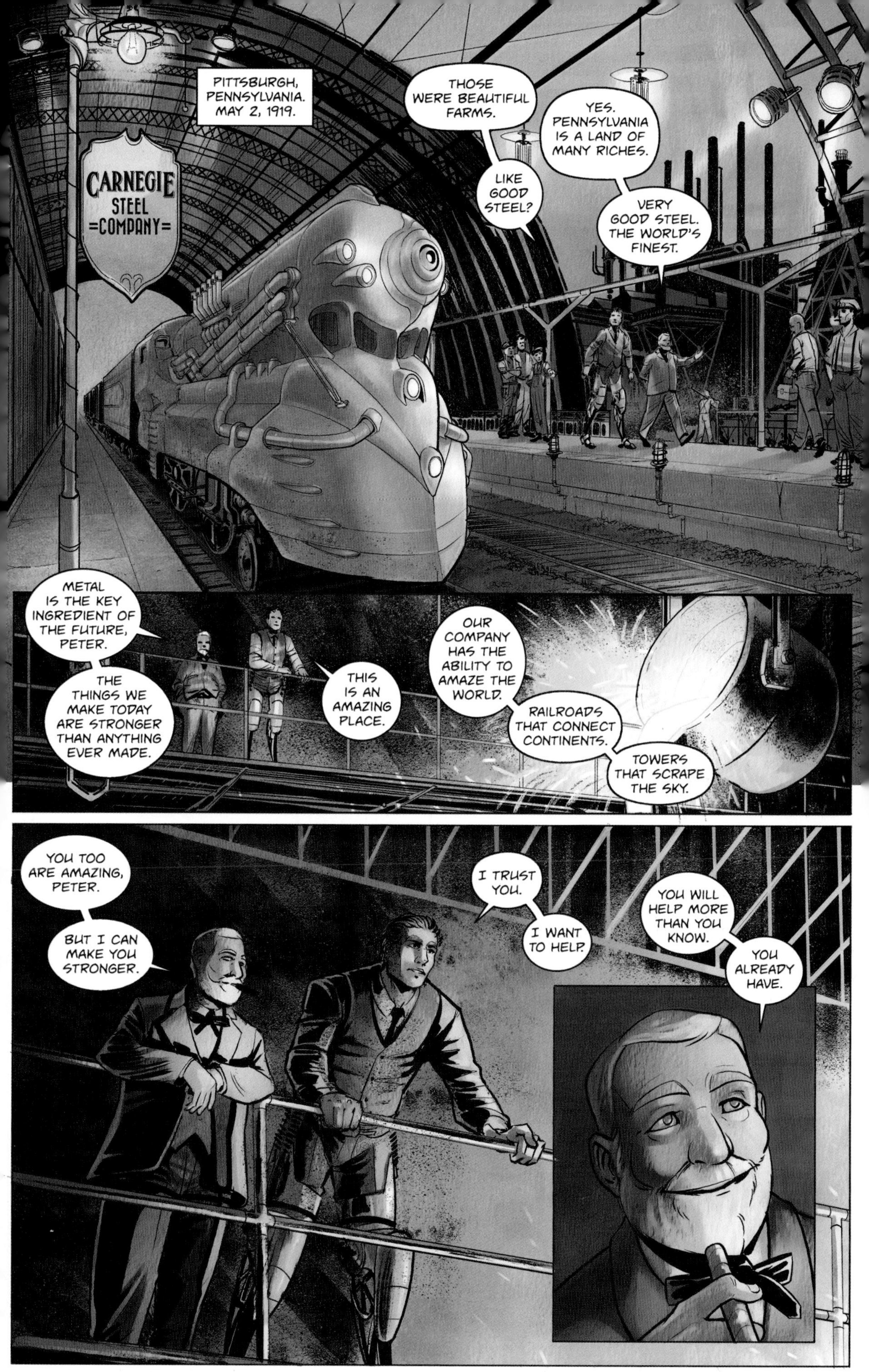
PITTSBURGH, PENNSYLVANIA. MAY 2, 1919.
CARNEGIE STEEL =COMPANY=
THOSE WERE BEAUTIFUL FARMS.
LIKE GOOD STEEL?
YES. PENNSYLVANIA IS A LAND OF MANY RICHES.
VERY GOOD STEEL. THE WORLD'S FINEST.
METAL IS THE KEY INGREDIENT OF THE FUTURE, PETER.
THE THINGS WE MAKE TODAY ARE STRONGER THAN ANYTHING EVER MADE.
THIS IS AN AMAZING PLACE.
OUR COMPANY HAS THE ABILITY TO AMAZE THE WORLD.
RAILROADS THAT CONNECT CONTINENTS.
TOWERS THAT SCRAPE THE SKY.
YOU TOO ARE AMAZING, PETER.
BUT I CAN MAKE YOU STRONGER.
I TRUST YOU.
I WANT TO HELP.
YOU WILL HELP MORE THAN YOU KNOW.
YOU ALREADY HAVE.

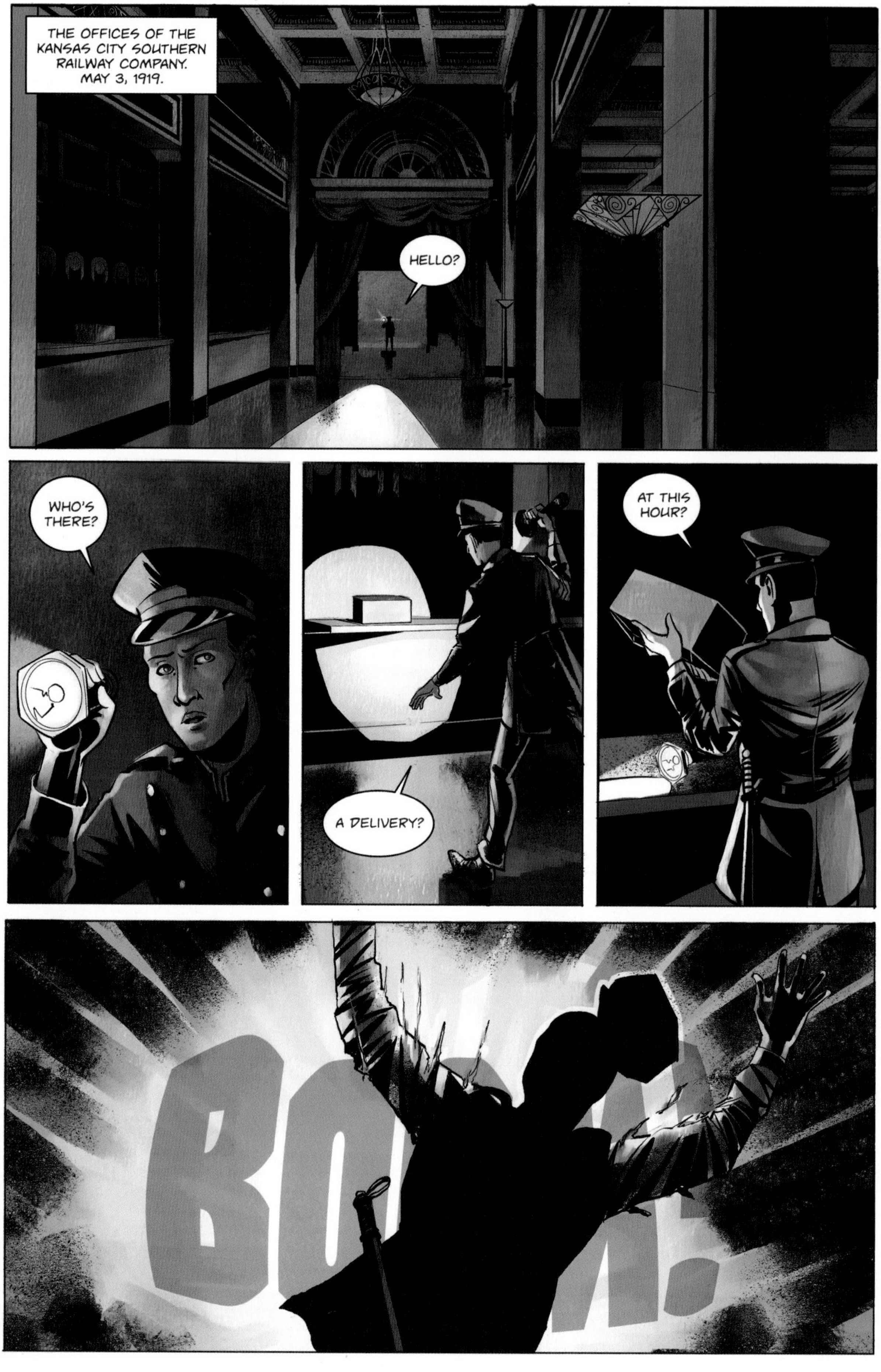
THE OFFICES OF THE KANSAS CITY SOUTHERN RAILWAY COMPANY. MAY 3, 1919.
HELLO?
WHO'S THERE?
A DELIVERY?
AT THIS HOUR?

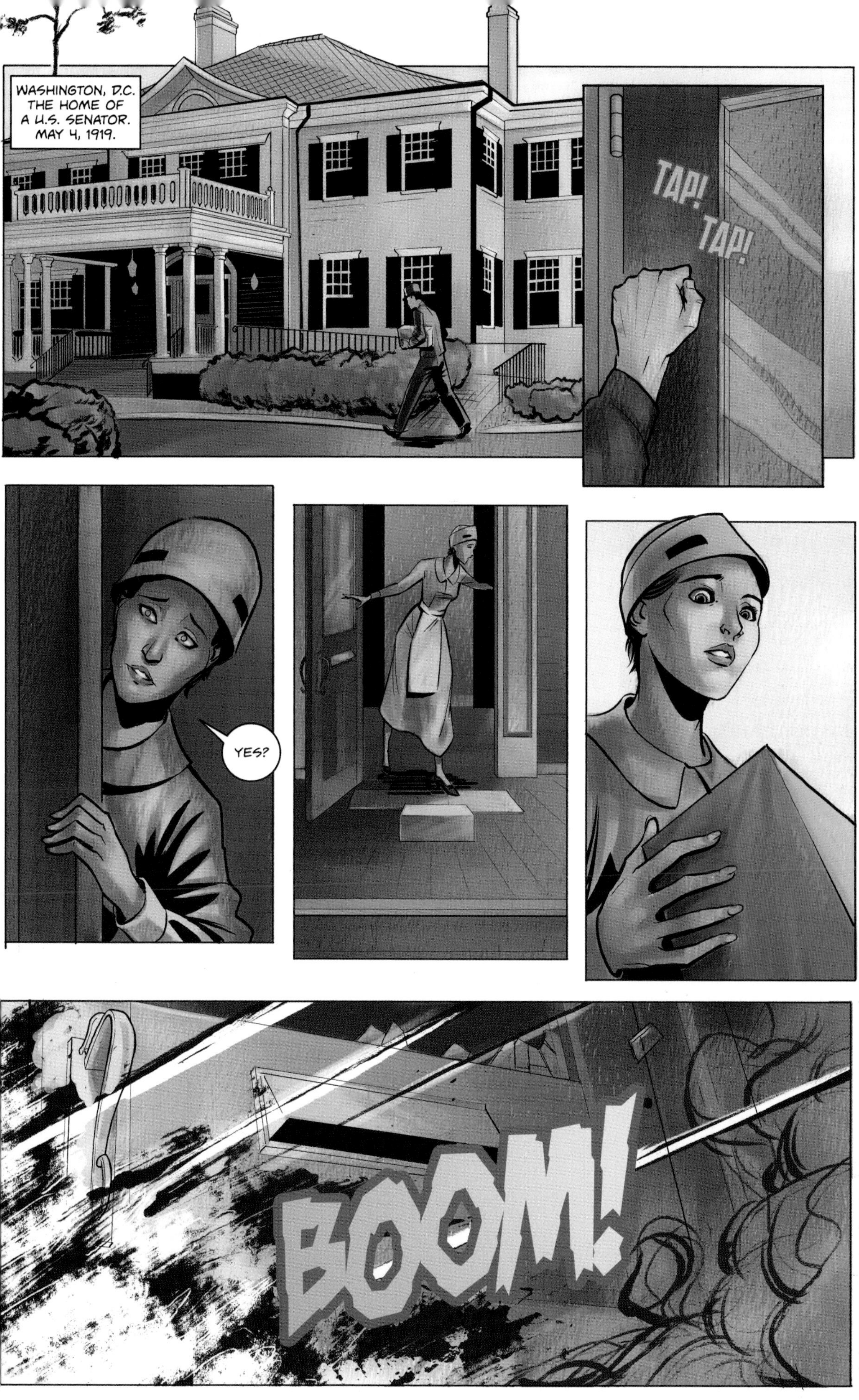
WASHINGTON, D.C.
THE HOME OF
A U.S. SENATOR.
MAY 4, 1919.
TAP!
TAP!
YES?
BOOM!

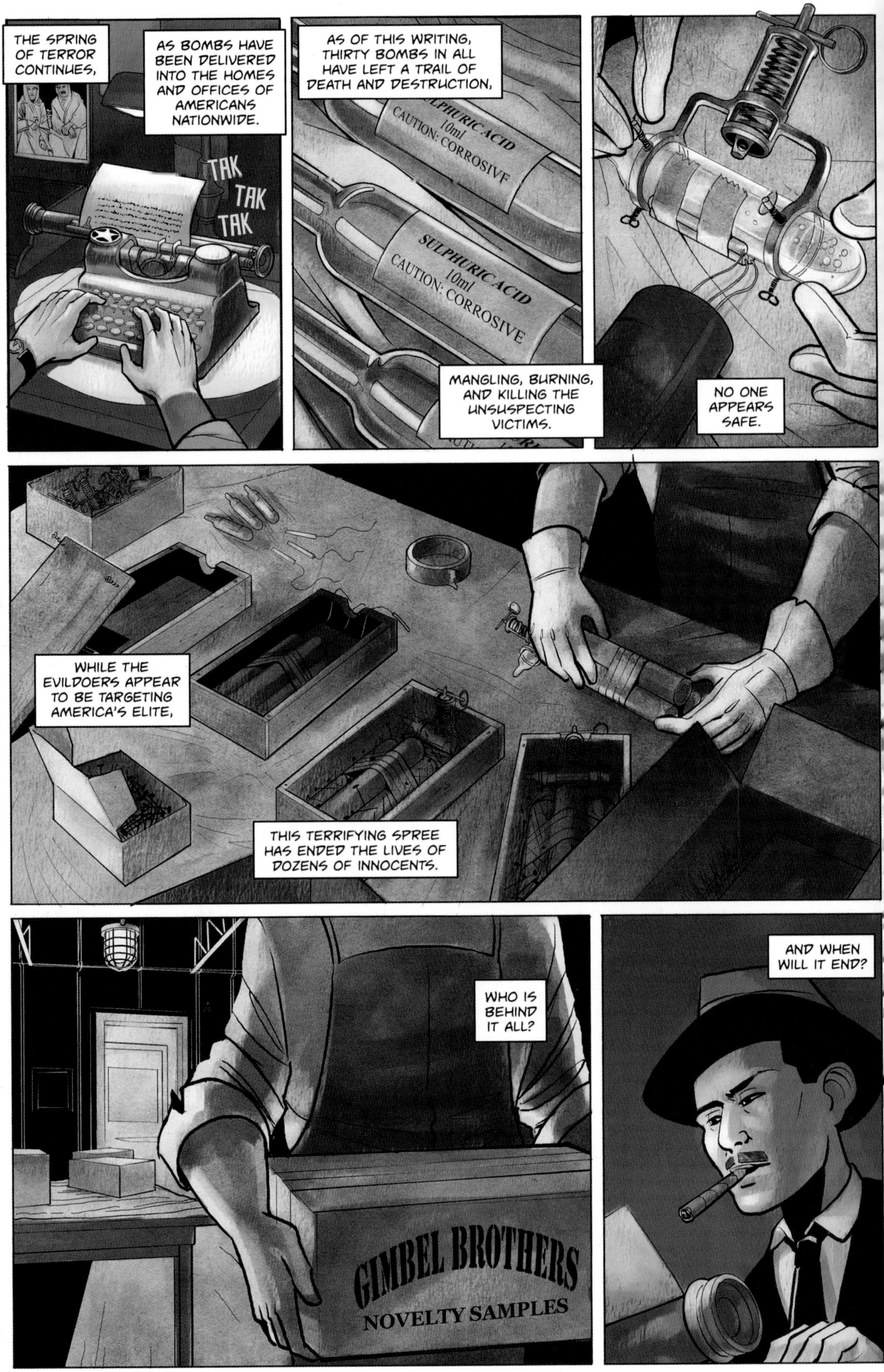
THE SPRING OF TERROR CONTINUES,
AS BOMBS HAVE BEEN DELIVERED INTO THE HOMES AND OFFICES OF AMERICANS NATIONWIDE.
TAK
TAK
TAK
AS OF THIS WRITING, THIRTY BOMBS IN ALL HAVE LEFT A TRAIL OF DEATH AND DESTRUCTION,
SULPHURICACID
10ml
CAUTION: CORROSIVE
SULPHURICACID
10ml
CAUTION: CORROSIVE
MANGLING, BURNING, AND KILLING THE UNSUSPECTING VICTIMS.
NO ONE APPEARS SAFE.
WHILE THE EVILDOERS APPEAR TO BE TARGETING AMERICA'S ELITE,
THIS TERRIFYING SPREE HAS ENDED THE LIVES OF DOZENS OF INNOCENTS.
WHO IS BEHIND IT ALL?
GIMBEL BROTHERS
NOVELTY SAMPLES
AND WHEN WILL IT END?

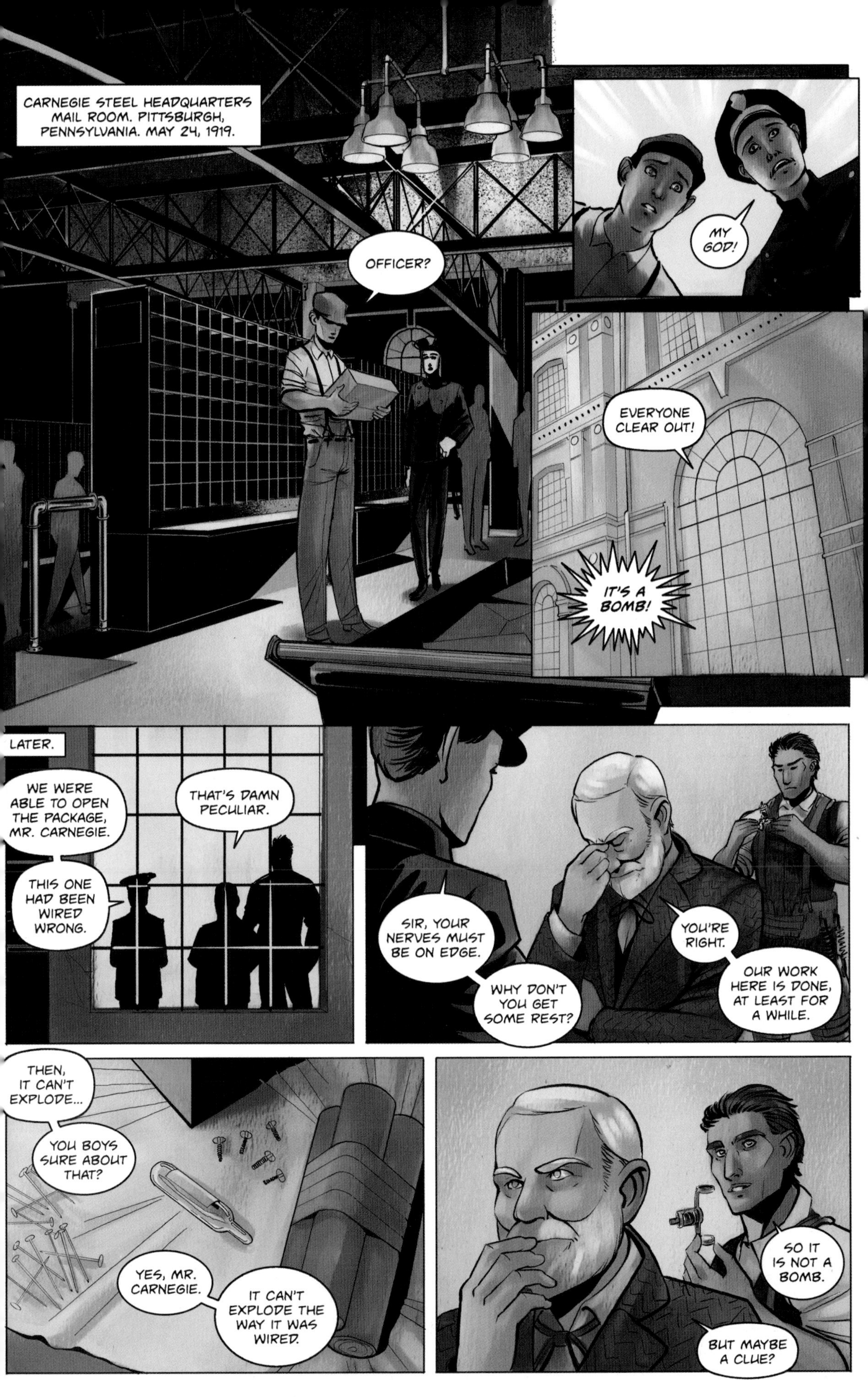
CARNEGIE STEEL HEADQUARTERS MAIL ROOM. PITTSBURGH, PENNSYLVANIA. MAY 24, 1919.
OFFICER?
MY GOD!
EVERYONE CLEAR OUT!
IT'S A BOMB!
LATER.
WE WERE ABLE TO OPEN THE PACKAGE, MR. CARNEGIE.
THIS ONE HAD BEEN WIRED WRONG.
THAT'S DAMN PECULIAR.
SIR, YOUR NERVES MUST BE ON EDGE.
WHY DON'T YOU GET SOME REST?
YOU'RE RIGHT.
OUR WORK HERE IS DONE, AT LEAST FOR A WHILE.
THEN, IT CAN'T EXPLODE...
YOU BOYS SURE ABOUT THAT?
YES, MR. CARNEGIE.
IT CAN'T EXPLODE THE WAY IT WAS WIRED.
SO IT IS NOT A BOMB.
BUT MAYBE A CLUE?

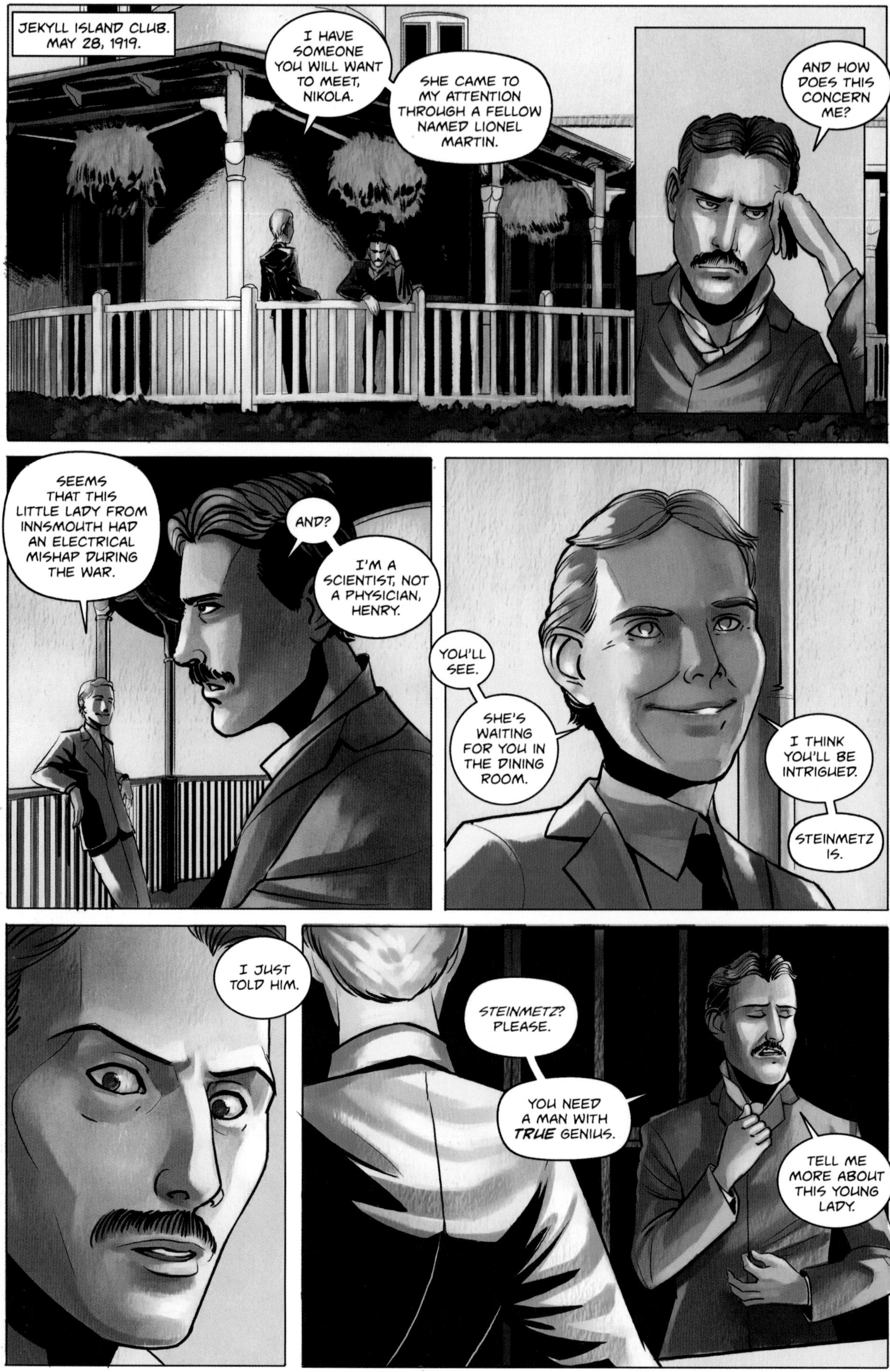
JEKYLL ISLAND CLUB. MAY 28, 1919.
I HAVE SOMEONE YOU WILL WANT TO MEET, NIKOLA.
SHE CAME TO MY ATTENTION THROUGH A FELLOW NAMED LIONEL MARTIN.
AND HOW DOES THIS CONCERN ME?
SEEMS THAT THIS LITTLE LADY FROM INNSMOUTH HAD AN ELECTRICAL MISHAP DURING THE WAR.
AND?
I'M A SCIENTIST, NOT A PHYSICIAN, HENRY.
YOU'LL SEE.
SHE'S WAITING FOR YOU IN THE DINING ROOM.
I THINK YOU'LL BE INTRIGUED.
STEINMETZ IS.
I JUST TOLD HIM.
STEINMETZ? PLEASE.
YOU NEED A MAN WITH TRUE GENIUS.
TELL ME MORE ABOUT THIS YOUNG LADY.

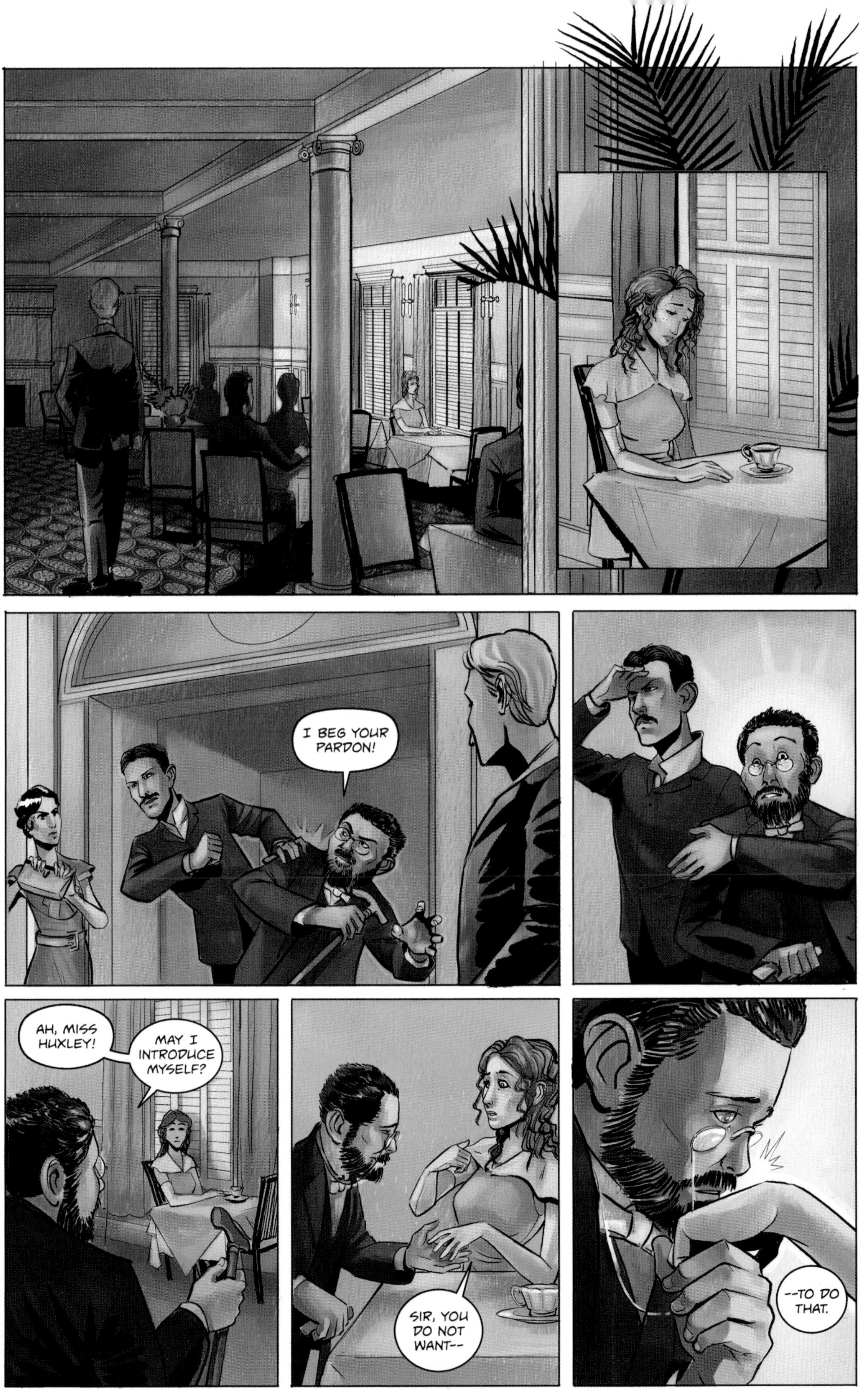

I BEG YOUR PARDON!
AH, MISS HUXLEY!
MAY I INTRODUCE MYSELF?
SIR, YOU DO NOT WANT--
--TO DO THAT.

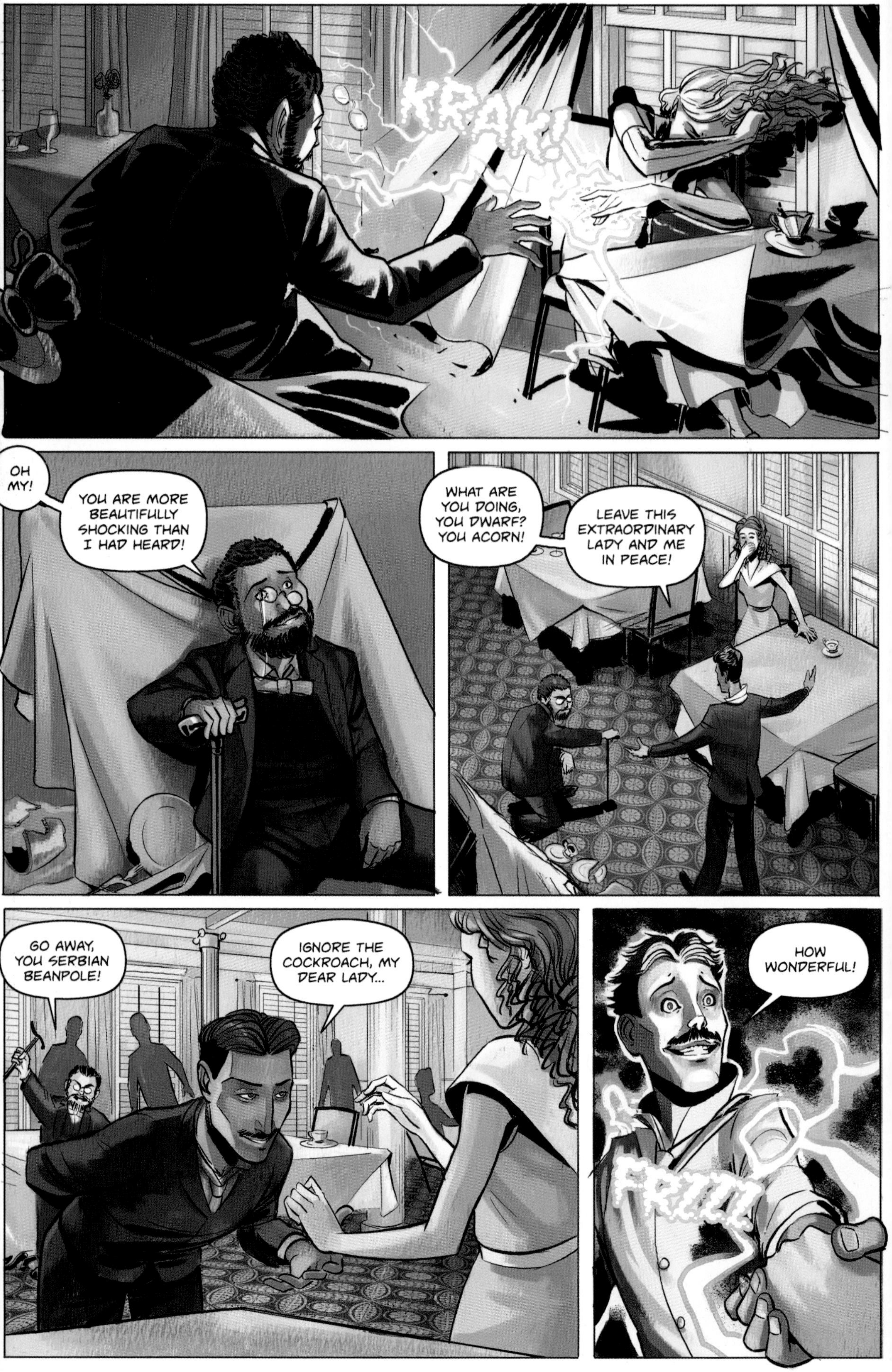
KRAK!
OH MY!
YOU ARE MORE BEAUTIFULLY SHOCKING THAN I HAD HEARD!
WHAT ARE YOU DOING, YOU DWARF? YOU ACORN!
LEAVE THIS EXTRAORDINARY LADY AND ME IN PEACE!
GO AWAY, YOU SERBIAN BEANPOLE!
IGNORE THE COCKROACH, MY DEAR LADY...
HOW WONDERFUL!
FRZZZ

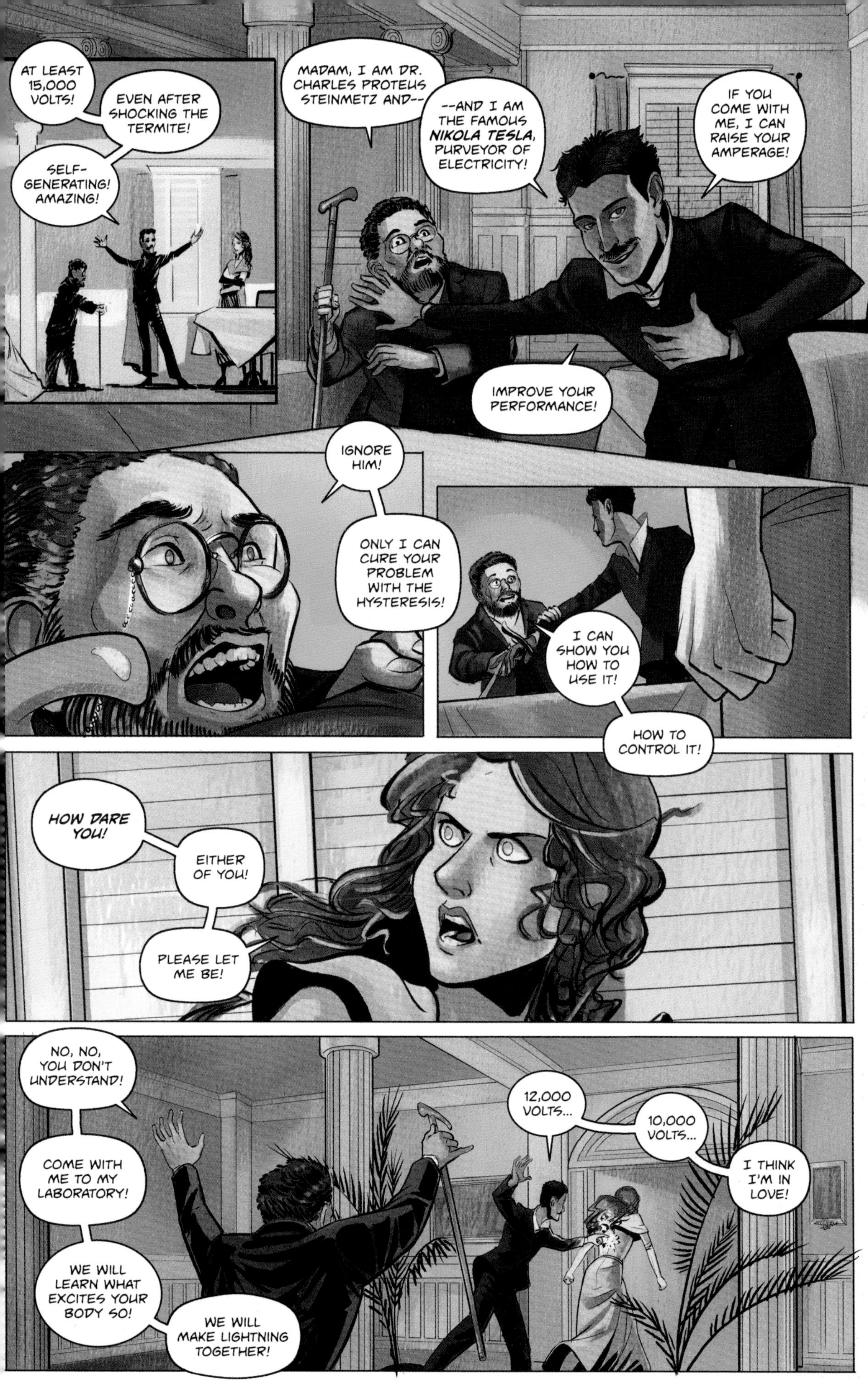
AT LEAST 15,000 VOLTS!
EVEN AFTER SHOCKING THE TERMITE!
SELF-GENERATING! AMAZING!
MADAM, I AM DR. CHARLES PROTEUS STEINMETZ AND--
--AND I AM THE FAMOUS *NIKOLA TESLA*, PURVEYOR OF ELECTRICITY!
IF YOU COME WITH ME, I CAN RAISE YOUR AMPERAGE!
IMPROVE YOUR PERFORMANCE!
IGNORE HIM!
ONLY I CAN CURE YOUR PROBLEM WITH THE HYSTERESIS!
I CAN SHOW YOU HOW TO USE IT!
HOW TO CONTROL IT!
HOW DARE YOU!
EITHER OF YOU!
PLEASE LET ME BE!
NO, NO, YOU DON'T UNDERSTAND!
COME WITH ME TO MY LABORATORY!
WE WILL LEARN WHAT EXCITES YOUR BODY SO!
WE WILL MAKE LIGHTNING TOGETHER!
12,000 VOLTS...
10,000 VOLTS...
I THINK I'M IN LOVE!

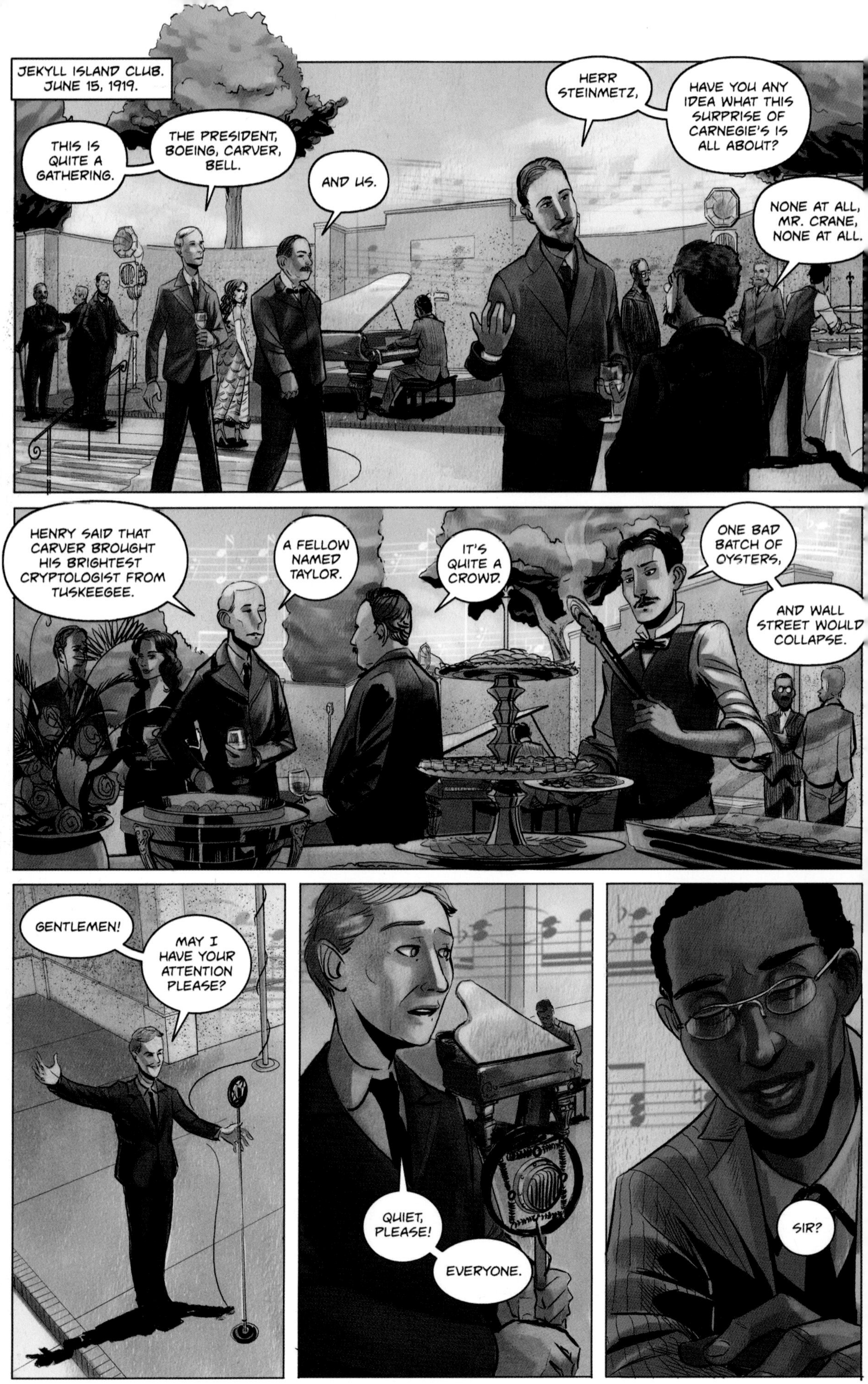
JEKYLL ISLAND CLUB. JUNE 15, 1919.
THIS IS QUITE A GATHERING.
THE PRESIDENT, BOEING, CARVER, BELL.
AND US.
HERR STEINMETZ,
HAVE YOU ANY IDEA WHAT THIS SURPRISE OF CARNEGIE'S IS ALL ABOUT?
NONE AT ALL, MR. CRANE, NONE AT ALL.
HENRY SAID THAT CARVER BROUGHT HIS BRIGHTEST CRYPTOLOGIST FROM TUSKEEGEE.
A FELLOW NAMED TAYLOR.
IT'S QUITE A CROWD.
ONE BAD BATCH OF OYSTERS,
AND WALL STREET WOULD COLLAPSE.
GENTLEMEN!
MAY I HAVE YOUR ATTENTION PLEASE?
QUIET, PLEASE!
EVERYONE.
SIR?

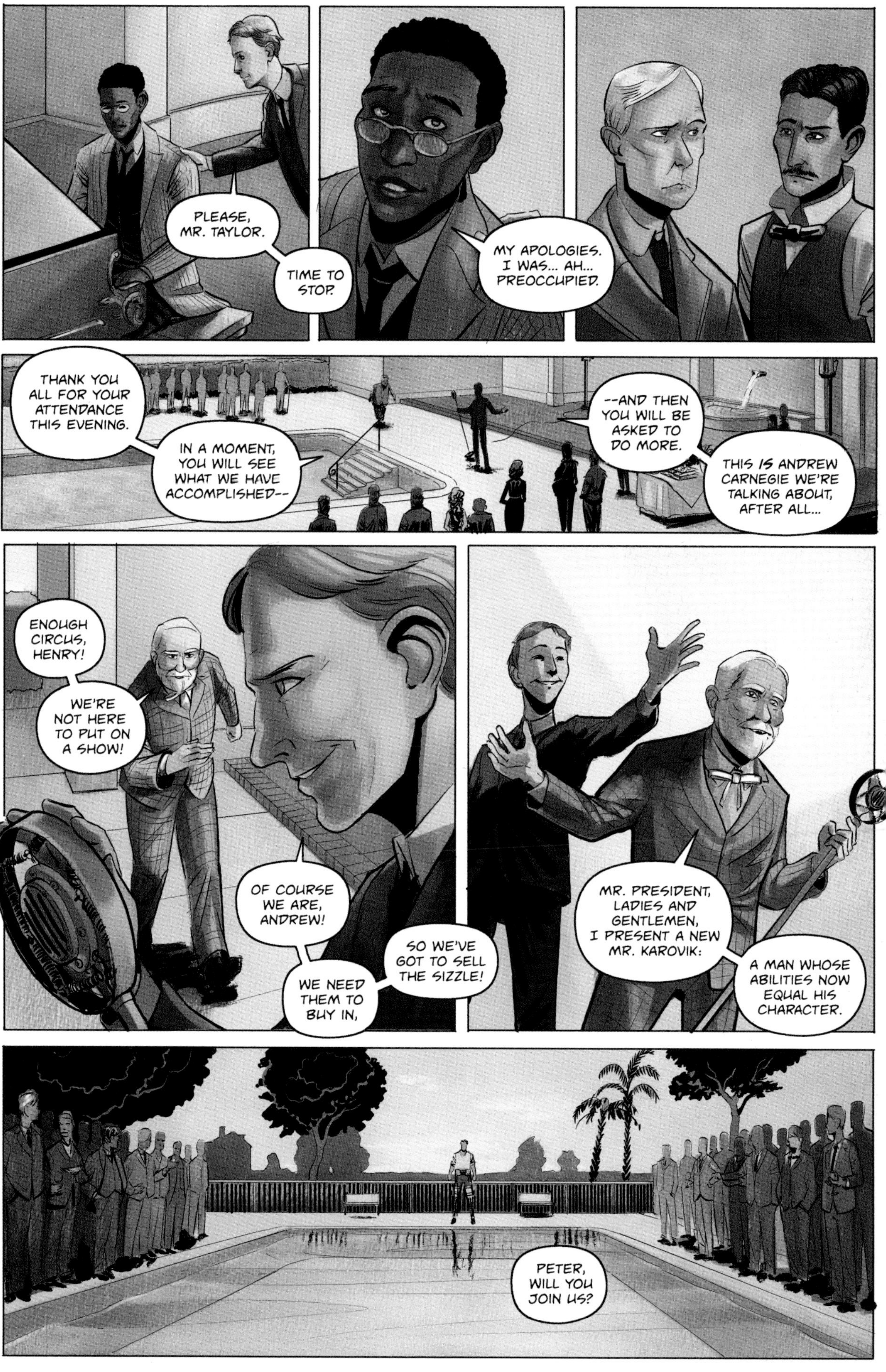
PLEASE, MR. TAYLOR.
TIME TO STOP.
MY APOLOGIES. I WAS... AH... PREOCCUPIED.
THANK YOU ALL FOR YOUR ATTENDANCE THIS EVENING.
IN A MOMENT, YOU WILL SEE WHAT WE HAVE ACCOMPLISHED--
--AND THEN YOU WILL BE ASKED TO DO MORE.
THIS *IS* ANDREW CARNEGIE WE'RE TALKING ABOUT, AFTER ALL...
ENOUGH CIRCUS, HENRY!
WE'RE NOT HERE TO PUT ON A SHOW!
OF COURSE WE ARE, ANDREW!
WE NEED THEM TO BUY IN,
SO WE'VE GOT TO SELL THE SIZZLE!
MR. PRESIDENT, LADIES AND GENTLEMEN, I PRESENT A NEW MR. KAROVIK:
A MAN WHOSE ABILITIES NOW EQUAL HIS CHARACTER.
PETER, WILL YOU JOIN US?

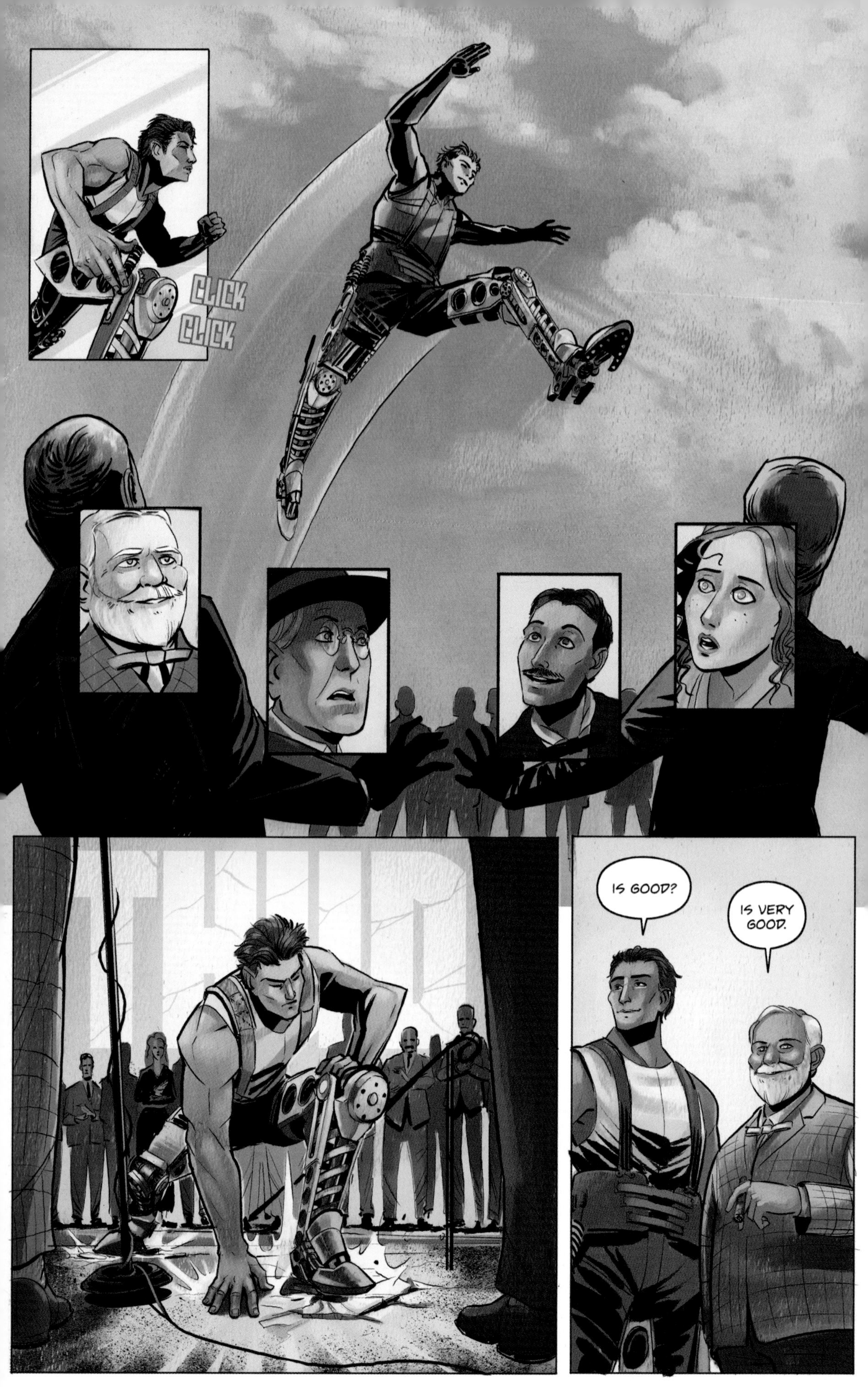
CLICK
CLICK
IS GOOD?
IS VERY GOOD.

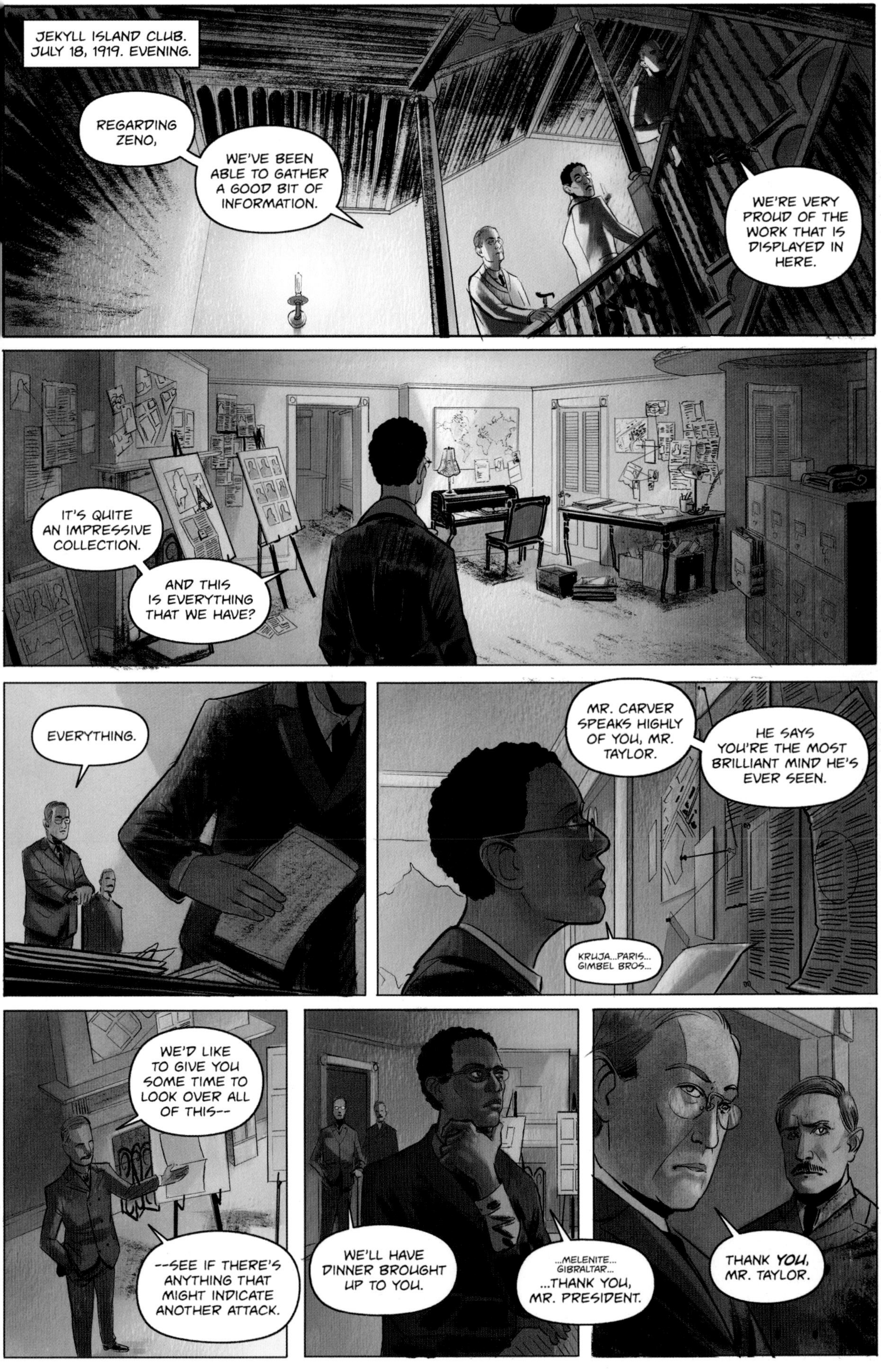
JEKYLL ISLAND CLUB.
JULY 18, 1919. EVENING.
REGARDING ZENO,
WE'VE BEEN ABLE TO GATHER A GOOD BIT OF INFORMATION.
WE'RE VERY PROUD OF THE WORK THAT IS DISPLAYED IN HERE.
IT'S QUITE AN IMPRESSIVE COLLECTION.
AND THIS IS EVERYTHING THAT WE HAVE?
EVERYTHING.
MR. CARVER SPEAKS HIGHLY OF YOU, MR. TAYLOR.
HE SAYS YOU'RE THE MOST BRILLIANT MIND HE'S EVER SEEN.
KRUJA...PARIS... GIMBEL BROS...
WE'D LIKE TO GIVE YOU SOME TIME TO LOOK OVER ALL OF THIS--
--SEE IF THERE'S ANYTHING THAT MIGHT INDICATE ANOTHER ATTACK.
WE'LL HAVE DINNER BROUGHT UP TO YOU.
...MELENITE... GIBRALTAR...
...THANK YOU, MR. PRESIDENT.
THANK *YOU*, MR. TAYLOR.

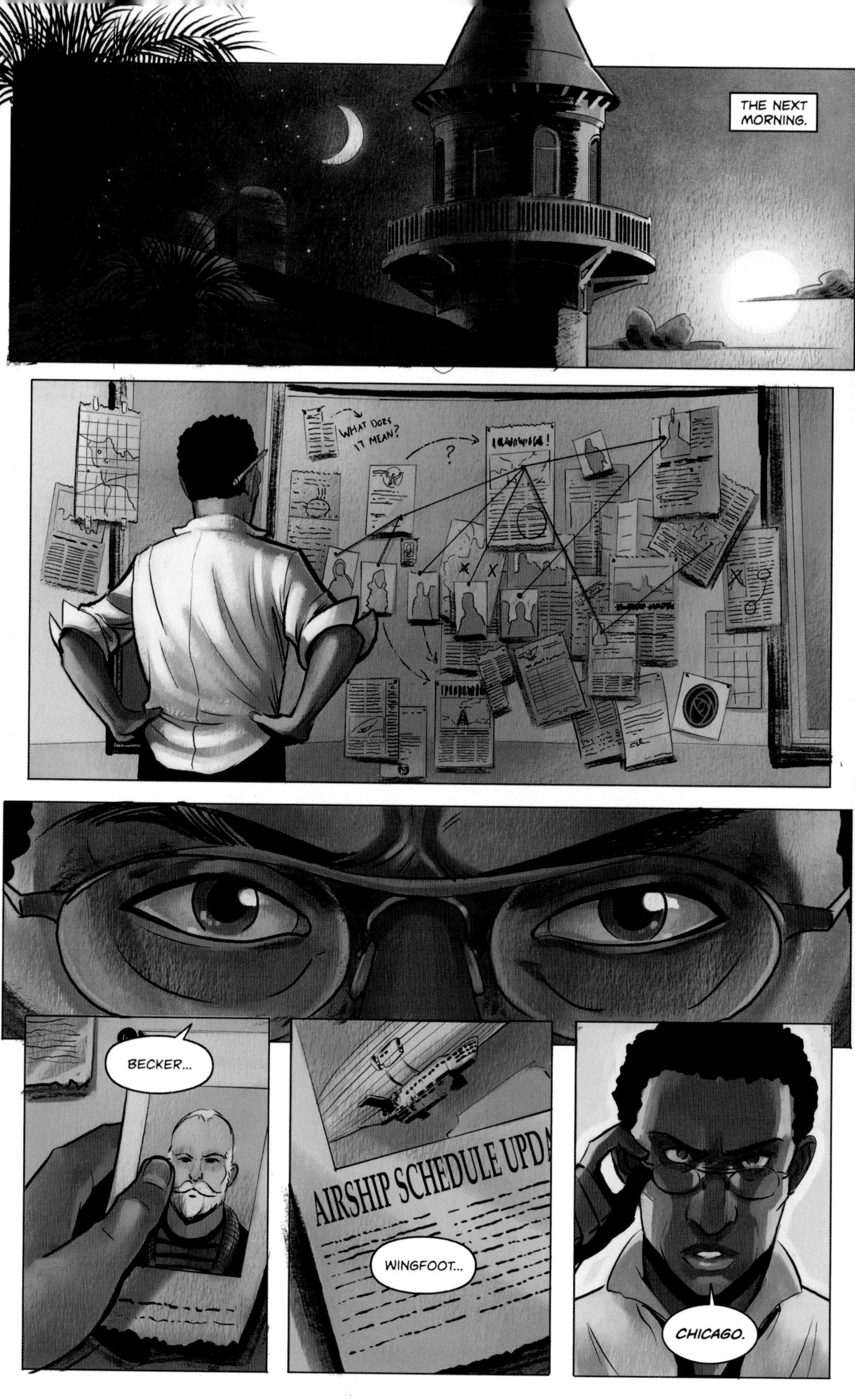
THE NEXT MORNING.
WHAT DOES IT MEAN?
?
BECKER...
AIRSHIP SCHEDULE UPD
WINGFOOT...
CHICAGO.

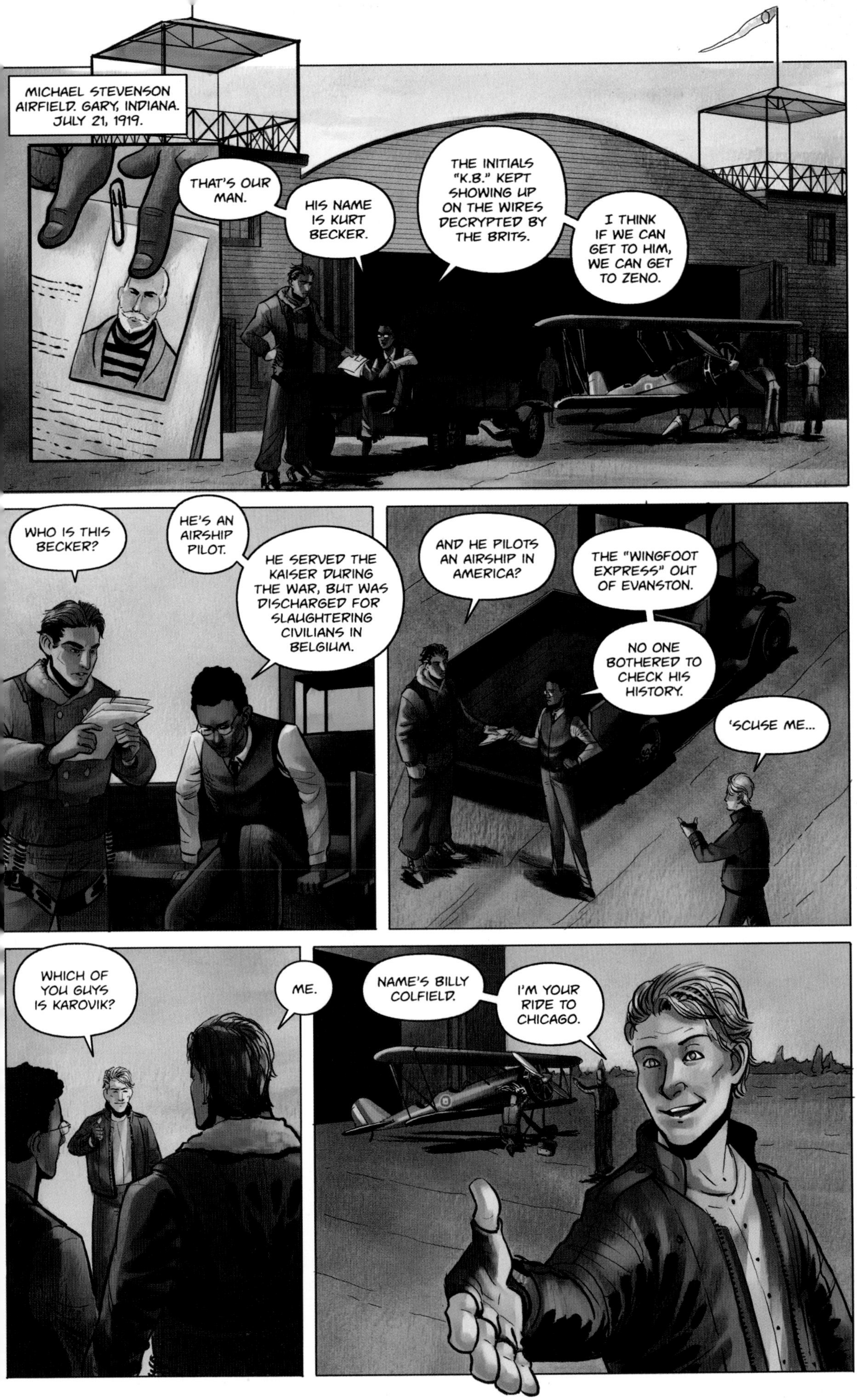
MICHAEL STEVENSON AIRFIELD. GARY, INDIANA. JULY 21, 1919.
THAT'S OUR MAN.
HIS NAME IS KURT BECKER.
THE INITIALS "K.B." KEPT SHOWING UP ON THE WIRES DECRYPTED BY THE BRITS.
I THINK IF WE CAN GET TO HIM, WE CAN GET TO ZENO.
WHO IS THIS BECKER?
HE'S AN AIRSHIP PILOT.
HE SERVED THE KAISER DURING THE WAR, BUT WAS DISCHARGED FOR SLAUGHTERING CIVILIANS IN BELGIUM.
AND HE PILOTS AN AIRSHIP IN AMERICA?
THE "WINGFOOT EXPRESS" OUT OF EVANSTON.
NO ONE BOTHERED TO CHECK HIS HISTORY.
'SCUSE ME...
WHICH OF YOU GUYS IS KAROVIK?
ME.
NAME'S BILLY COLFIELD.
I'M YOUR RIDE TO CHICAGO.

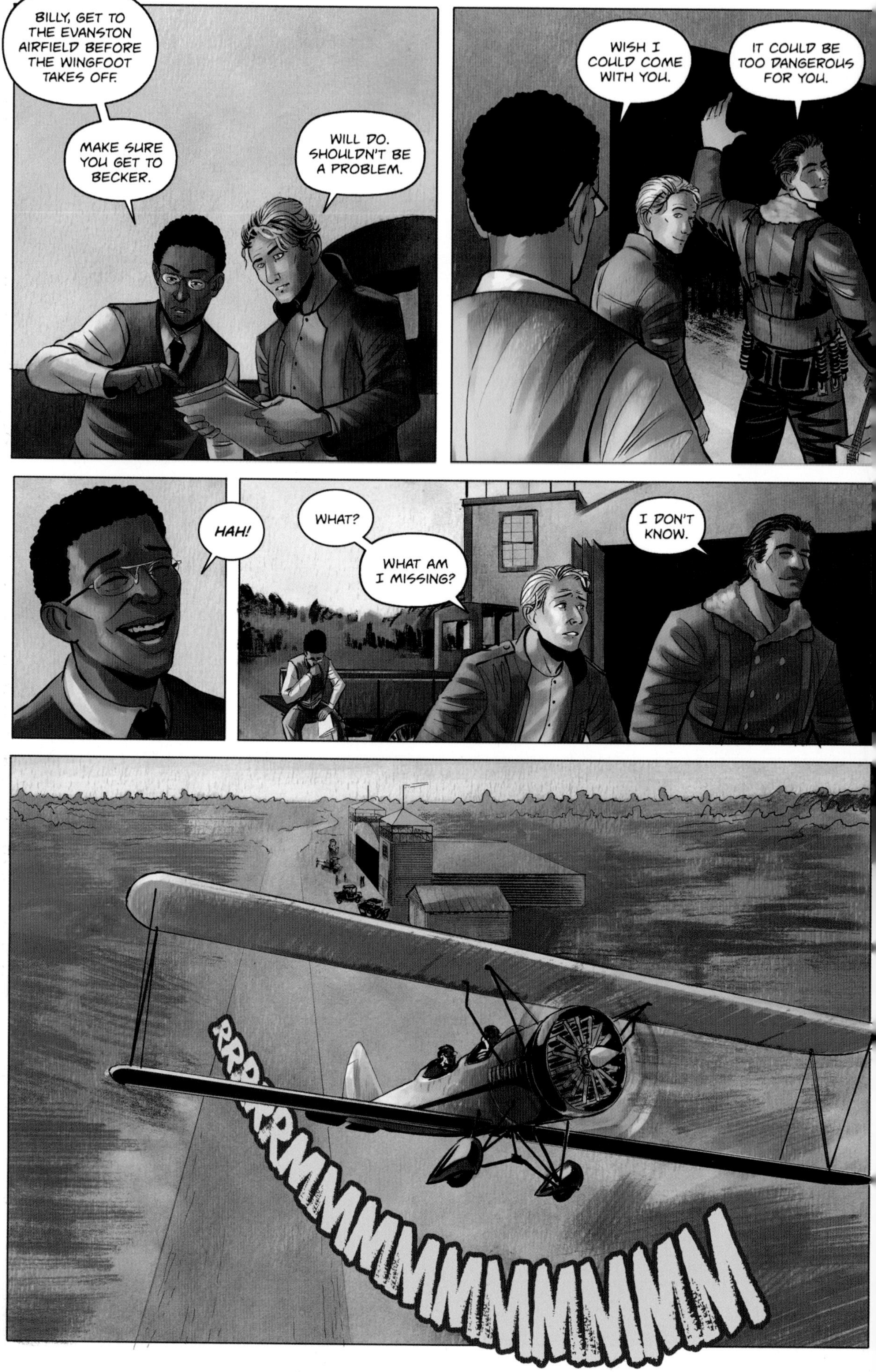
BILLY, GET TO THE EVANSTON AIRFIELD BEFORE THE WINGFOOT TAKES OFF.
MAKE SURE YOU GET TO BECKER.
WILL DO. SHOULDN'T BE A PROBLEM.
WISH I COULD COME WITH YOU.
IT COULD BE TOO DANGEROUS FOR YOU.
HAH!
WHAT?
WHAT AM I MISSING?
I DON'T KNOW.
RRRRMMMMMMMMMMMM

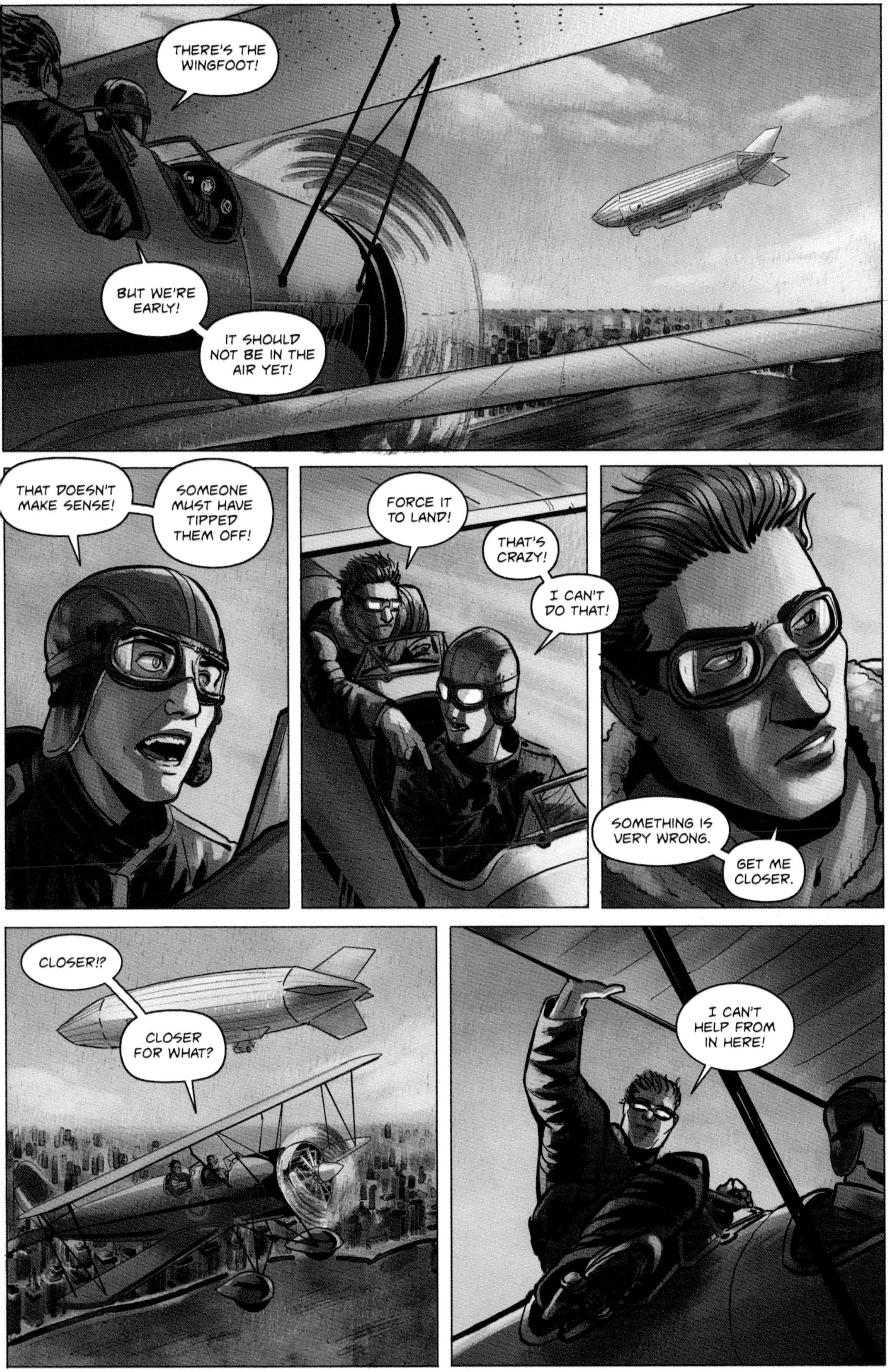

THERE'S THE WINGFOOT!
BUT WE'RE EARLY!
IT SHOULD NOT BE IN THE AIR YET!
THAT DOESN'T MAKE SENSE!
SOMEONE MUST HAVE TIPPED THEM OFF!
FORCE IT TO LAND!
THAT'S CRAZY!
I CAN'T DO THAT!
SOMETHING IS VERY WRONG.
GET ME CLOSER.
CLOSER!?
CLOSER FOR WHAT?
I CAN'T HELP FROM IN HERE!

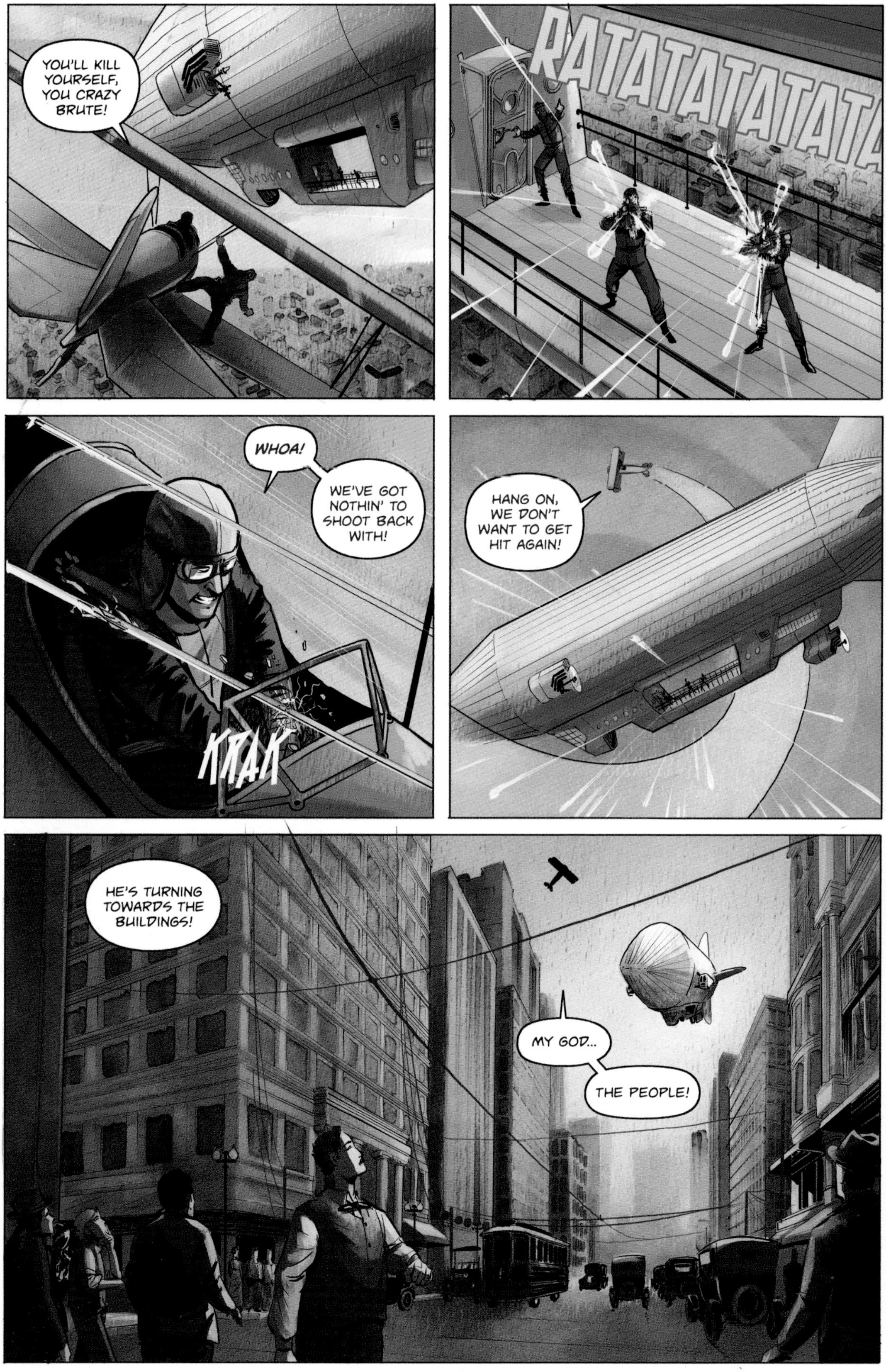
YOU'LL KILL YOURSELF, YOU CRAZY BRUTE!
RATATATATATATA
WHOA!
WE'VE GOT NOTHIN' TO SHOOT BACK WITH!
KRAK
HANG ON, WE DON'T WANT TO GET HIT AGAIN!
HE'S TURNING TOWARDS THE BUILDINGS!
MY GOD...
THE PEOPLE!

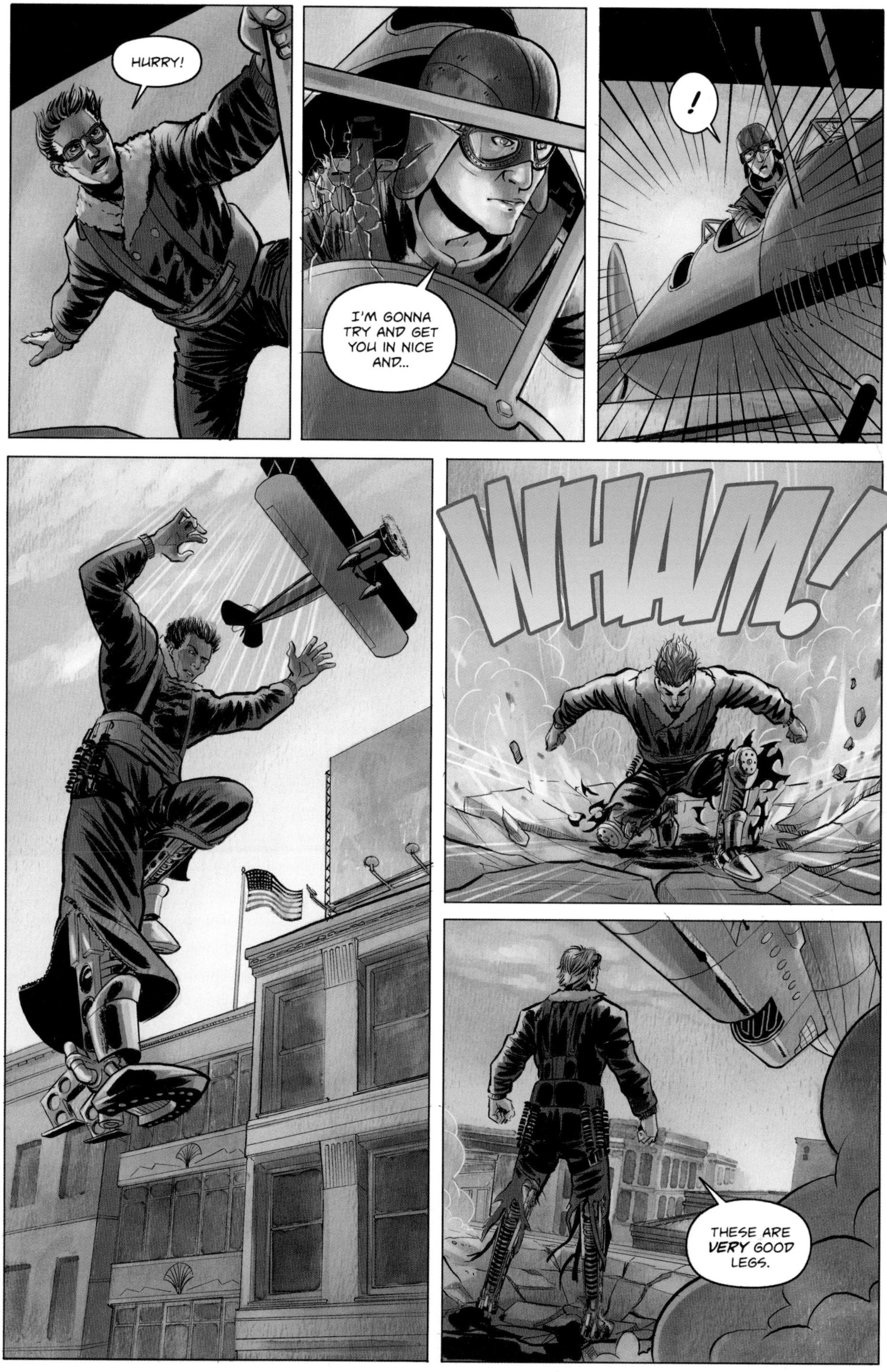
HURRY!
I'M GONNA TRY AND GET YOU IN NICE AND...
!
WHAM!
THESE ARE **VERY** GOOD LEGS.

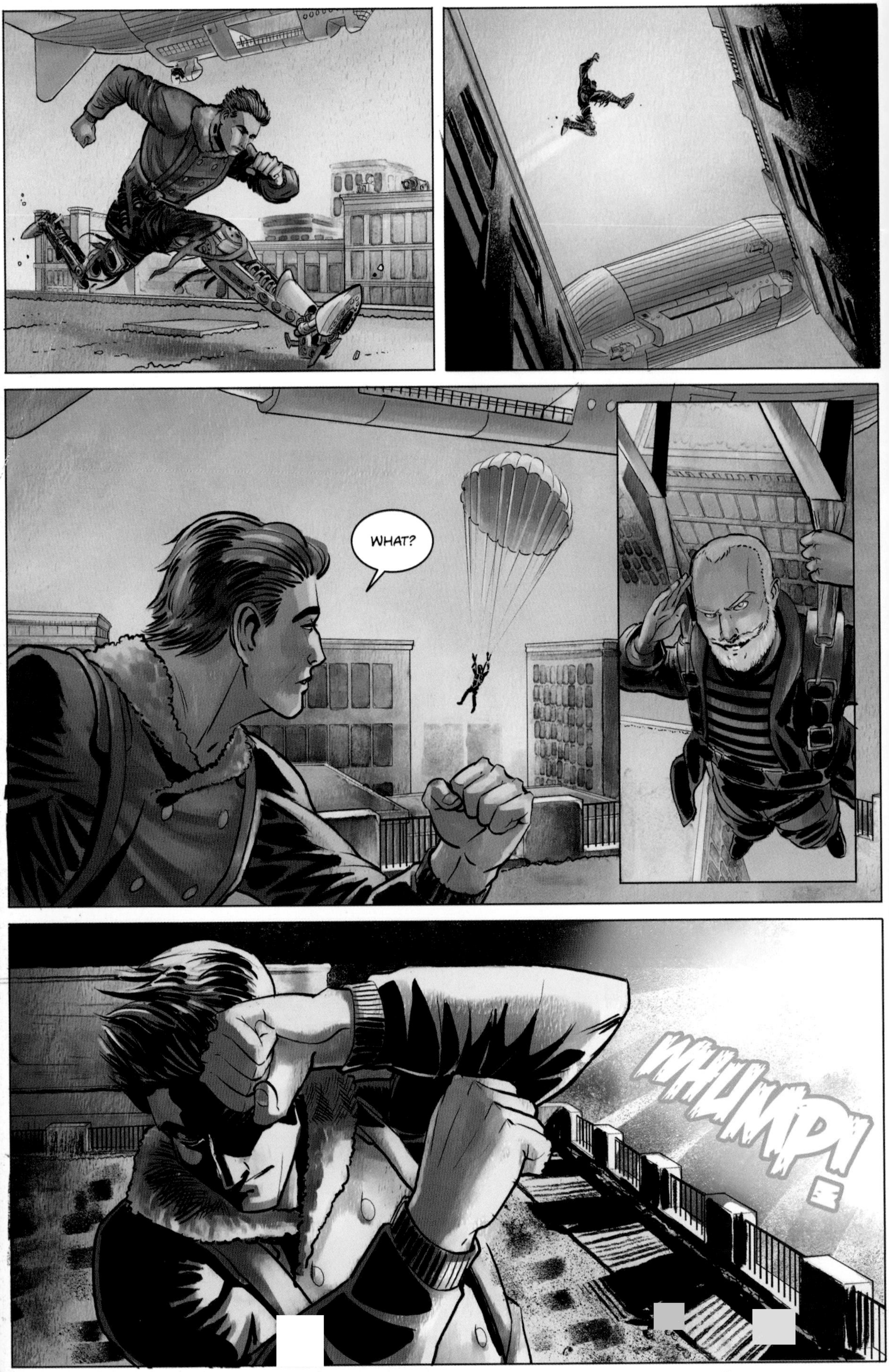
WHAT?
WHUMP!

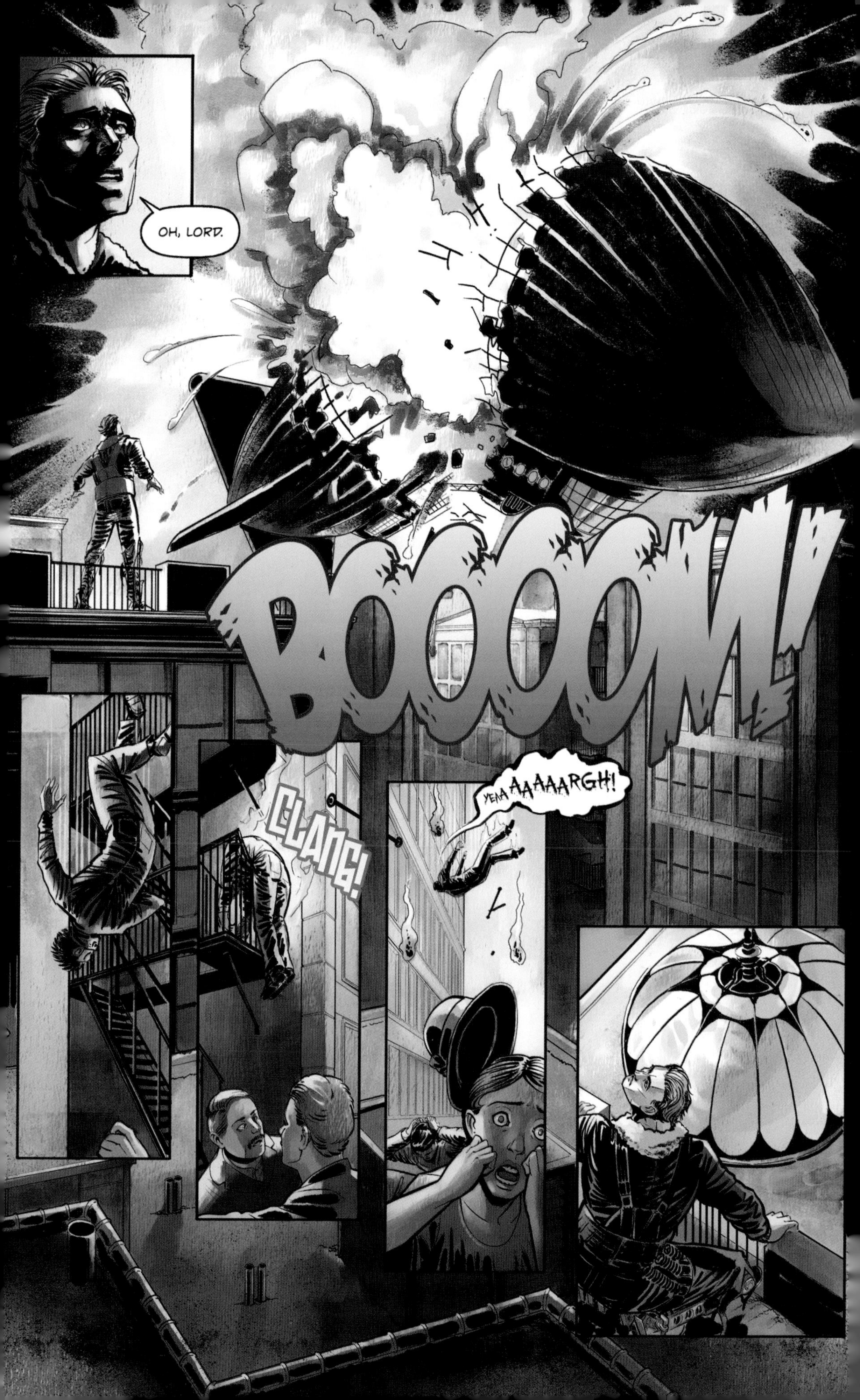
OH, LORD.
BOOOOOM!
CLANG!
YEAA AAAAARGH!

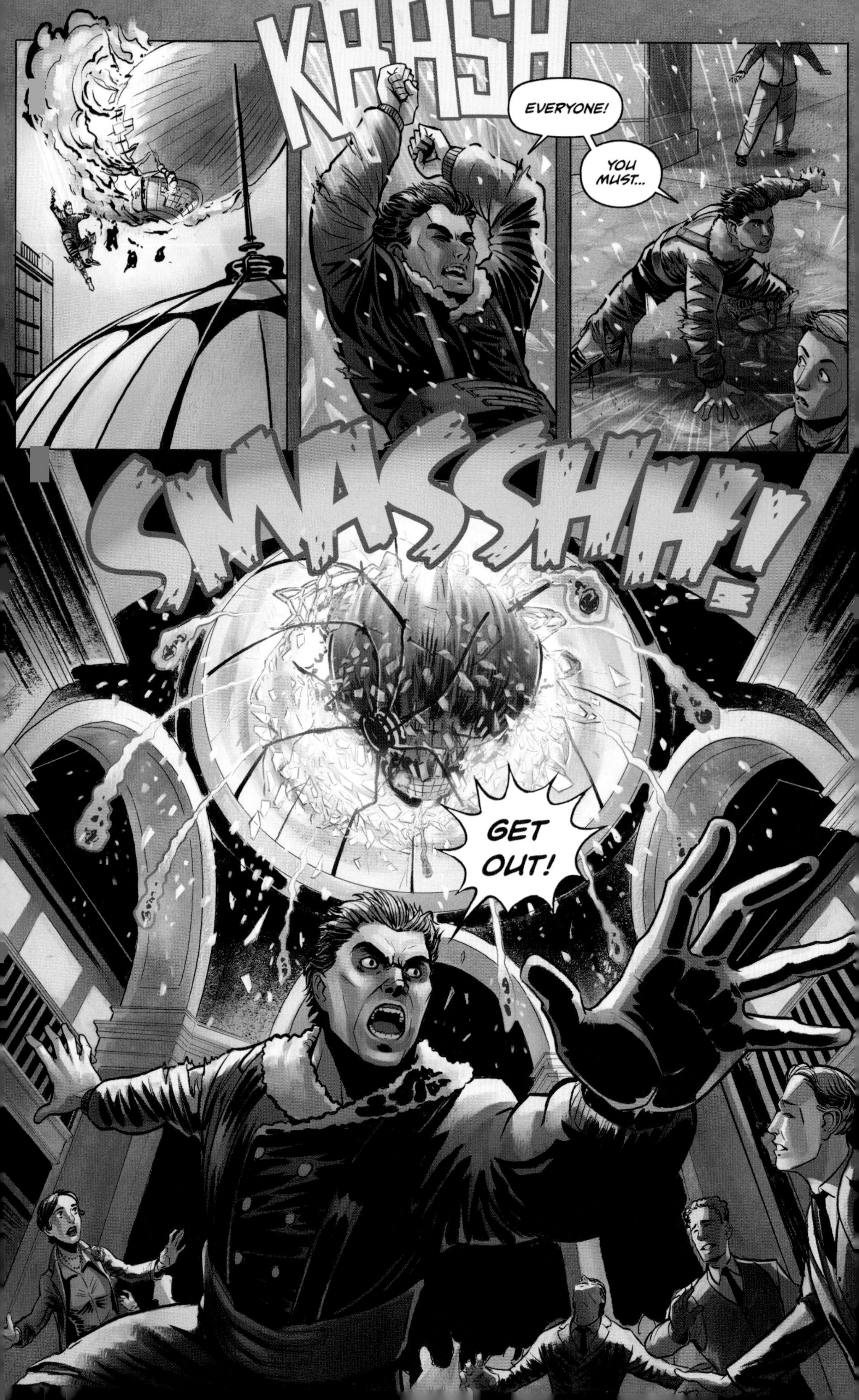
KRASH
EVERYONE!
YOU MUST...
SMASSHH!
GET OUT!

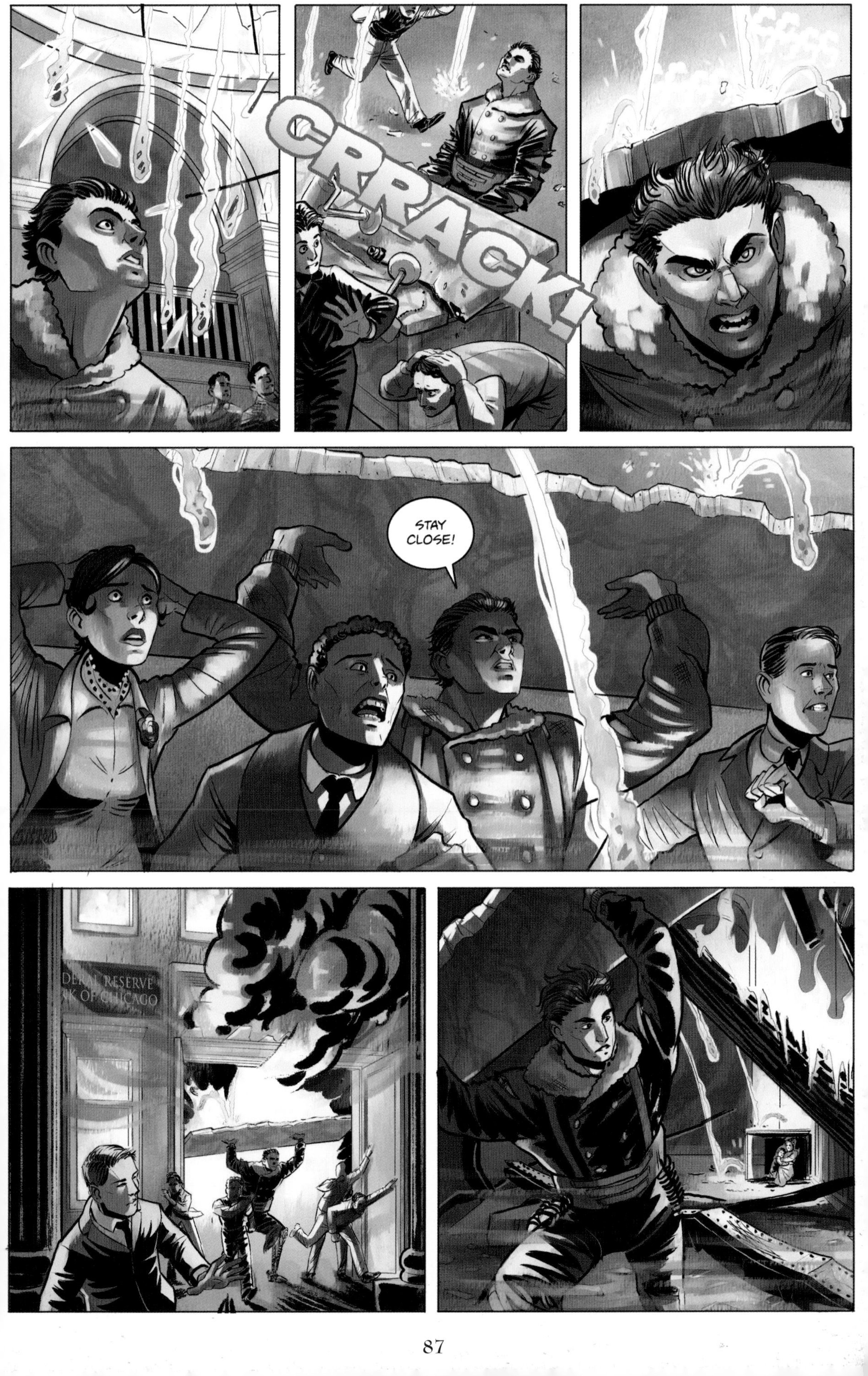
CRRACK!
STAY CLOSE!
DERAL RESERVE
K OF CHICAGO

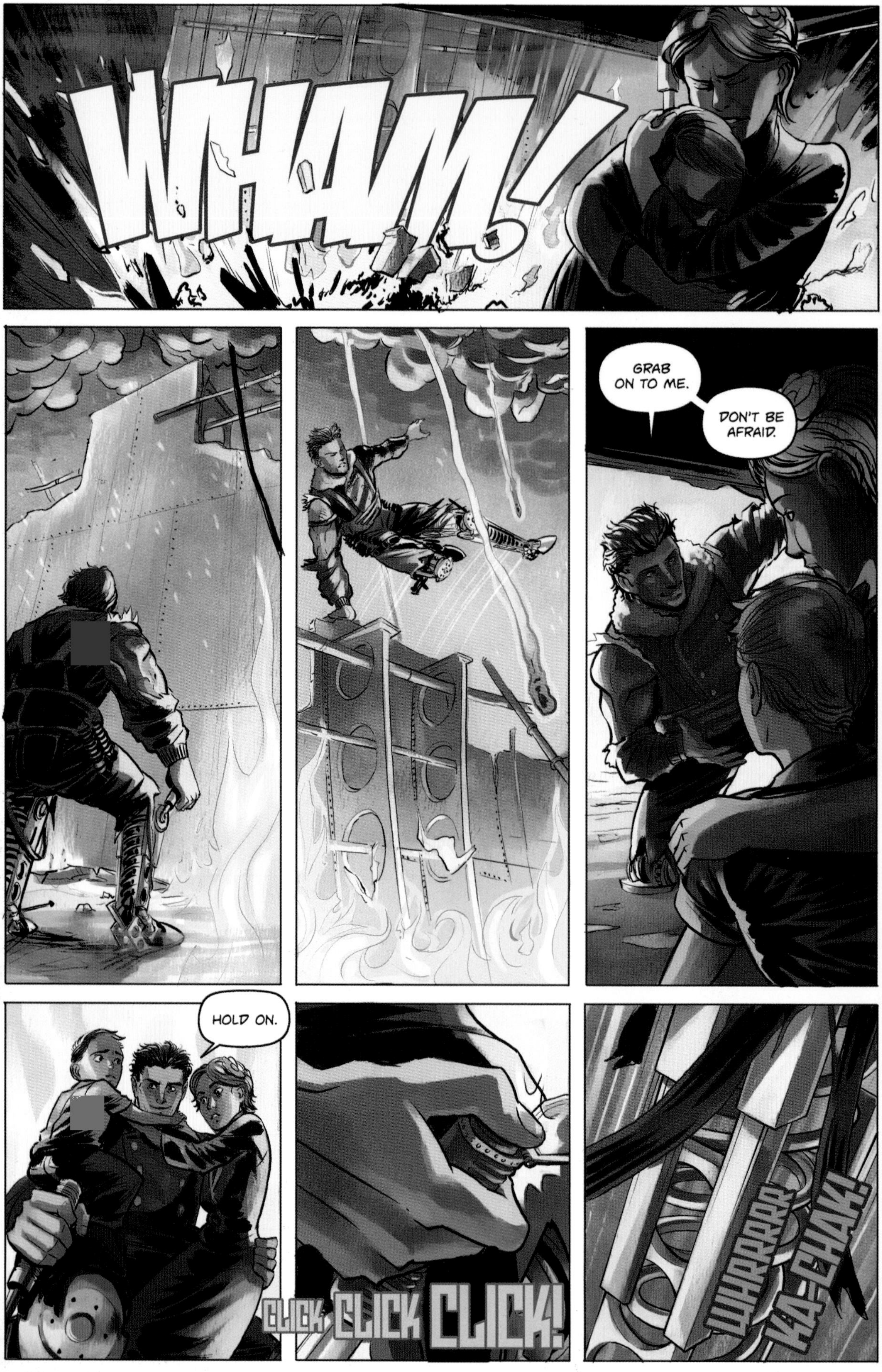

WHAM!
GRAB ON TO ME.
DON'T BE AFRAID.
HOLD ON.
CLICK CLICK CLICK!
WHRRRR
KA-CHAK!

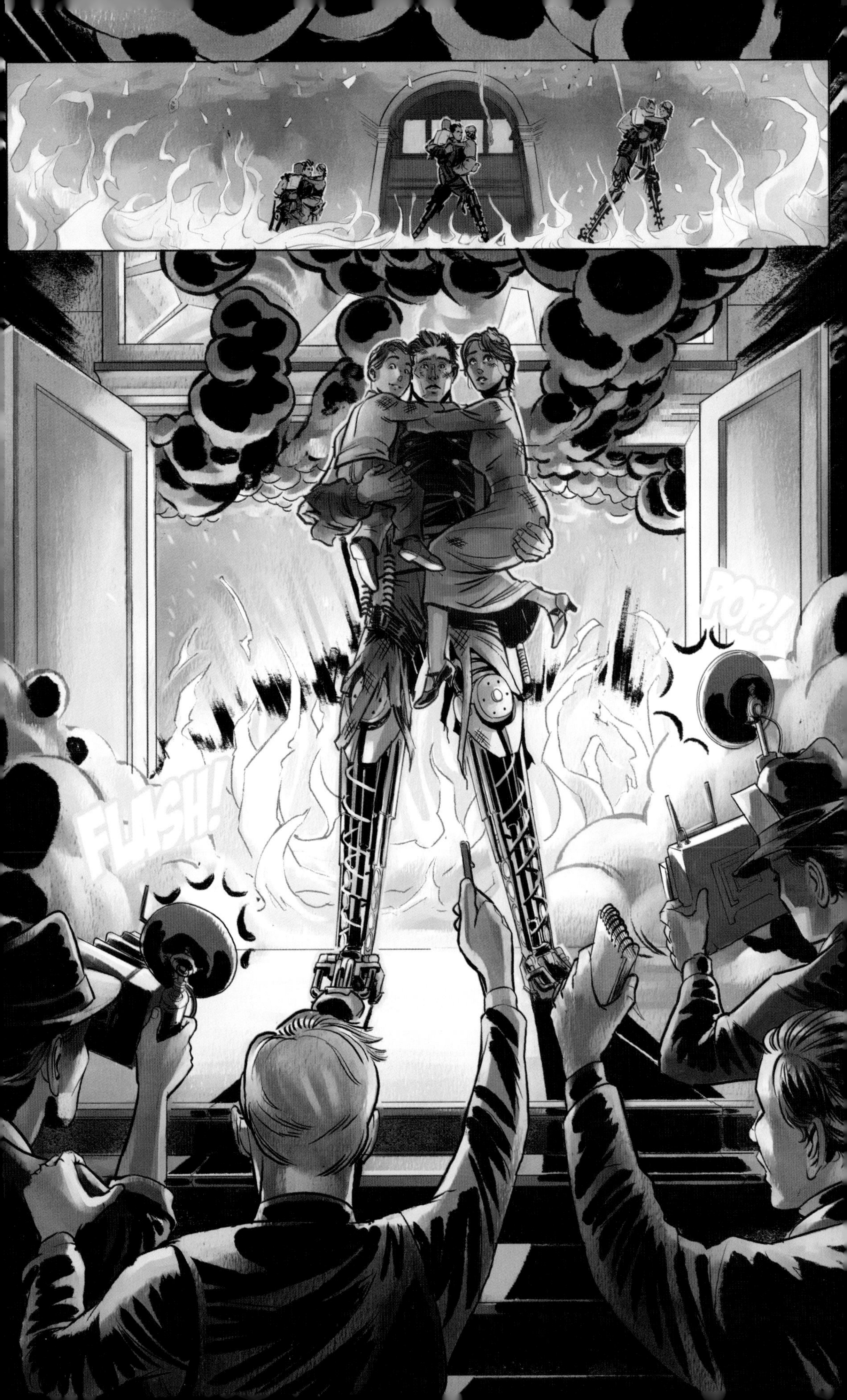
POP!
FLASH!

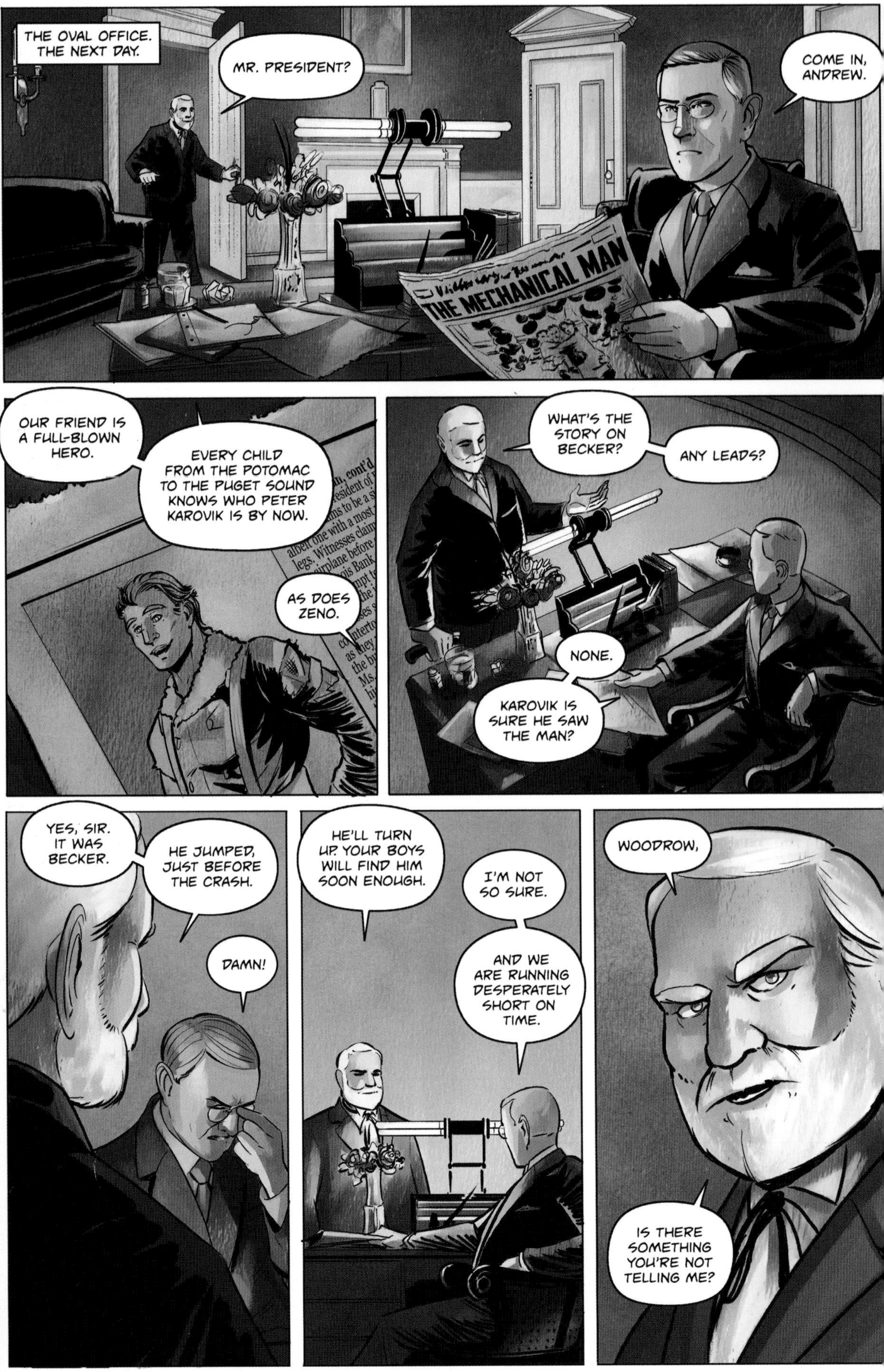
THE OVAL OFFICE. THE NEXT DAY.
MR. PRESIDENT?
COME IN, ANDREW.
THE MECHANICAL MAN
OUR FRIEND IS A FULL-BLOWN HERO.
EVERY CHILD FROM THE POTOMAC TO THE PUGET SOUND KNOWS WHO PETER KAROVIK IS BY NOW.
AS DOES ZENO.
WHAT'S THE STORY ON BECKER?
ANY LEADS?
NONE.
KAROVIK IS SURE HE SAW THE MAN?
YES, SIR. IT WAS BECKER.
HE JUMPED, JUST BEFORE THE CRASH.
DAMN!
HE'LL TURN UP. YOUR BOYS WILL FIND HIM SOON ENOUGH.
I'M NOT SO SURE.
AND WE ARE RUNNING DESPERATELY SHORT ON TIME.
WOODROW,
IS THERE SOMETHING YOU'RE NOT TELLING ME?

ZENO IS ONE SHARP BASTARD.

WE CAN'T AFFORD TO ALLOW HIM ANY MORE PRACTICE RUNS.

...PRACTICE RUNS?

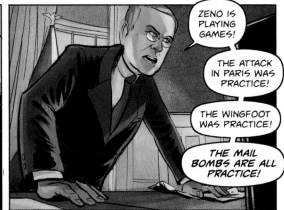

ZENO IS PLAYING GAMES!

THE ATTACK IN PARIS WAS PRACTICE!

THE WINGFOOT WAS PRACTICE!

THE MAIL BOMBS ARE ALL PRACTICE!

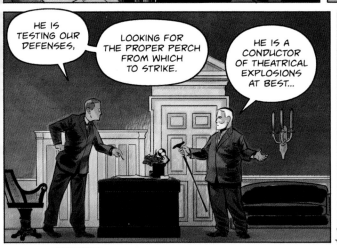

HE IS TESTING OUR DEFENSES,

LOOKING FOR THE PROPER PERCH FROM WHICH TO STRIKE.

HE IS A CONDUCTOR OF THEATRICAL EXPLOSIONS AT BEST...

NO.

HE POSSESSES TWO RAILCARS' WORTH OF AN EXPERIMENTAL NEW GAS... A *NERVE GAS.*

WHAT!?

WE FOUND THESE IN THE WINGFOOT WRECKAGE, AS WELL AS IN PARIS.

THE SERIAL NUMBERS MATCH THOSE FROM A SHIPMENT THAT WENT MISSING IN GIBRALTAR.

NERVE GAS. GOOD LORD...

SO THAT'S WHAT HAPPENED IN THE TUNNEL.

WE NEVER KNEW...

WORK FAST, ANDREW.

WE NEED MORE PEOPLE LIKE KAROVIK,

AND WE NEED THEM PREPARED FOR ANYTHING.

ZENO IS NOT SIMPLY MAIL BOMBS AND THEATRICS--

--HE'S AFTER SOMETHING MUCH WORSE.

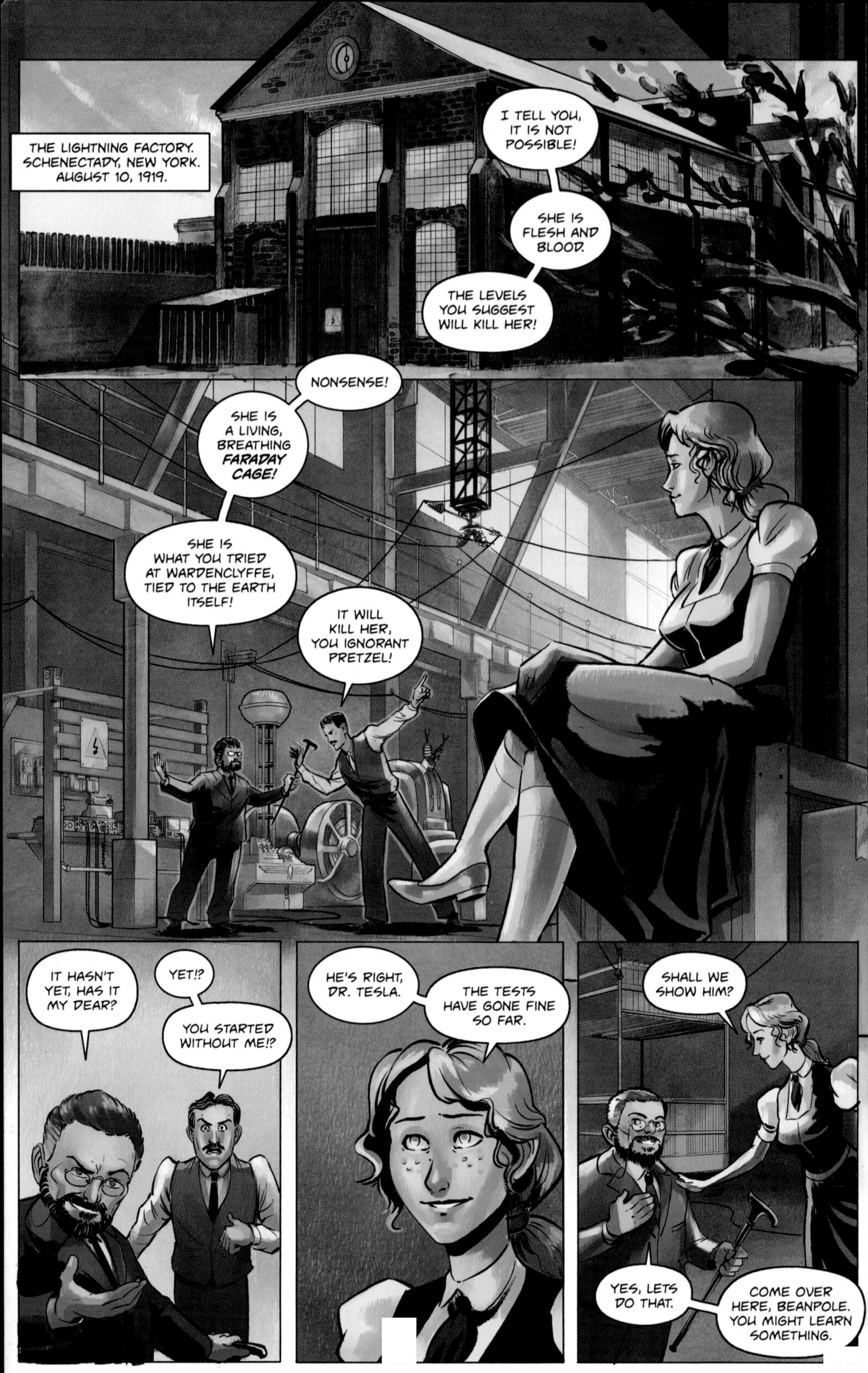
THE LIGHTNING FACTORY. SCHENECTADY, NEW YORK. AUGUST 10, 1919.
I TELL YOU, IT IS NOT POSSIBLE!
SHE IS FLESH AND BLOOD.
THE LEVELS YOU SUGGEST WILL KILL HER!
NONSENSE!
SHE IS A LIVING, BREATHING *FARADAY CAGE!*
SHE IS WHAT YOU TRIED AT WARDENCLYFFE, TIED TO THE EARTH ITSELF!
IT WILL KILL HER, YOU IGNORANT PRETZEL!
IT HASN'T YET, HAS IT MY DEAR?
YET!?
YOU STARTED WITHOUT ME!?
HE'S RIGHT, DR. TESLA.
THE TESTS HAVE GONE FINE SO FAR.
SHALL WE SHOW HIM?
YES, LETS DO THAT.
COME OVER HERE, BEANPOLE. YOU MIGHT LEARN SOMETHING.

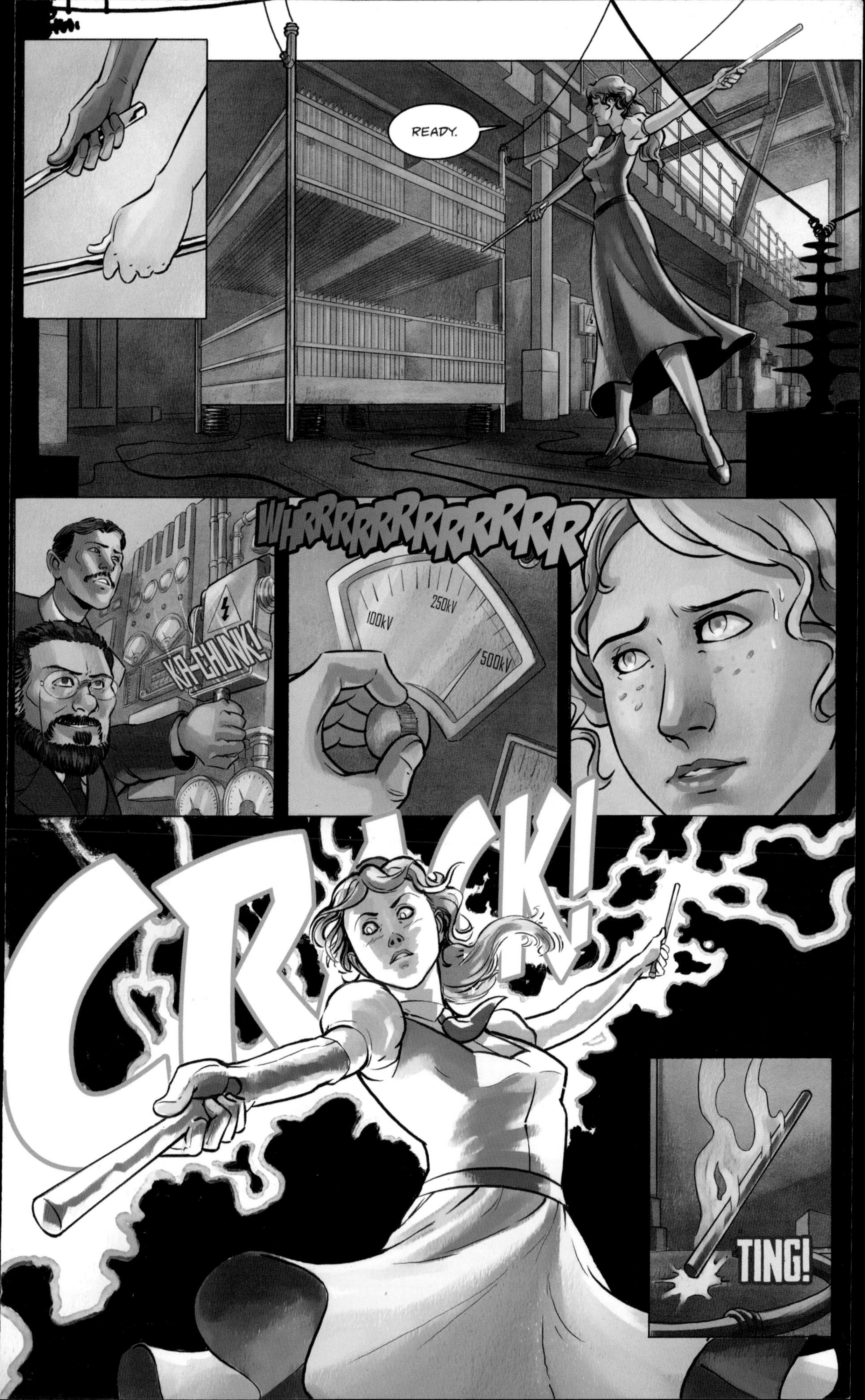
READY.
WHRRRRRRRRRRRRR
KA-CHUNK!
100kV
250kV
500kV
CRACK!
TING!

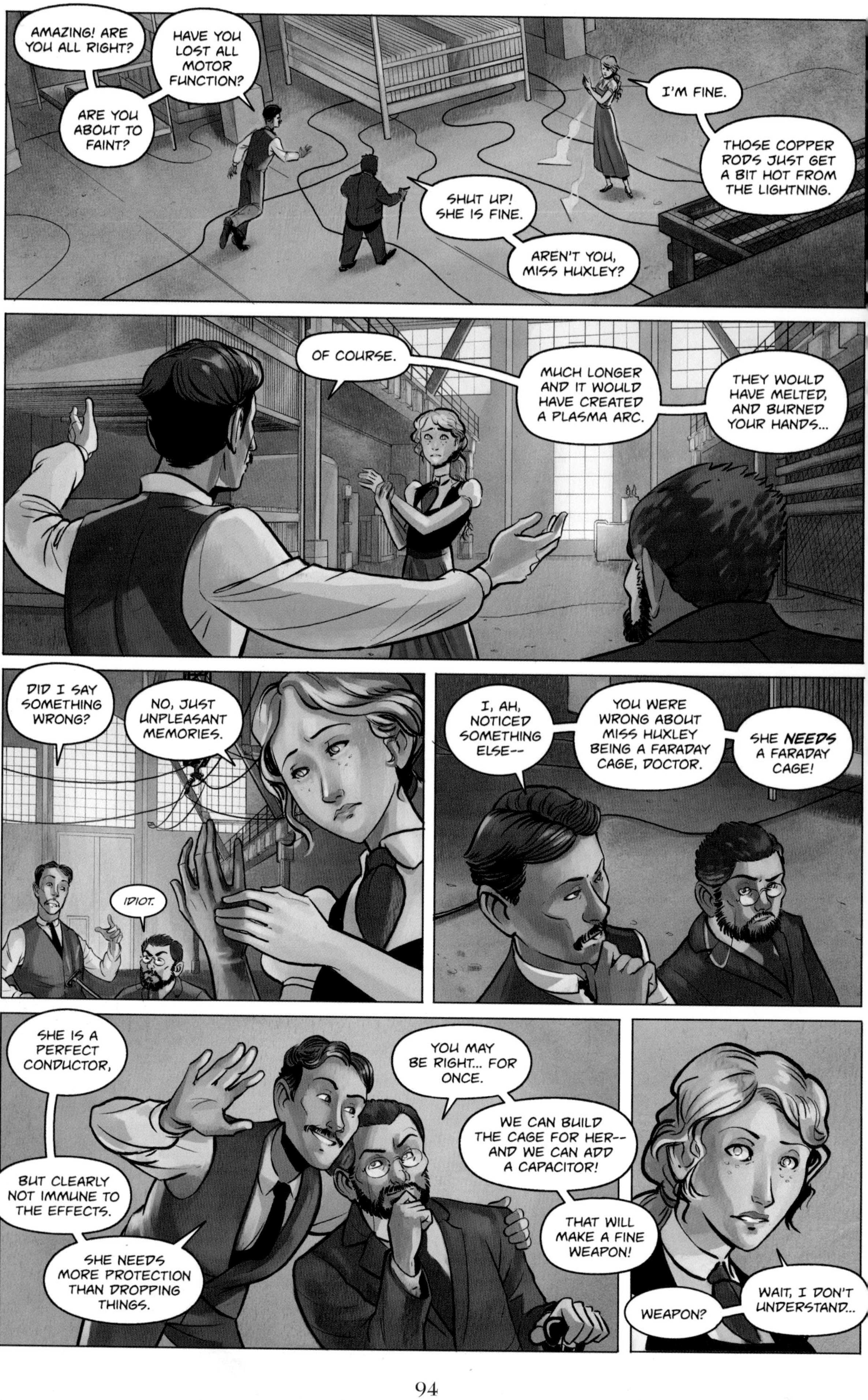
AMAZING! ARE YOU ALL RIGHT?
ARE YOU ABOUT TO FAINT?
HAVE YOU LOST ALL MOTOR FUNCTION?
SHUT UP! SHE IS FINE.
AREN'T YOU, MISS HUXLEY?
I'M FINE.
THOSE COPPER RODS JUST GET A BIT HOT FROM THE LIGHTNING.
OF COURSE.
MUCH LONGER AND IT WOULD HAVE CREATED A PLASMA ARC.
THEY WOULD HAVE MELTED, AND BURNED YOUR HANDS...
DID I SAY SOMETHING WRONG?
NO, JUST UNPLEASANT MEMORIES.
IDIOT.
I, AH, NOTICED SOMETHING ELSE--
YOU WERE WRONG ABOUT MISS HUXLEY BEING A FARADAY CAGE, DOCTOR.
SHE NEEDS A FARADAY CAGE!
SHE IS A PERFECT CONDUCTOR,
BUT CLEARLY NOT IMMUNE TO THE EFFECTS.
SHE NEEDS MORE PROTECTION THAN DROPPING THINGS.
YOU MAY BE RIGHT... FOR ONCE.
WE CAN BUILD THE CAGE FOR HER-- AND WE CAN ADD A CAPACITOR!
THAT WILL MAKE A FINE WEAPON!
WEAPON?
WAIT, I DON'T UNDERSTAND...

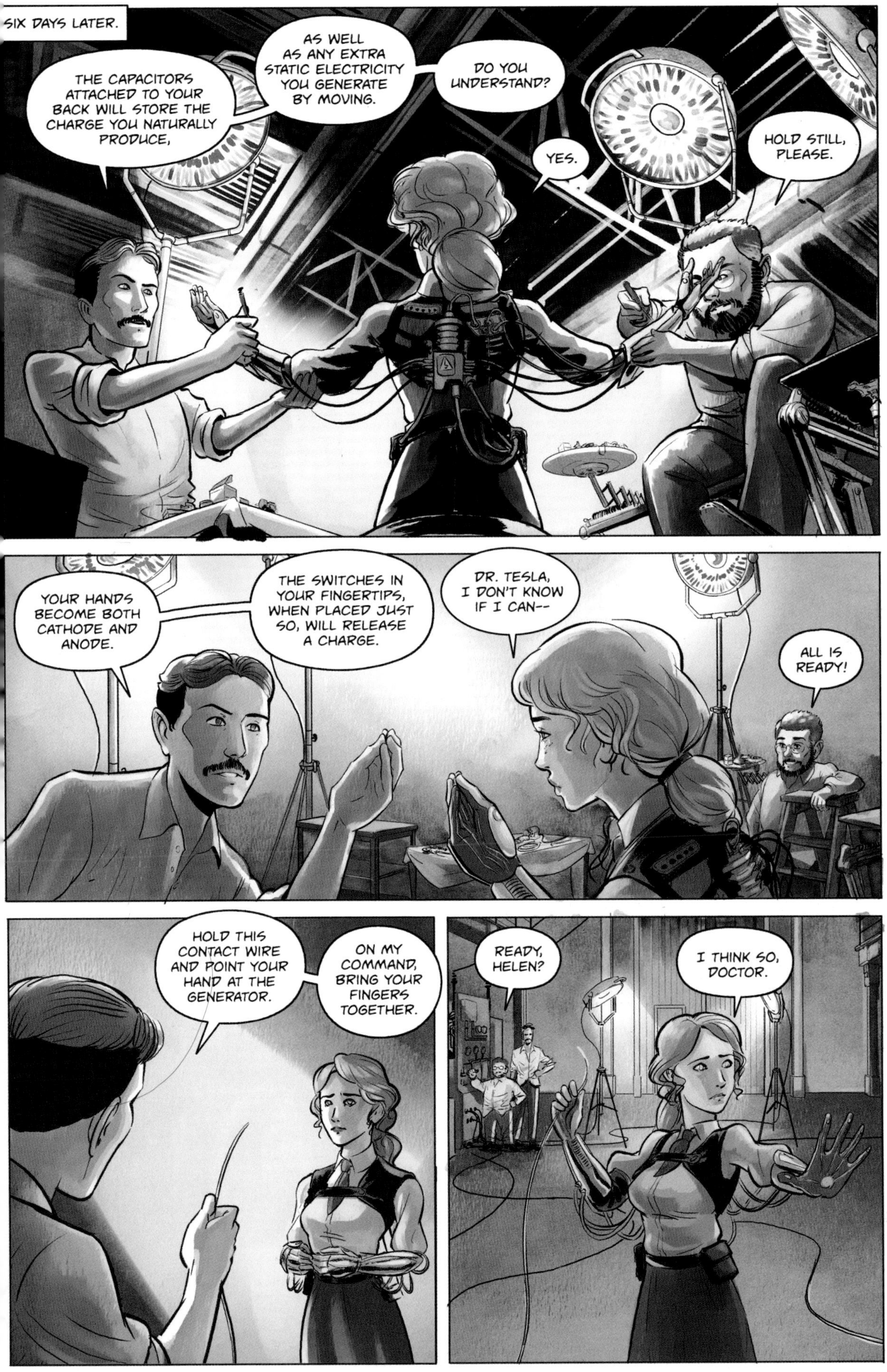
SIX DAYS LATER.
THE CAPACITORS ATTACHED TO YOUR BACK WILL STORE THE CHARGE YOU NATURALLY PRODUCE,
AS WELL AS ANY EXTRA STATIC ELECTRICITY YOU GENERATE BY MOVING.
DO YOU UNDERSTAND?
YES.
HOLD STILL, PLEASE.
YOUR HANDS BECOME BOTH CATHODE AND ANODE.
THE SWITCHES IN YOUR FINGERTIPS, WHEN PLACED JUST SO, WILL RELEASE A CHARGE.
DR. TESLA, I DON'T KNOW IF I CAN--
ALL IS READY!
HOLD THIS CONTACT WIRE AND POINT YOUR HAND AT THE GENERATOR.
ON MY COMMAND, BRING YOUR FINGERS TOGETHER.
READY, HELEN?
I THINK SO, DOCTOR.

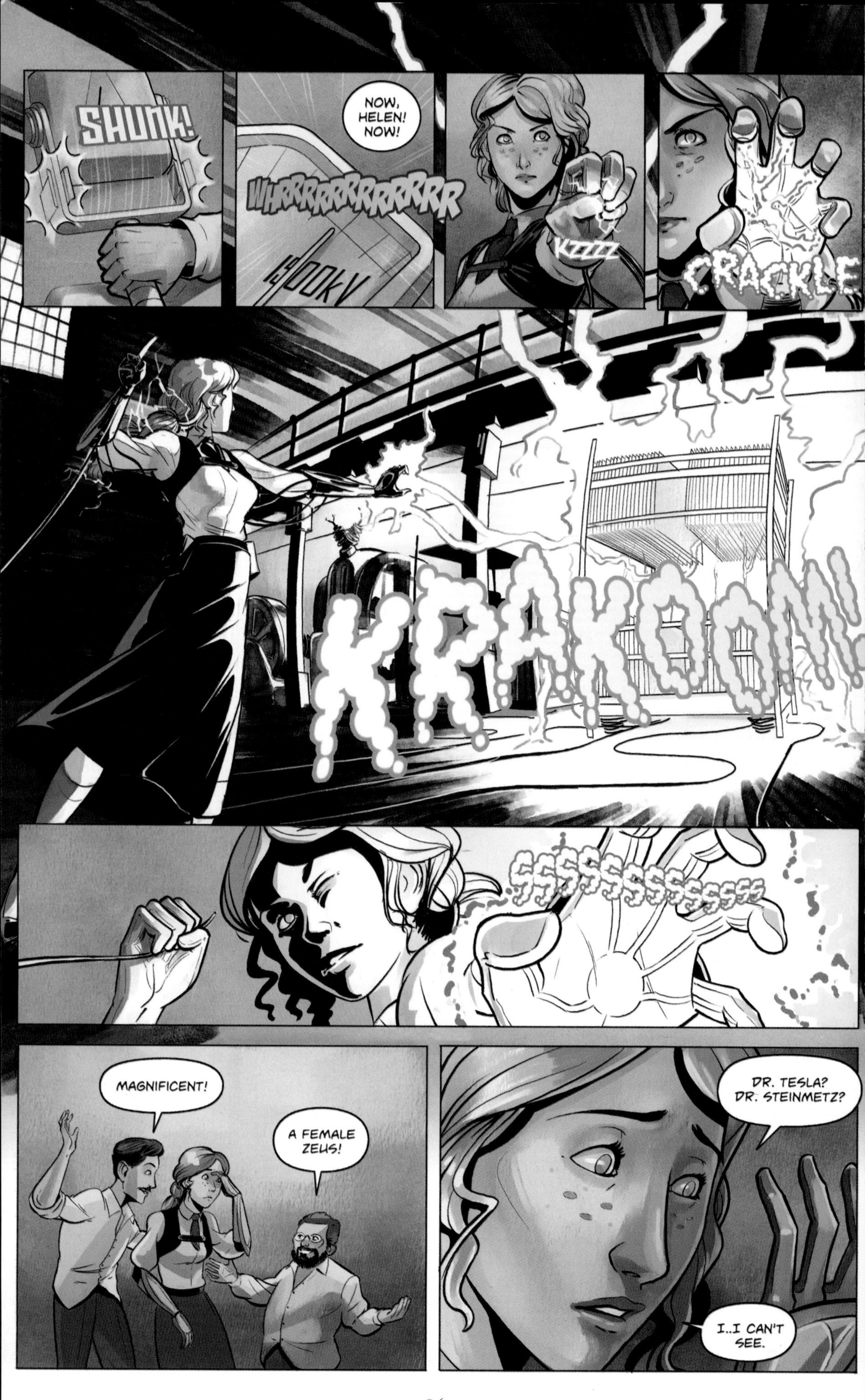
SHUNK!
NOW, HELEN! NOW!
WHRRRRRRRRRRRR
400KV
KZZZZ
CRACKLE
KRAKOOM!
SSSSSSSSSSSSSS
MAGNIFICENT!
A FEMALE ZEUS!
DR. TESLA? DR. STEINMETZ?
I..I CAN'T SEE.

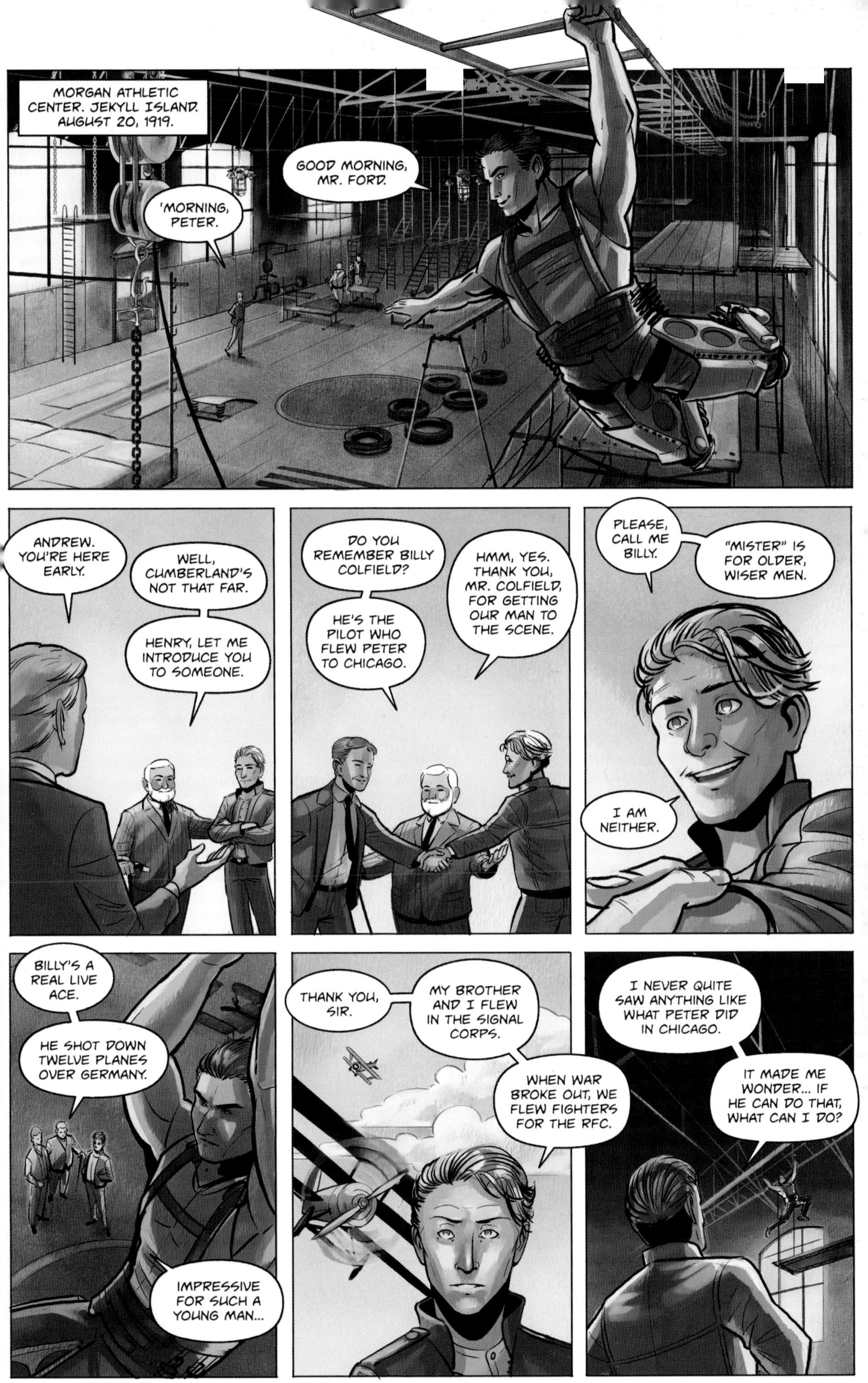
MORGAN ATHLETIC CENTER. JEKYLL ISLAND. AUGUST 20, 1919.
GOOD MORNING, MR. FORD.
'MORNING, PETER.
ANDREW. YOU'RE HERE EARLY.
WELL, CUMBERLAND'S NOT THAT FAR.
HENRY, LET ME INTRODUCE YOU TO SOMEONE.
DO YOU REMEMBER BILLY COLFIELD?
HE'S THE PILOT WHO FLEW PETER TO CHICAGO.
HMM, YES. THANK YOU, MR. COLFIELD, FOR GETTING OUR MAN TO THE SCENE.
PLEASE, CALL ME BILLY.
"MISTER" IS FOR OLDER, WISER MEN.
I AM NEITHER.
BILLY'S A REAL LIVE ACE.
HE SHOT DOWN TWELVE PLANES OVER GERMANY.
IMPRESSIVE FOR SUCH A YOUNG MAN...
THANK YOU, SIR.
MY BROTHER AND I FLEW IN THE SIGNAL CORPS.
WHEN WAR BROKE OUT, WE FLEW FIGHTERS FOR THE RFC.
I NEVER QUITE SAW ANYTHING LIKE WHAT PETER DID IN CHICAGO.
IT MADE ME WONDER... IF HE CAN DO THAT, WHAT CAN I DO?

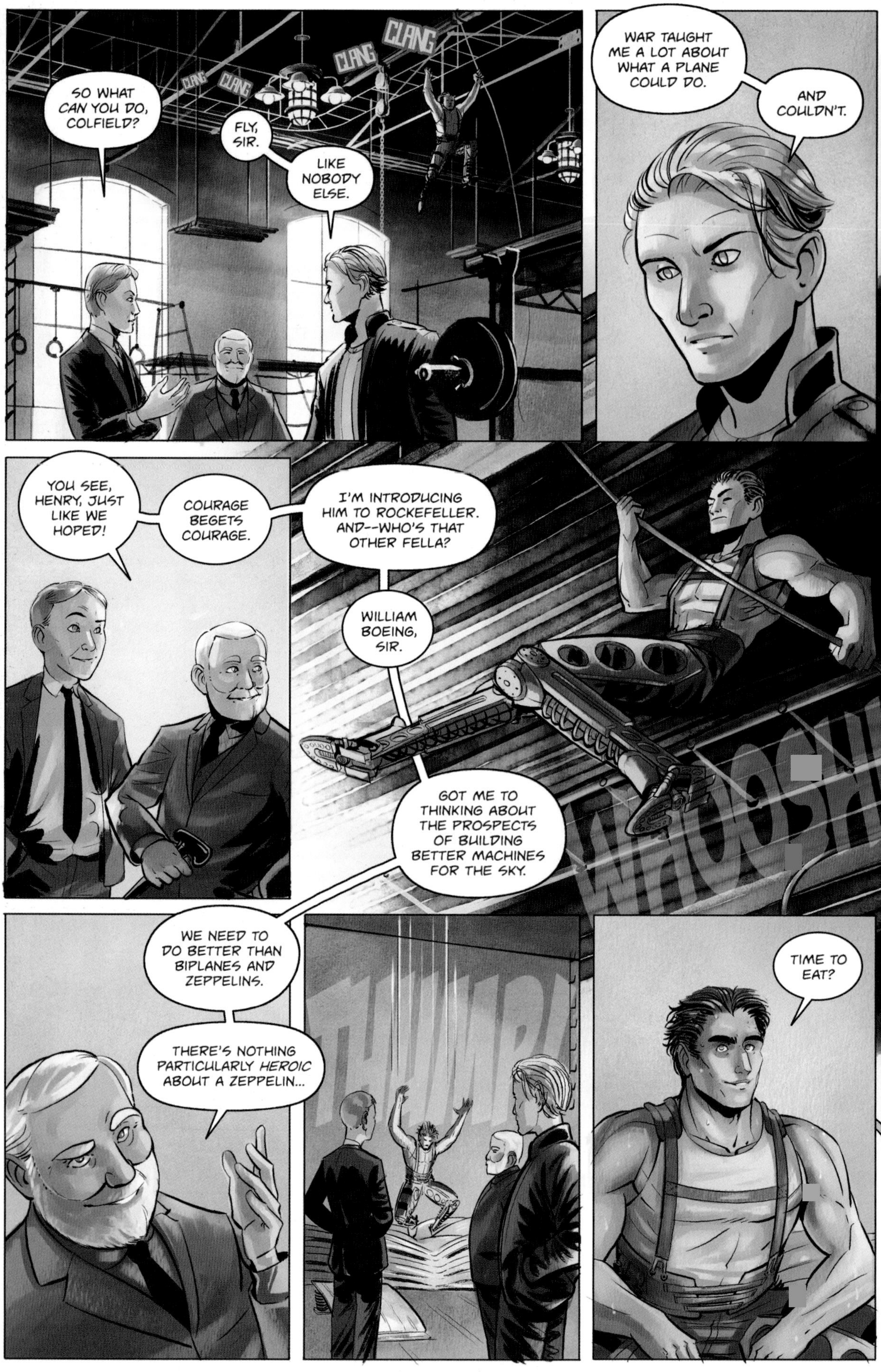
CLANG
CLANG
CLANG
CLANG
SO WHAT CAN YOU DO, COLFIELD?
FLY, SIR.
LIKE NOBODY ELSE.
WAR TAUGHT ME A LOT ABOUT WHAT A PLANE COULD DO.
AND COULDN'T.
YOU SEE, HENRY, JUST LIKE WE HOPED!
COURAGE BEGETS COURAGE.
I'M INTRODUCING HIM TO ROCKEFELLER. AND--WHO'S THAT OTHER FELLA?
WILLIAM BOEING, SIR.
GOT ME TO THINKING ABOUT THE PROSPECTS OF BUILDING BETTER MACHINES FOR THE SKY.
WHOOSH!
WE NEED TO DO BETTER THAN BIPLANES AND ZEPPELINS.
THERE'S NOTHING PARTICULARLY *HEROIC* ABOUT A ZEPPELIN...
THUMP!
TIME TO EAT?

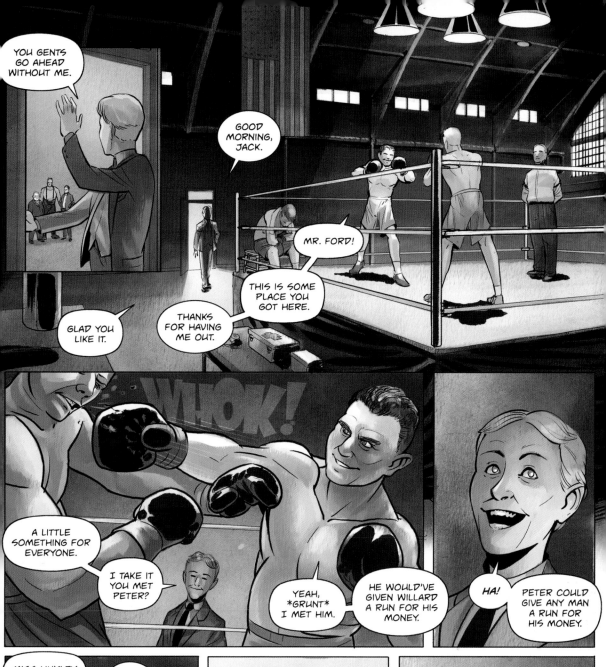

YOU GENTS GO AHEAD WITHOUT ME.

GOOD MORNING, JACK.

MR. FORD!

THIS IS SOME PLACE YOU GOT HERE.

THANKS FOR HAVING ME OUT.

GLAD YOU LIKE IT.

WHOK!

A LITTLE SOMETHING FOR EVERYONE.

I TAKE IT YOU MET PETER?

YEAH, *GRUNT* I MET HIM.

HE WOULD'VE GIVEN WILLARD A RUN FOR HIS MONEY.

HA!

PETER COULD GIVE ANY MAN A RUN FOR HIS MONEY.

MISS HUXLEY HERE YET?

SOON.

SHE HAD A BIT OF AN EYE INJURY, BUT SHE'S ON THE MEND.

I'M LOOKING FORWARD TO MEETING HER.

I HEAR SHE'S QUITE THE WOMAN.

OH, SHE'S A REAL LIVE WIRE.

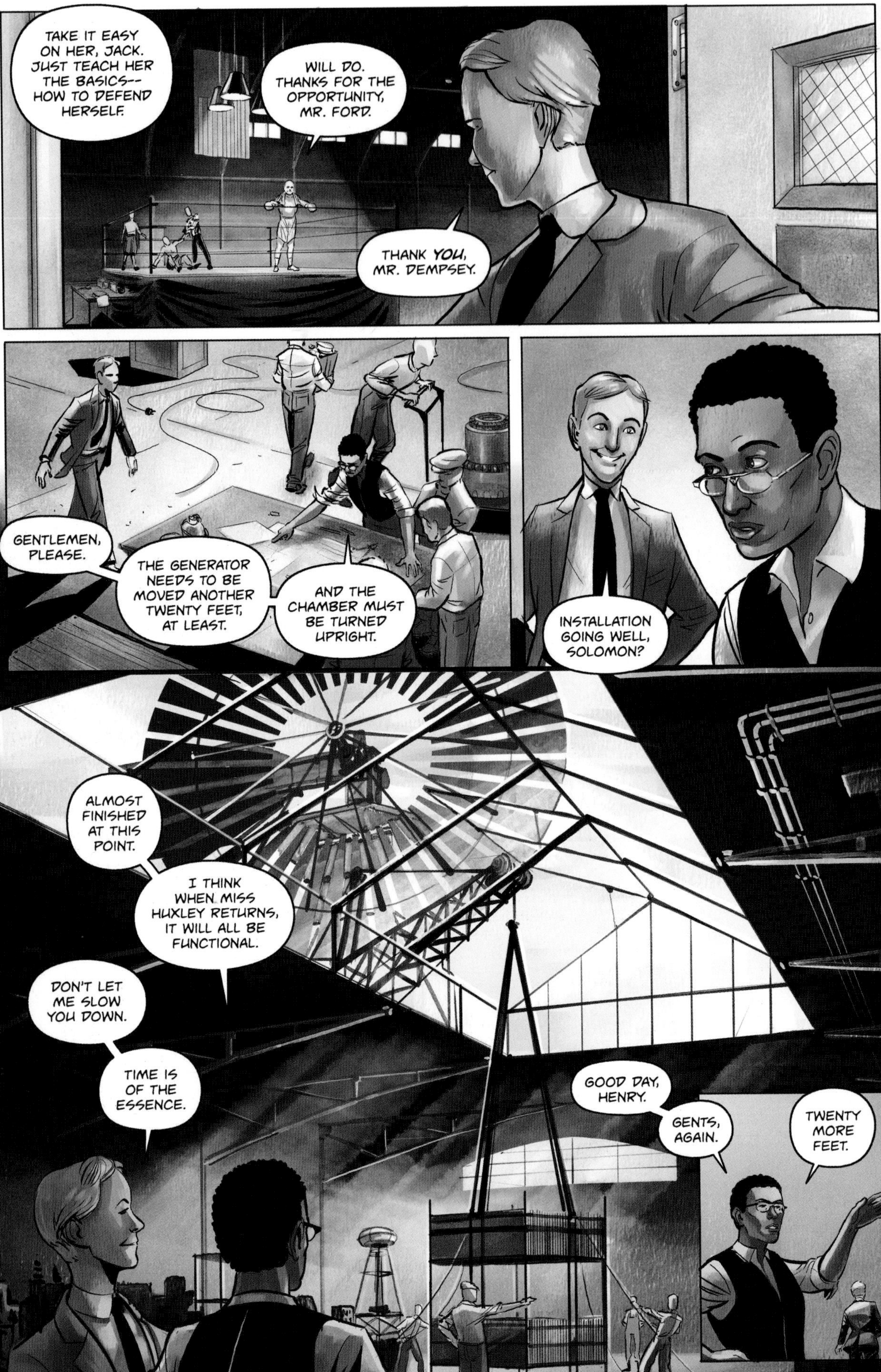
TAKE IT EASY ON HER, JACK. JUST TEACH HER THE BASICS-- HOW TO DEFEND HERSELF.
WILL DO. THANKS FOR THE OPPORTUNITY, MR. FORD.
THANK YOU, MR. DEMPSEY.
GENTLEMEN, PLEASE.
THE GENERATOR NEEDS TO BE MOVED ANOTHER TWENTY FEET, AT LEAST.
AND THE CHAMBER MUST BE TURNED UPRIGHT.
INSTALLATION GOING WELL, SOLOMON?
ALMOST FINISHED AT THIS POINT.
I THINK WHEN MISS HUXLEY RETURNS, IT WILL ALL BE FUNCTIONAL.
DON'T LET ME SLOW YOU DOWN.
TIME IS OF THE ESSENCE.
GOOD DAY, HENRY.
GENTS, AGAIN.
TWENTY MORE FEET.

OCCIDENTAL RESTAURANT. WASHINGTON, D.C. AUGUST 28, 1919.

WHEN ANDREW TOLD ME ABOUT YOU, I SIMPLY HAD TO MEET YOU, MISS HUXLEY.

AND EDITH DOESN'T WANT ME DINING ALONE WITH OTHER BEAUTIFUL WOMEN.

YOU HAVE QUITE AN AMAZING STORY, HELEN.

YOU ARE LUCKY TO BE ALIVE.

YES.

LUCKY...

IS IT TRUE THAT YOUR BODY CARRIES A CHARGE?

THAT YOU EMIT A SHOCK?

UNFORTUNATELY, IT IS TRUE.

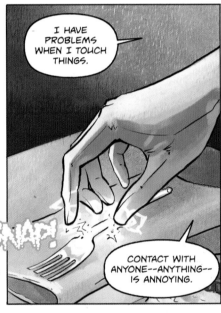

I HAVE PROBLEMS WHEN I TOUCH THINGS.

SNAP!

CONTACT WITH ANYONE--ANYTHING-- IS ANNOYING.

IMAGINE RUBBING YOUR FEET ON A CARPET, THEN TOUCHING A DOORKNOB.

THAT'S KIND OF WHAT HAPPENS.

ONLY, ALL THE TIME.

ZZZOT

REMARKABLE.

REMARKABLY IRRITATING...

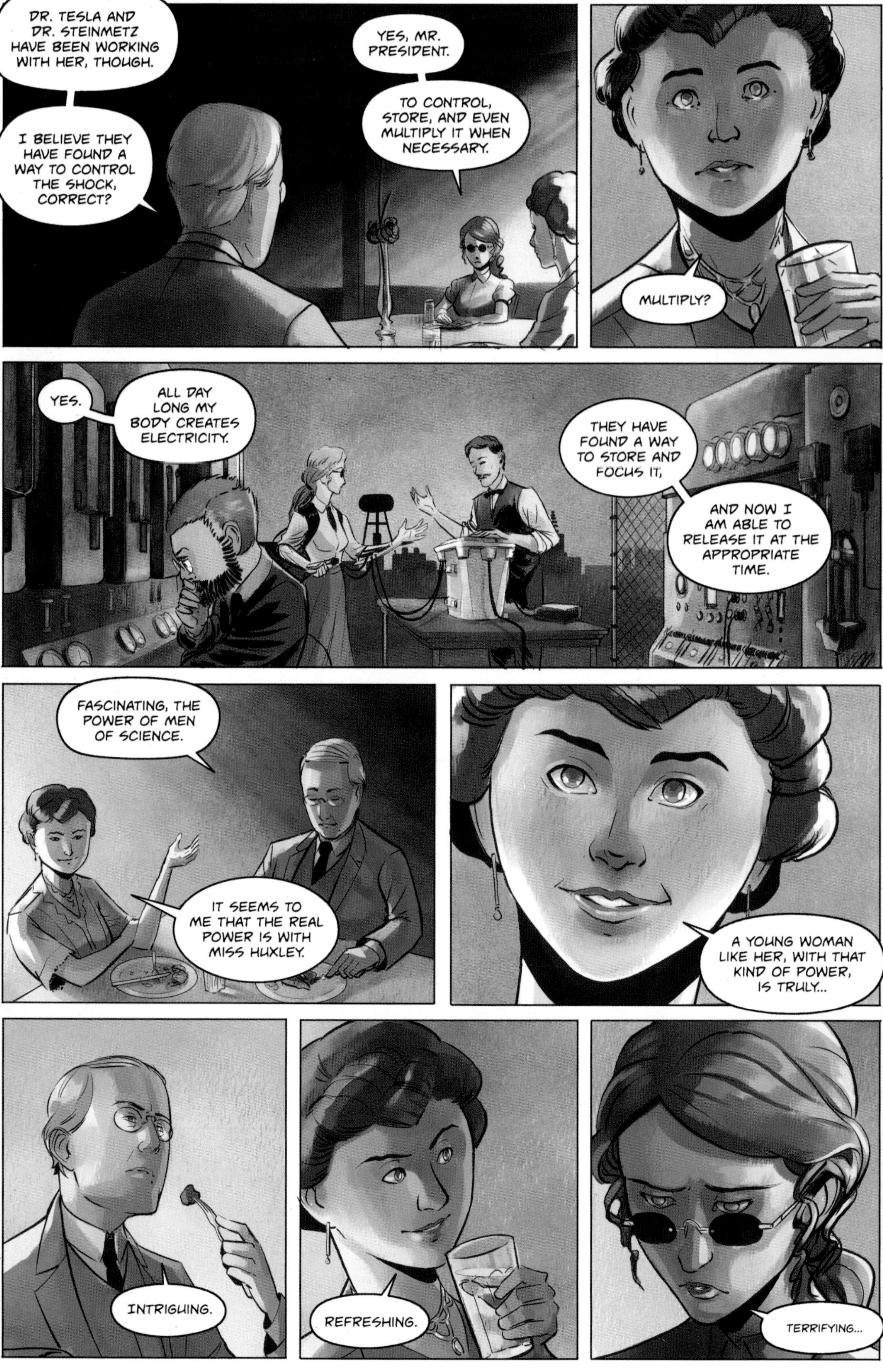

DR. TESLA AND DR. STEINMETZ HAVE BEEN WORKING WITH HER, THOUGH.
I BELIEVE THEY HAVE FOUND A WAY TO CONTROL THE SHOCK, CORRECT?
YES, MR. PRESIDENT.
TO CONTROL, STORE, AND EVEN MULTIPLY IT WHEN NECESSARY.
MULTIPLY?
YES.
ALL DAY LONG MY BODY CREATES ELECTRICITY.
THEY HAVE FOUND A WAY TO STORE AND FOCUS IT,
AND NOW I AM ABLE TO RELEASE IT AT THE APPROPRIATE TIME.
FASCINATING, THE POWER OF MEN OF SCIENCE.
IT SEEMS TO ME THAT THE REAL POWER IS WITH MISS HUXLEY.
A YOUNG WOMAN LIKE HER, WITH THAT KIND OF POWER, IS TRULY...
INTRIGUING.
REFRESHING.
TERRIFYING...

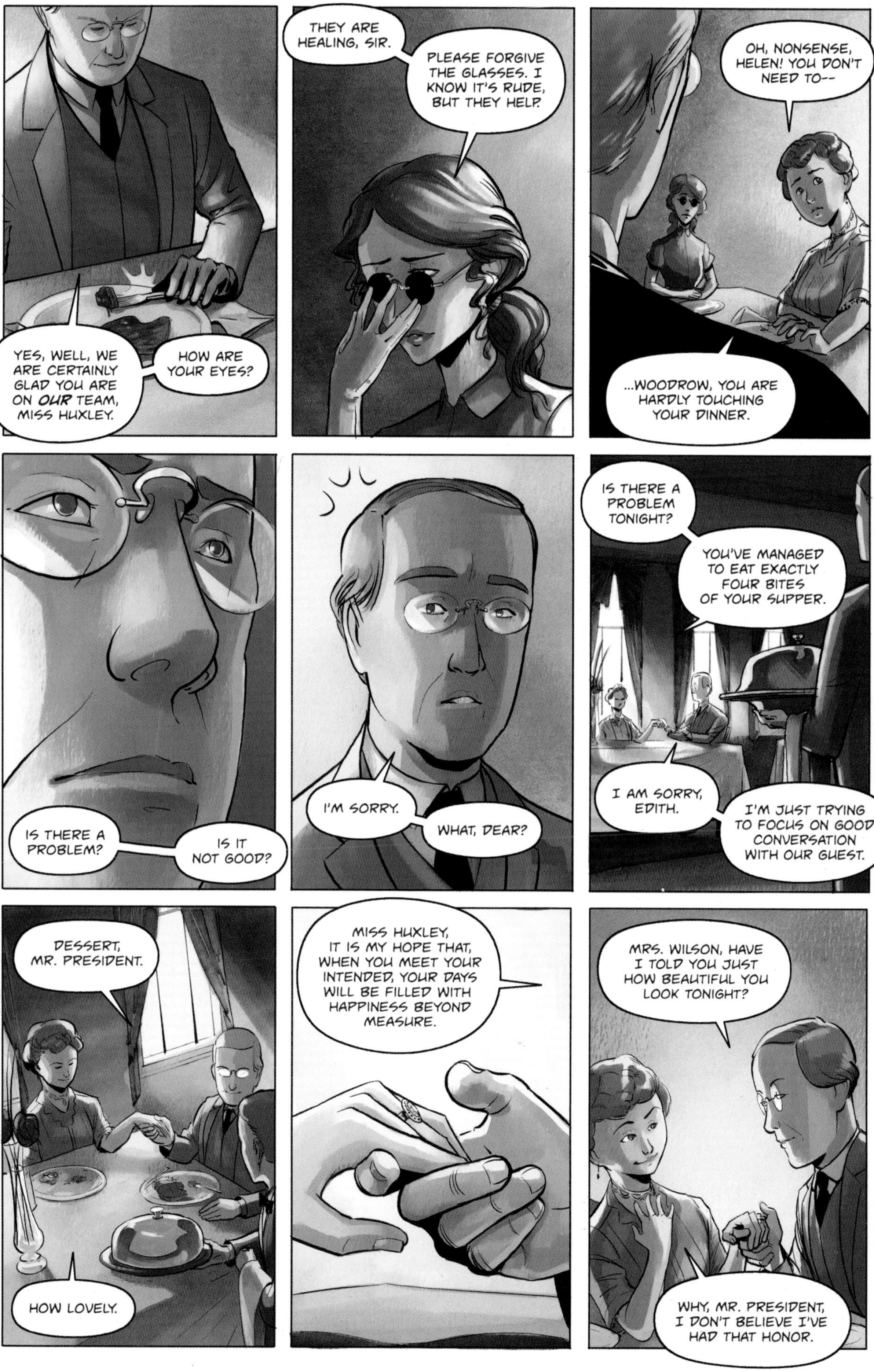
YES, WELL, WE ARE CERTAINLY GLAD YOU ARE ON OUR TEAM, MISS HUXLEY.
HOW ARE YOUR EYES?
THEY ARE HEALING, SIR.
PLEASE FORGIVE THE GLASSES. I KNOW IT'S RUDE, BUT THEY HELP.
OH, NONSENSE, HELEN! YOU DON'T NEED TO--
...WOODROW, YOU ARE HARDLY TOUCHING YOUR DINNER.
IS THERE A PROBLEM?
IS IT NOT GOOD?
I'M SORRY.
WHAT, DEAR?
IS THERE A PROBLEM TONIGHT?
YOU'VE MANAGED TO EAT EXACTLY FOUR BITES OF YOUR SUPPER.
I AM SORRY, EDITH.
I'M JUST TRYING TO FOCUS ON GOOD CONVERSATION WITH OUR GUEST.
DESSERT, MR. PRESIDENT.
HOW LOVELY.
MISS HUXLEY, IT IS MY HOPE THAT, WHEN YOU MEET YOUR INTENDED, YOUR DAYS WILL BE FILLED WITH HAPPINESS BEYOND MEASURE.
MRS. WILSON, HAVE I TOLD YOU JUST HOW BEAUTIFUL YOU LOOK TONIGHT?
WHY, MR. PRESIDENT, I DON'T BELIEVE I'VE HAD THAT HONOR.

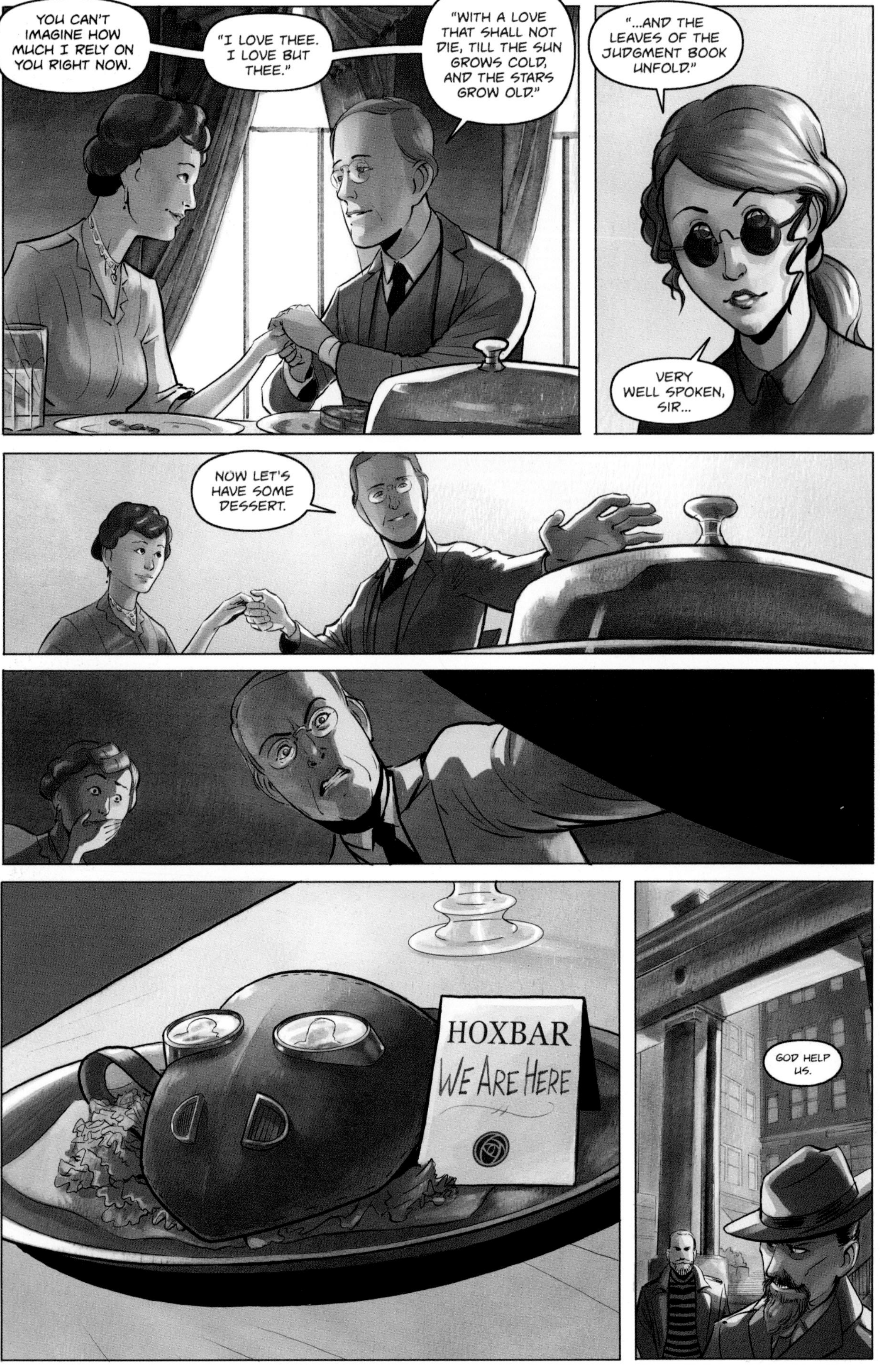
YOU CAN'T IMAGINE HOW MUCH I RELY ON YOU RIGHT NOW.
"I LOVE THEE. I LOVE BUT THEE."
"WITH A LOVE THAT SHALL NOT DIE, TILL THE SUN GROWS COLD, AND THE STARS GROW OLD."
"...AND THE LEAVES OF THE JUDGMENT BOOK UNFOLD."
VERY WELL SPOKEN, SIR...
NOW LET'S HAVE SOME DESSERT.
HOXBAR
WE ARE HERE
GOD HELP US.

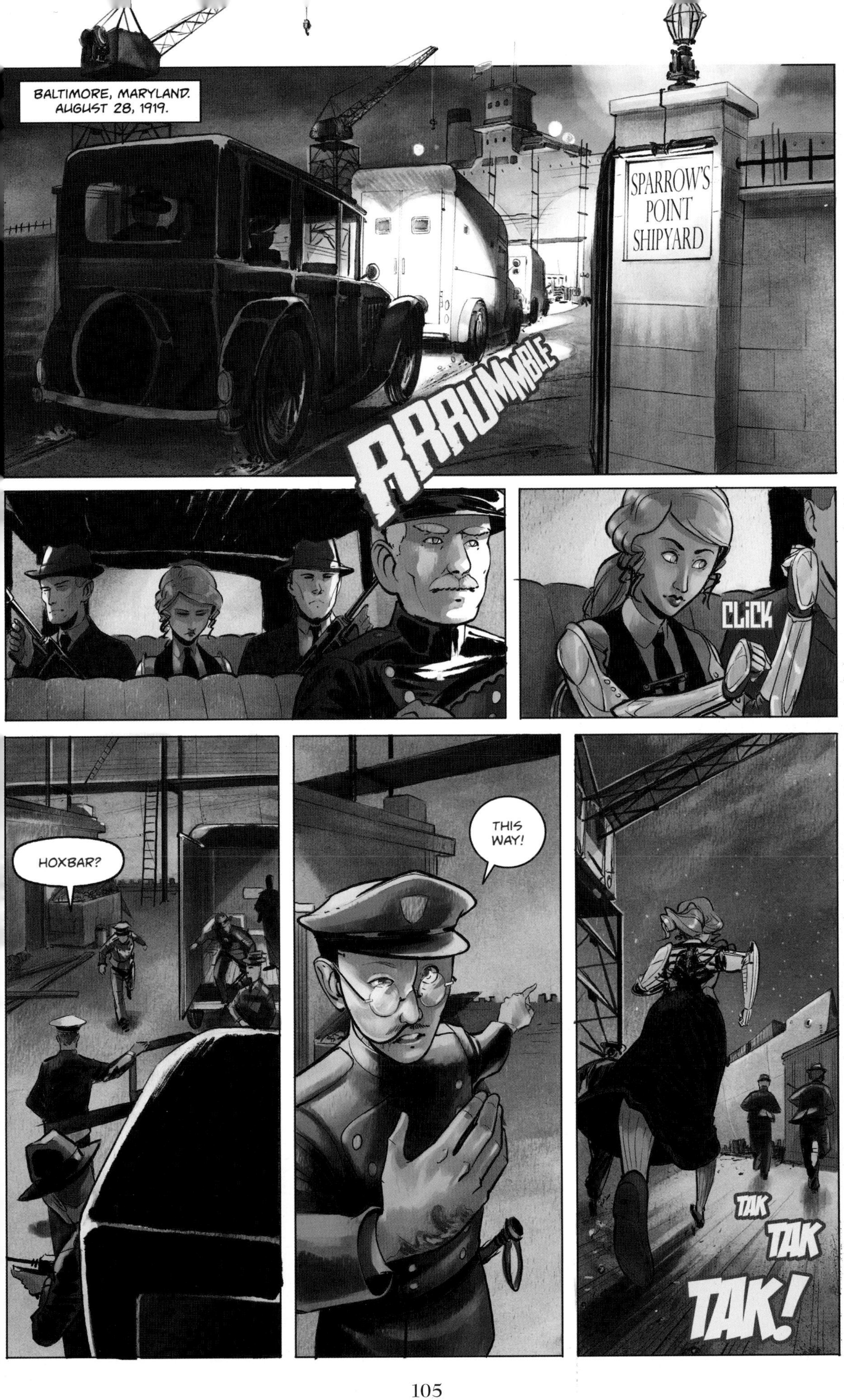
BALTIMORE, MARYLAND. AUGUST 28, 1919.
SPARROW'S POINT SHIPYARD
RRRUMMBLE
CLICK
HOXBAR?
THIS WAY!
TAK
TAK
TAK!

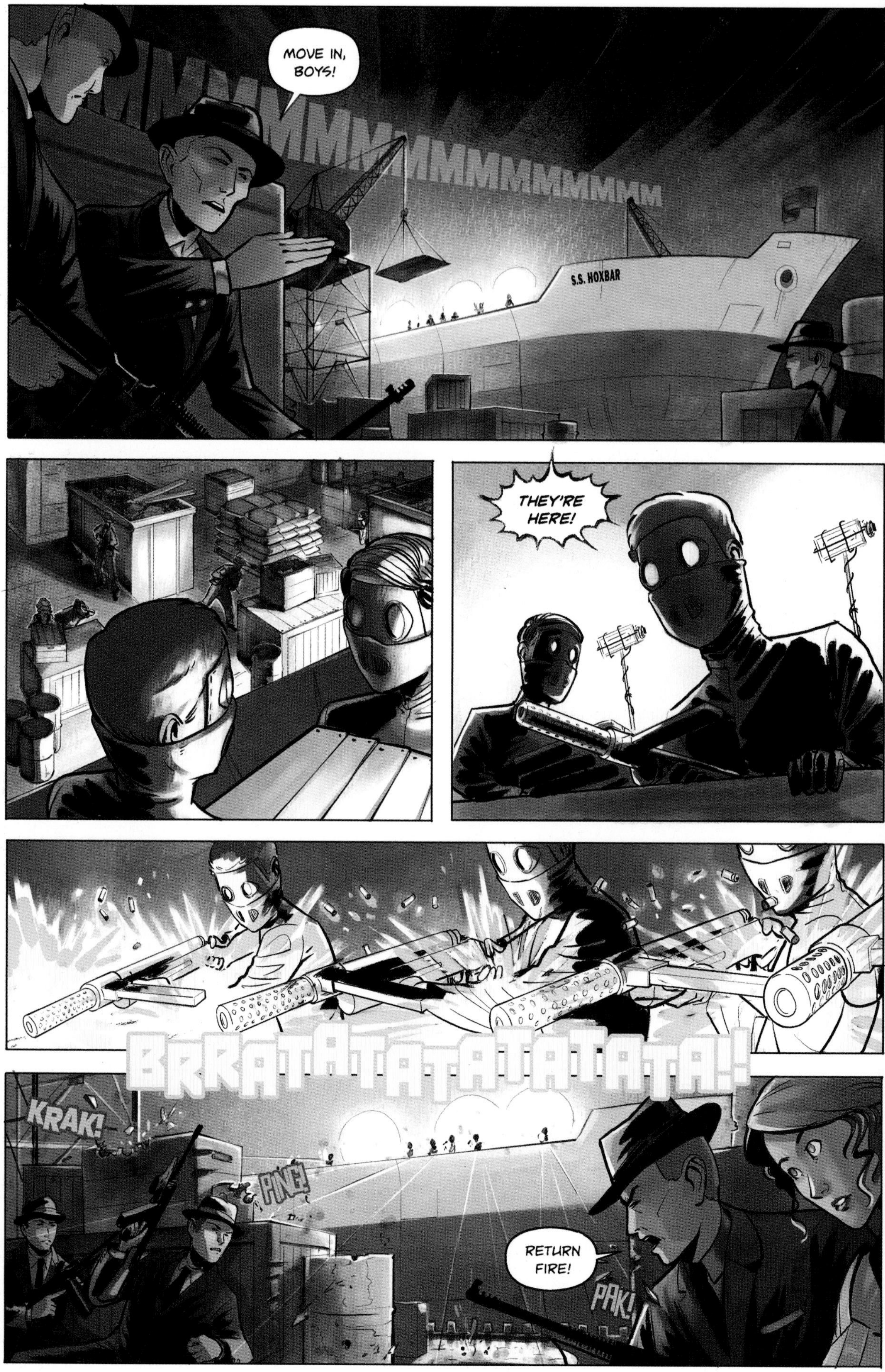
MOVE IN, BOYS!
MMMMMMMMMMMMMMMMM
S.S. HOXBAR
THEY'RE HERE!
BRRATATATATATATA!!
KRAK!
PING!
RETURN FIRE!
PAK!

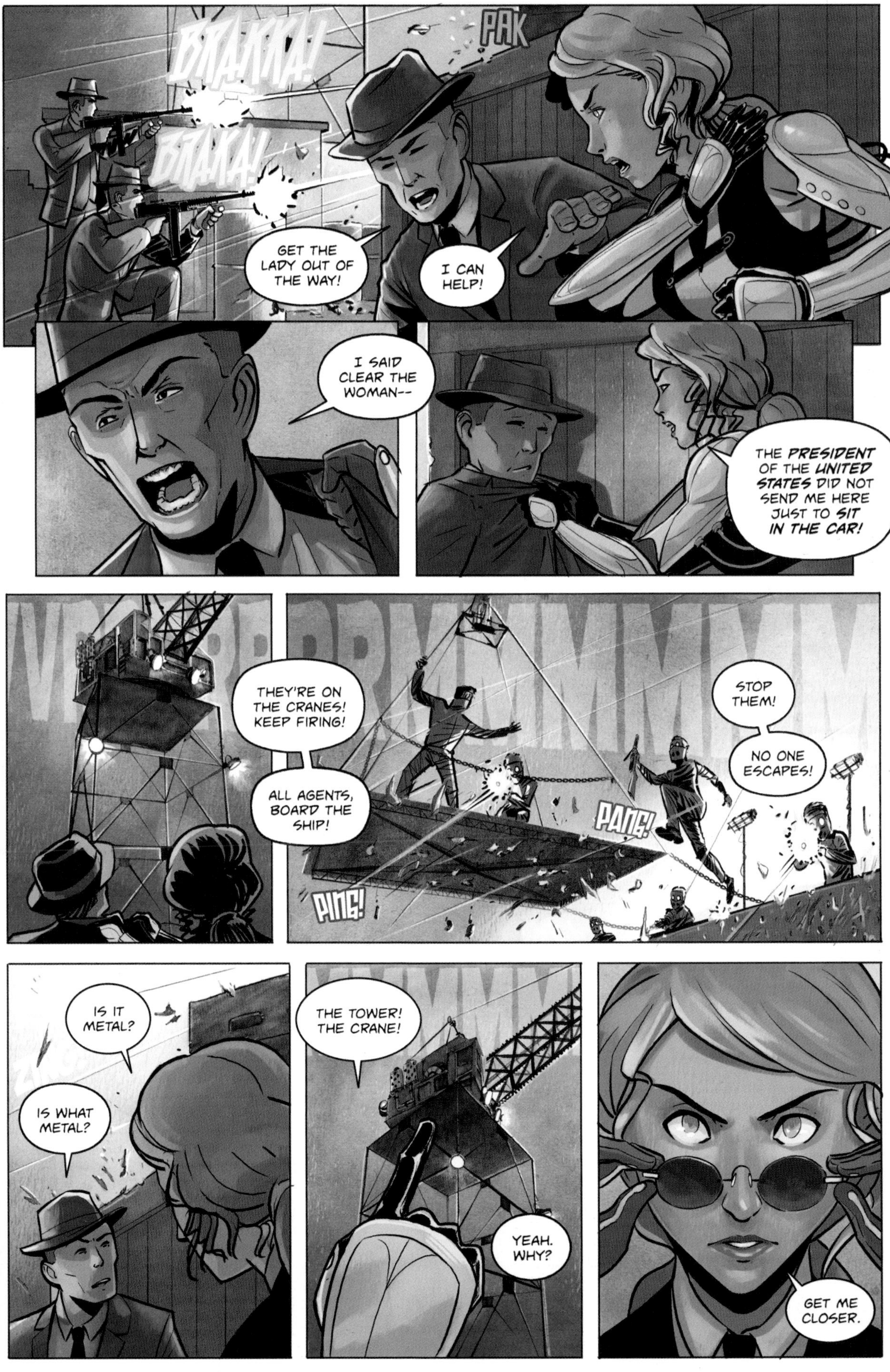
BRAKKA!
BRAKA!
PAK
GET THE LADY OUT OF THE WAY!
I CAN HELP!
I SAID CLEAR THE WOMAN--
THE PRESIDENT OF THE UNITED STATES DID NOT SEND ME HERE JUST TO SIT IN THE CAR!
THEY'RE ON THE CRANES! KEEP FIRING!
ALL AGENTS, BOARD THE SHIP!
STOP THEM!
NO ONE ESCAPES!
PANG!
PING!
IS IT METAL?
IS WHAT METAL?
THE TOWER! THE CRANE!
YEAH. WHY?
GET ME CLOSER.

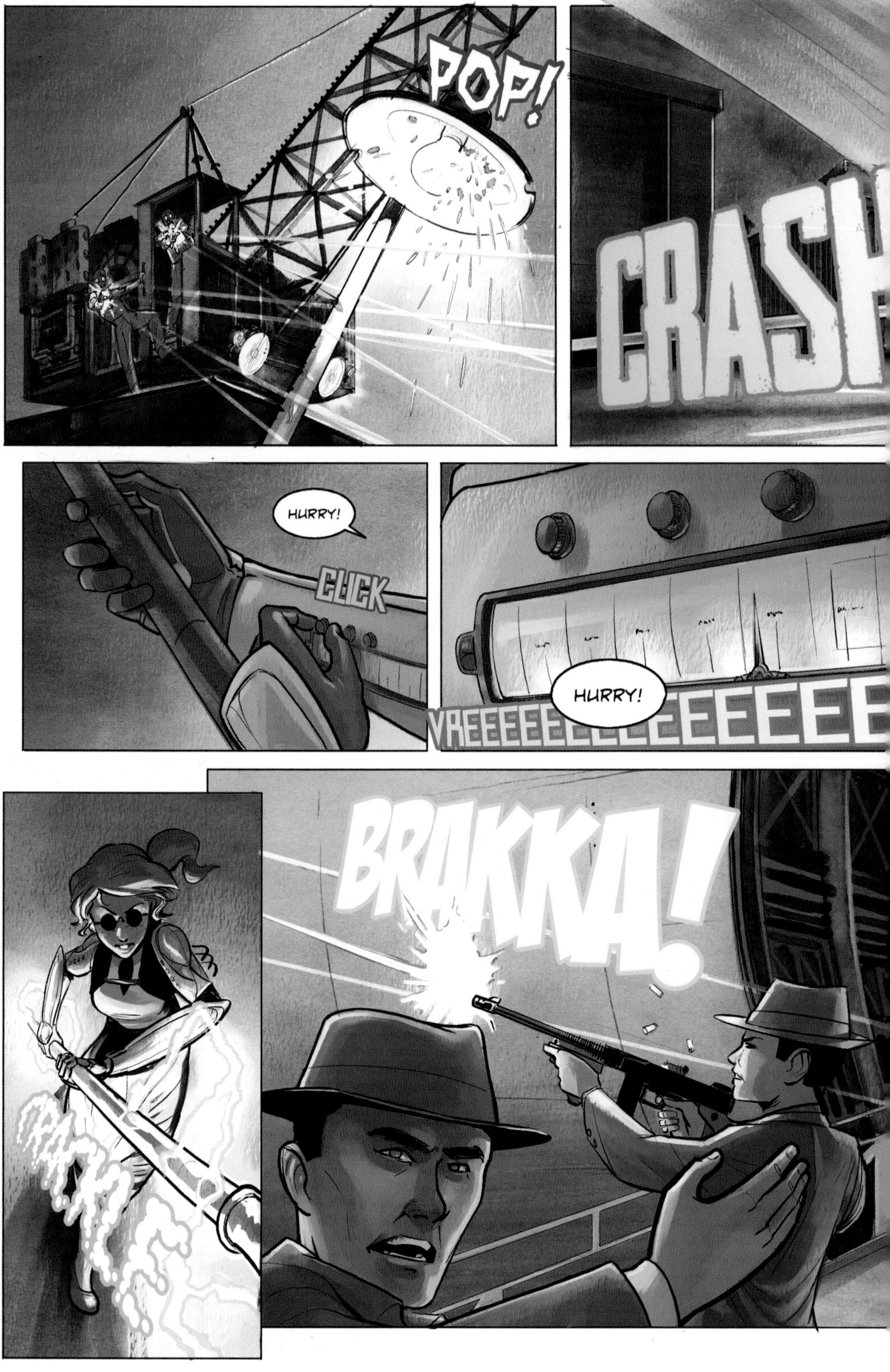
POP!
CRASH
HURRY!
CLICK
HURRY!
VREEEEEEEEEEEEE
BRAKKA!

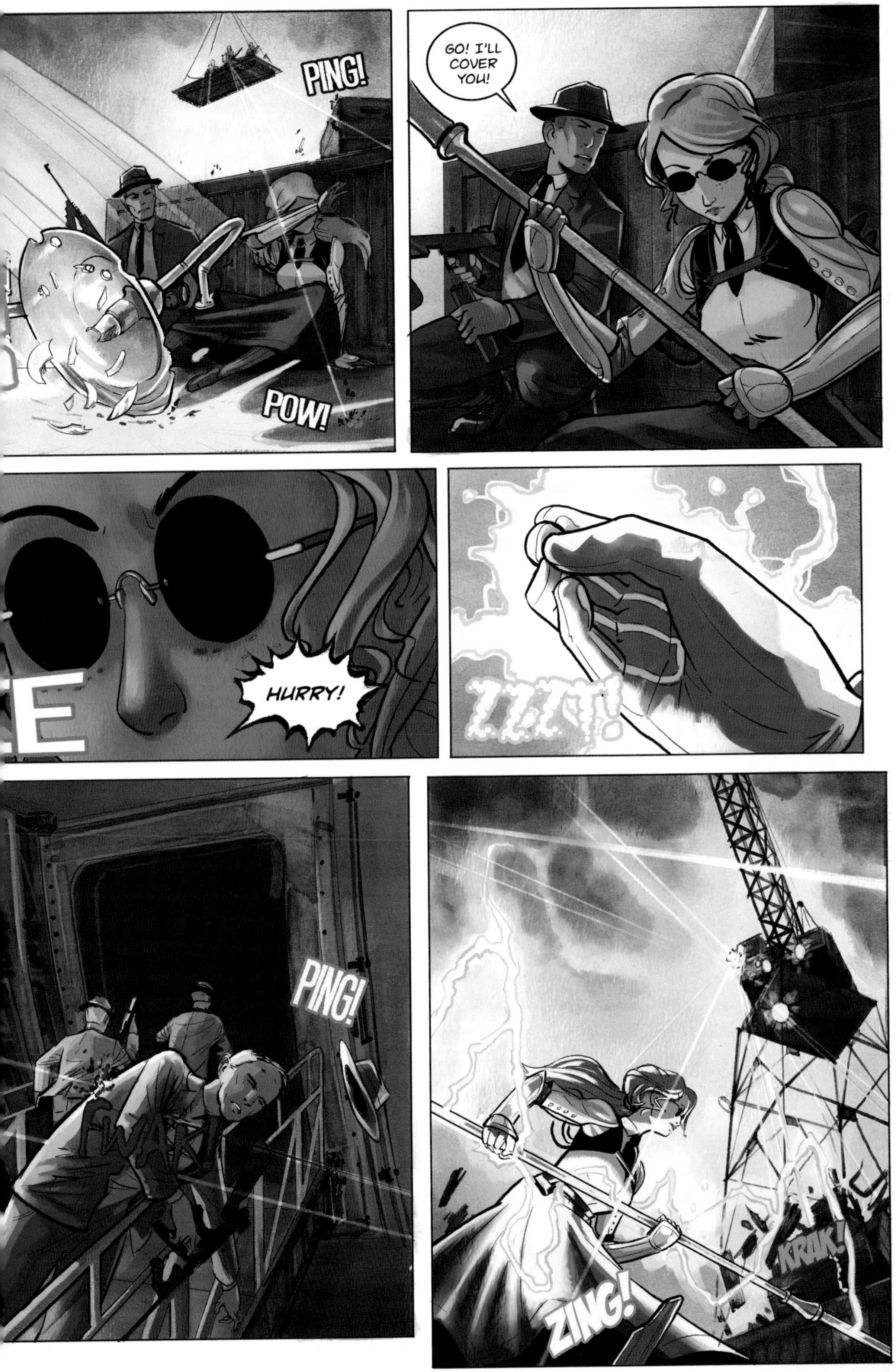
PING!
POW!
GO! I'LL COVER YOU!
HURRY!
ZZZT!
PING!
KRAK!
ZING!

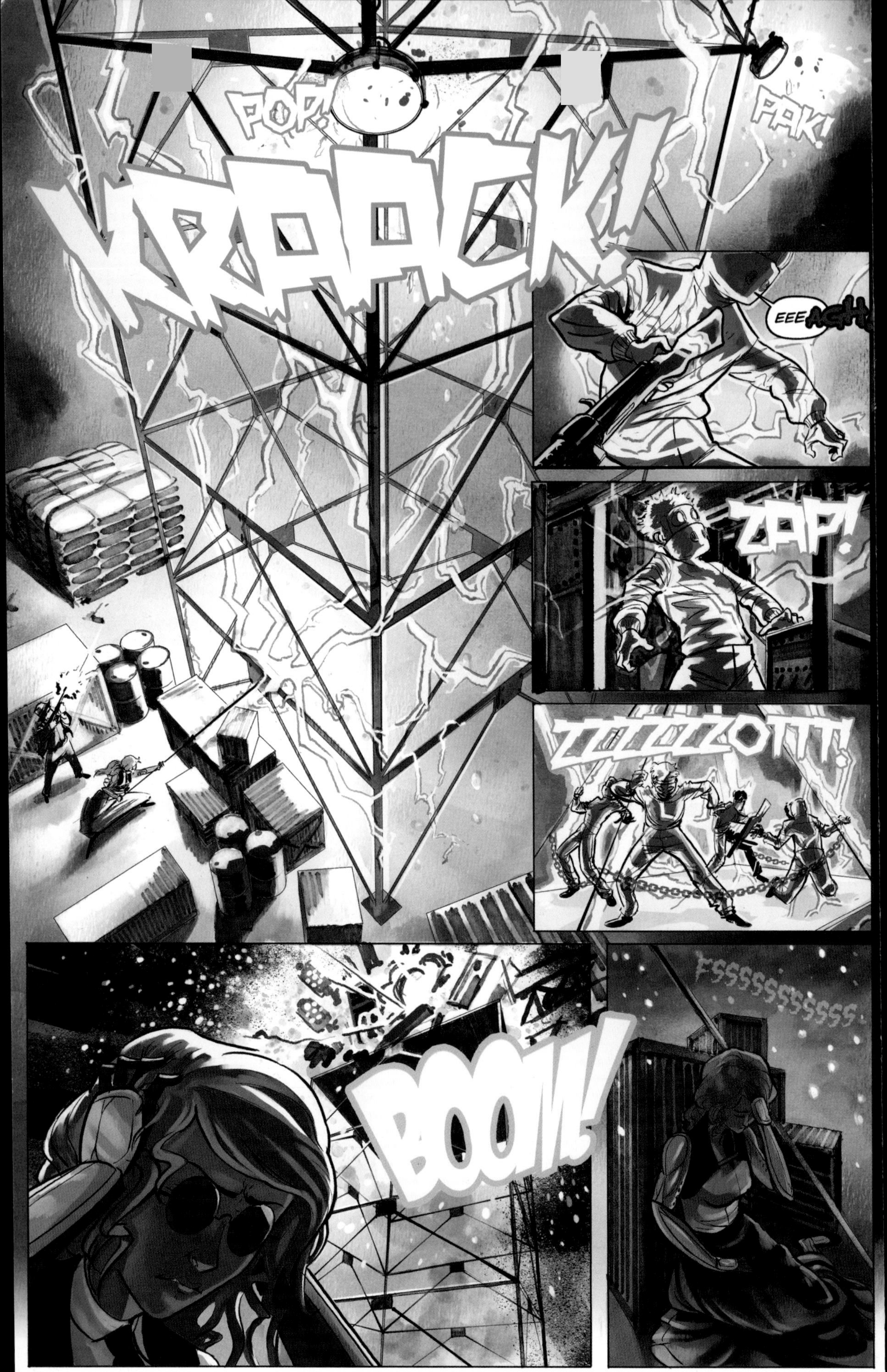
POP!
PAK!
KRAACK!
EEEAGH!
ZAP!
ZZZZZOTTT!
BOOM!
FSSSSSSSSSSS

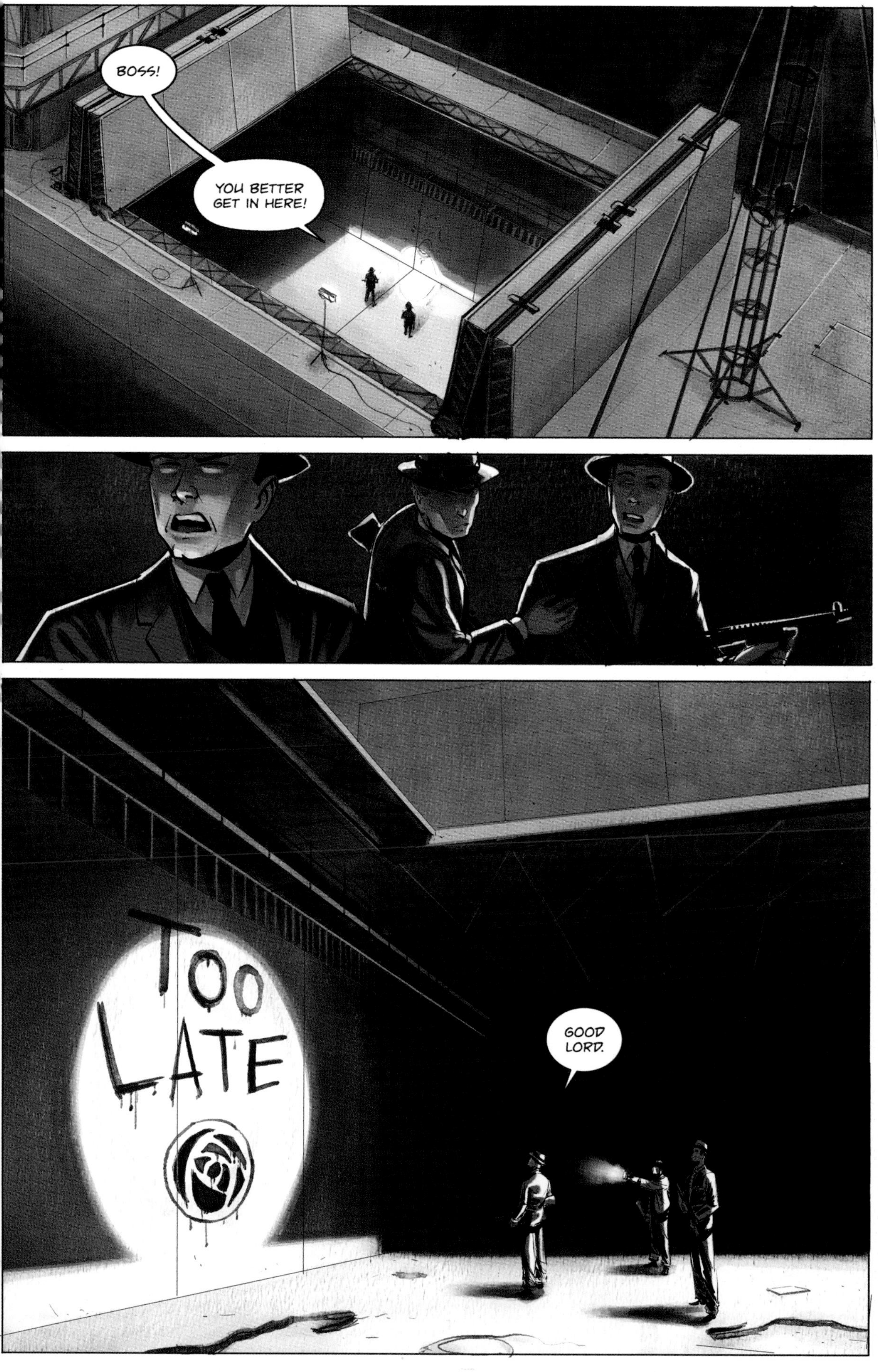
BOSS!
YOU BETTER GET IN HERE!
TOO LATE
GOOD LORD.

MOVE, QUICKLY!

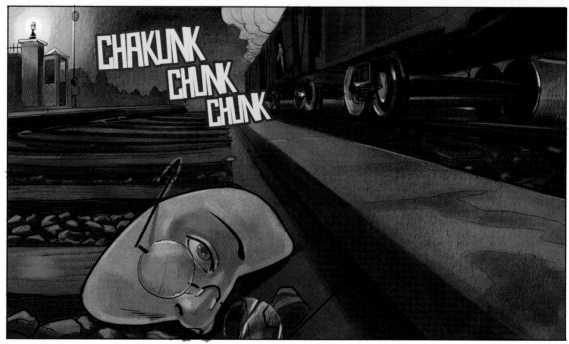

CHAKUNK
CHUNK
CHUNK

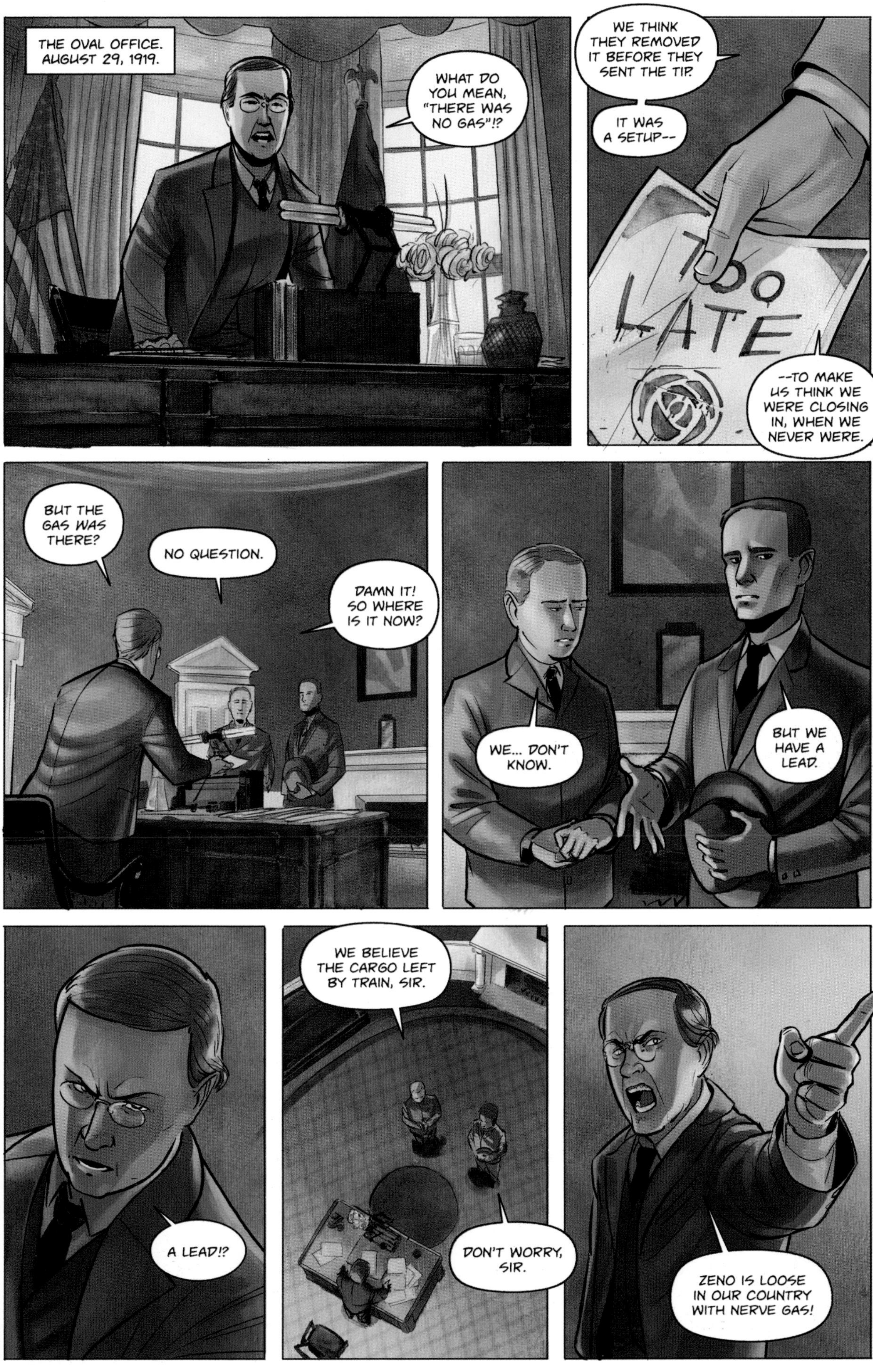
THE OVAL OFFICE. AUGUST 29, 1919.
WHAT DO YOU MEAN, "THERE WAS NO GAS"!?
WE THINK THEY REMOVED IT BEFORE THEY SENT THE TIP.
IT WAS A SETUP--
TOO LATE
--TO MAKE US THINK WE WERE CLOSING IN, WHEN WE NEVER WERE.
BUT THE GAS WAS THERE?
NO QUESTION.
DAMN IT! SO WHERE IS IT NOW?
WE... DON'T KNOW.
BUT WE HAVE A LEAD.
A LEAD!?
WE BELIEVE THE CARGO LEFT BY TRAIN, SIR.
DON'T WORRY, SIR.
ZENO IS LOOSE IN OUR COUNTRY WITH NERVE GAS!

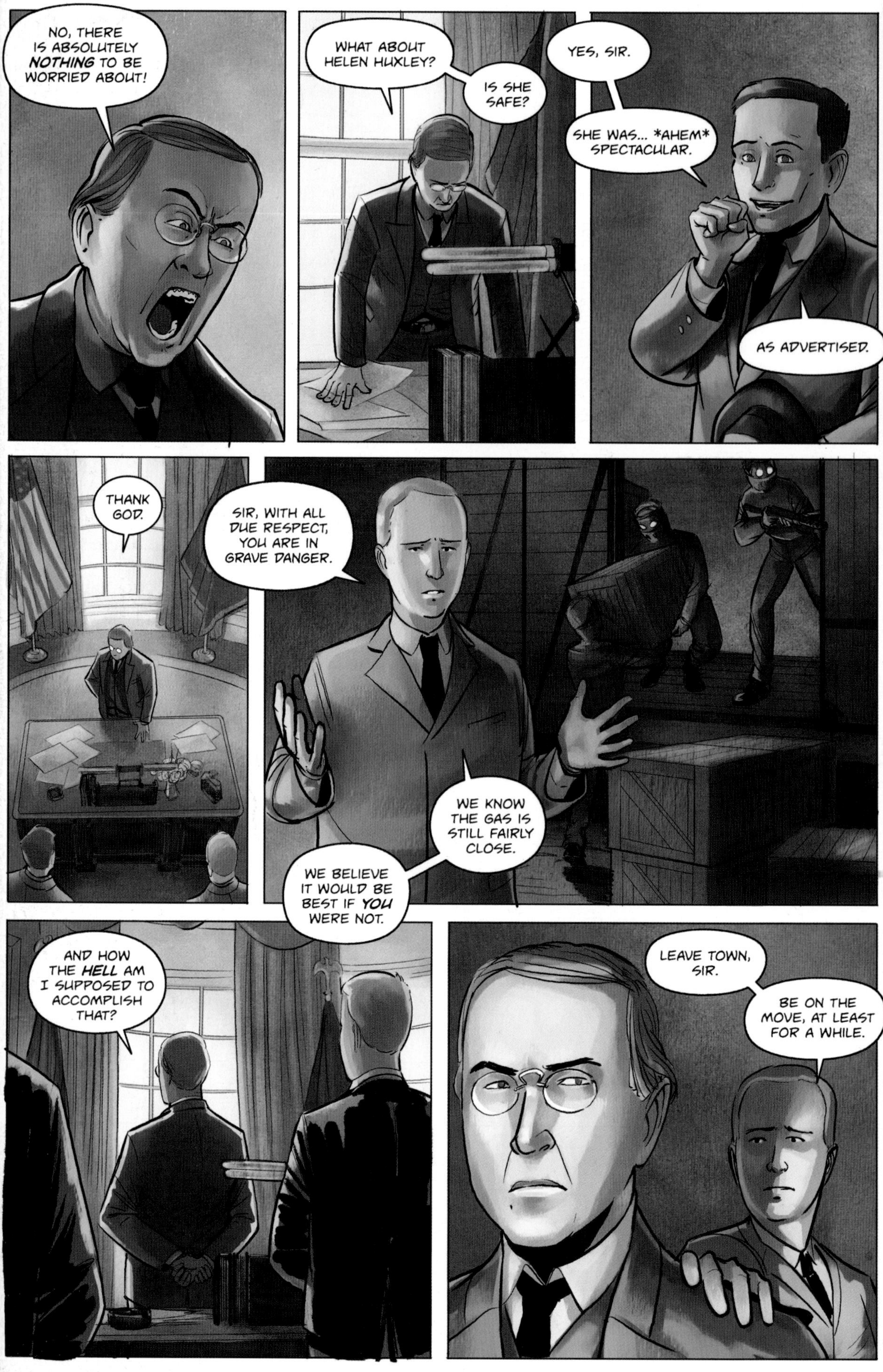

NO, THERE IS ABSOLUTELY ***NOTHING*** TO BE WORRIED ABOUT!
WHAT ABOUT HELEN HUXLEY?
IS SHE SAFE?
YES, SIR.
SHE WAS... *AHEM* SPECTACULAR.
AS ADVERTISED.
THANK GOD.
SIR, WITH ALL DUE RESPECT, YOU ARE IN GRAVE DANGER.
WE KNOW THE GAS IS STILL FAIRLY CLOSE.
WE BELIEVE IT WOULD BE BEST IF ***YOU*** WERE NOT.
AND HOW THE ***HELL*** AM I SUPPOSED TO ACCOMPLISH THAT?
LEAVE TOWN, SIR.
BE ON THE MOVE, AT LEAST FOR A WHILE.

Vol. LXIX No. 4536 WASHINGTON, D.C. SEPTEMBER 26, 1919. TWO CENTS

THE WASHINGTON LEDGER

EXHAUSTED WILSON RETURNS HOME

Presidential Journey Derailed

Over three weeks ago, President Wilson left Washington D.C., embarking on a national tour to muster support for the League of Nations. In an effort to gain a lasting peace, he made forty speeches in twenty cities. In three weeks, the President covered almost 10,000 miles.

President Wilson reportedly suffered from excrutiating headaches during the trip before collapsing from exhaustion yesterday in Colorado. The President's personal secretary, Joseph Tumulty, informed the press that the tour has been cancelled and the President will be returning to the White House. Wilson reportedly made the trip against his doctor's orders.

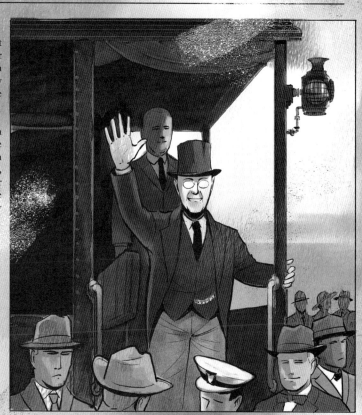

Happier Times. Wilson, shown here on September 3, boards a train from Washington, embarking on his extended journey.

FORT COLLINS
DENVER
COLORADO
PUEBLO

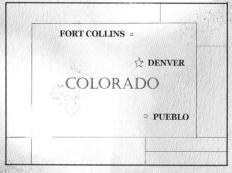

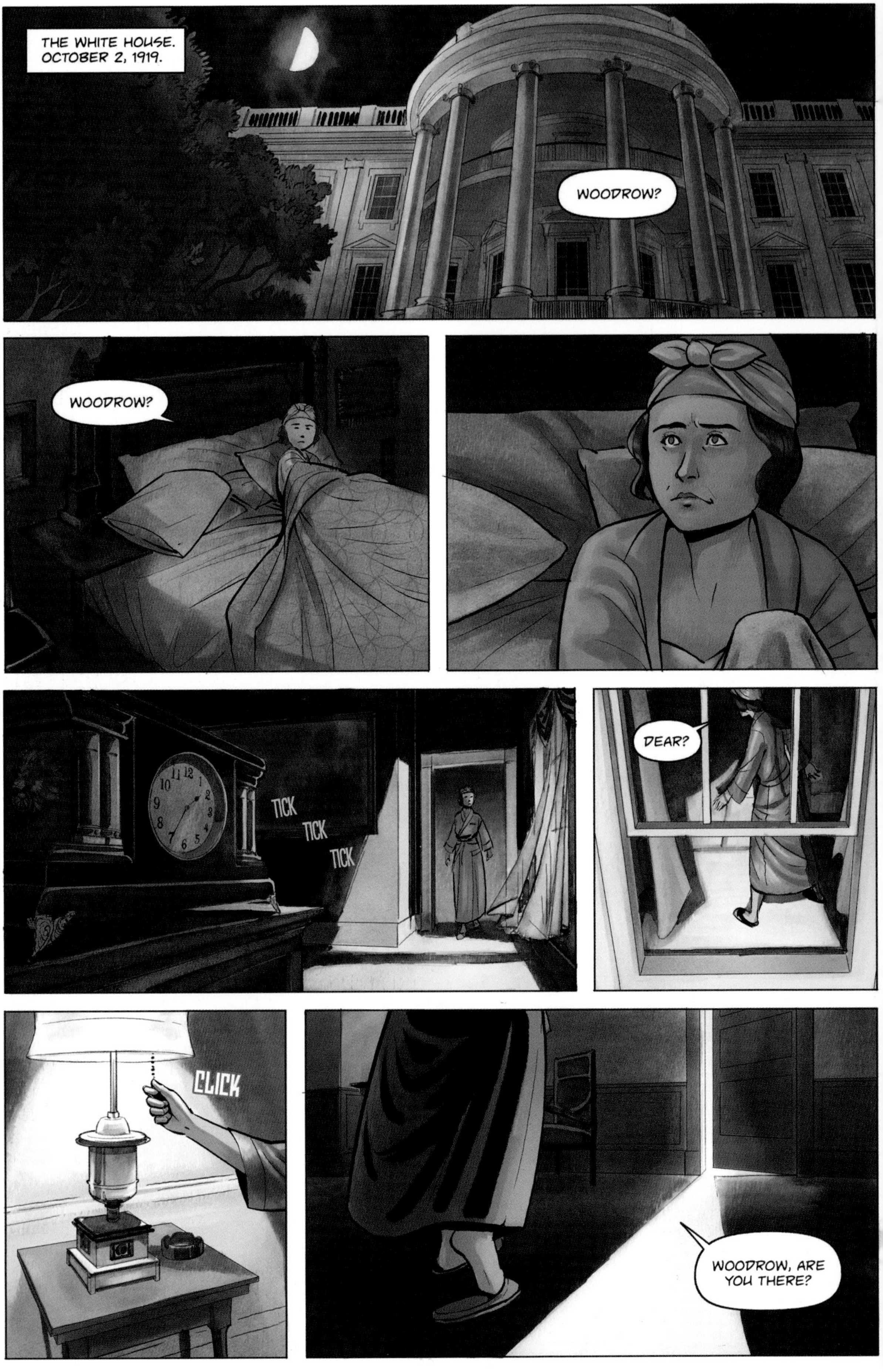
THE WHITE HOUSE.
OCTOBER 2, 1919.
WOODROW?
WOODROW?
TICK
TICK
TICK
DEAR?
CLICK
WOODROW, ARE YOU THERE?

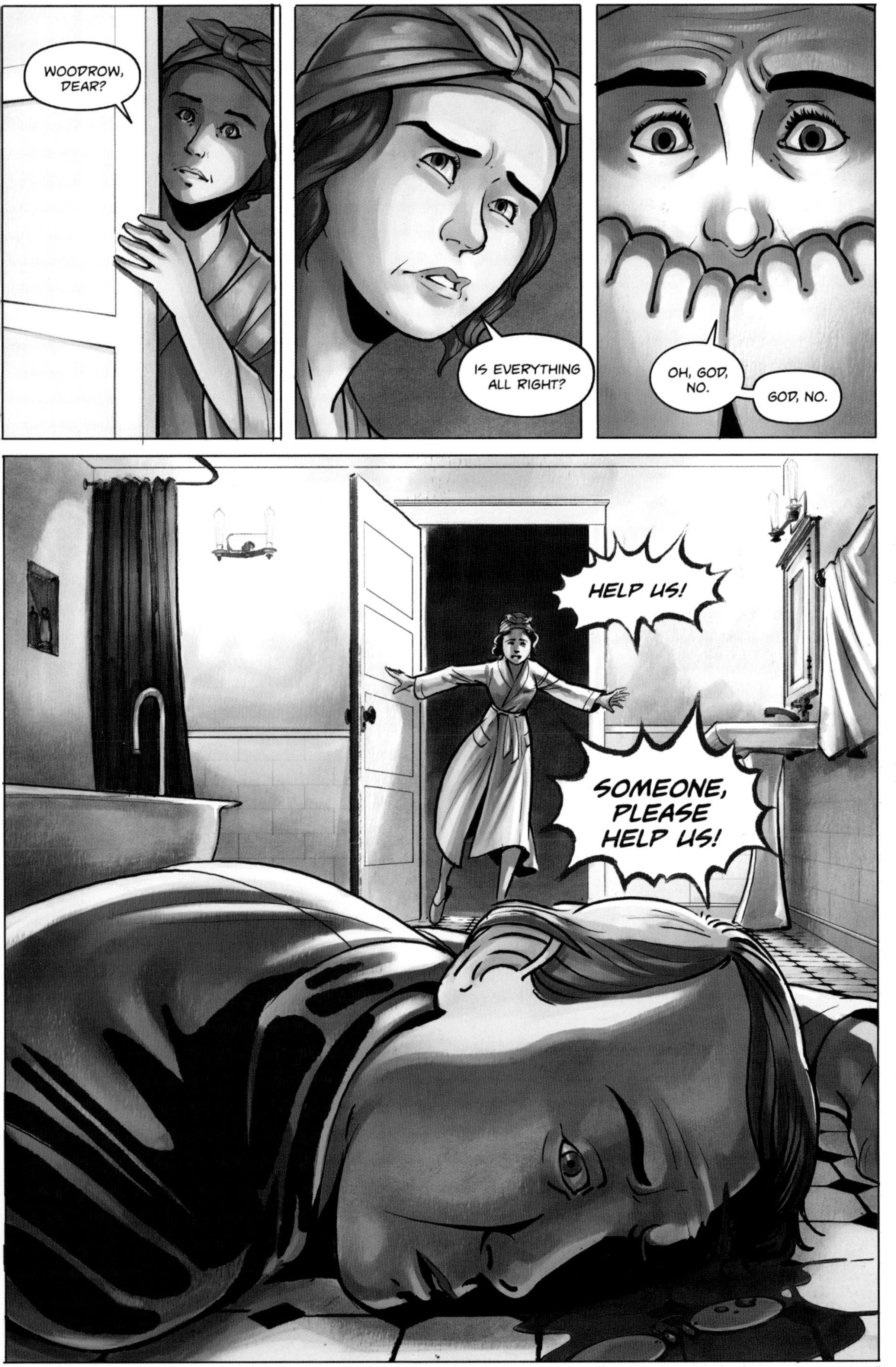
WOODROW, DEAR?
IS EVERYTHING ALL RIGHT?
OH, GOD, NO.
GOD, NO.
HELP US!
SOMEONE, PLEASE HELP US!

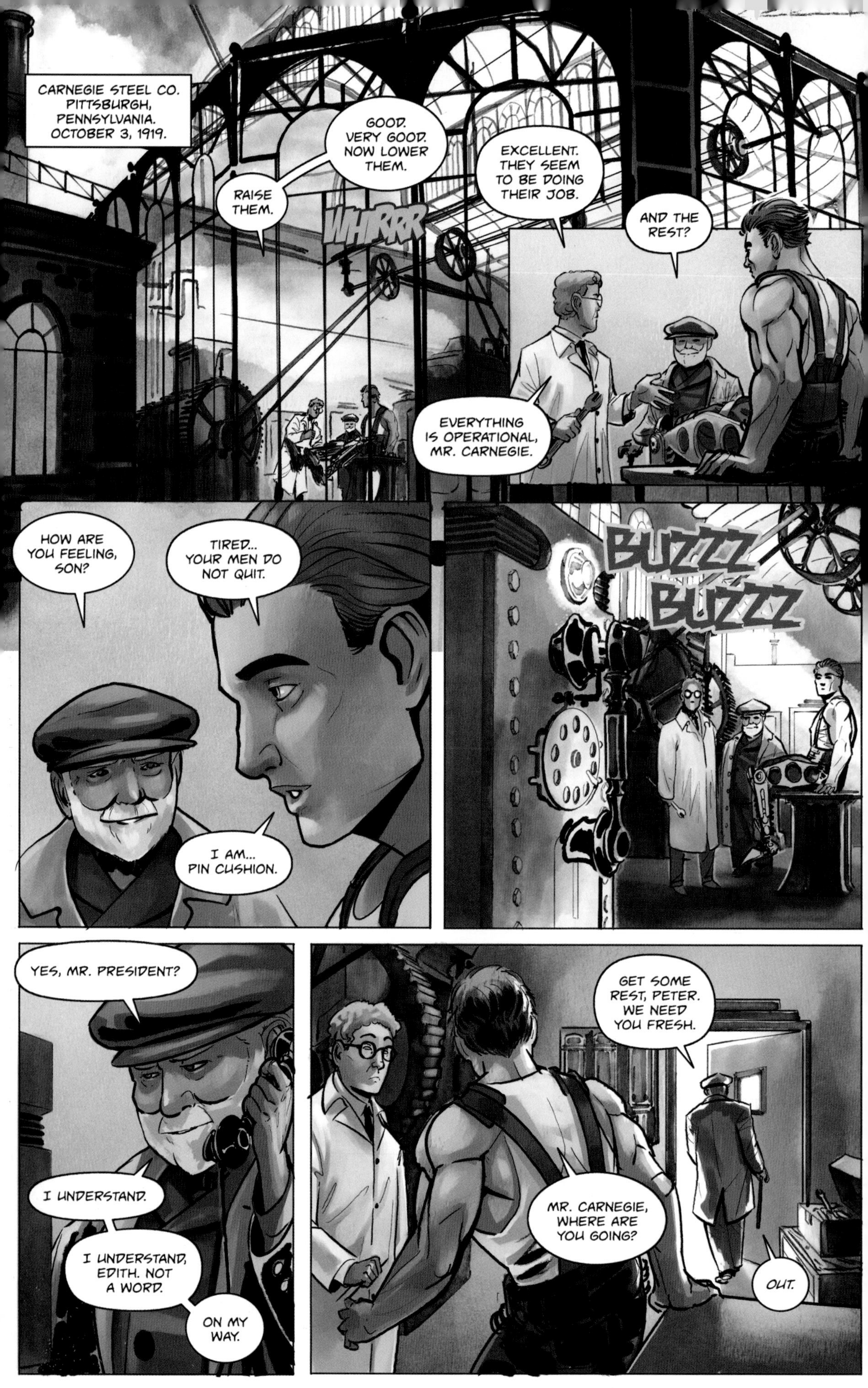
CARNEGIE STEEL CO.
PITTSBURGH,
PENNSYLVANIA.
OCTOBER 3, 1919.
RAISE THEM.
WHIRRR
GOOD. VERY GOOD. NOW LOWER THEM.
EXCELLENT. THEY SEEM TO BE DOING THEIR JOB.
AND THE REST?
EVERYTHING IS OPERATIONAL, MR. CARNEGIE.
HOW ARE YOU FEELING, SON?
TIRED... YOUR MEN DO NOT QUIT.
I AM... PIN CUSHION.
BUZZZ
BUZZZ
YES, MR. PRESIDENT?
I UNDERSTAND.
I UNDERSTAND, EDITH. NOT A WORD.
ON MY WAY.
GET SOME REST, PETER. WE NEED YOU FRESH.
MR. CARNEGIE, WHERE ARE YOU GOING?
OUT.

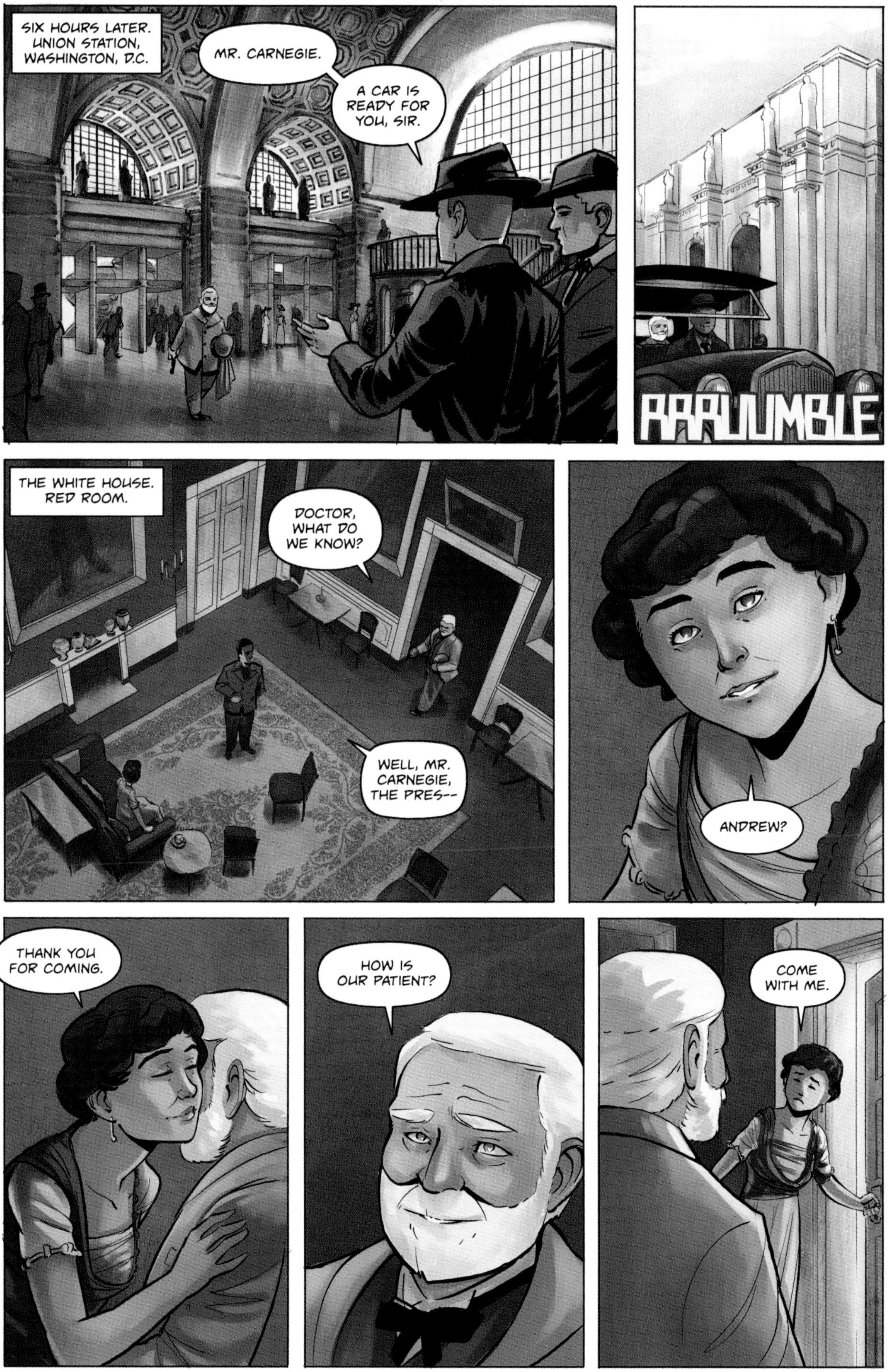

SIX HOURS LATER. UNION STATION, WASHINGTON, D.C.
MR. CARNEGIE.
A CAR IS READY FOR YOU, SIR.
RRRUUMBLE
THE WHITE HOUSE. RED ROOM.
DOCTOR, WHAT DO WE KNOW?
WELL, MR. CARNEGIE, THE PRES--
ANDREW?
THANK YOU FOR COMING.
HOW IS OUR PATIENT?
COME WITH ME.

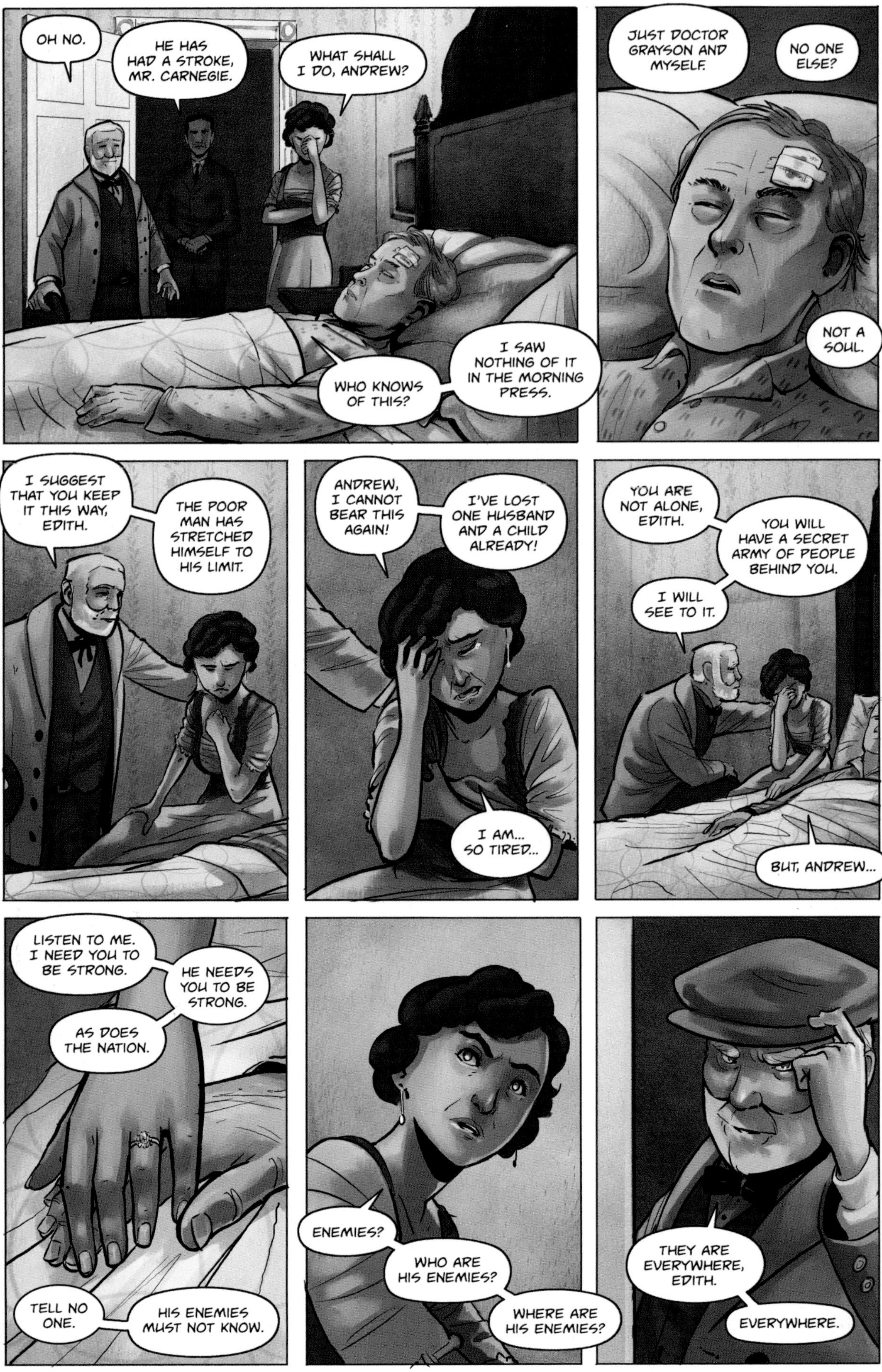
OH NO.
HE HAS HAD A STROKE, MR. CARNEGIE.
WHAT SHALL I DO, ANDREW?
WHO KNOWS OF THIS?
I SAW NOTHING OF IT IN THE MORNING PRESS.
JUST DOCTOR GRAYSON AND MYSELF.
NO ONE ELSE?
NOT A SOUL.
I SUGGEST THAT YOU KEEP IT THIS WAY, EDITH.
THE POOR MAN HAS STRETCHED HIMSELF TO HIS LIMIT.
ANDREW, I CANNOT BEAR THIS AGAIN!
I'VE LOST ONE HUSBAND AND A CHILD ALREADY!
I AM... SO TIRED...
YOU ARE NOT ALONE, EDITH.
YOU WILL HAVE A SECRET ARMY OF PEOPLE BEHIND YOU.
I WILL SEE TO IT.
BUT, ANDREW...
LISTEN TO ME. I NEED YOU TO BE STRONG.
HE NEEDS YOU TO BE STRONG.
AS DOES THE NATION.
TELL NO ONE.
HIS ENEMIES MUST NOT KNOW.
ENEMIES?
WHO ARE HIS ENEMIES?
WHERE ARE HIS ENEMIES?
THEY ARE EVERYWHERE, EDITH.
EVERYWHERE.

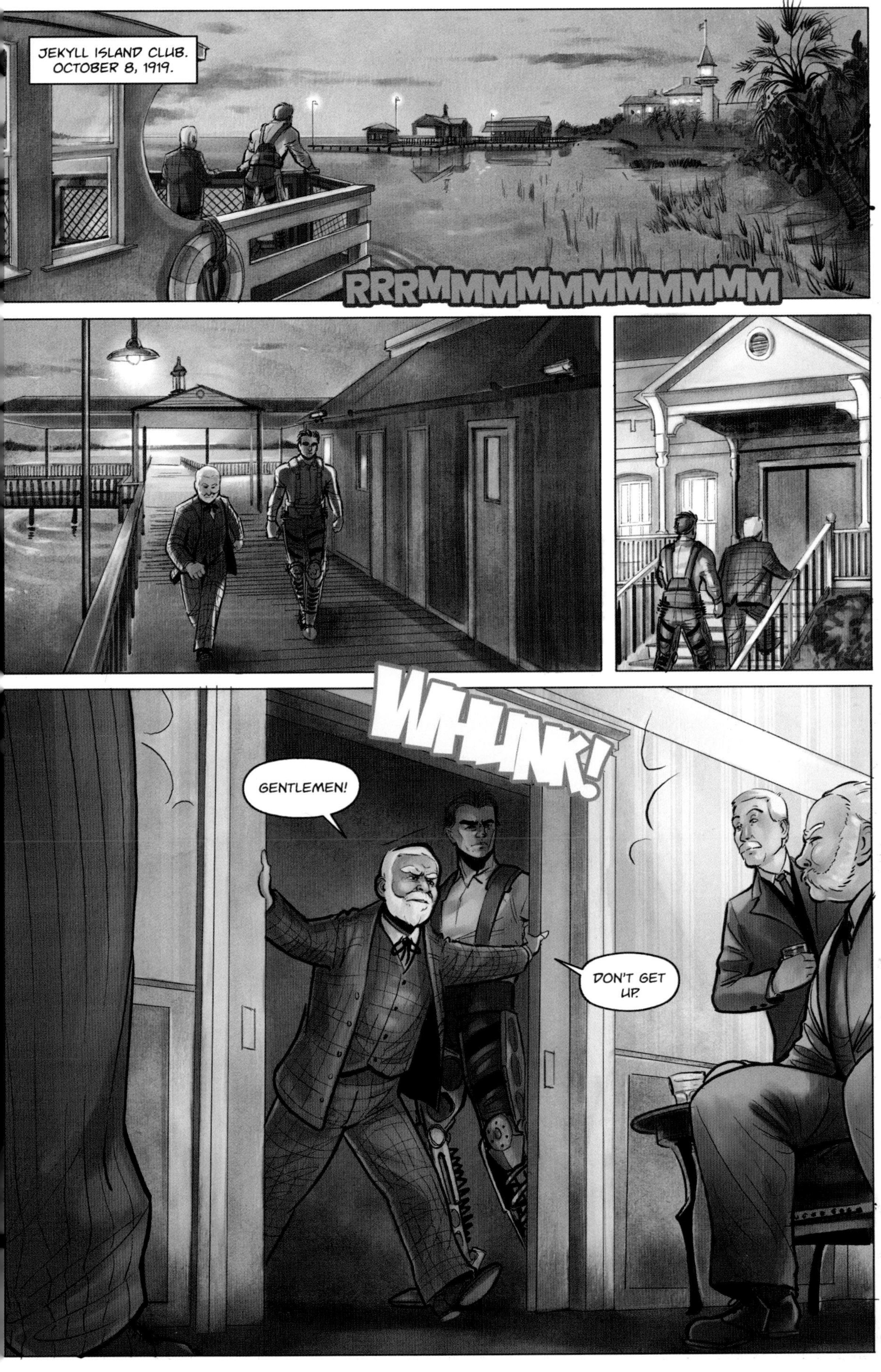
JEKYLL ISLAND CLUB.
OCTOBER 8, 1919.
RRRMMMMMMMMMMMM
WHUNK!
GENTLEMEN!
DON'T GET UP.

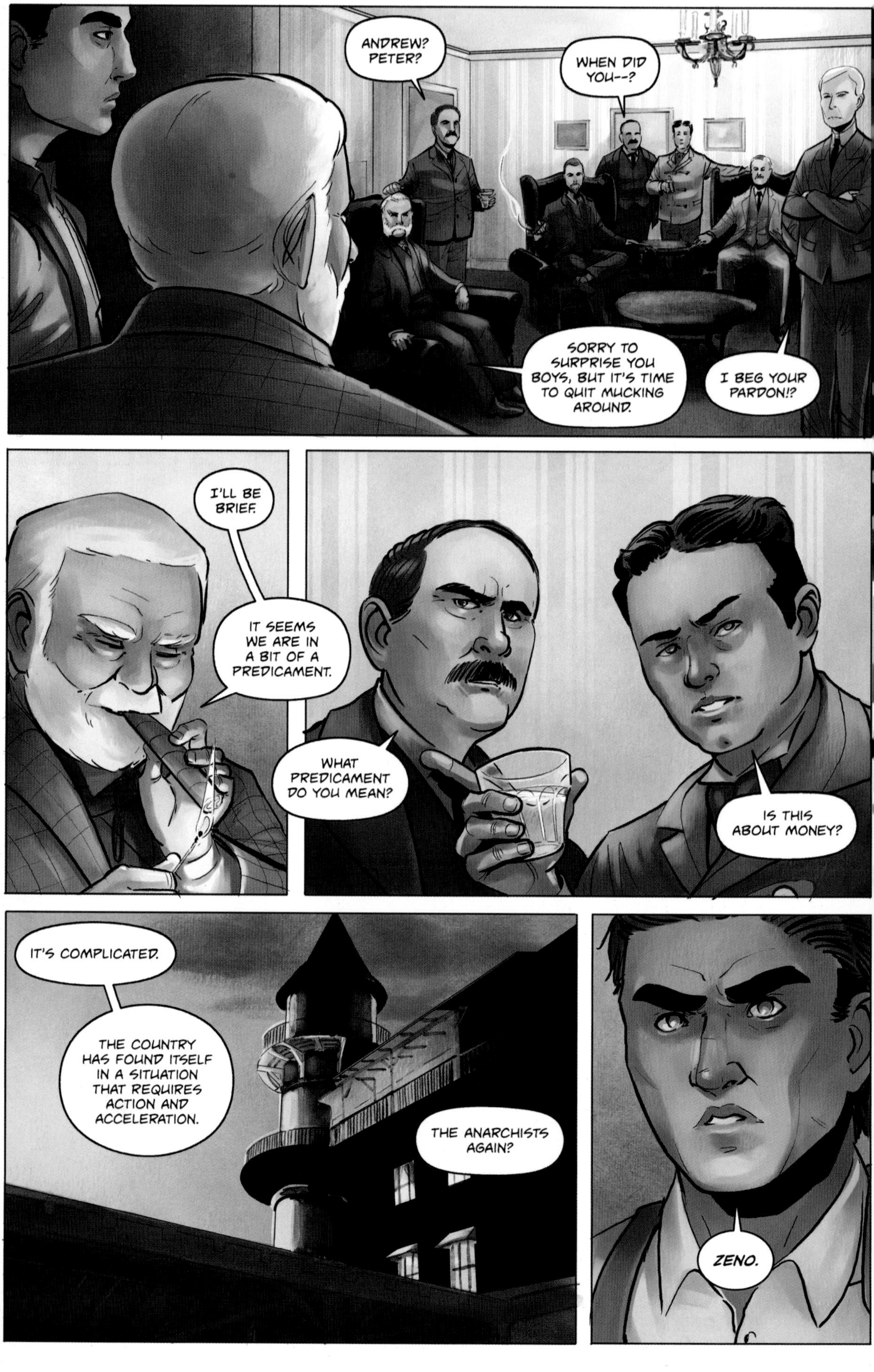
ANDREW? PETER?
WHEN DID YOU--?
SORRY TO SURPRISE YOU BOYS, BUT IT'S TIME TO QUIT MUCKING AROUND.
I BEG YOUR PARDON!?
I'LL BE BRIEF.
IT SEEMS WE ARE IN A BIT OF A PREDICAMENT.
WHAT PREDICAMENT DO YOU MEAN?
IS THIS ABOUT MONEY?
IT'S COMPLICATED.
THE COUNTRY HAS FOUND ITSELF IN A SITUATION THAT REQUIRES ACTION AND ACCELERATION.
THE ANARCHISTS AGAIN?
ZENO.

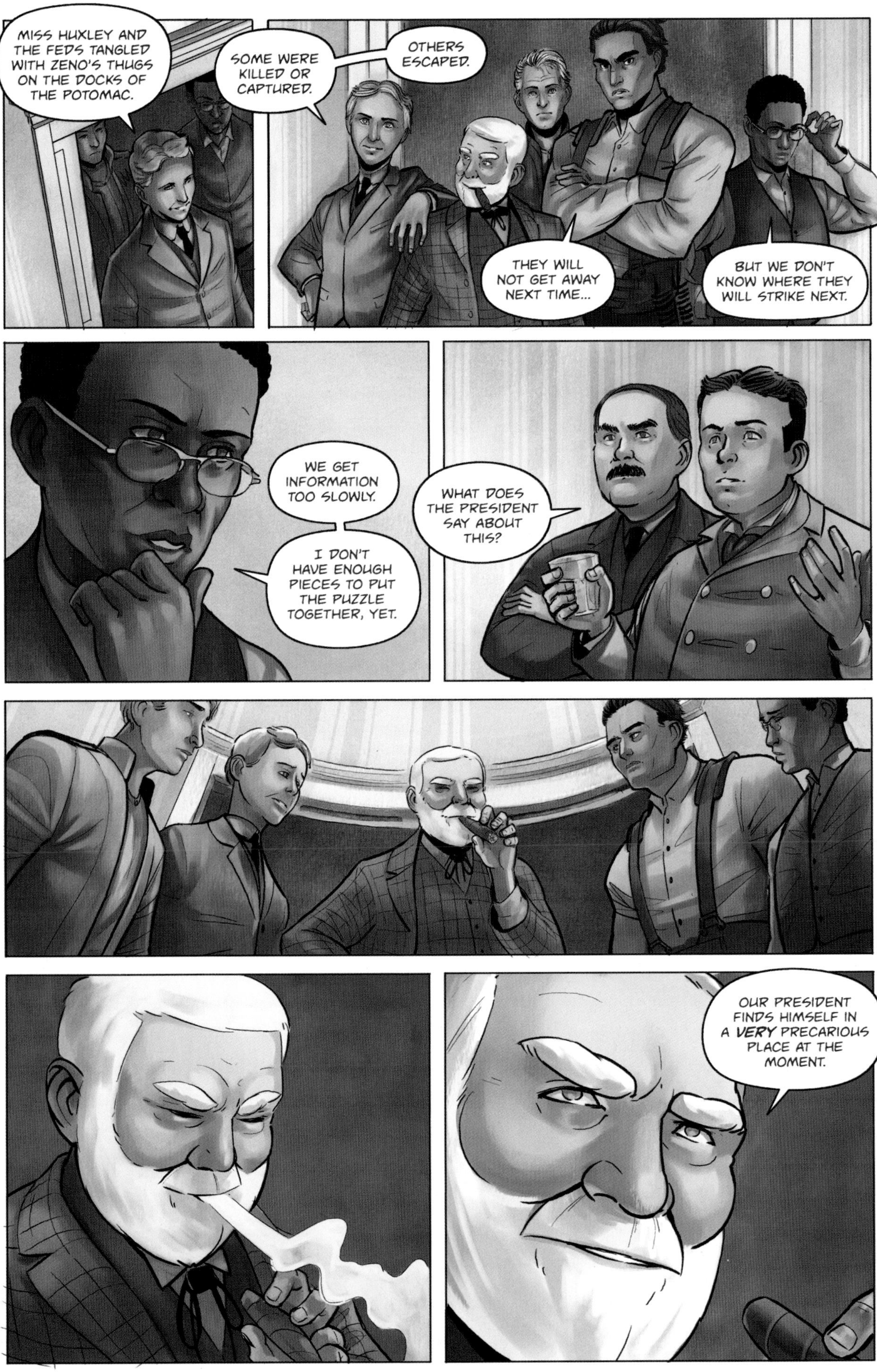
MISS HUXLEY AND THE FEDS TANGLED WITH ZENO'S THUGS ON THE DOCKS OF THE POTOMAC.
SOME WERE KILLED OR CAPTURED.
OTHERS ESCAPED.
THEY WILL NOT GET AWAY NEXT TIME...
BUT WE DON'T KNOW WHERE THEY WILL STRIKE NEXT.
WE GET INFORMATION TOO SLOWLY.
I DON'T HAVE ENOUGH PIECES TO PUT THE PUZZLE TOGETHER, YET.
WHAT DOES THE PRESIDENT SAY ABOUT THIS?
OUR PRESIDENT FINDS HIMSELF IN A **VERY** PRECARIOUS PLACE AT THE MOMENT.

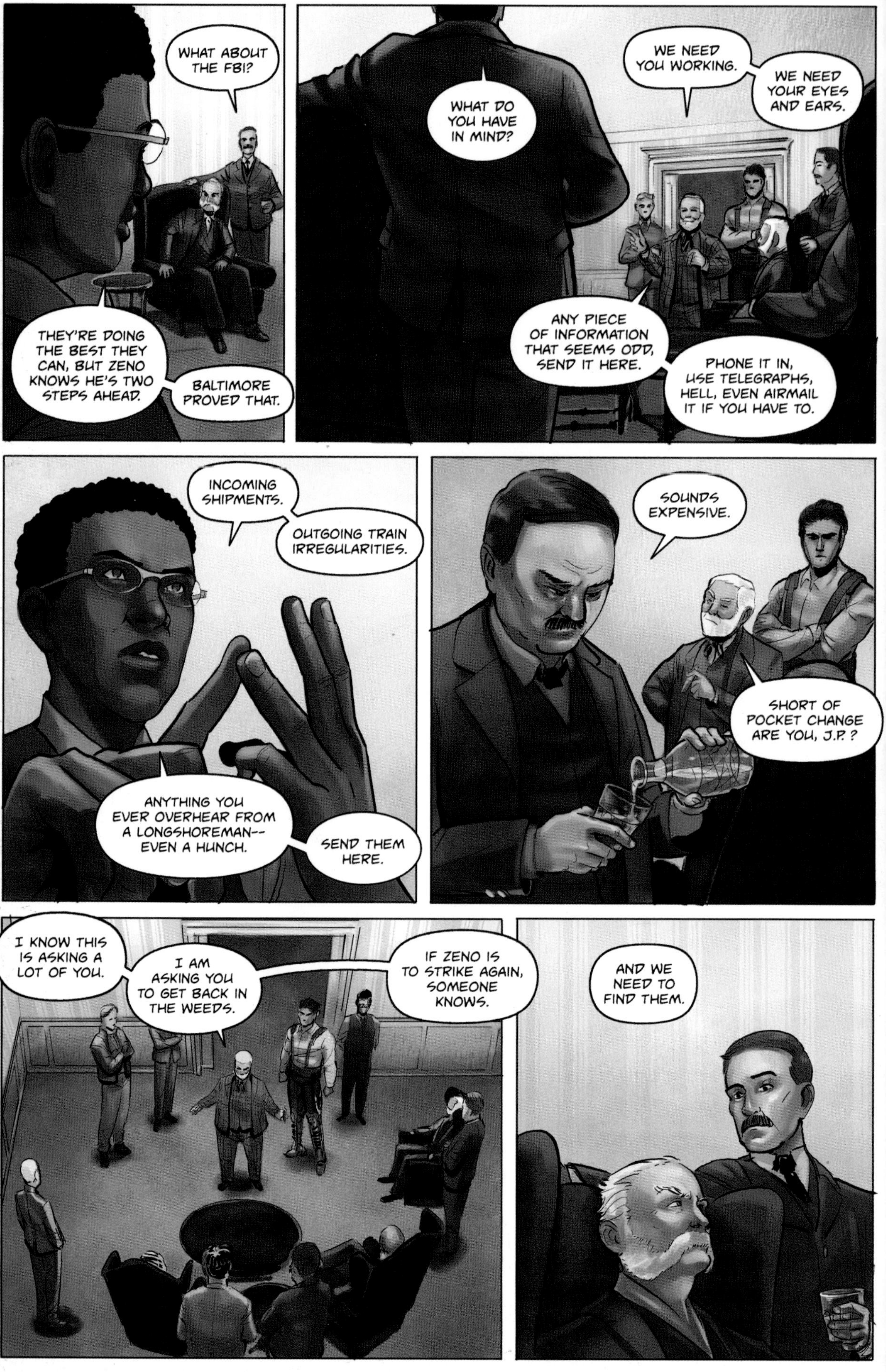
WHAT ABOUT THE FBI?
THEY'RE DOING THE BEST THEY CAN, BUT ZENO KNOWS HE'S TWO STEPS AHEAD.
BALTIMORE PROVED THAT.
WHAT DO YOU HAVE IN MIND?
WE NEED YOU WORKING.
WE NEED YOUR EYES AND EARS.
ANY PIECE OF INFORMATION THAT SEEMS ODD, SEND IT HERE.
PHONE IT IN, USE TELEGRAPHS, HELL, EVEN AIRMAIL IT IF YOU HAVE TO.
INCOMING SHIPMENTS.
OUTGOING TRAIN IRREGULARITIES.
ANYTHING YOU EVER OVERHEAR FROM A LONGSHOREMAN-- EVEN A HUNCH.
SEND THEM HERE.
SOUNDS EXPENSIVE.
SHORT OF POCKET CHANGE ARE YOU, J.P. ?
I KNOW THIS IS ASKING A LOT OF YOU.
I AM ASKING YOU TO GET BACK IN THE WEEDS.
IF ZENO IS TO STRIKE AGAIN, SOMEONE KNOWS.
AND WE NEED TO FIND THEM.

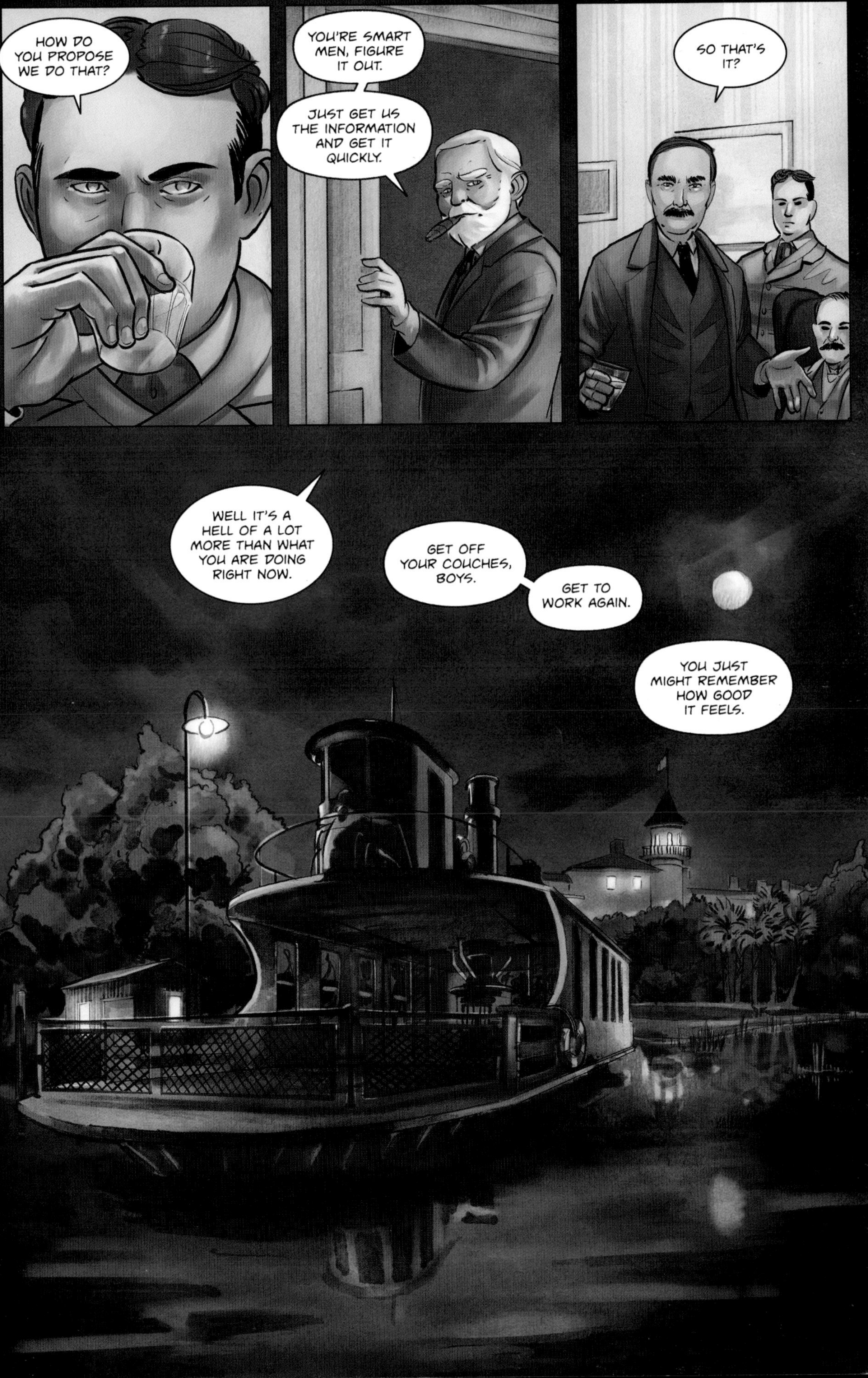
HOW DO YOU PROPOSE WE DO THAT?
YOU'RE SMART MEN, FIGURE IT OUT.
JUST GET US THE INFORMATION AND GET IT QUICKLY.
SO THAT'S IT?
WELL IT'S A HELL OF A LOT MORE THAN WHAT YOU ARE DOING RIGHT NOW.
GET OFF YOUR COUCHES, BOYS.
GET TO WORK AGAIN.
YOU JUST MIGHT REMEMBER HOW GOOD IT FEELS.

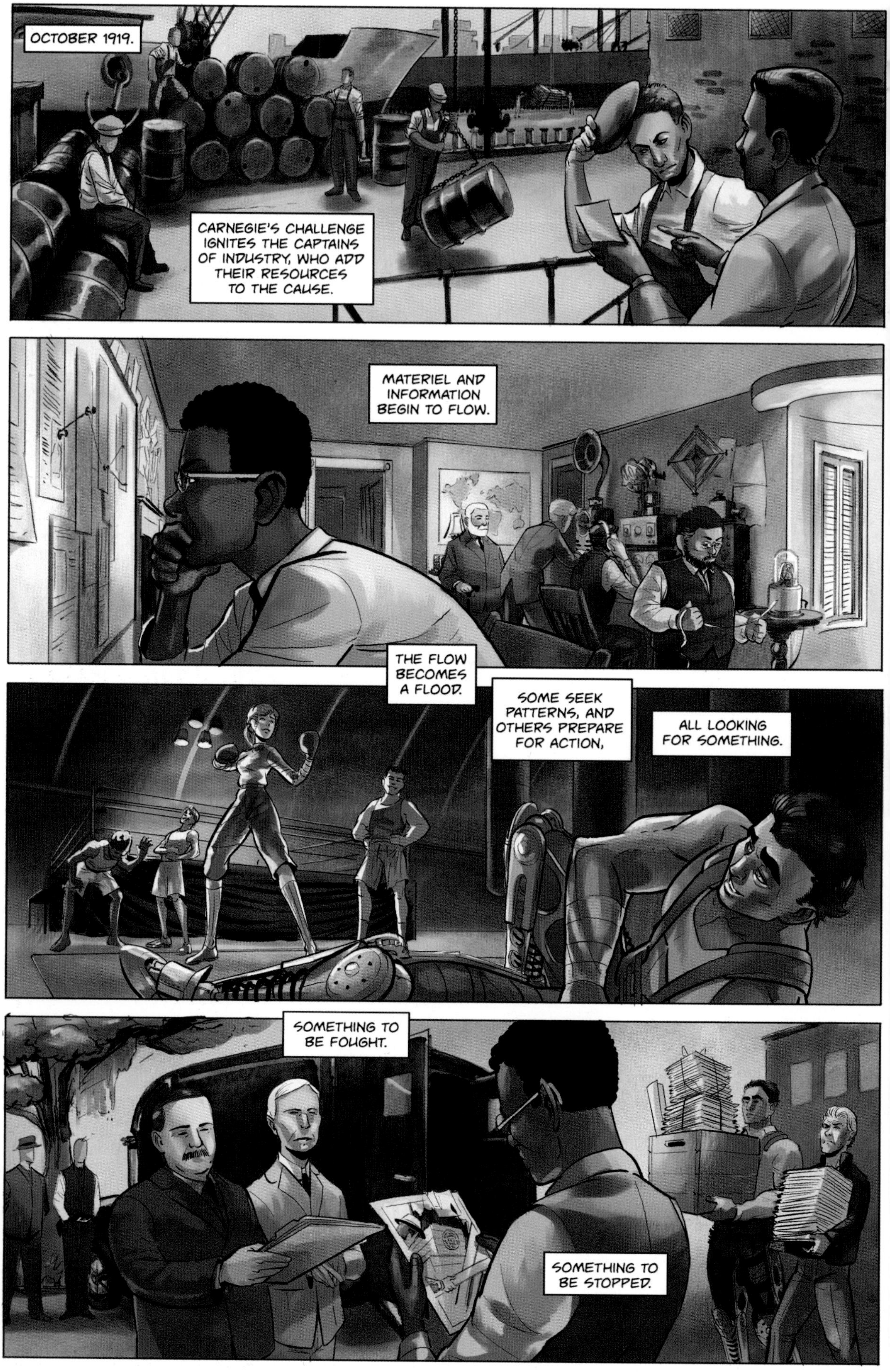
OCTOBER 1919.
CARNEGIE'S CHALLENGE IGNITES THE CAPTAINS OF INDUSTRY, WHO ADD THEIR RESOURCES TO THE CAUSE.
MATERIEL AND INFORMATION BEGIN TO FLOW.
THE FLOW BECOMES A FLOOD.
SOME SEEK PATTERNS, AND OTHERS PREPARE FOR ACTION,
ALL LOOKING FOR SOMETHING.
SOMETHING TO BE FOUGHT.
SOMETHING TO BE STOPPED.

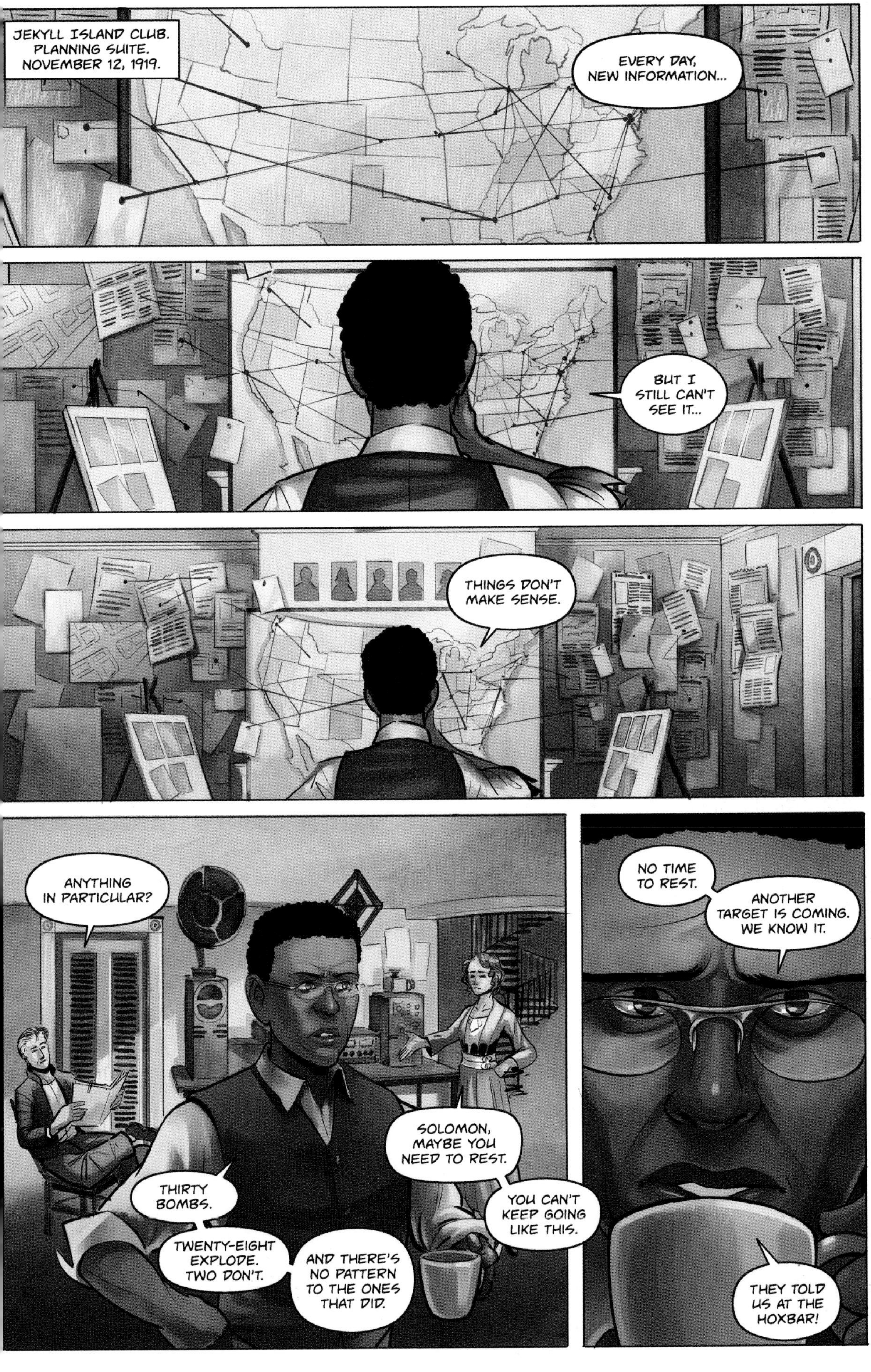
JEKYLL ISLAND CLUB. PLANNING SUITE. NOVEMBER 12, 1919.
EVERY DAY, NEW INFORMATION...
BUT I STILL CAN'T SEE IT...
THINGS DON'T MAKE SENSE.
ANYTHING IN PARTICULAR?
THIRTY BOMBS.
TWENTY-EIGHT EXPLODE. TWO DON'T.
AND THERE'S NO PATTERN TO THE ONES THAT DID.
SOLOMON, MAYBE YOU NEED TO REST.
YOU CAN'T KEEP GOING LIKE THIS.
NO TIME TO REST.
ANOTHER TARGET IS COMING. WE KNOW IT.
THEY TOLD US AT THE HOXBAR!

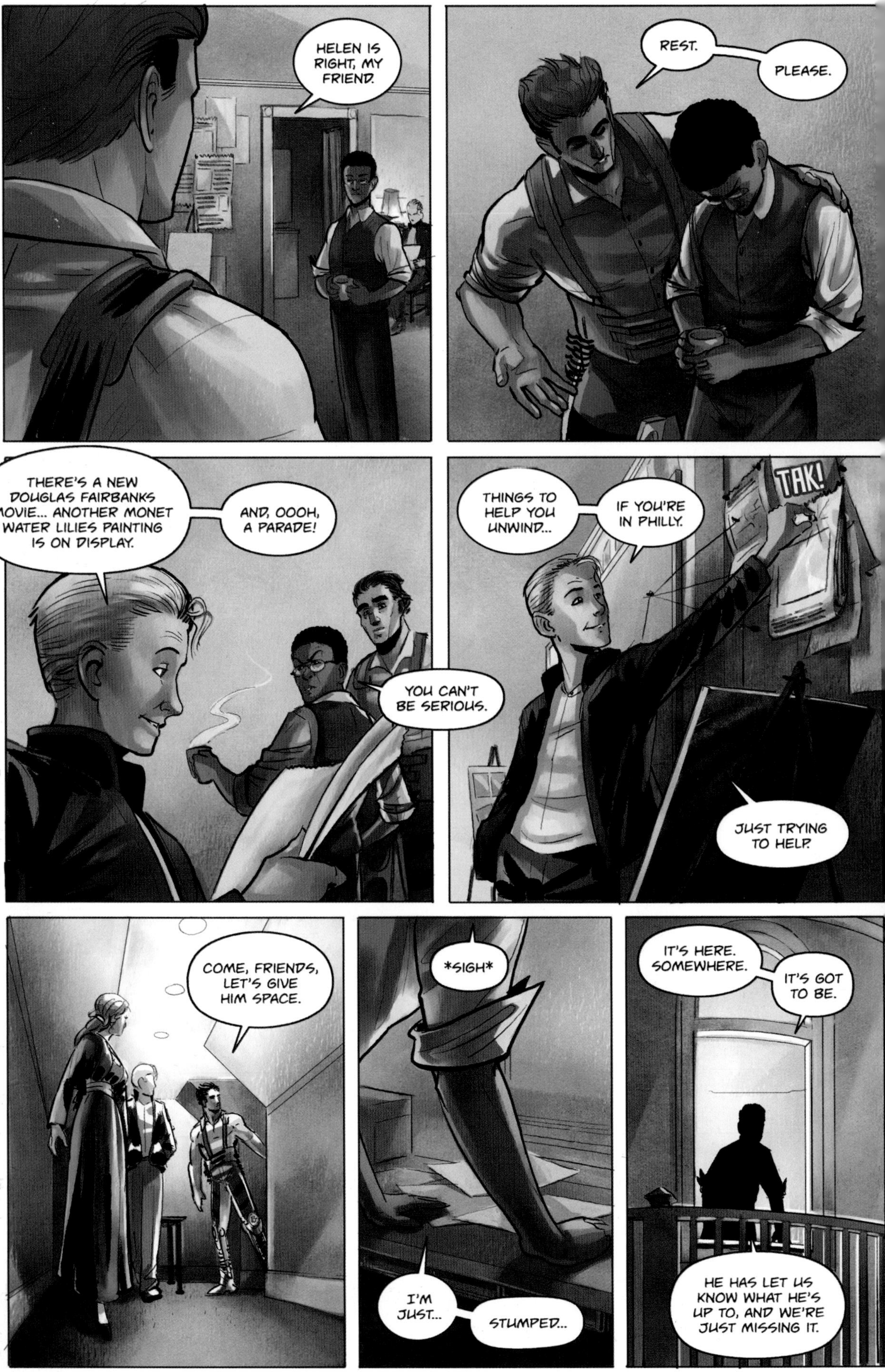
HELEN IS RIGHT, MY FRIEND.
REST.
PLEASE.
THERE'S A NEW DOUGLAS FAIRBANKS MOVIE... ANOTHER MONET WATER LILIES PAINTING IS ON DISPLAY.
AND, OOOH, A PARADE!
YOU CAN'T BE SERIOUS.
THINGS TO HELP YOU UNWIND...
IF YOU'RE IN PHILLY.
TAK!
JUST TRYING TO HELP.
COME, FRIENDS, LET'S GIVE HIM SPACE.
SIGH
I'M JUST...
STUMPED...
IT'S HERE. SOMEWHERE.
IT'S GOT TO BE.
HE HAS LET US KNOW WHAT HE'S UP TO, AND WE'RE JUST MISSING IT.

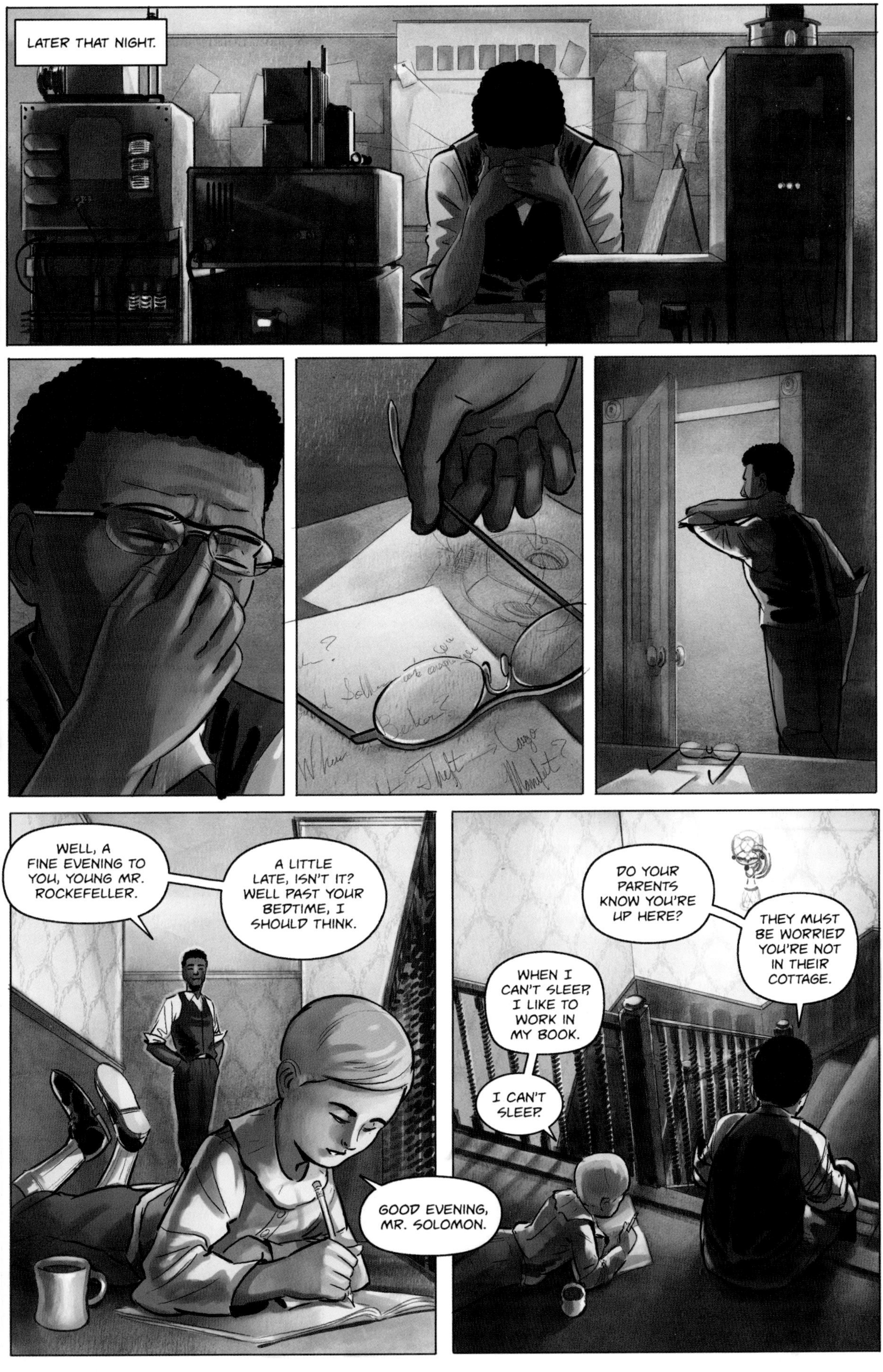
LATER THAT NIGHT.
WELL, A FINE EVENING TO YOU, YOUNG MR. ROCKEFELLER.
A LITTLE LATE, ISN'T IT? WELL PAST YOUR BEDTIME, I SHOULD THINK.
GOOD EVENING, MR. SOLOMON.
DO YOUR PARENTS KNOW YOU'RE UP HERE?
THEY MUST BE WORRIED YOU'RE NOT IN THEIR COTTAGE.
WHEN I CAN'T SLEEP, I LIKE TO WORK IN MY BOOK.
I CAN'T SLEEP.

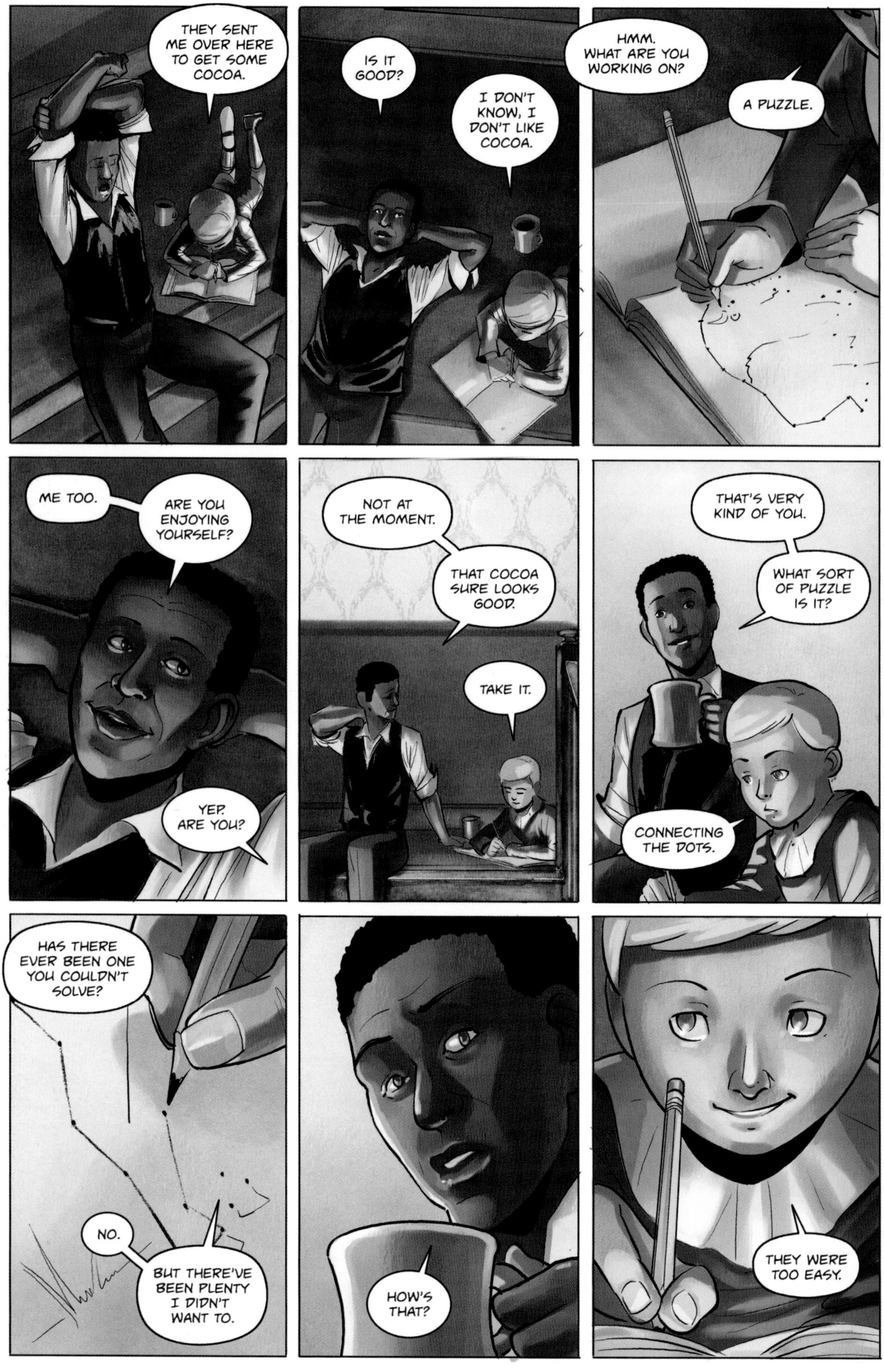
THEY SENT ME OVER HERE TO GET SOME COCOA.
IS IT GOOD?
I DON'T KNOW, I DON'T LIKE COCOA.
HMM. WHAT ARE YOU WORKING ON?
A PUZZLE.
ME TOO.
ARE YOU ENJOYING YOURSELF?
YEP. ARE YOU?
NOT AT THE MOMENT.
THAT COCOA SURE LOOKS GOOD.
TAKE IT.
THAT'S VERY KIND OF YOU.
WHAT SORT OF PUZZLE IS IT?
CONNECTING THE DOTS.
HAS THERE EVER BEEN ONE YOU COULDN'T SOLVE?
NO.
BUT THERE'VE BEEN PLENTY I DIDN'T WANT TO.
HOW'S THAT?
THEY WERE TOO EASY.

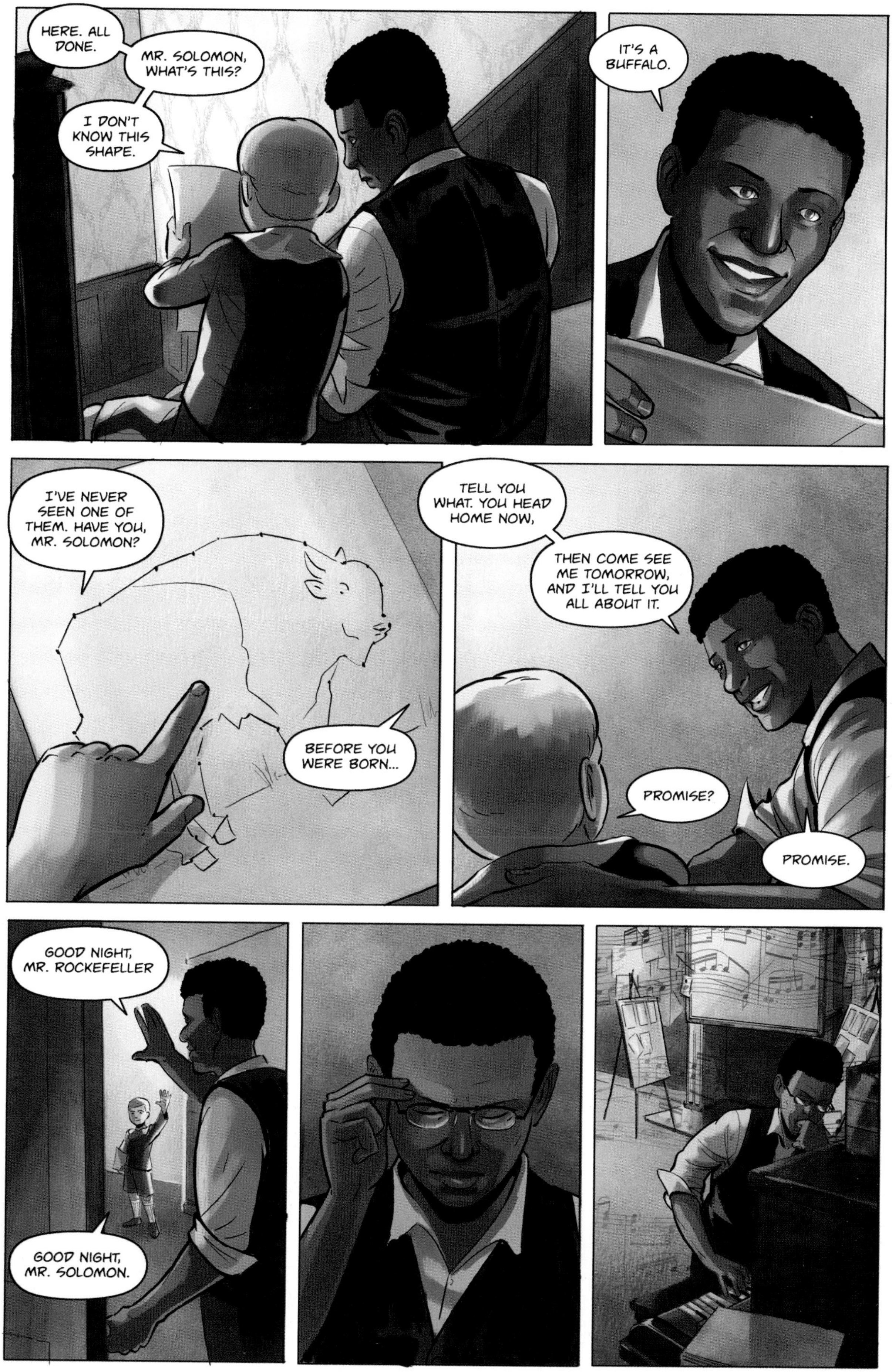
HERE. ALL DONE.
MR. SOLOMON, WHAT'S THIS?
I DON'T KNOW THIS SHAPE.
IT'S A BUFFALO.
I'VE NEVER SEEN ONE OF THEM. HAVE YOU, MR. SOLOMON?
BEFORE YOU WERE BORN...
TELL YOU WHAT. YOU HEAD HOME NOW,
THEN COME SEE ME TOMORROW, AND I'LL TELL YOU ALL ABOUT IT.
PROMISE?
PROMISE.
GOOD NIGHT, MR. ROCKEFELLER
GOOD NIGHT, MR. SOLOMON.

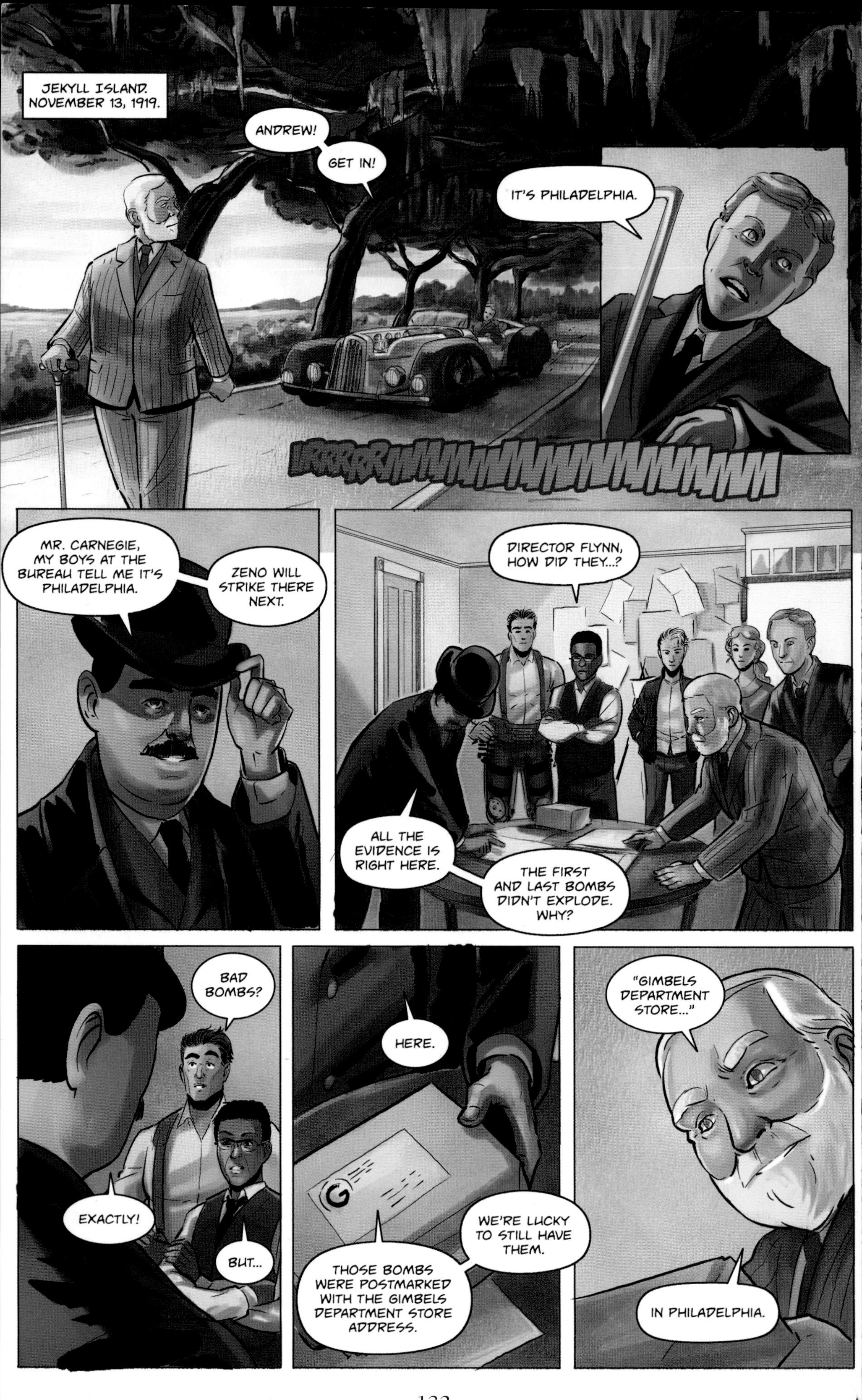
JEKYLL ISLAND. NOVEMBER 13, 1919.
ANDREW!
GET IN!
IT'S PHILADELPHIA.
URRRRRMMMMMMMMMMMMMMMMMMM
MR. CARNEGIE, MY BOYS AT THE BUREAU TELL ME IT'S PHILADELPHIA.
ZENO WILL STRIKE THERE NEXT.
DIRECTOR FLYNN, HOW DID THEY...?
ALL THE EVIDENCE IS RIGHT HERE.
THE FIRST AND LAST BOMBS DIDN'T EXPLODE. WHY?
BAD BOMBS?
EXACTLY!
BUT...
HERE.
THOSE BOMBS WERE POSTMARKED WITH THE GIMBELS DEPARTMENT STORE ADDRESS.
WE'RE LUCKY TO STILL HAVE THEM.
"GIMBELS DEPARTMENT STORE..."
IN PHILADELPHIA.

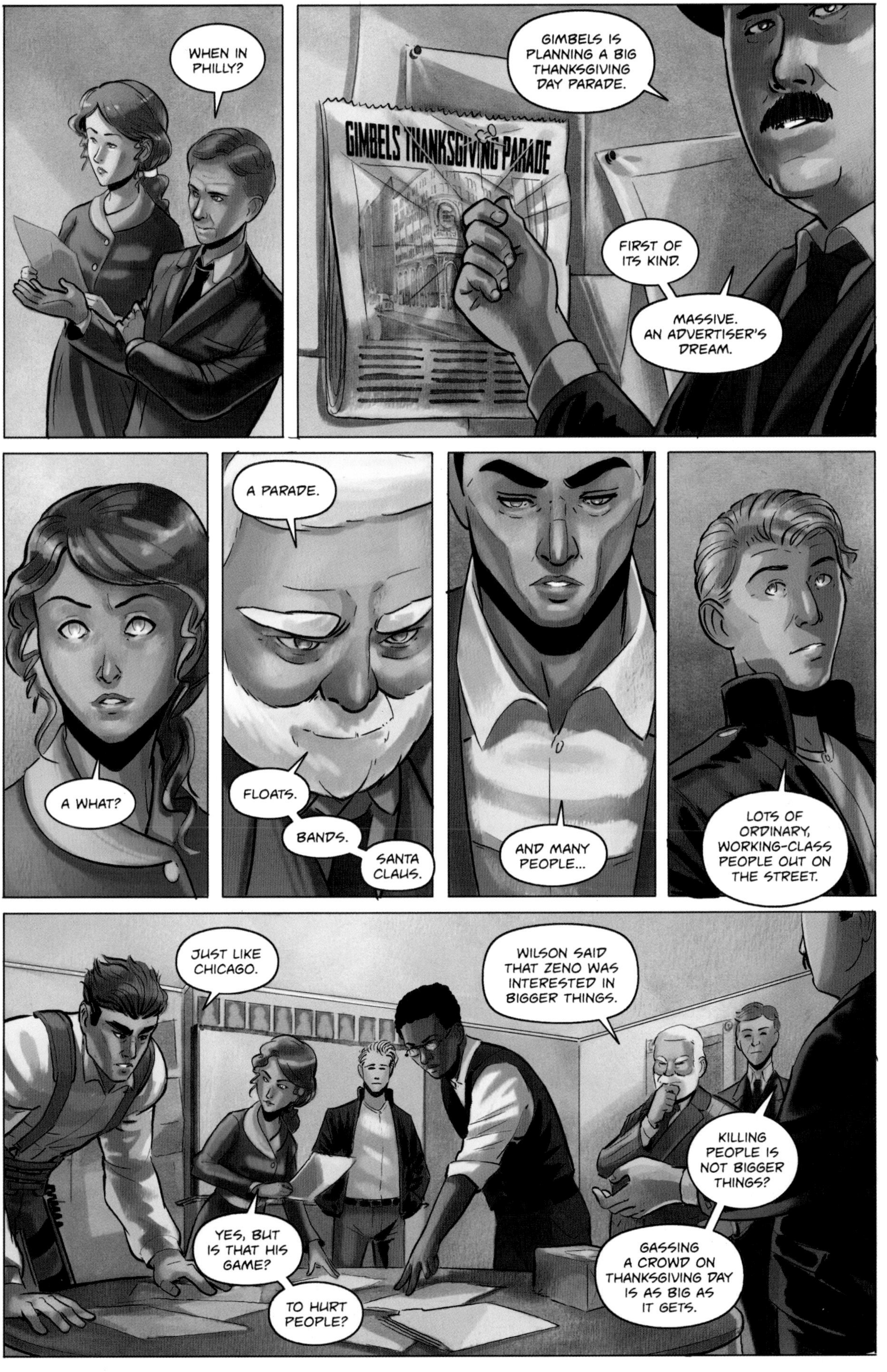
WHEN IN PHILLY?
GIMBELS IS PLANNING A BIG THANKSGIVING DAY PARADE.
GIMBELS THANKSGIVING PARADE
FIRST OF ITS KIND.
MASSIVE. AN ADVERTISER'S DREAM.
A WHAT?
A PARADE.
FLOATS.
BANDS.
SANTA CLAUS.
AND MANY PEOPLE...
LOTS OF ORDINARY, WORKING-CLASS PEOPLE OUT ON THE STREET.
JUST LIKE CHICAGO.
WILSON SAID THAT ZENO WAS INTERESTED IN BIGGER THINGS.
KILLING PEOPLE IS NOT BIGGER THINGS?
YES, BUT IS THAT HIS GAME?
TO HURT PEOPLE?
GASSING A CROWD ON THANKSGIVING DAY IS AS BIG AS IT GETS.

WE HAVE EVERY REASON TO BELIEVE THIS IS THE TARGET.

IT DOESN'T ADD UP...

NO?

EVERYTHING THUS FAR POINTS TO PHILLY.

KILLING THOUSANDS AT ONCE WOULD BE HIS BIGGEST STATEMENT YET.

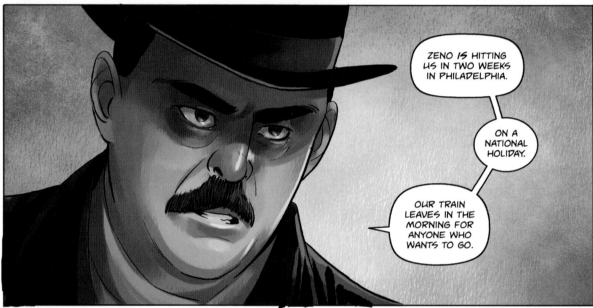

ZENO IS HITTING US IN TWO WEEKS IN PHILADELPHIA.

ON A NATIONAL HOLIDAY.

OUR TRAIN LEAVES IN THE MORNING FOR ANYONE WHO WANTS TO GO.

YOU COMING, SOLOMON?

I'M NOT GOING TO PHILADELPHIA.

I DON'T UNDERSTAND.

THIS PUZZLE IS TOO EASY.

NOTHING WILL HAPPEN IN PHILLY.

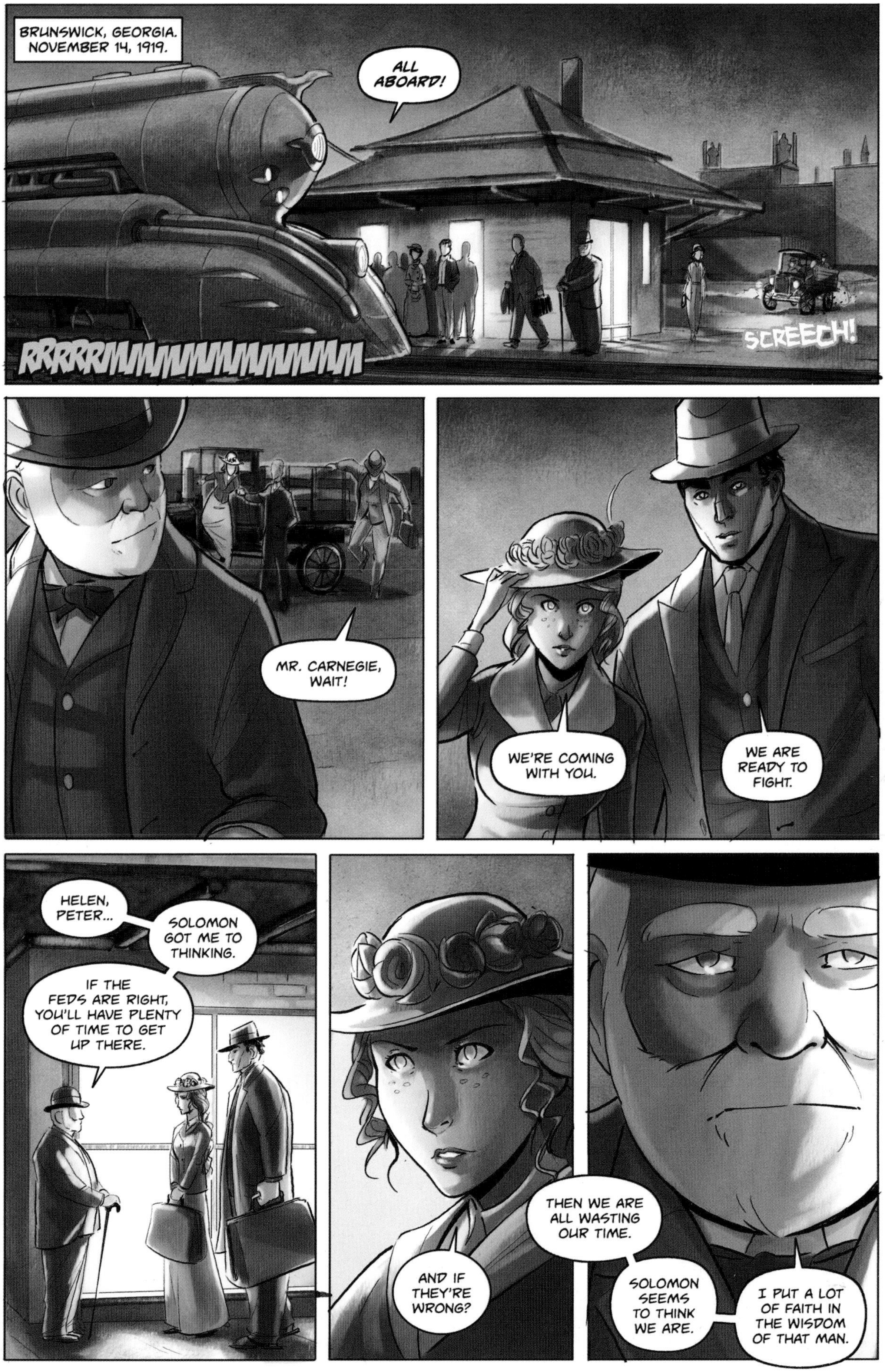
BRUNSWICK, GEORGIA. NOVEMBER 14, 1919.
ALL ABOARD!
RRRRRMMMMMMMMMMMMM
SCREECH!
MR. CARNEGIE, WAIT!
WE'RE COMING WITH YOU.
WE ARE READY TO FIGHT.
HELEN, PETER...
SOLOMON GOT ME TO THINKING.
IF THE FEDS ARE RIGHT, YOU'LL HAVE PLENTY OF TIME TO GET UP THERE.
AND IF THEY'RE WRONG?
THEN WE ARE ALL WASTING OUR TIME.
SOLOMON SEEMS TO THINK WE ARE.
I PUT A LOT OF FAITH IN THE WISDOM OF THAT MAN.

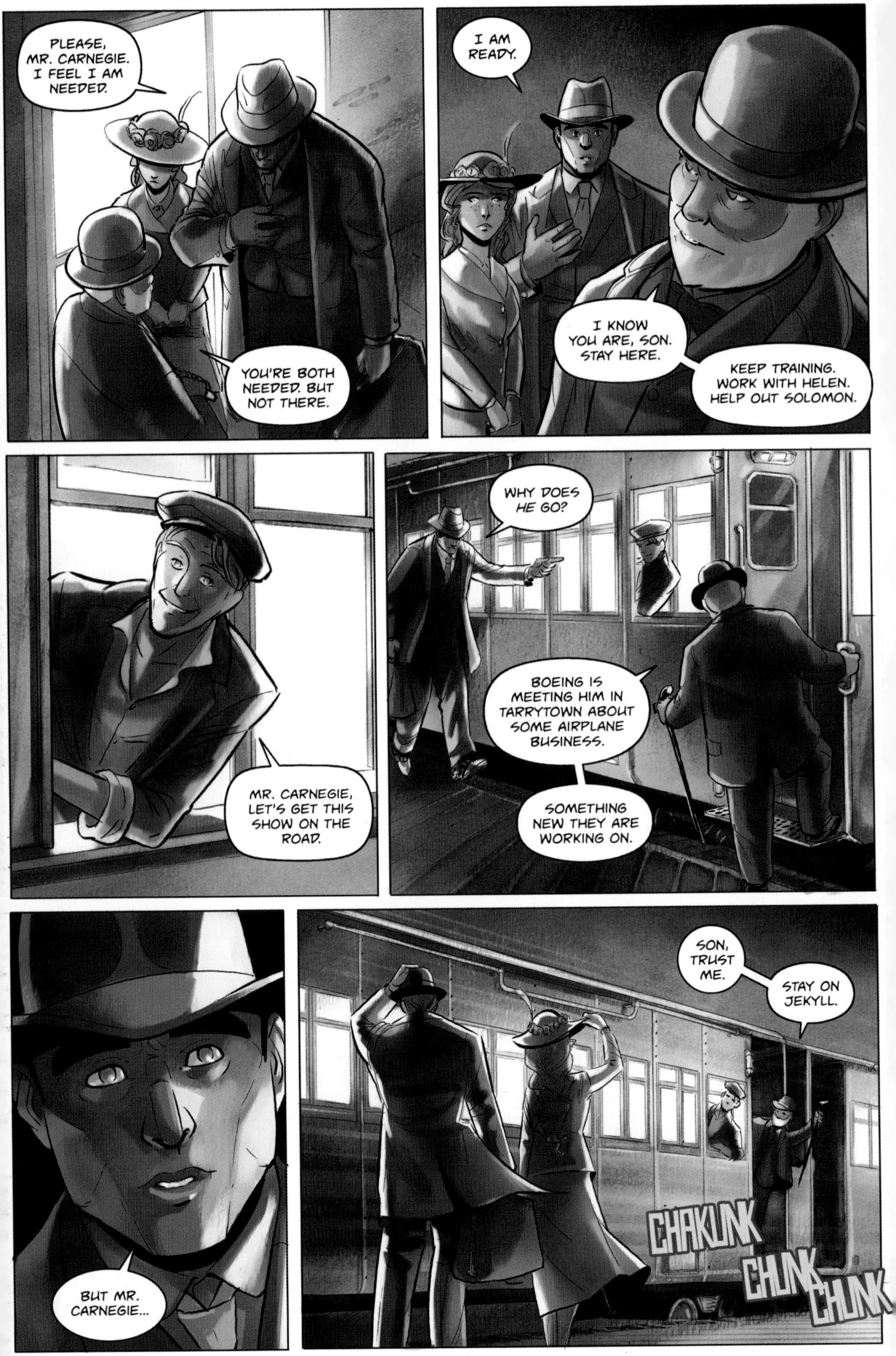
PLEASE, MR. CARNEGIE. I FEEL I AM NEEDED.
YOU'RE BOTH NEEDED. BUT NOT THERE.
I AM READY.
I KNOW YOU ARE, SON. STAY HERE.
KEEP TRAINING. WORK WITH HELEN. HELP OUT SOLOMON.
MR. CARNEGIE, LET'S GET THIS SHOW ON THE ROAD.
WHY DOES HE GO?
BOEING IS MEETING HIM IN TARRYTOWN ABOUT SOME AIRPLANE BUSINESS.
SOMETHING NEW THEY ARE WORKING ON.
BUT MR. CARNEGIE...
SON, TRUST ME.
STAY ON JEKYLL.
CHAKUNK
CHUNK CHUNK

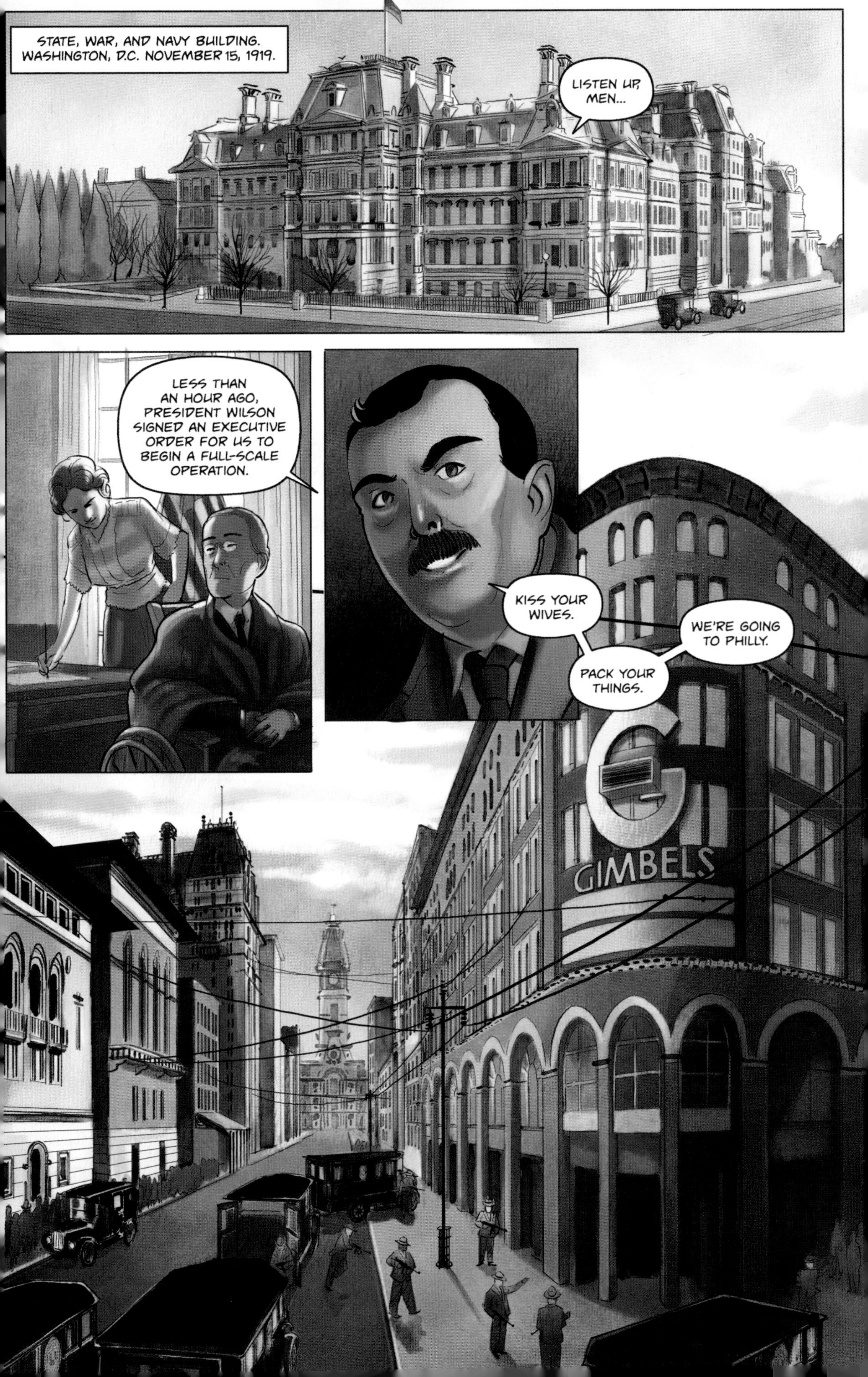
STATE, WAR, AND NAVY BUILDING.
WASHINGTON, D.C. NOVEMBER 15, 1919.
LISTEN UP, MEN...
LESS THAN AN HOUR AGO, PRESIDENT WILSON SIGNED AN EXECUTIVE ORDER FOR US TO BEGIN A FULL-SCALE OPERATION.
KISS YOUR WIVES.
PACK YOUR THINGS.
WE'RE GOING TO PHILLY.
GIMBELS

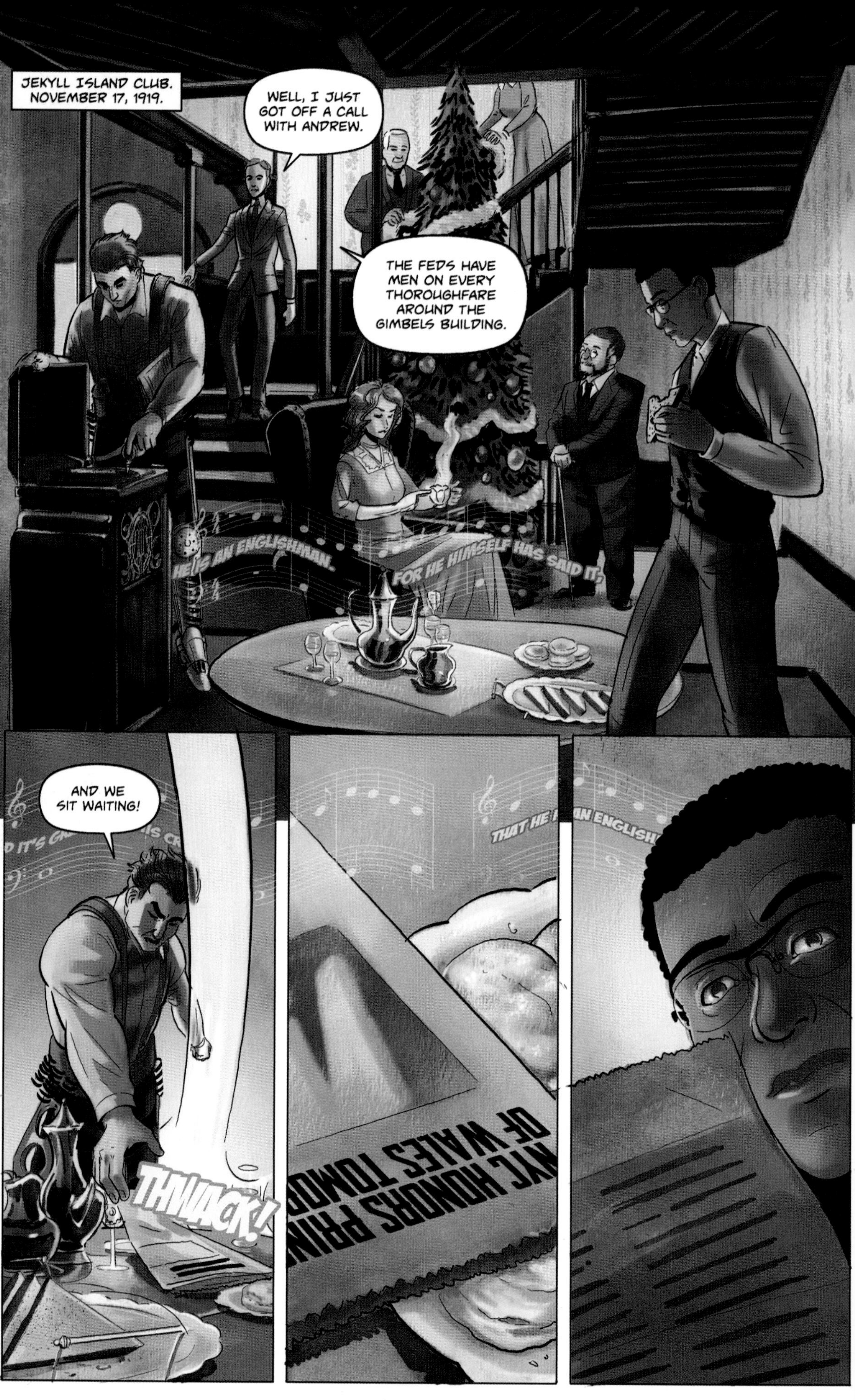
JEKYLL ISLAND CLUB. NOVEMBER 17, 1919.
WELL, I JUST GOT OFF A CALL WITH ANDREW.
THE FEDS HAVE MEN ON EVERY THOROUGHFARE AROUND THE GIMBELS BUILDING.
HE IS AN ENGLISHMAN..
FOR HE HIMSELF HAS SAID IT,
AND WE SIT WAITING!
THWACK!
NYC HONORS PRIN
OF WALES TOMO

BUT IN SPITE OF ALL TEMPTATIONS TO BELONG TO OTHER NATIONS,

H.M.S. Pinafore
GILBERT & SULLIVAN

WELL...

I'LL

BE

DAMNED...

HE REMAINS AN ENGLISHMAN!

WHAT?

IF I WERE ZENO, WHERE COULD I REMOVE GOVERNMENTS...

...THE NEXT KING AND A VICE PRESIDENT...

...IN ONE FELL SWOOP?

NYC HO... OF WALE... PRINCE TOMORROW

THIS IS WHERE I WOULD BE.

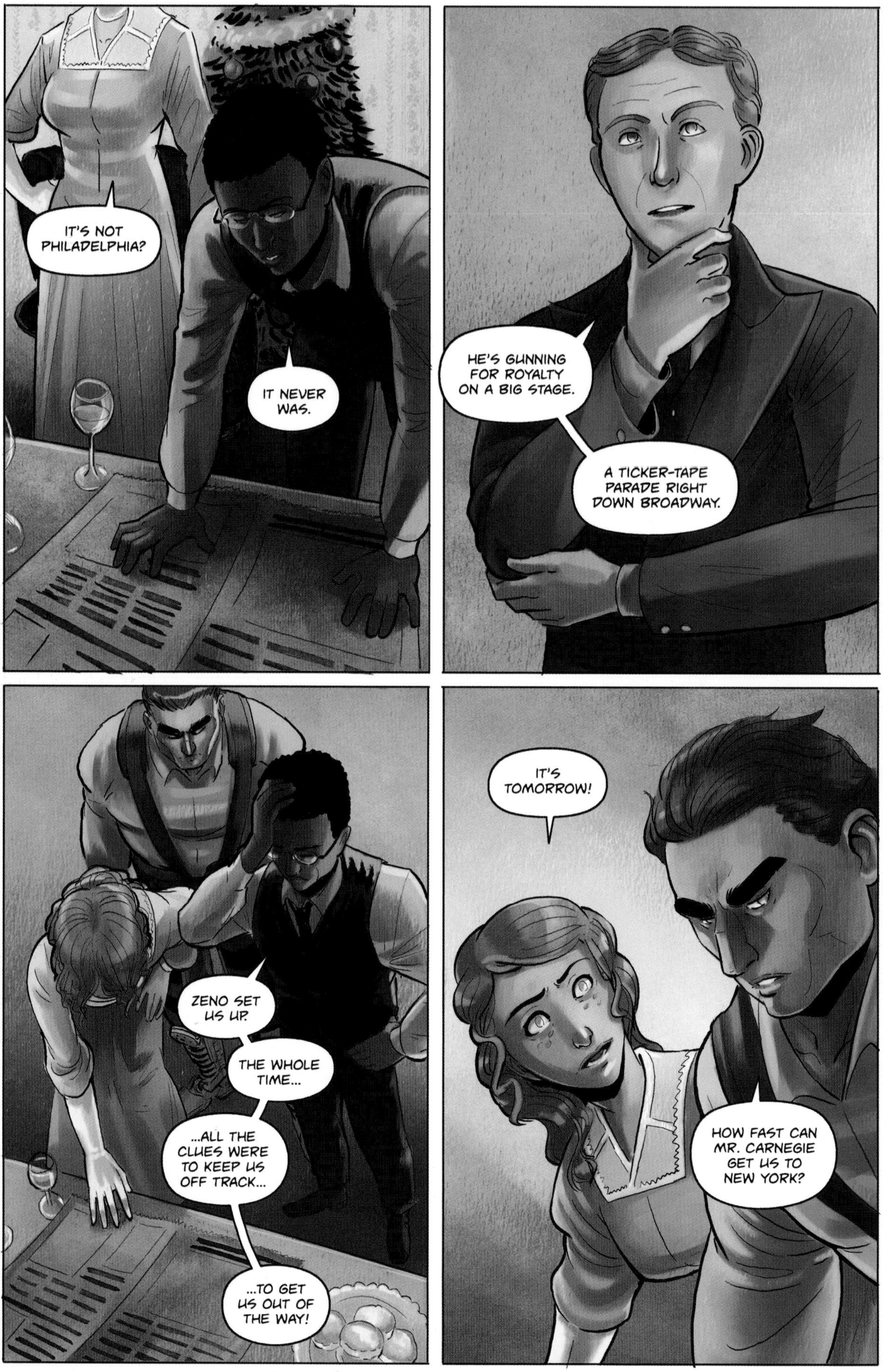
IT'S NOT PHILADELPHIA?
IT NEVER WAS.
HE'S GUNNING FOR ROYALTY ON A BIG STAGE.
A TICKER-TAPE PARADE RIGHT DOWN BROADWAY.
ZENO SET US UP.
THE WHOLE TIME...
...ALL THE CLUES WERE TO KEEP US OFF TRACK...
...TO GET US OUT OF THE WAY!
IT'S TOMORROW!
HOW FAST CAN MR. CARNEGIE GET US TO NEW YORK?

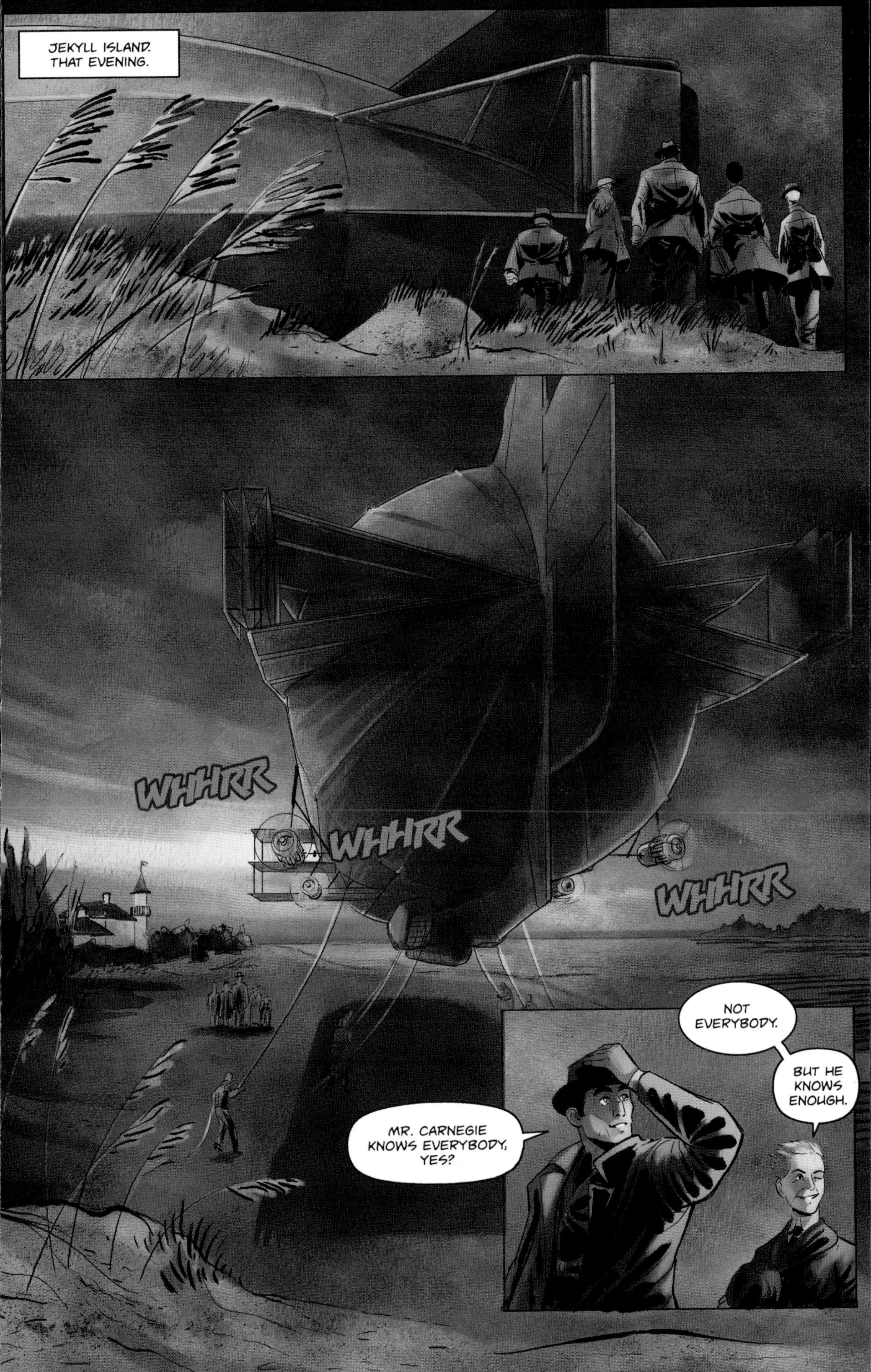

JEKYLL ISLAND. THAT EVENING.
WHHRR
WHHRR
WHHRR
MR. CARNEGIE KNOWS EVERYBODY, YES?
NOT EVERYBODY.
BUT HE KNOWS ENOUGH.

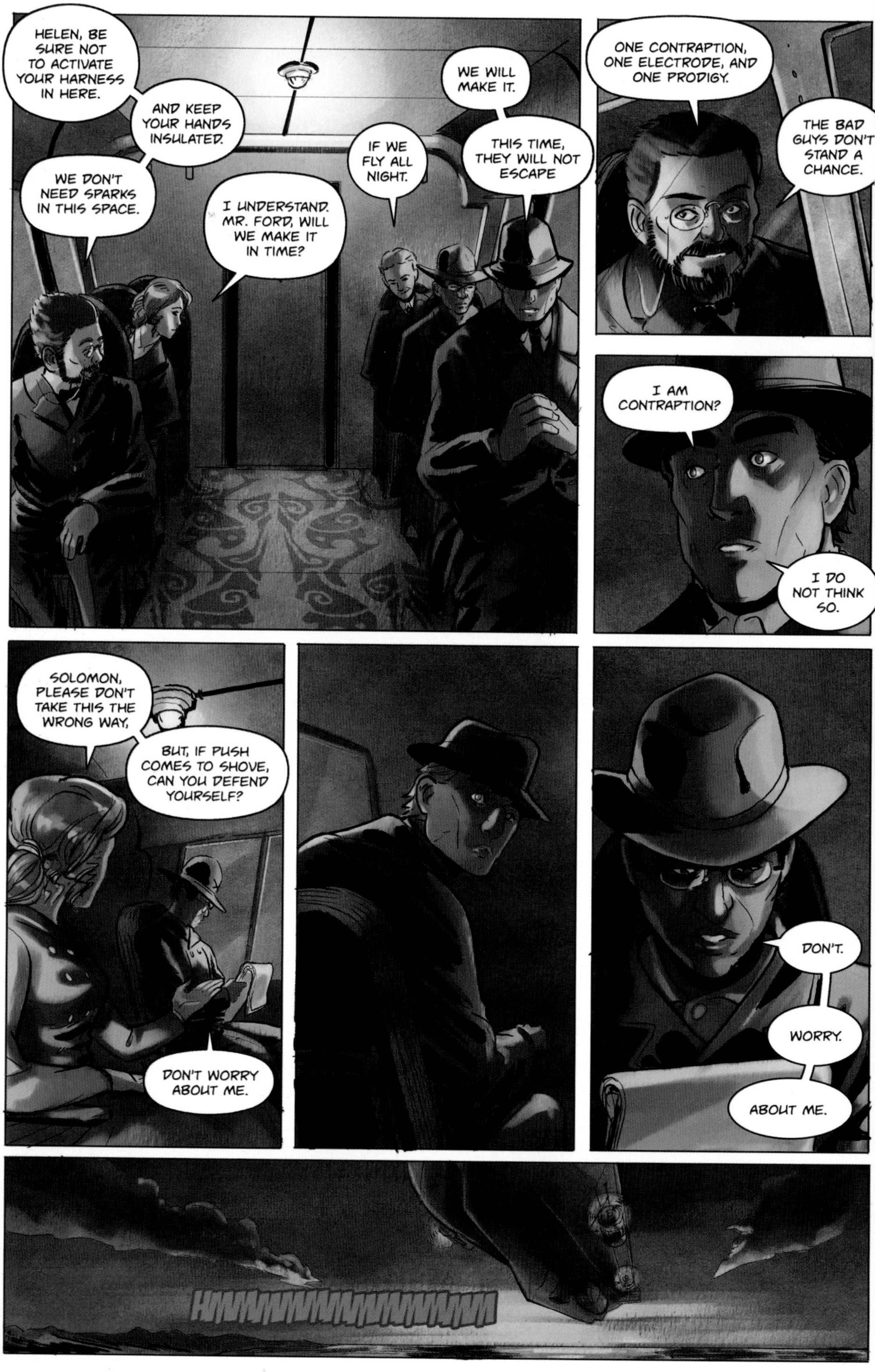
HELEN, BE SURE NOT TO ACTIVATE YOUR HARNESS IN HERE.
AND KEEP YOUR HANDS INSULATED.
WE DON'T NEED SPARKS IN THIS SPACE.
I UNDERSTAND. MR. FORD, WILL WE MAKE IT IN TIME?
IF WE FLY ALL NIGHT.
WE WILL MAKE IT.
THIS TIME, THEY WILL NOT ESCAPE
ONE CONTRAPTION, ONE ELECTRODE, AND ONE PRODIGY.
THE BAD GUYS DON'T STAND A CHANCE.
I AM CONTRAPTION?
I DO NOT THINK SO.
SOLOMON, PLEASE DON'T TAKE THIS THE WRONG WAY,
BUT, IF PUSH COMES TO SHOVE, CAN YOU DEFEND YOURSELF?
DON'T WORRY ABOUT ME.
DON'T.
WORRY.
ABOUT ME.
HMMMMMMMMMMMMMMMMMM

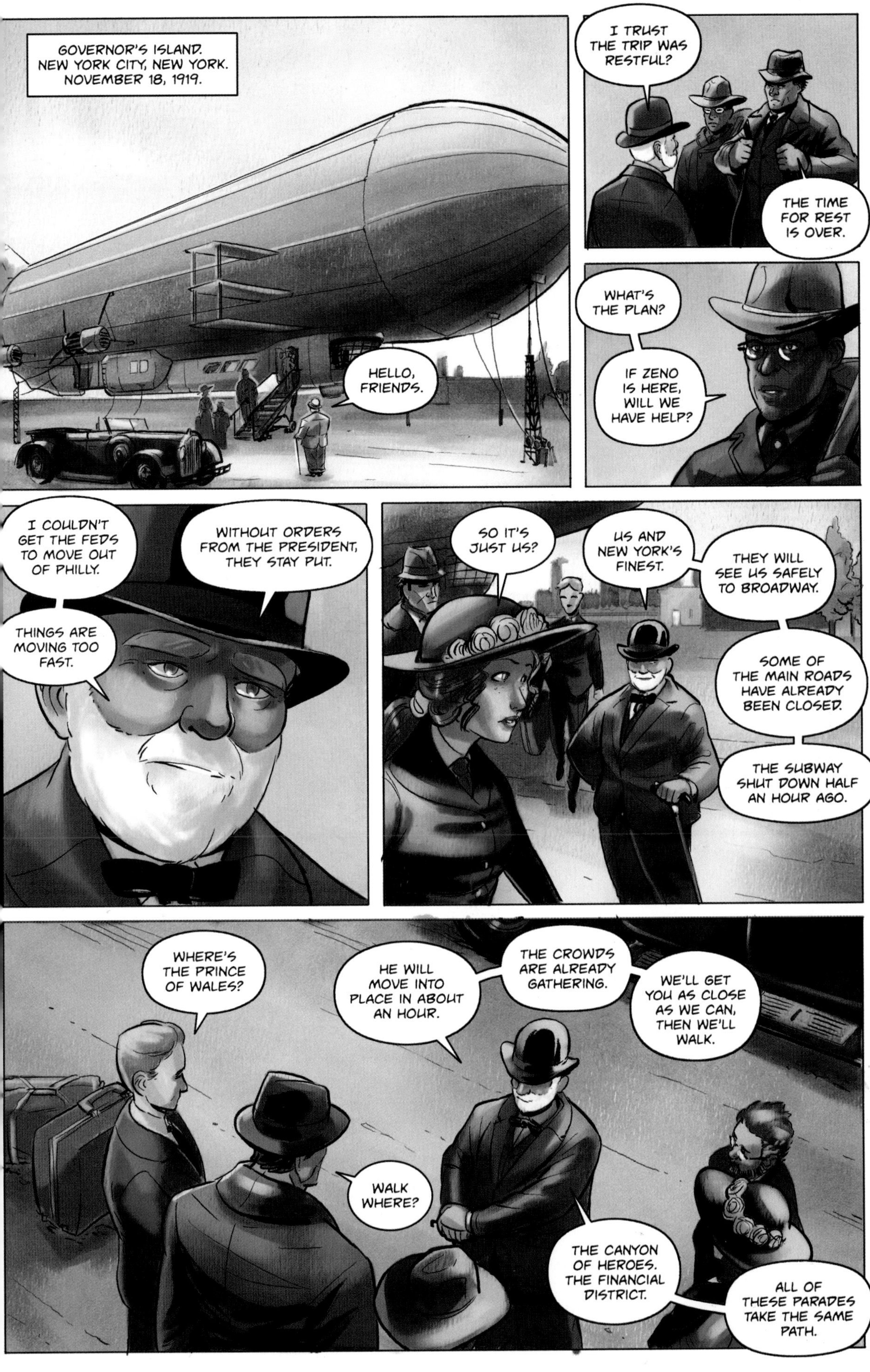
GOVERNOR'S ISLAND. NEW YORK CITY, NEW YORK. NOVEMBER 18, 1919.
HELLO, FRIENDS.
I TRUST THE TRIP WAS RESTFUL?
THE TIME FOR REST IS OVER.
WHAT'S THE PLAN?
IF ZENO IS HERE, WILL WE HAVE HELP?
I COULDN'T GET THE FEDS TO MOVE OUT OF PHILLY.
WITHOUT ORDERS FROM THE PRESIDENT, THEY STAY PUT.
THINGS ARE MOVING TOO FAST.
SO IT'S JUST US?
US AND NEW YORK'S FINEST.
THEY WILL SEE US SAFELY TO BROADWAY.
SOME OF THE MAIN ROADS HAVE ALREADY BEEN CLOSED.
THE SUBWAY SHUT DOWN HALF AN HOUR AGO.
WHERE'S THE PRINCE OF WALES?
HE WILL MOVE INTO PLACE IN ABOUT AN HOUR.
THE CROWDS ARE ALREADY GATHERING.
WE'LL GET YOU AS CLOSE AS WE CAN, THEN WE'LL WALK.
WALK WHERE?
THE CANYON OF HEROES. THE FINANCIAL DISTRICT.
ALL OF THESE PARADES TAKE THE SAME PATH.

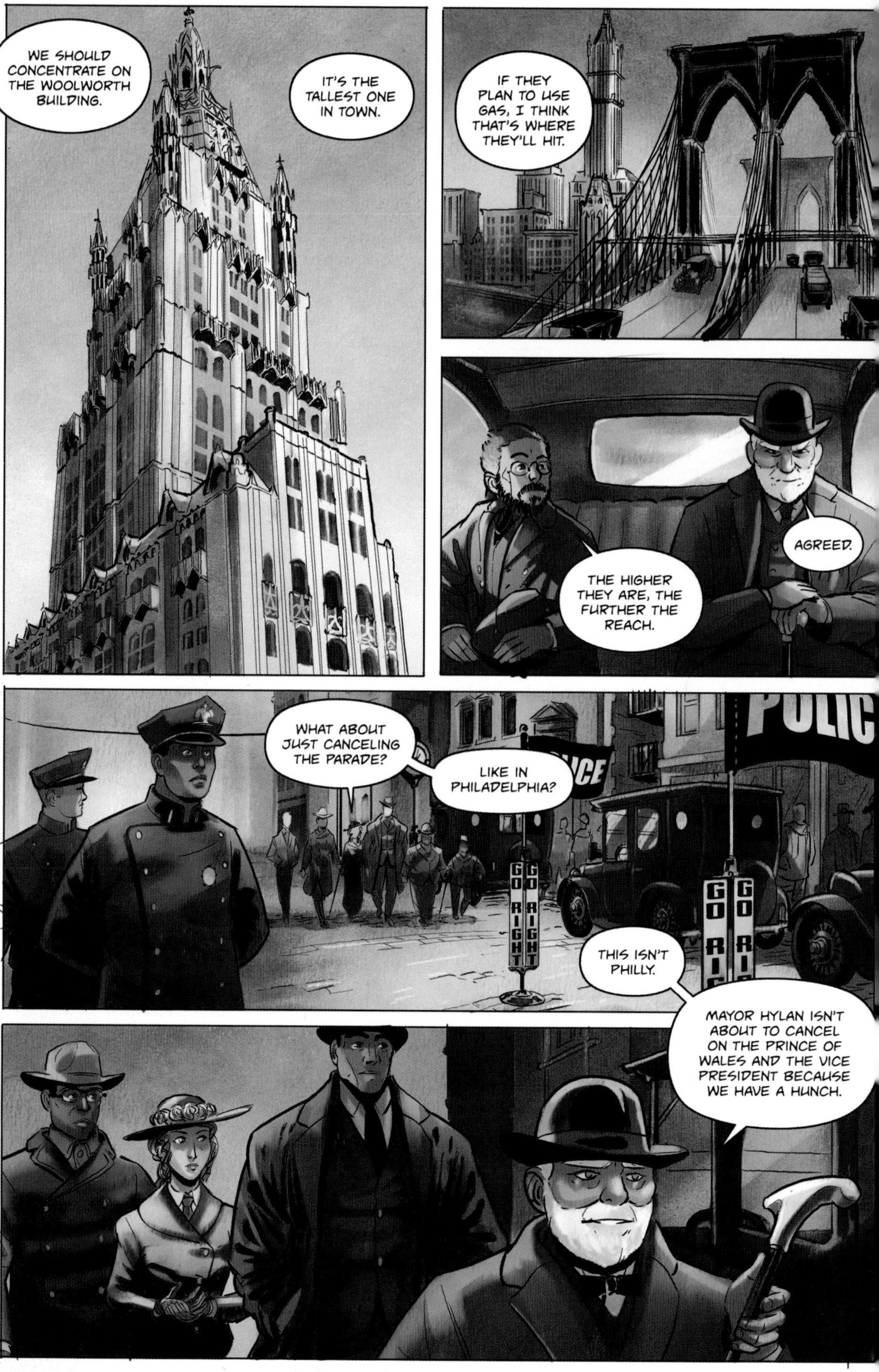
WE SHOULD CONCENTRATE ON THE WOOLWORTH BUILDING.
IT'S THE TALLEST ONE IN TOWN.
IF THEY PLAN TO USE GAS, I THINK THAT'S WHERE THEY'LL HIT.
THE HIGHER THEY ARE, THE FURTHER THE REACH.
AGREED.
POLIC
WHAT ABOUT JUST CANCELING THE PARADE?
LIKE IN PHILADELPHIA?
GO RIGHT
GO RIGHT
THIS ISN'T PHILLY.
MAYOR HYLAN ISN'T ABOUT TO CANCEL ON THE PRINCE OF WALES AND THE VICE PRESIDENT BECAUSE WE HAVE A HUNCH.

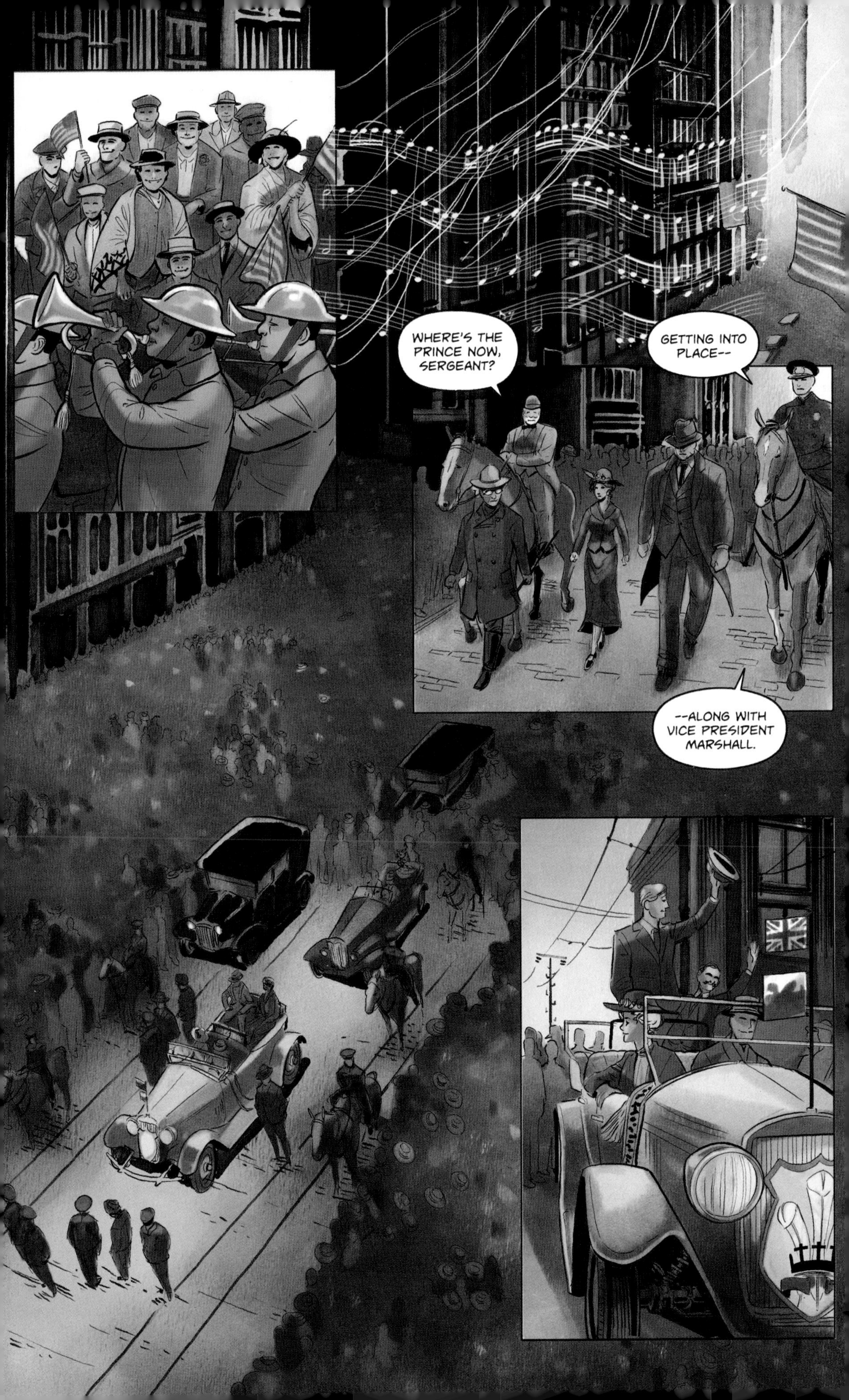
WHERE'S THE PRINCE NOW, SERGEANT?
GETTING INTO PLACE--
--ALONG WITH VICE PRESIDENT MARSHALL.

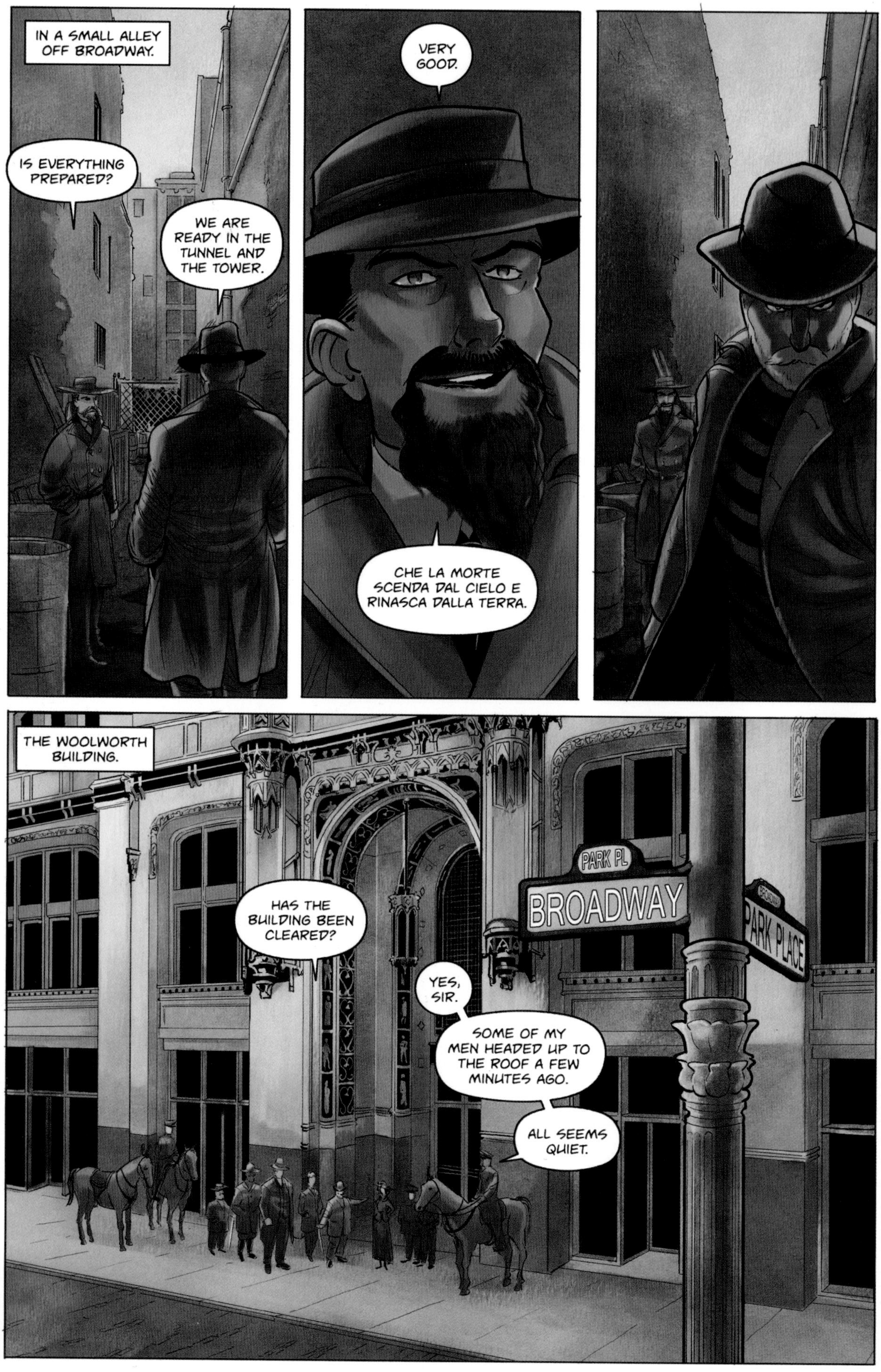
IN A SMALL ALLEY OFF BROADWAY.
IS EVERYTHING PREPARED?
WE ARE READY IN THE TUNNEL AND THE TOWER.
VERY GOOD.
CHE LA MORTE SCENDA DAL CIELO E RINASCA DALLA TERRA.
THE WOOLWORTH BUILDING.
PARK PL
BROADWAY
PARK PLACE
HAS THE BUILDING BEEN CLEARED?
YES, SIR.
SOME OF MY MEN HEADED UP TO THE ROOF A FEW MINUTES AGO.
ALL SEEMS QUIET.

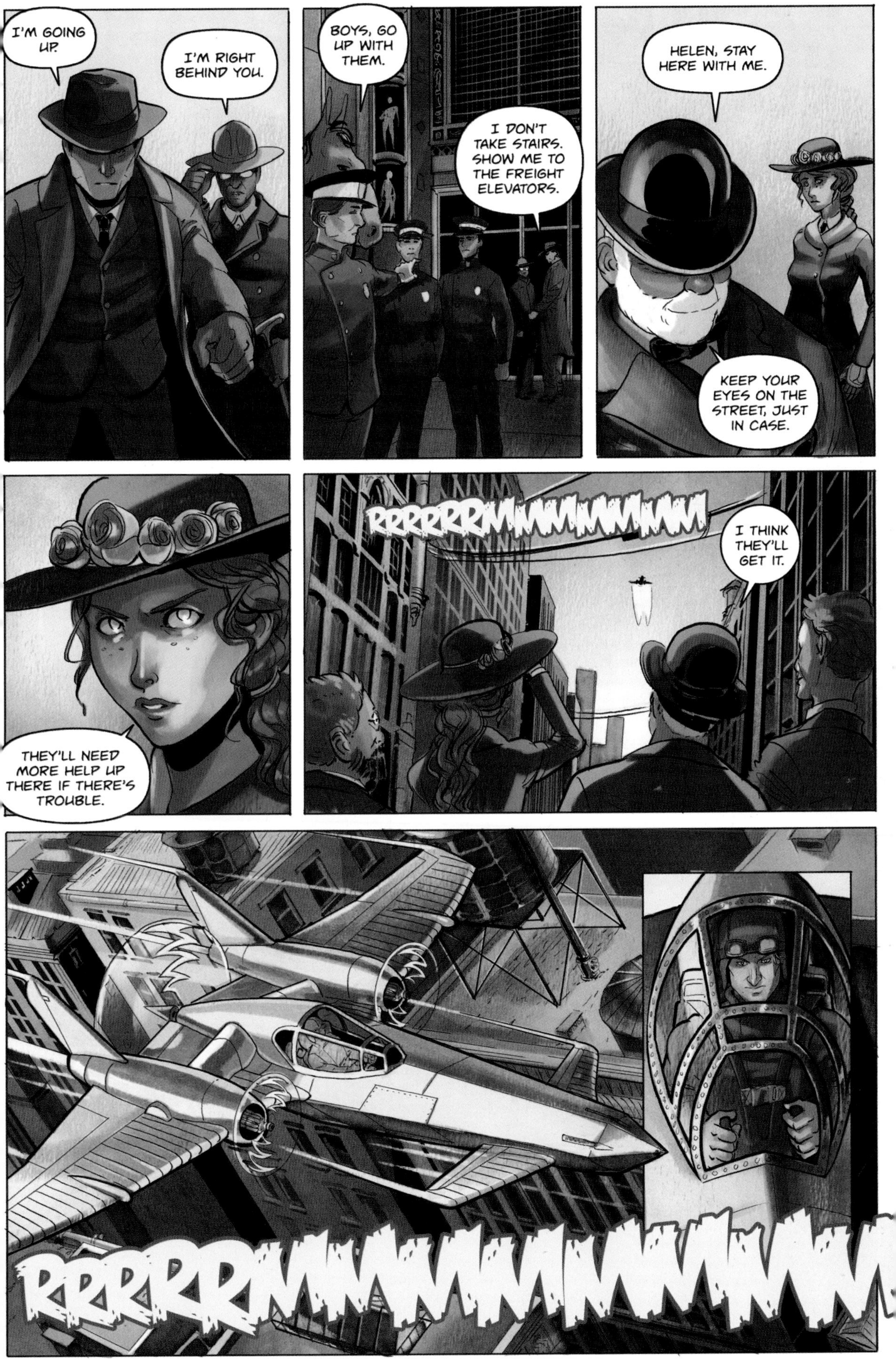
I'M GOING UP.
I'M RIGHT BEHIND YOU.
BOYS, GO UP WITH THEM.
I DON'T TAKE STAIRS. SHOW ME TO THE FREIGHT ELEVATORS.
HELEN, STAY HERE WITH ME.
KEEP YOUR EYES ON THE STREET, JUST IN CASE.
THEY'LL NEED MORE HELP UP THERE IF THERE'S TROUBLE.
RRRRRRMMMMMMMM
I THINK THEY'LL GET IT.
RRRRRMMMMMMMMMM

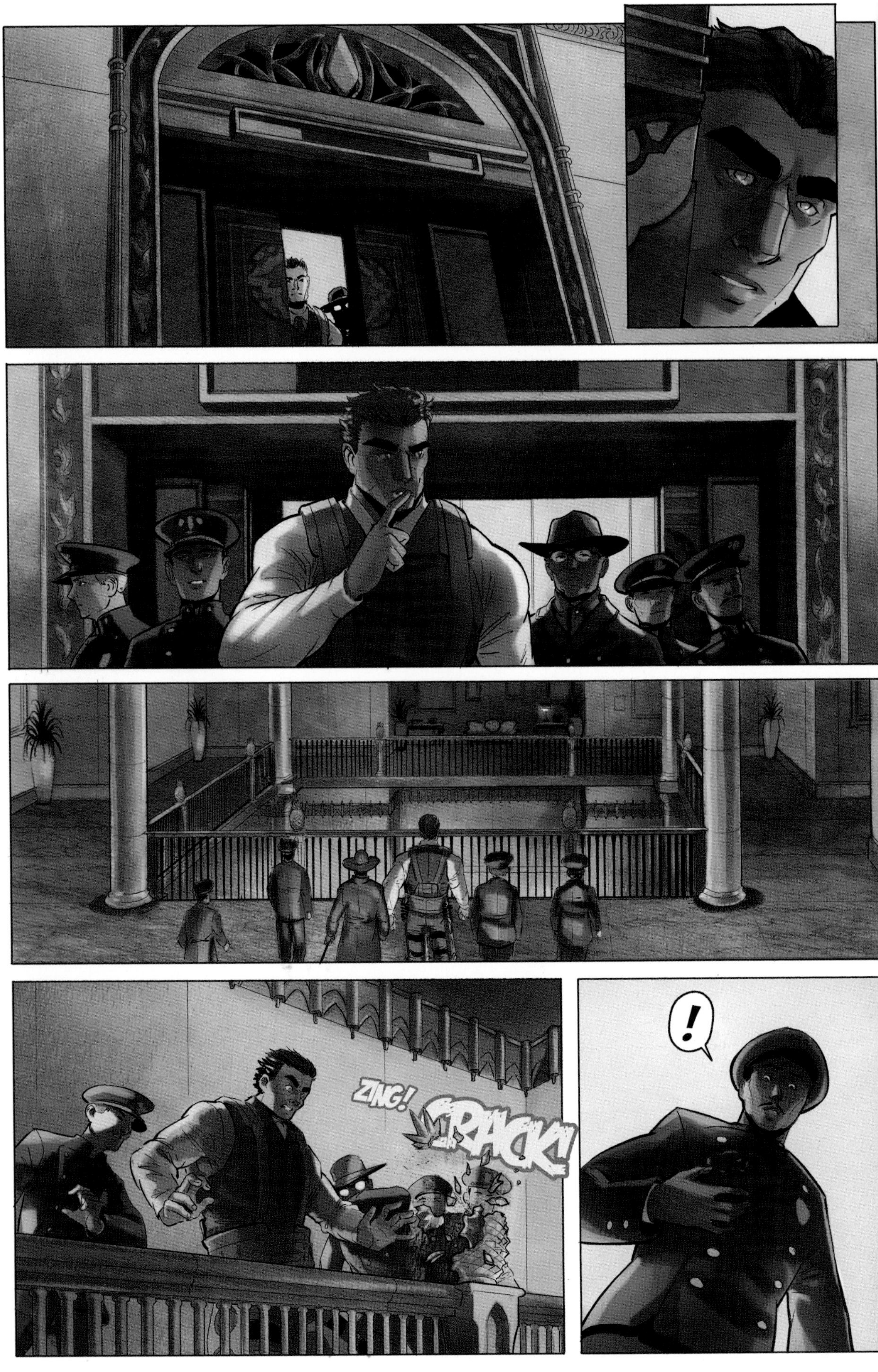
!
ZING!
CRACK!

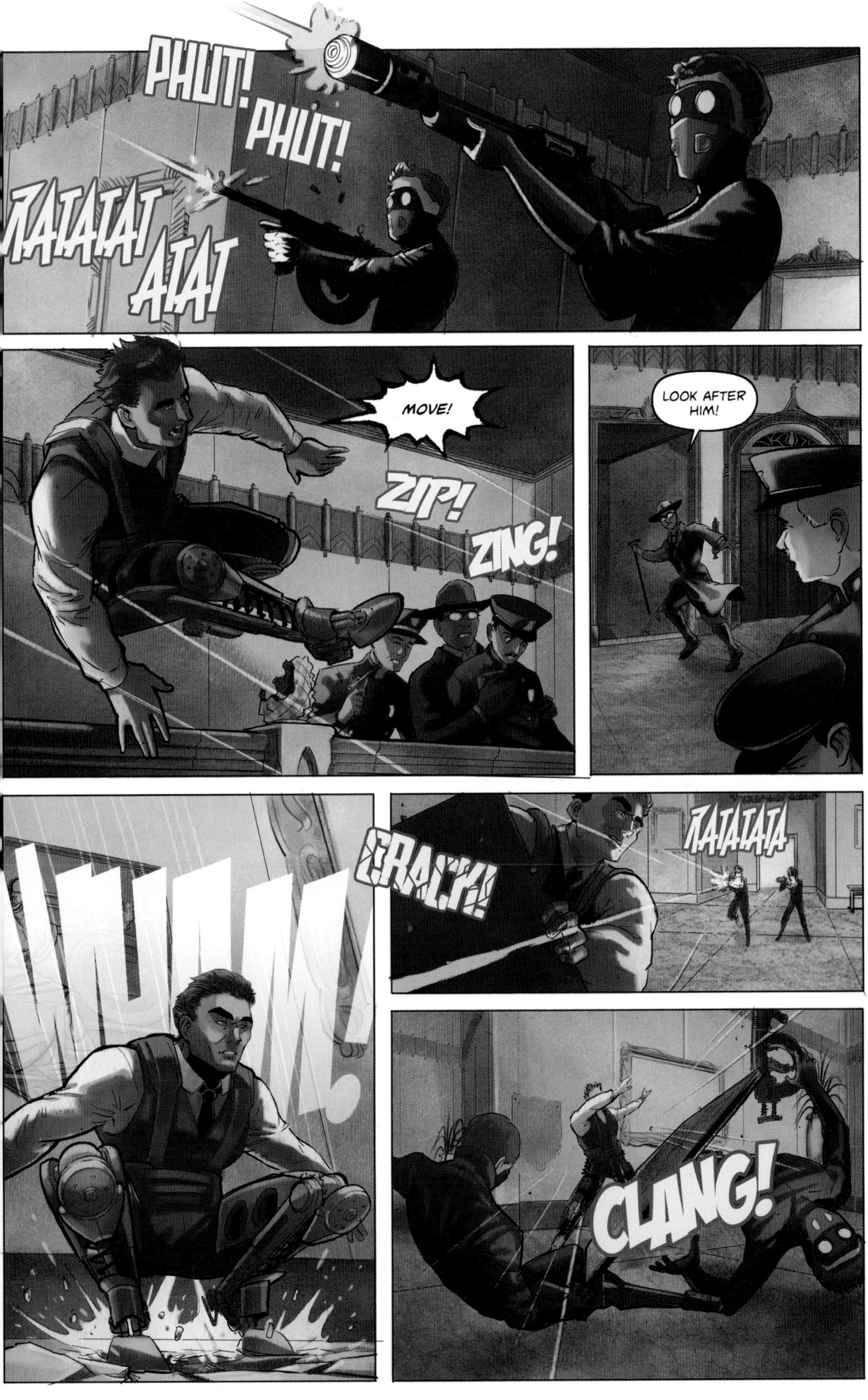
PHUT!
PHUT!
RATATAT
ATAT
MOVE!
ZIP!
ZING!
LOOK AFTER HIM!
CRACK!
RATATATA
CLANG!

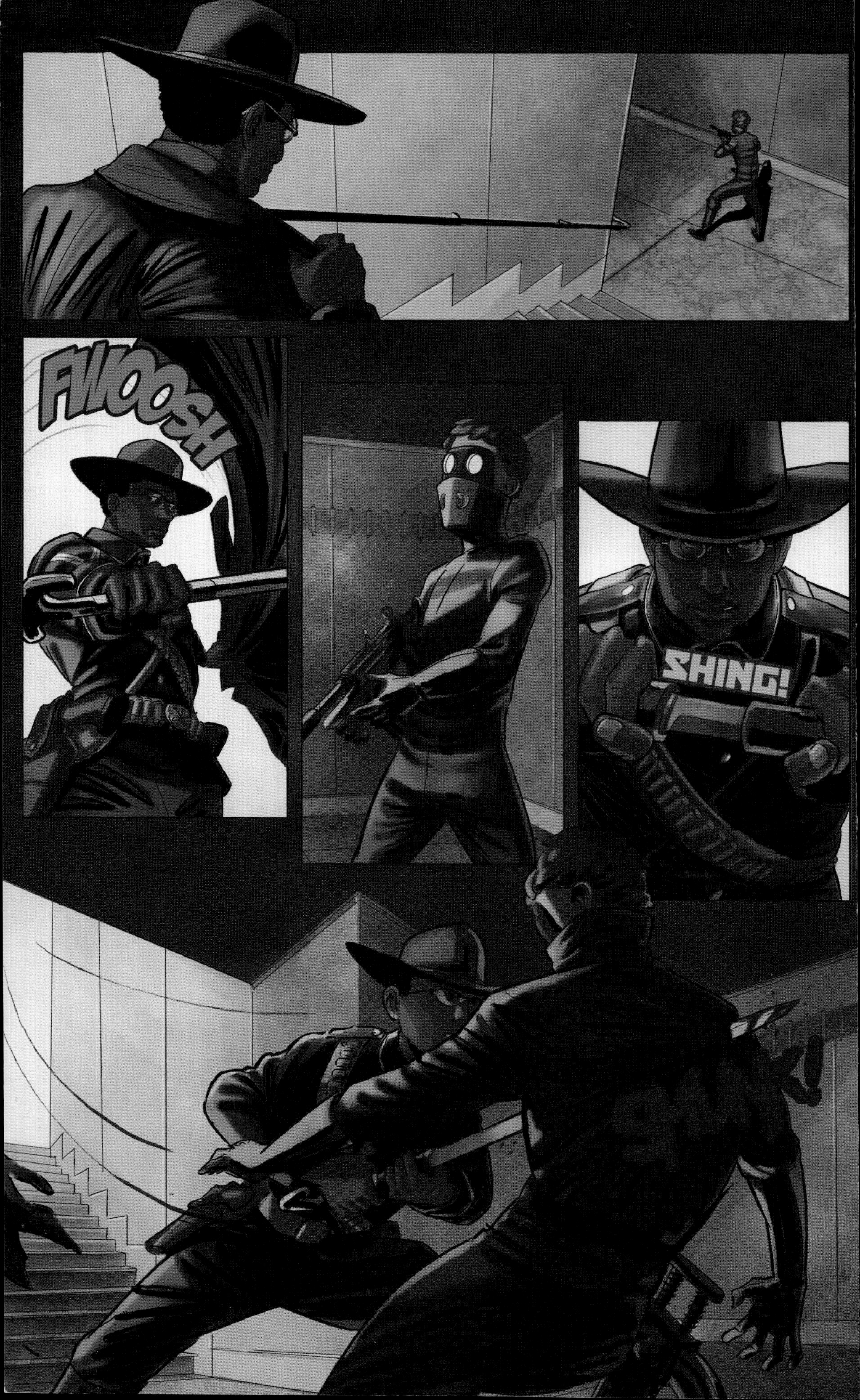
FWOOSH
SHING!

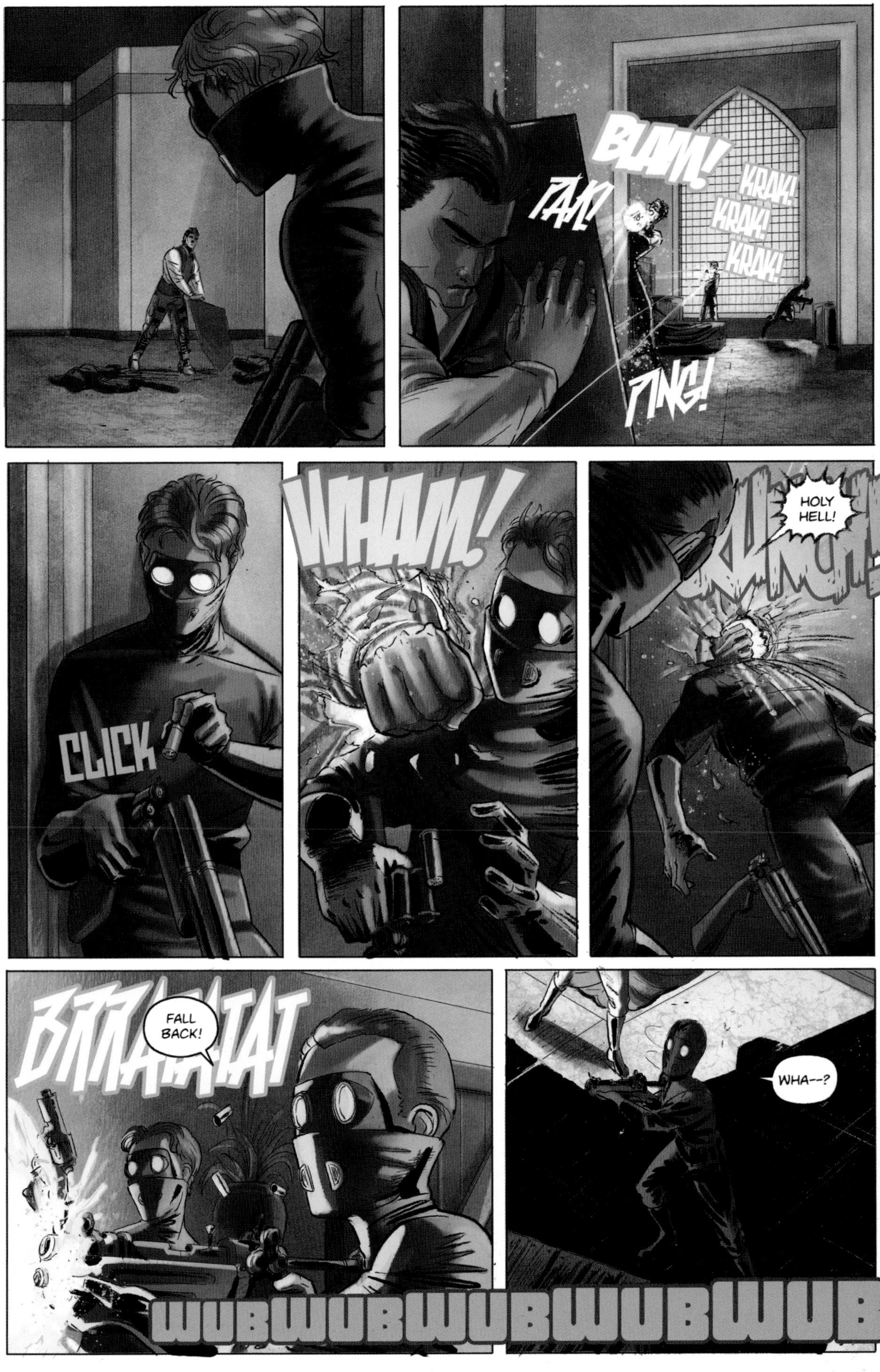
BLAM!
PAK!
KRAK!
KRAK!
KRAK!
PING!
CLICK
WHAM!
HOLY HELL!
FALL BACK!
WHA--?
WUBWUBWUBWUBWUB

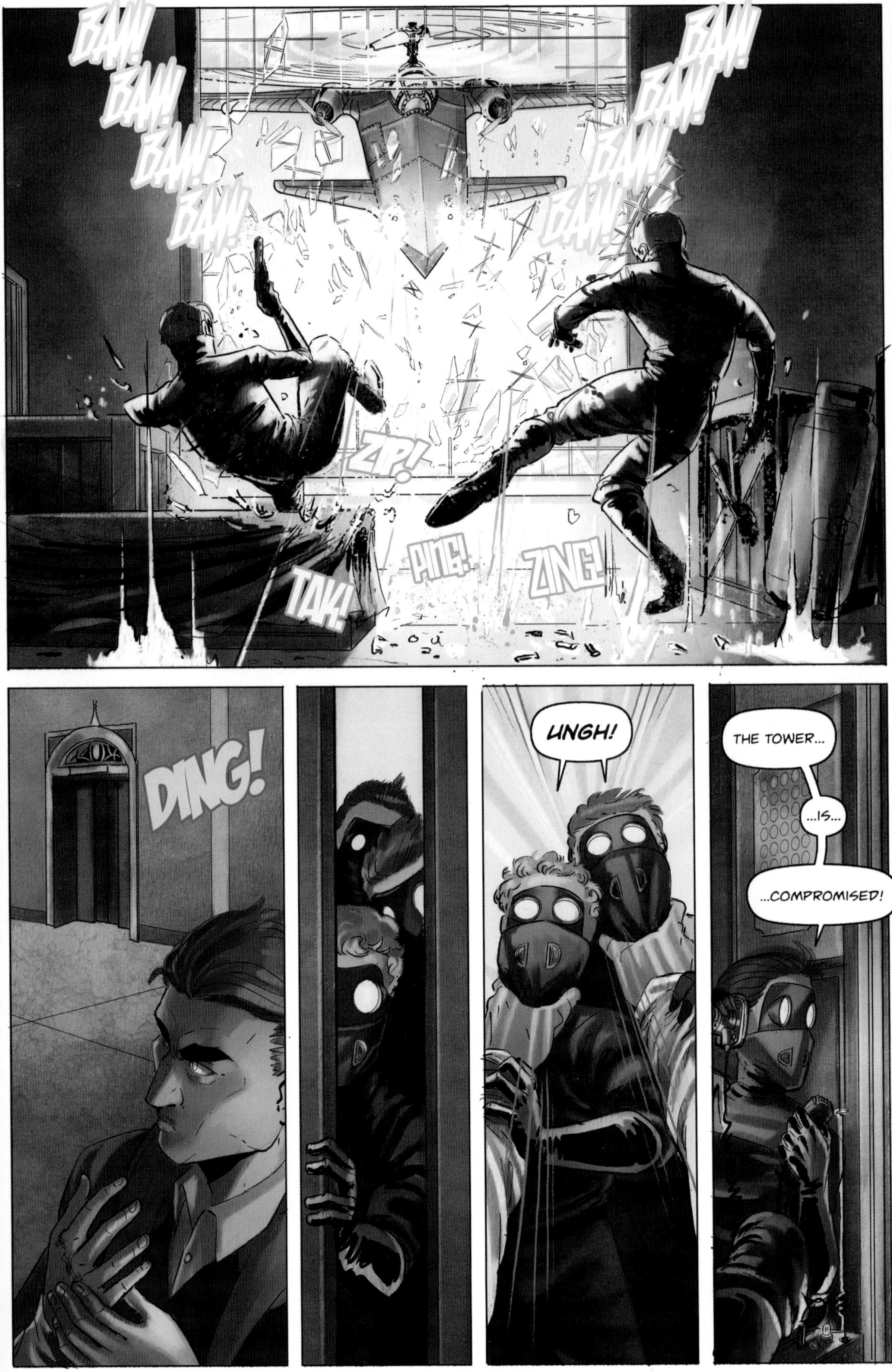
BAM! BAM! BAM! BAM!
BAM! BAM! BAM! BAM!
ZIP!
TAK!
PING!
ZING!
DING!
UNGH!
THE TOWER...
...IS...
...COMPROMISED!

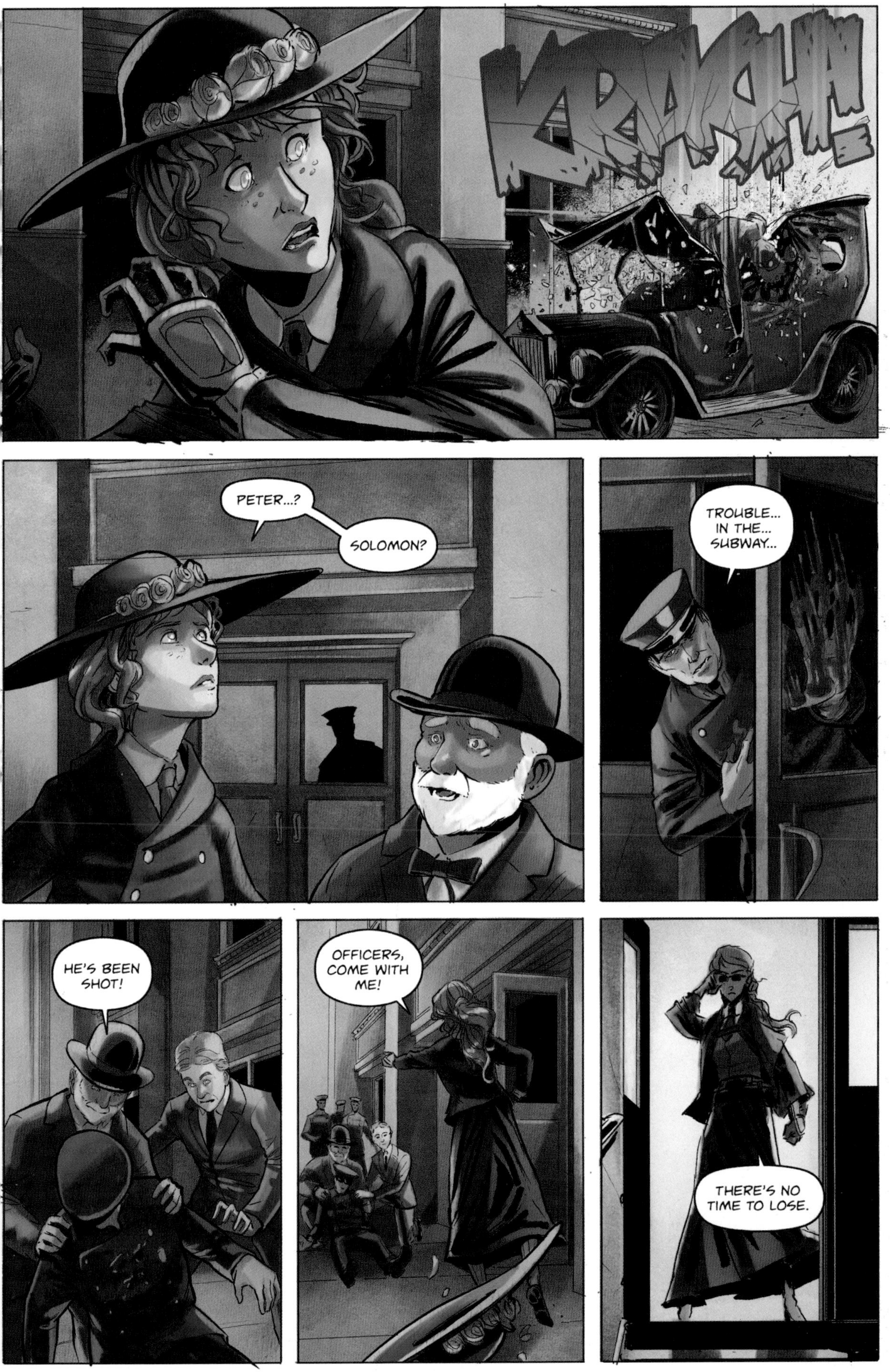
KRAKOOLLHH!
PETER...?
SOLOMON?
TROUBLE... IN THE... SUBWAY...
HE'S BEEN SHOT!
OFFICERS, COME WITH ME!
THERE'S NO TIME TO LOSE.

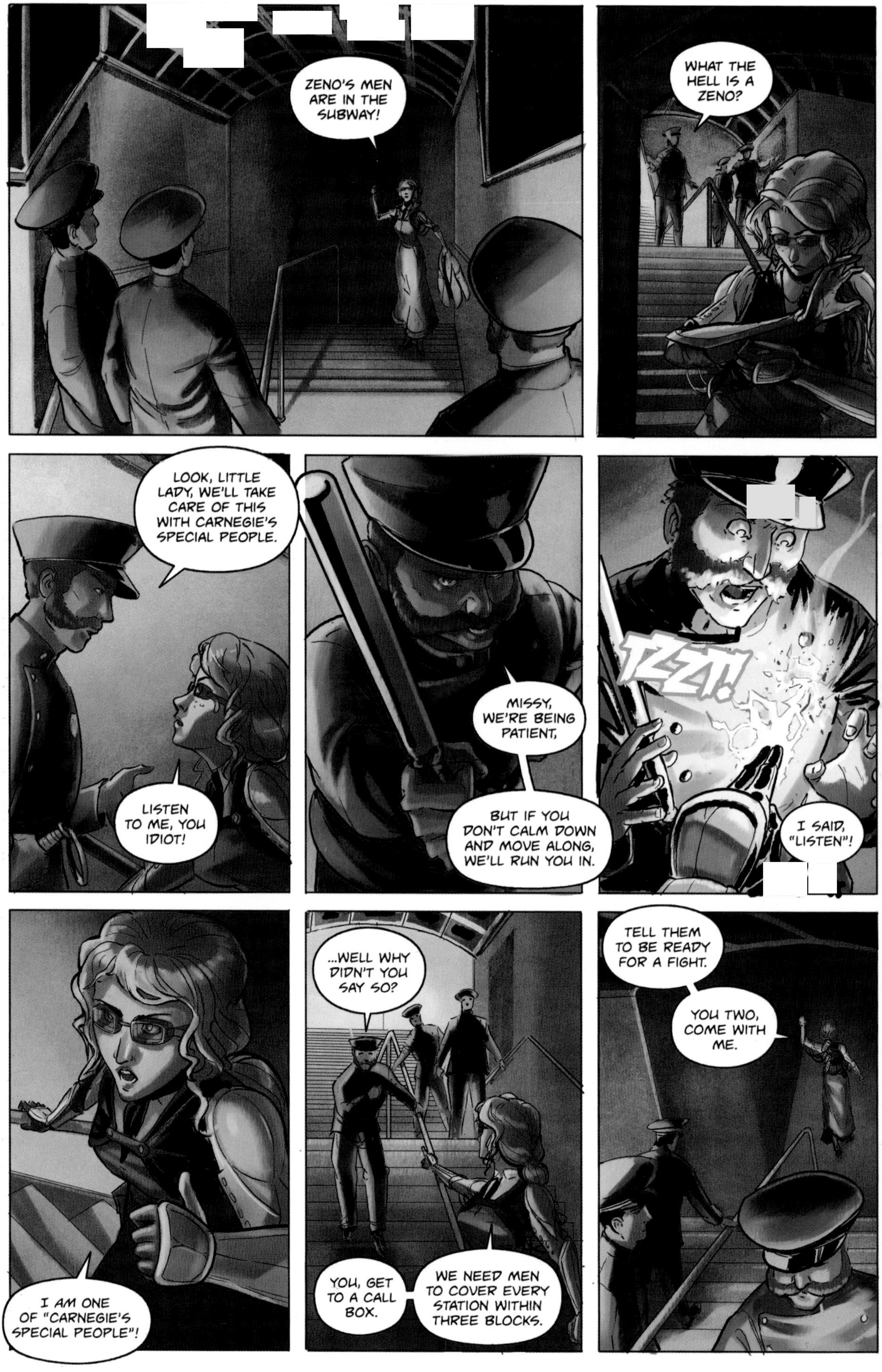
ZENO'S MEN ARE IN THE SUBWAY!
WHAT THE HELL IS A ZENO?
LOOK, LITTLE LADY, WE'LL TAKE CARE OF THIS WITH CARNEGIE'S SPECIAL PEOPLE.
LISTEN TO ME, YOU IDIOT!
MISSY, WE'RE BEING PATIENT,
BUT IF YOU DON'T CALM DOWN AND MOVE ALONG, WE'LL RUN YOU IN.
TZZAT!
I SAID, "LISTEN"!
I AM ONE OF "CARNEGIE'S SPECIAL PEOPLE"!
...WELL WHY DIDN'T YOU SAY SO?
WE NEED MEN TO COVER EVERY STATION WITHIN THREE BLOCKS.
YOU, GET TO A CALL BOX.
TELL THEM TO BE READY FOR A FIGHT.
YOU TWO, COME WITH ME.

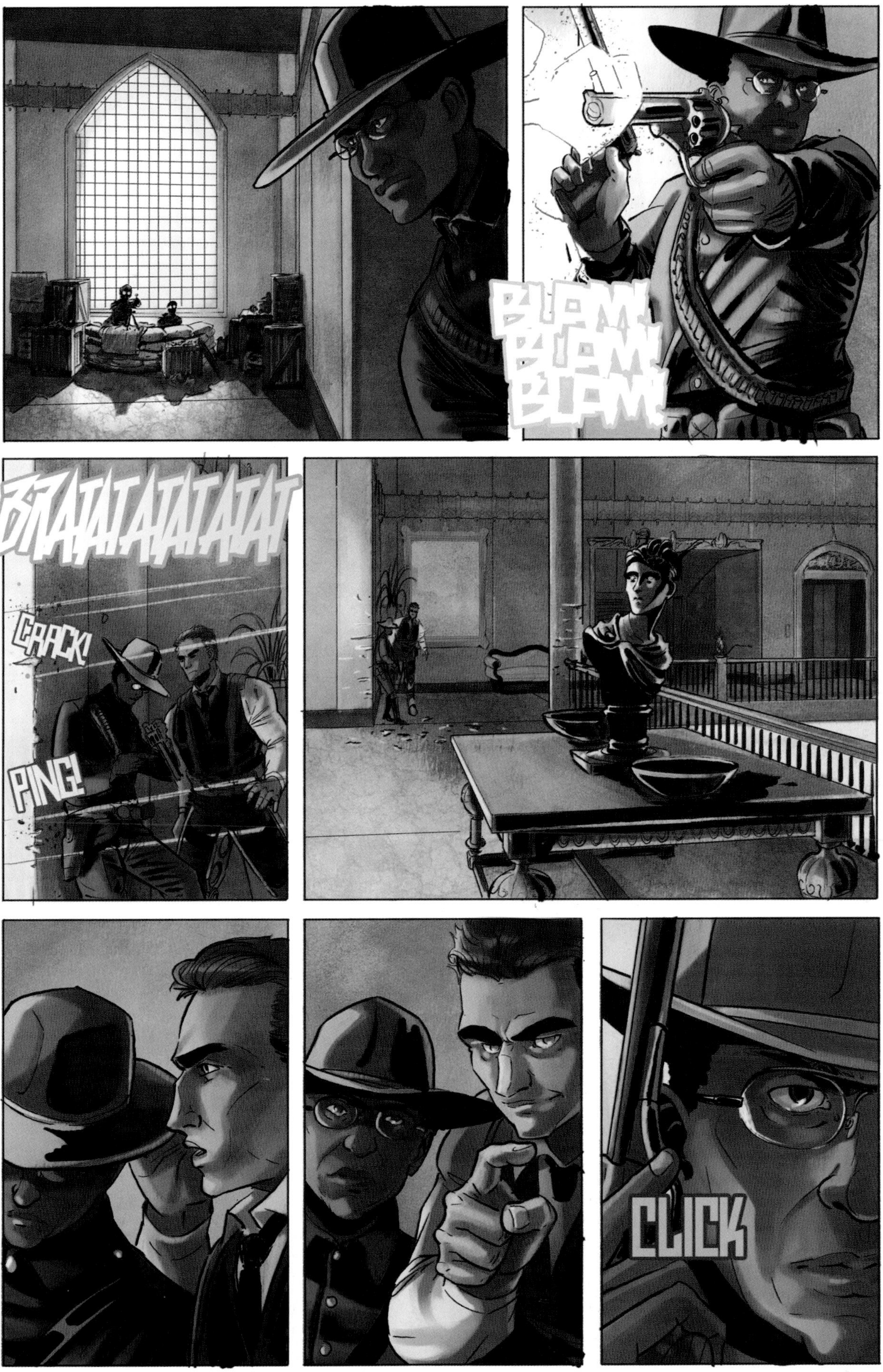
BLAM! BLAM! BLAM!
BRATATATATATAT
CRACK!
PING!
CLICK

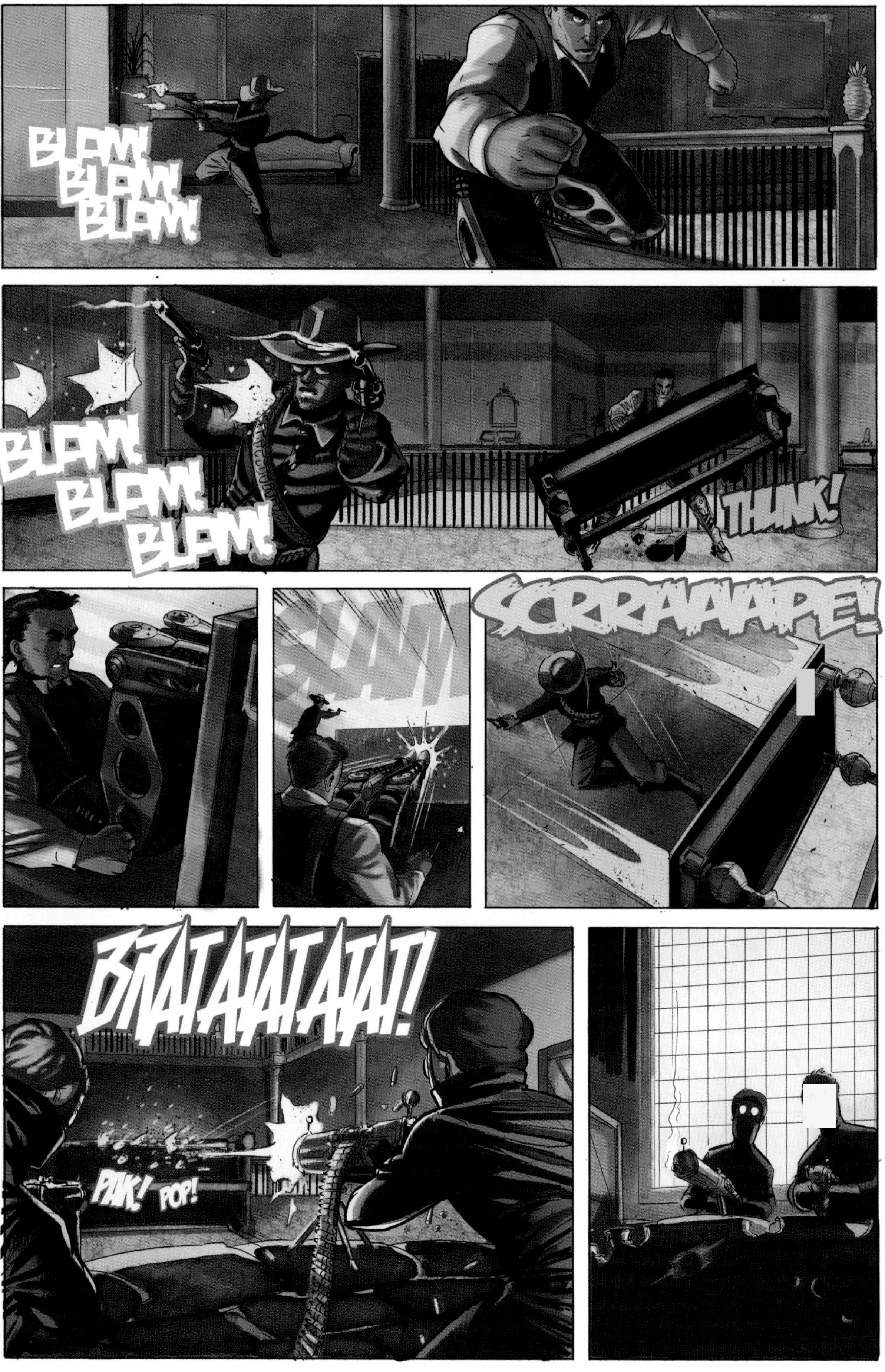
BLAM! BLAM! BLAM!
BLAM! BLAM! BLAM!
THUNK!
SCRRAAAAPE!
BRATATATAT!
PAK! POP!

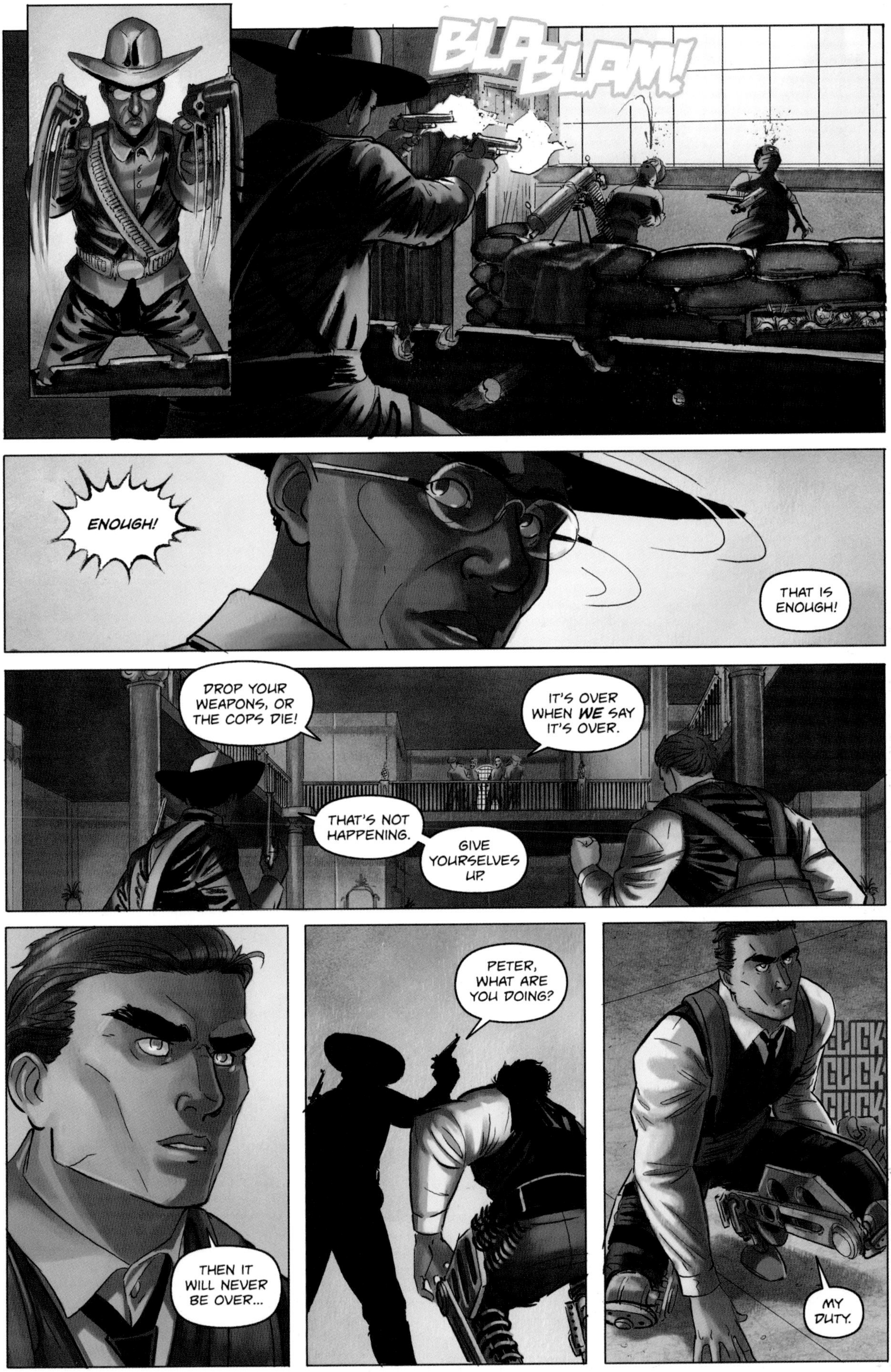
BLABLAM!
ENOUGH!
THAT IS ENOUGH!
DROP YOUR WEAPONS, OR THE COPS DIE!
IT'S OVER WHEN WE SAY IT'S OVER.
THAT'S NOT HAPPENING.
GIVE YOURSELVES UP.
THEN IT WILL NEVER BE OVER...
PETER, WHAT ARE YOU DOING?
CLICK
CLICK
CLICK
MY DUTY.

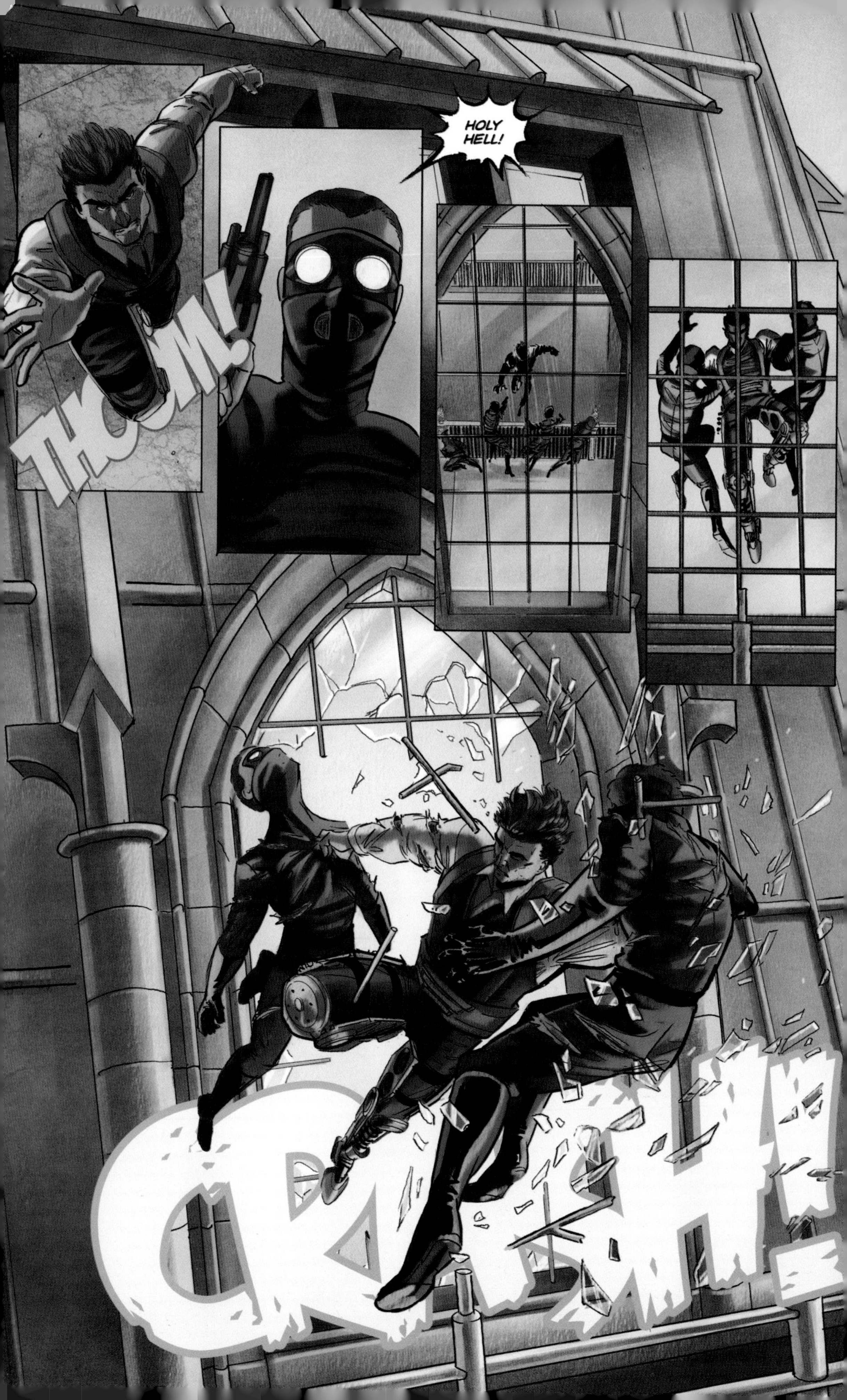
THOOM!
HOLY HELL!
CRASH!

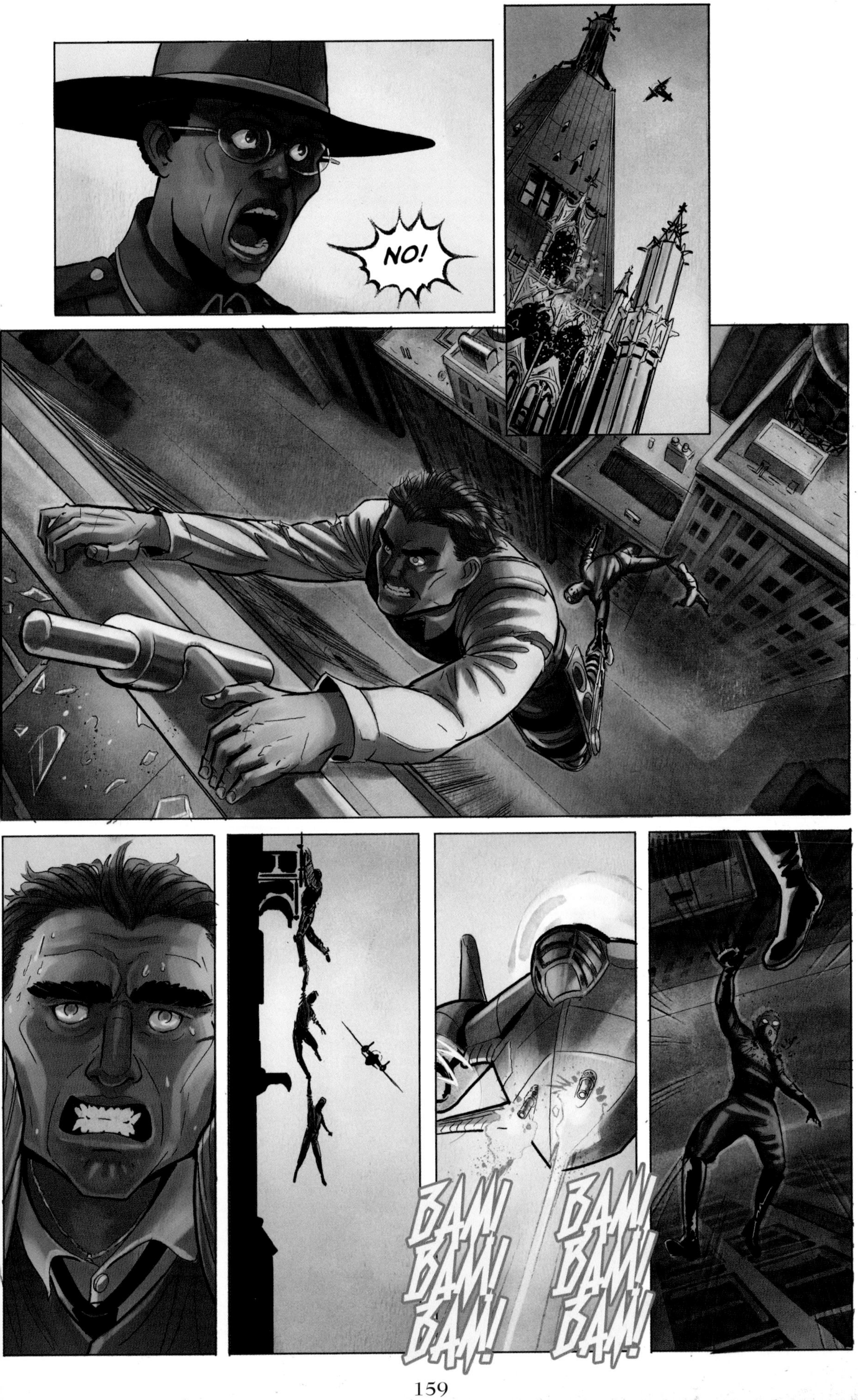
NO!
BAM! BAM! BAM!
BAM! BAM! BAM!

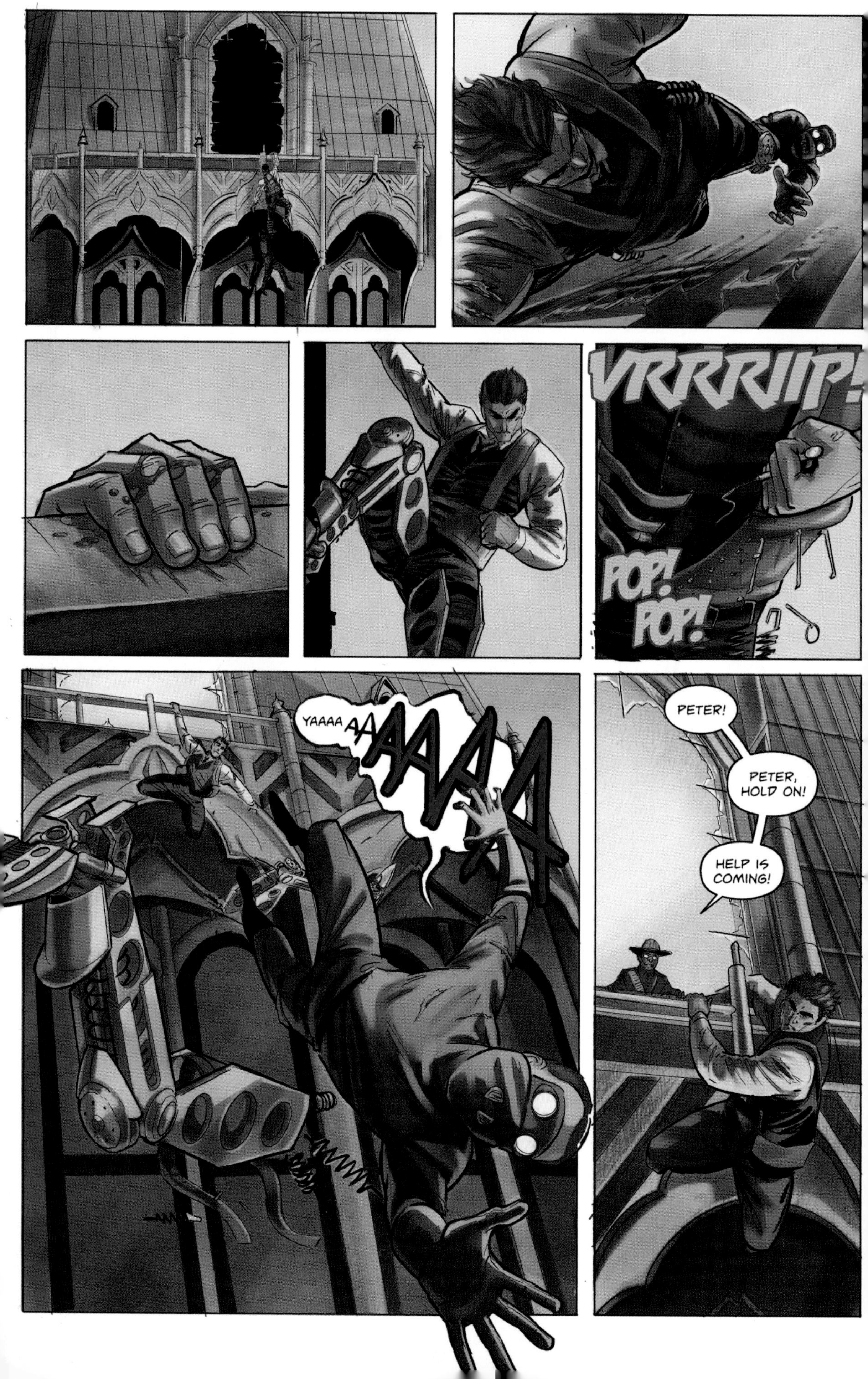
VRRRIIP!
POP!
POP!
YAAAAAAAAAA
PETER!
PETER, HOLD ON!
HELP IS COMING!

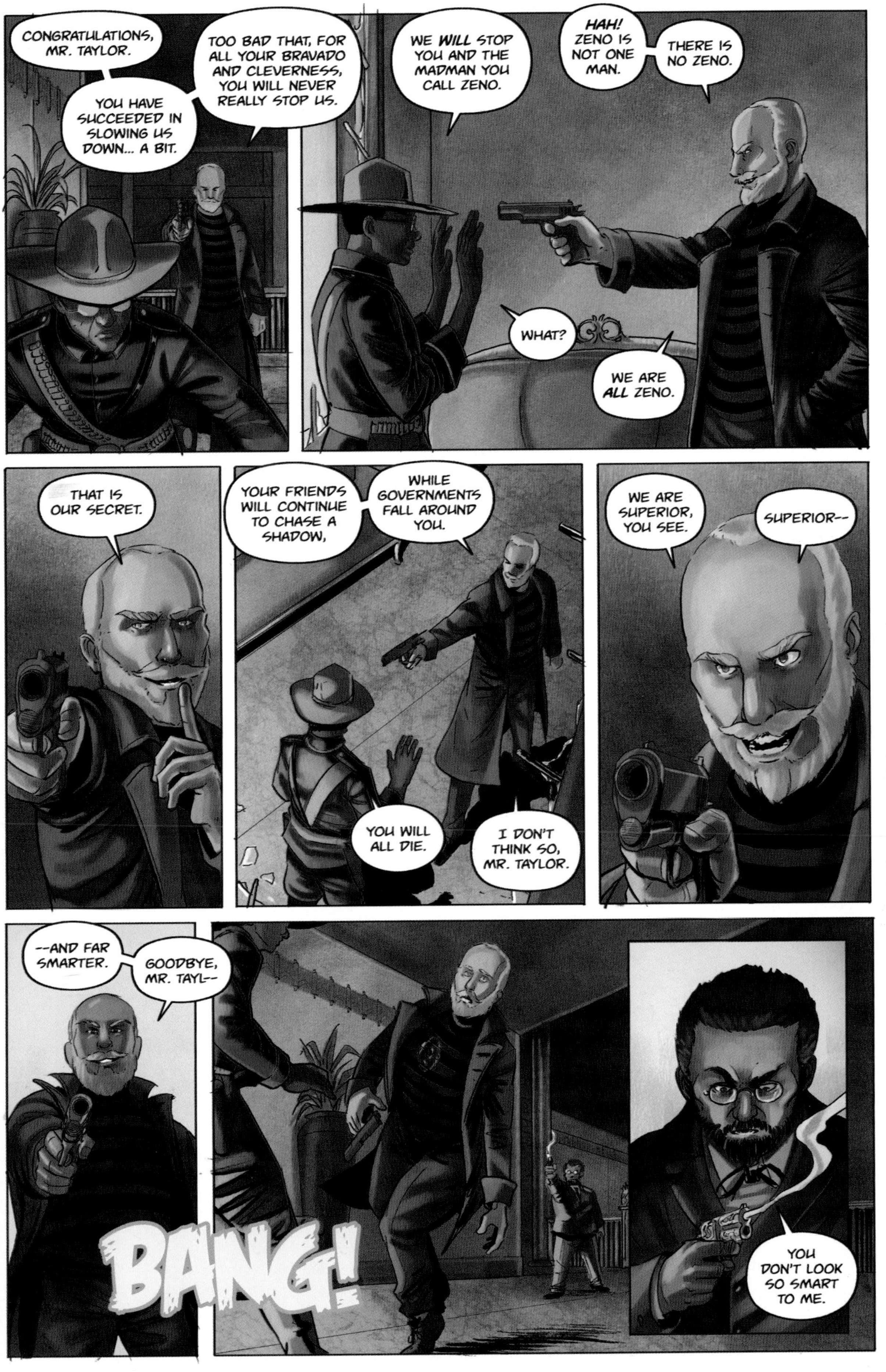
CONGRATULATIONS, MR. TAYLOR.
YOU HAVE SUCCEEDED IN SLOWING US DOWN... A BIT.
TOO BAD THAT, FOR ALL YOUR BRAVADO AND CLEVERNESS, YOU WILL NEVER REALLY STOP US.
WE WILL STOP YOU AND THE MADMAN YOU CALL ZENO.
HAH! ZENO IS NOT ONE MAN.
THERE IS NO ZENO.
WHAT?
WE ARE ALL ZENO.
THAT IS OUR SECRET.
YOUR FRIENDS WILL CONTINUE TO CHASE A SHADOW,
WHILE GOVERNMENTS FALL AROUND YOU.
YOU WILL ALL DIE.
I DON'T THINK SO, MR. TAYLOR.
WE ARE SUPERIOR, YOU SEE.
SUPERIOR--
--AND FAR SMARTER.
GOODBYE, MR. TAYL--
BANG!
YOU DON'T LOOK SO SMART TO ME.

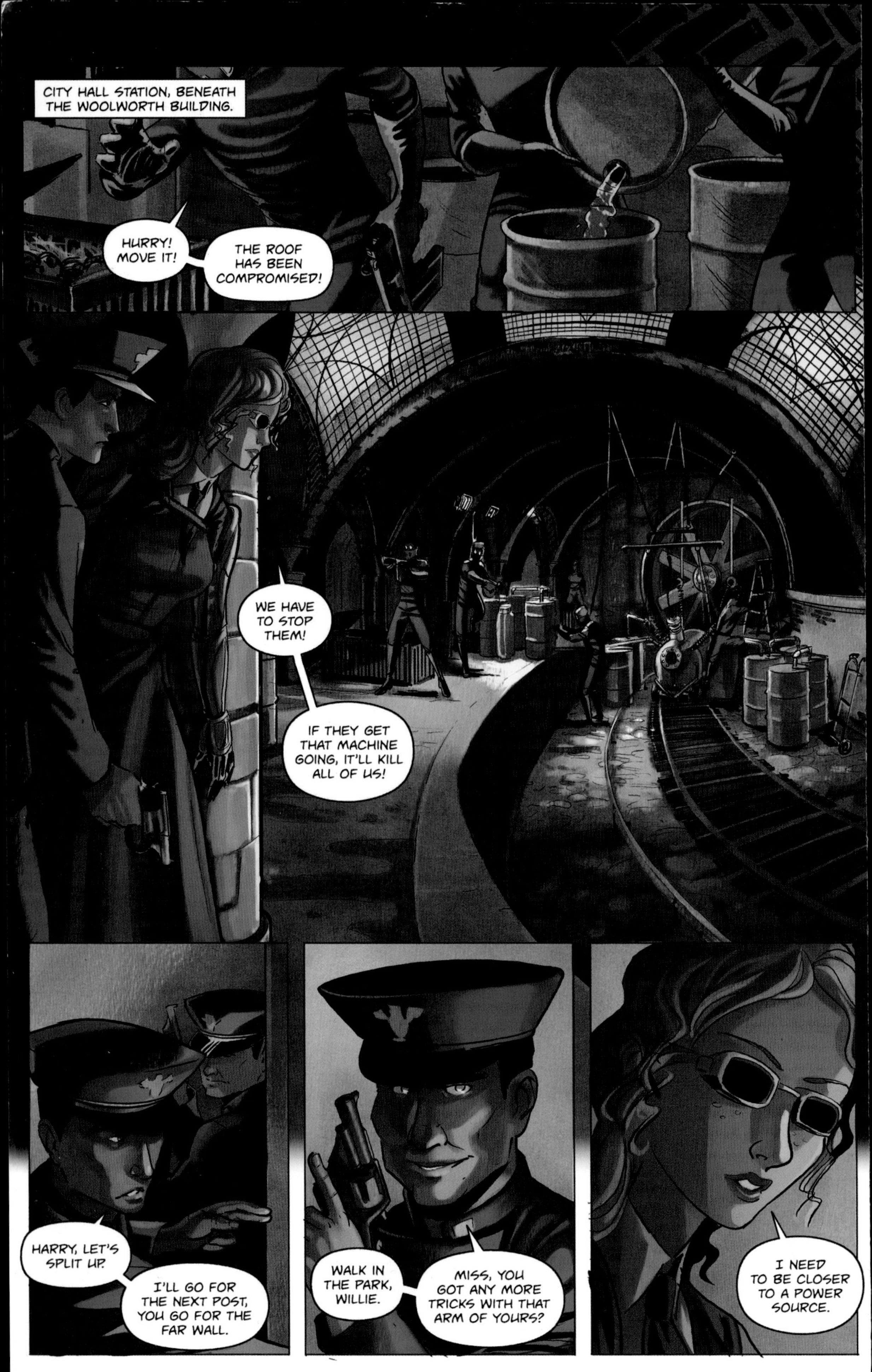

CITY HALL STATION, BENEATH THE WOOLWORTH BUILDING.
HURRY! MOVE IT!
THE ROOF HAS BEEN COMPROMISED!
WE HAVE TO STOP THEM!
IF THEY GET THAT MACHINE GOING, IT'LL KILL ALL OF US!
HARRY, LET'S SPLIT UP.
I'LL GO FOR THE NEXT POST, YOU GO FOR THE FAR WALL.
WALK IN THE PARK, WILLIE.
MISS, YOU GOT ANY MORE TRICKS WITH THAT ARM OF YOURS?
I NEED TO BE CLOSER TO A POWER SOURCE.

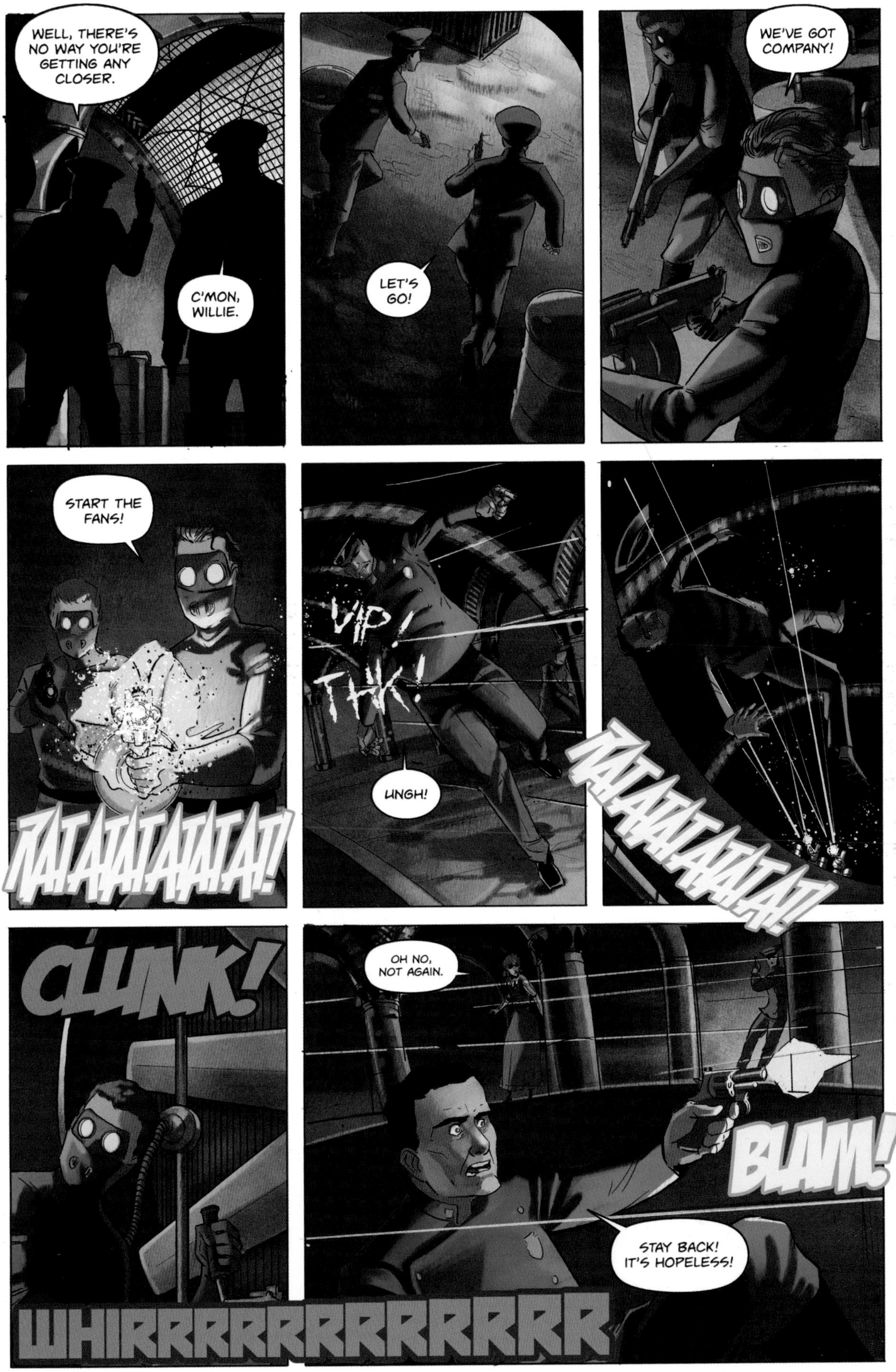
WELL, THERE'S NO WAY YOU'RE GETTING ANY CLOSER.
C'MON, WILLIE.
LET'S GO!
WE'VE GOT COMPANY!
START THE FANS!
RAT-A-TAT-A-TAT-A-TAT!
VIP!
THK!
UNGH!
RAT-A-TAT-A-TAT-A-TAT!
CLUNK!
WHIRRRRRRRRRRRR
OH NO, NOT AGAIN.
BLAM!
STAY BACK! IT'S HOPELESS!

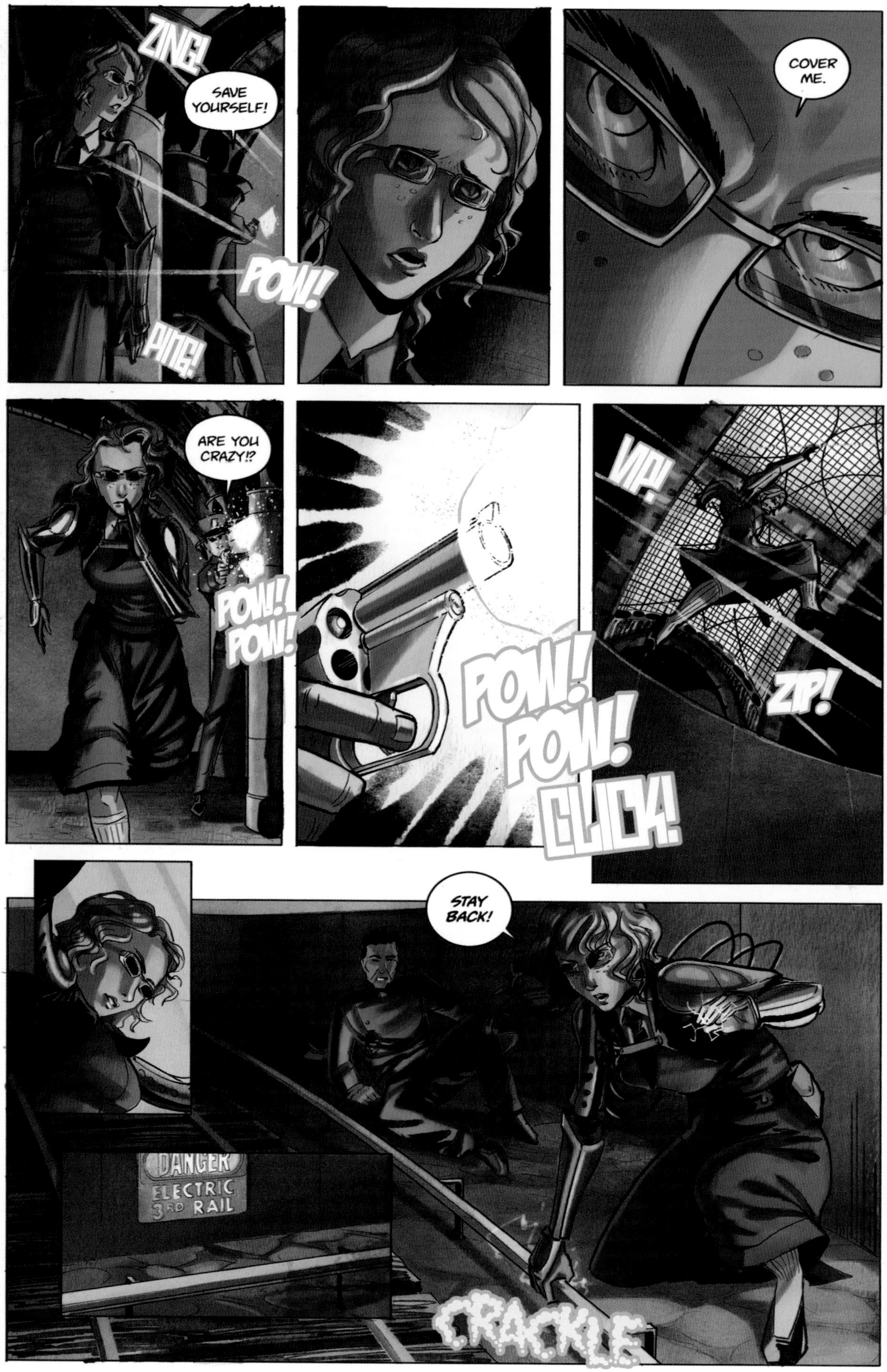
ZING!
SAVE YOURSELF!
POW!
PING!
COVER ME.
ARE YOU CRAZY!?
POW! POW!
POW! POW!
CLICK!
VIP!
ZIP!
STAY BACK!
DANGER
ELECTRIC
3RD RAIL
CRACKLE

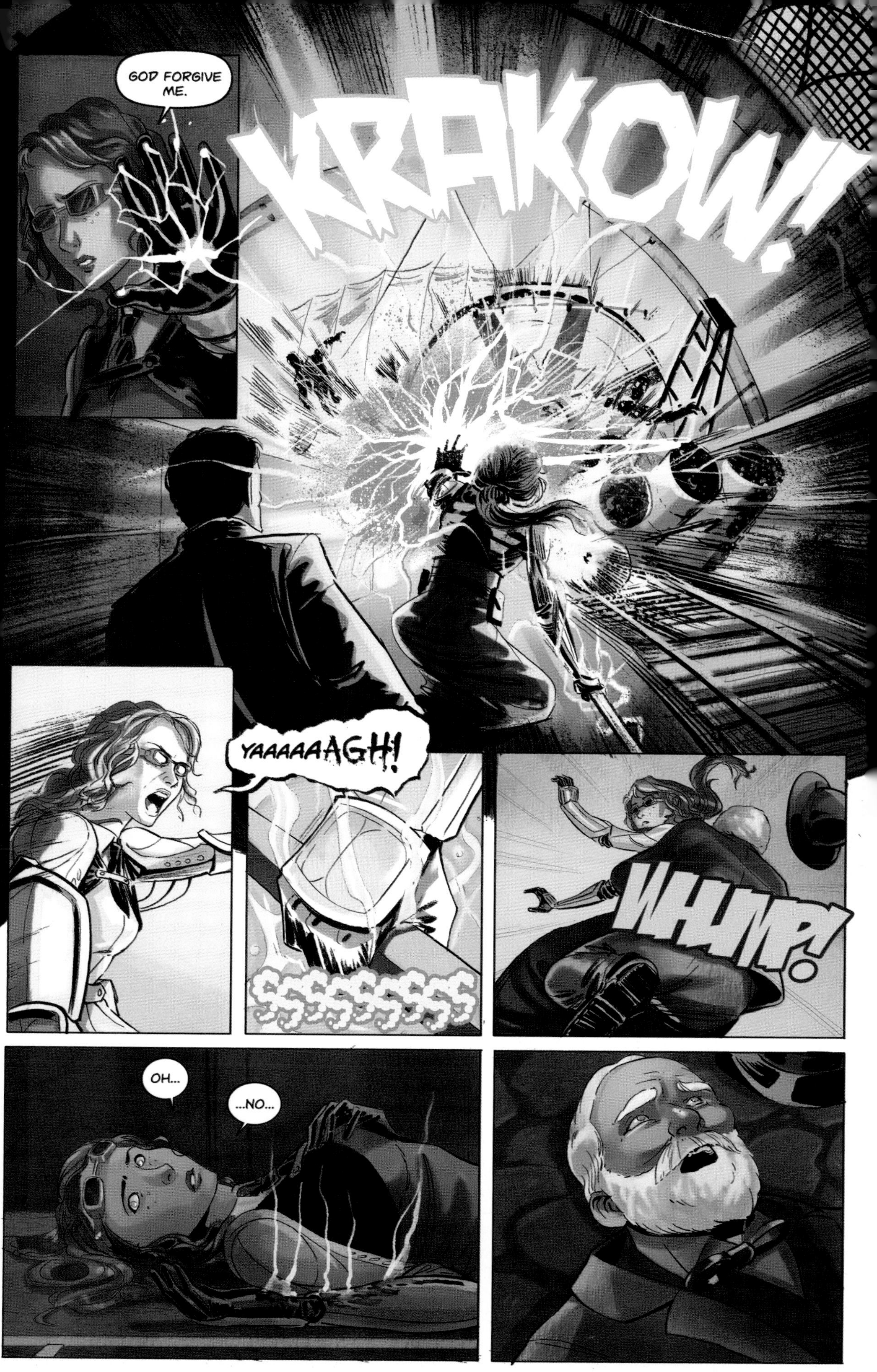
GOD FORGIVE ME.
KRAKOW!
YAAAAAAGH!
SSSSSSSS
WHUMP!
OH...
...NO...

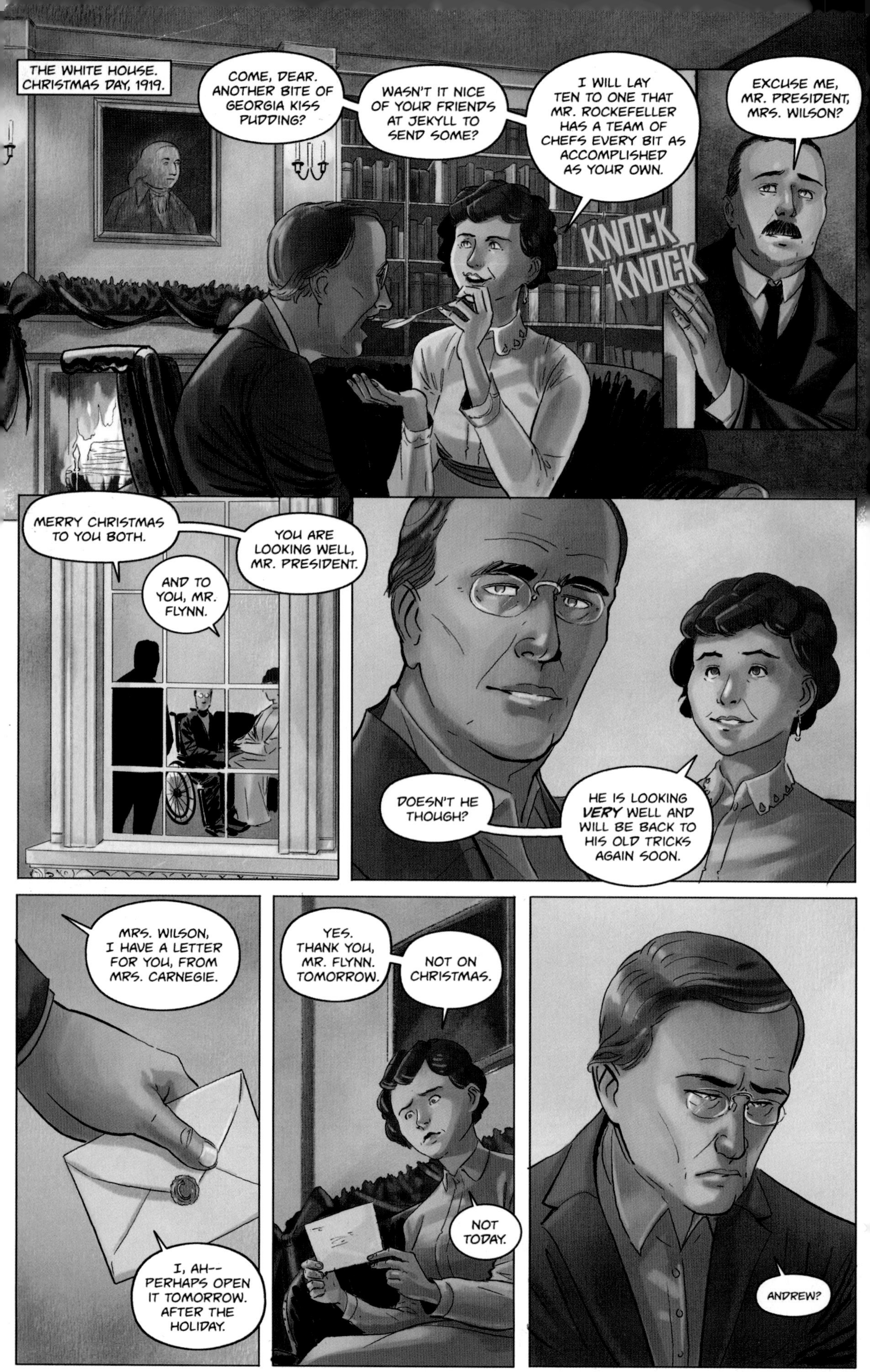
THE WHITE HOUSE. CHRISTMAS DAY, 1919.
COME, DEAR. ANOTHER BITE OF GEORGIA KISS PUDDING?
WASN'T IT NICE OF YOUR FRIENDS AT JEKYLL TO SEND SOME?
I WILL LAY TEN TO ONE THAT MR. ROCKEFELLER HAS A TEAM OF CHEFS EVERY BIT AS ACCOMPLISHED AS YOUR OWN.
KNOCK KNOCK
EXCUSE ME, MR. PRESIDENT, MRS. WILSON?
MERRY CHRISTMAS TO YOU BOTH.
YOU ARE LOOKING WELL, MR. PRESIDENT.
AND TO YOU, MR. FLYNN.
DOESN'T HE THOUGH?
HE IS LOOKING VERY WELL AND WILL BE BACK TO HIS OLD TRICKS AGAIN SOON.
MRS. WILSON, I HAVE A LETTER FOR YOU, FROM MRS. CARNEGIE.
I, AH-- PERHAPS OPEN IT TOMORROW. AFTER THE HOLIDAY.
YES. THANK YOU, MR. FLYNN. TOMORROW.
NOT ON CHRISTMAS.
NOT TODAY.
ANDREW?

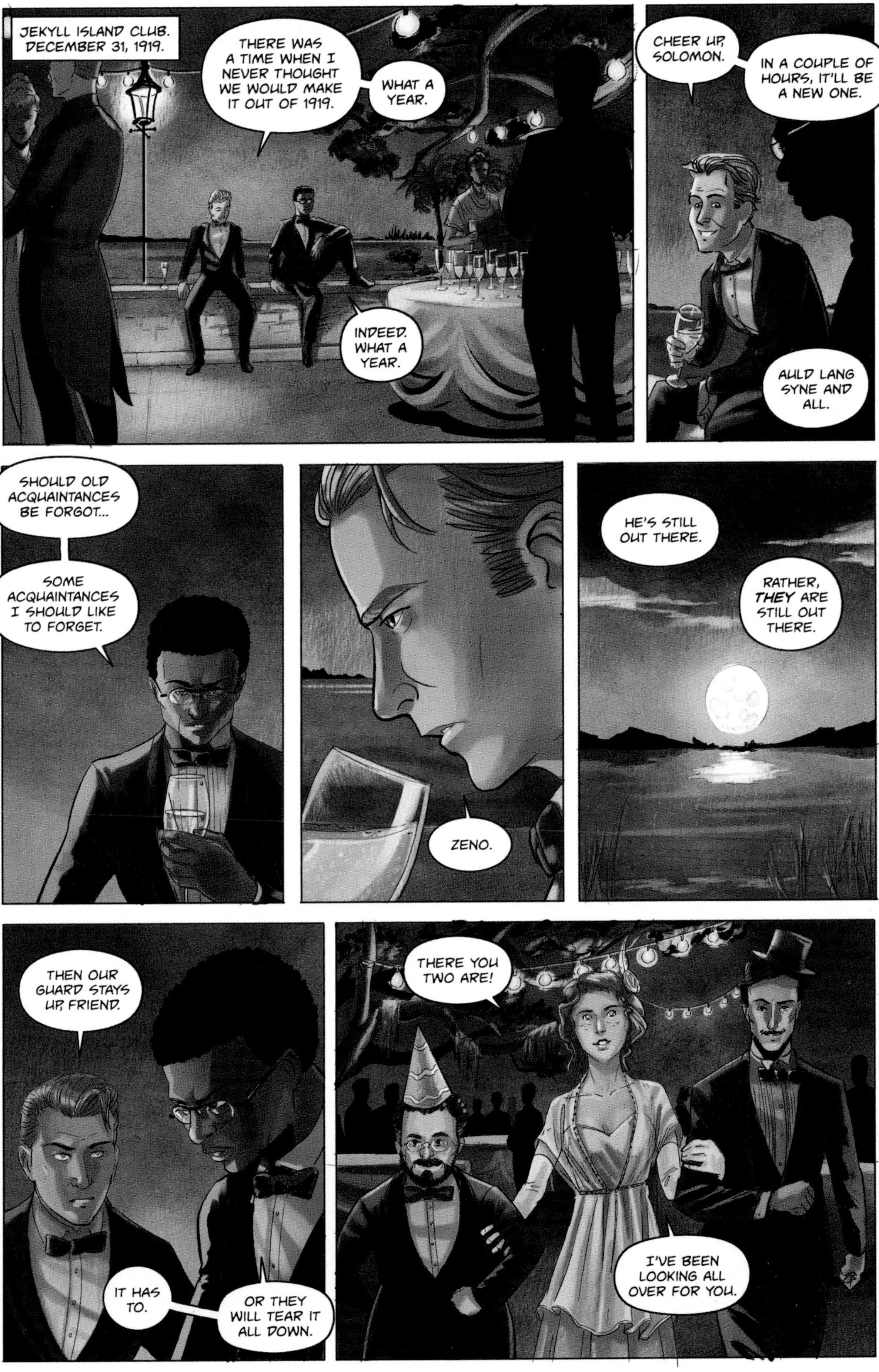
JEKYLL ISLAND CLUB. DECEMBER 31, 1919.
THERE WAS A TIME WHEN I NEVER THOUGHT WE WOULD MAKE IT OUT OF 1919.
WHAT A YEAR.
INDEED. WHAT A YEAR.
CHEER UP, SOLOMON.
IN A COUPLE OF HOURS, IT'LL BE A NEW ONE.
AULD LANG SYNE AND ALL.
SHOULD OLD ACQUAINTANCES BE FORGOT...
SOME ACQUAINTANCES I SHOULD LIKE TO FORGET.
ZENO.
HE'S STILL OUT THERE.
RATHER, *THEY* ARE STILL OUT THERE.
THEN OUR GUARD STAYS UP, FRIEND.
IT HAS TO.
OR THEY WILL TEAR IT ALL DOWN.
THERE YOU TWO ARE!
I'VE BEEN LOOKING ALL OVER FOR YOU.

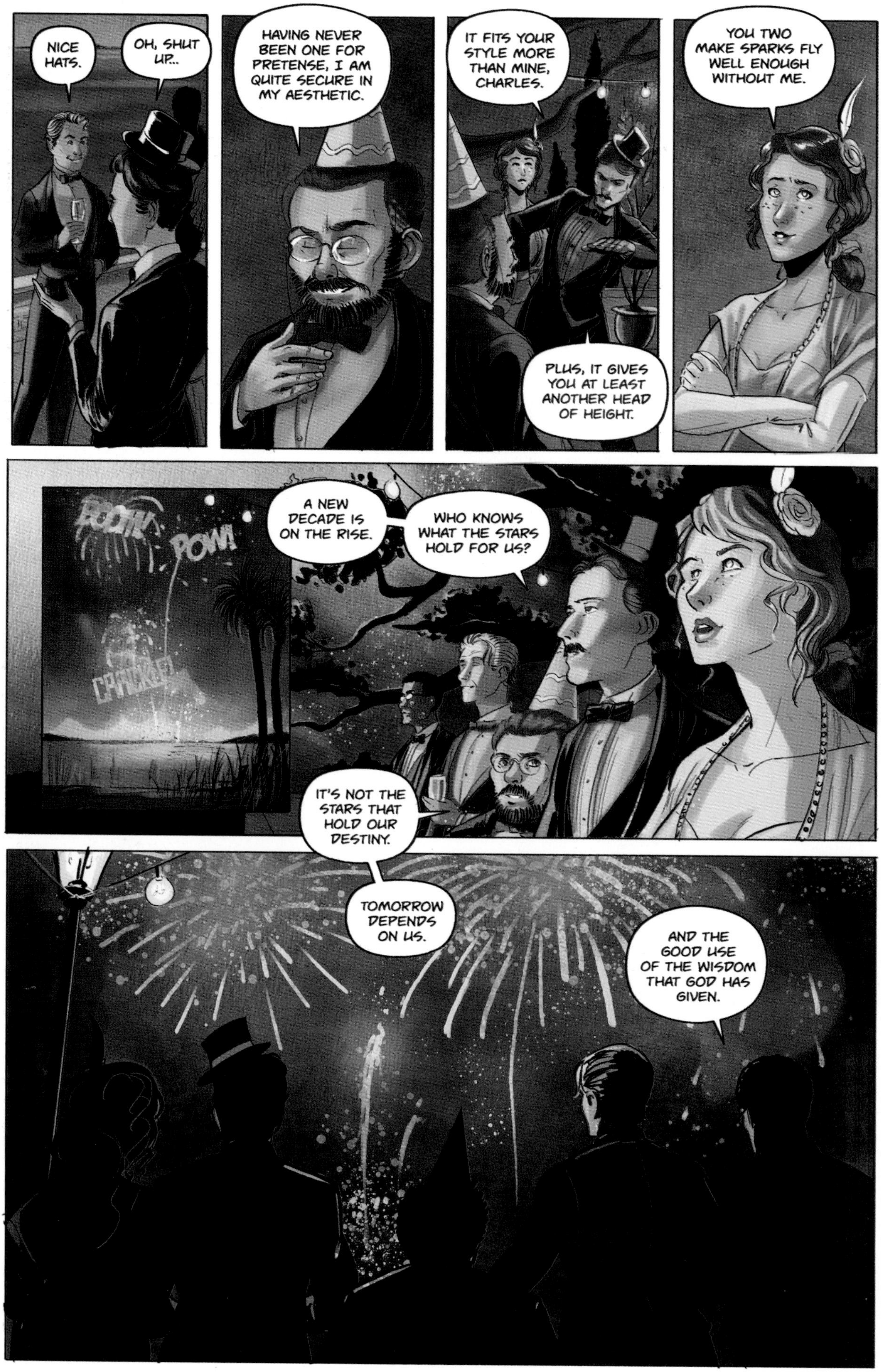
NICE HATS.
OH, SHUT UP...
HAVING NEVER BEEN ONE FOR PRETENSE, I AM QUITE SECURE IN MY AESTHETIC.
IT FITS YOUR STYLE MORE THAN MINE, CHARLES.
PLUS, IT GIVES YOU AT LEAST ANOTHER HEAD OF HEIGHT.
YOU TWO MAKE SPARKS FLY WELL ENOUGH WITHOUT ME.
BOOM!
POW!
CRACKLE!
A NEW DECADE IS ON THE RISE.
WHO KNOWS WHAT THE STARS HOLD FOR US?
IT'S NOT THE STARS THAT HOLD OUR DESTINY.
TOMORROW DEPENDS ON US.
AND THE GOOD USE OF THE WISDOM THAT GOD HAS GIVEN.

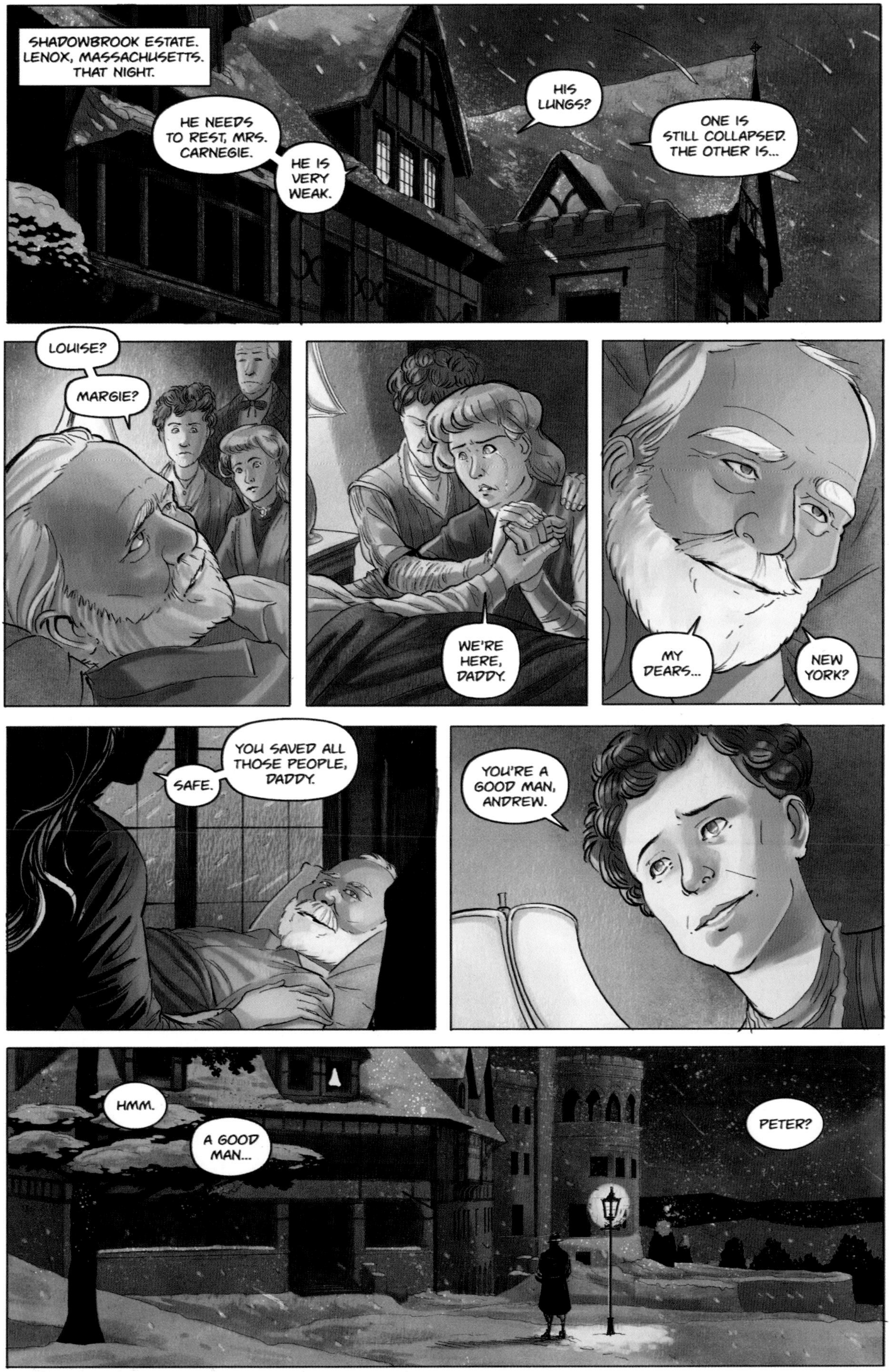
SHADOWBROOK ESTATE. LENOX, MASSACHUSETTS. THAT NIGHT.
HE NEEDS TO REST, MRS. CARNEGIE.
HE IS VERY WEAK.
HIS LUNGS?
ONE IS STILL COLLAPSED. THE OTHER IS...
LOUISE?
MARGIE?
WE'RE HERE, DADDY.
MY DEARS...
NEW YORK?
YOU SAVED ALL THOSE PEOPLE, DADDY.
SAFE.
YOU'RE A GOOD MAN, ANDREW.
HMM.
A GOOD MAN...
PETER?

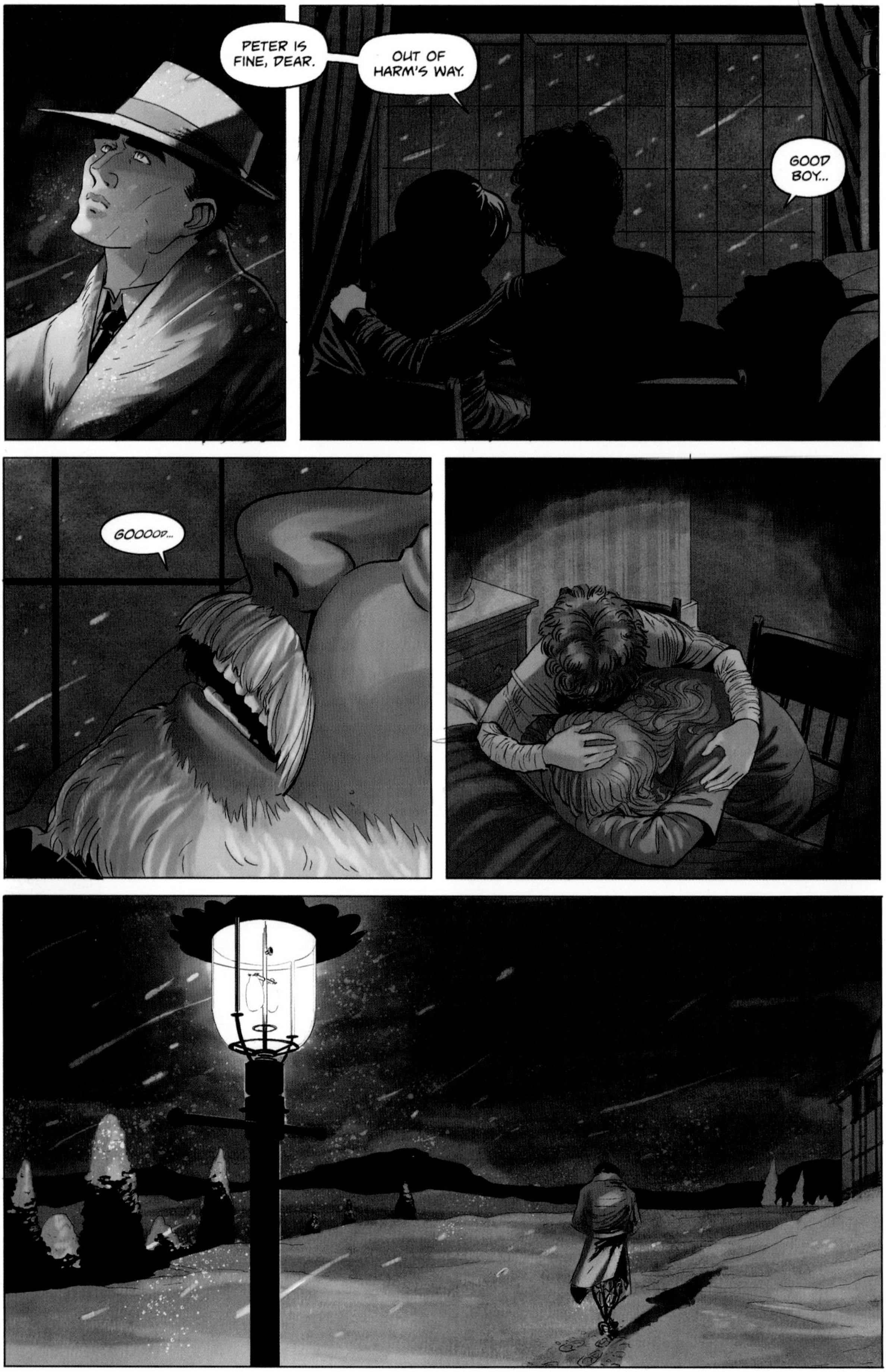
PETER IS FINE, DEAR.
OUT OF HARM'S WAY.
GOOD BOY...
GOOOOD...

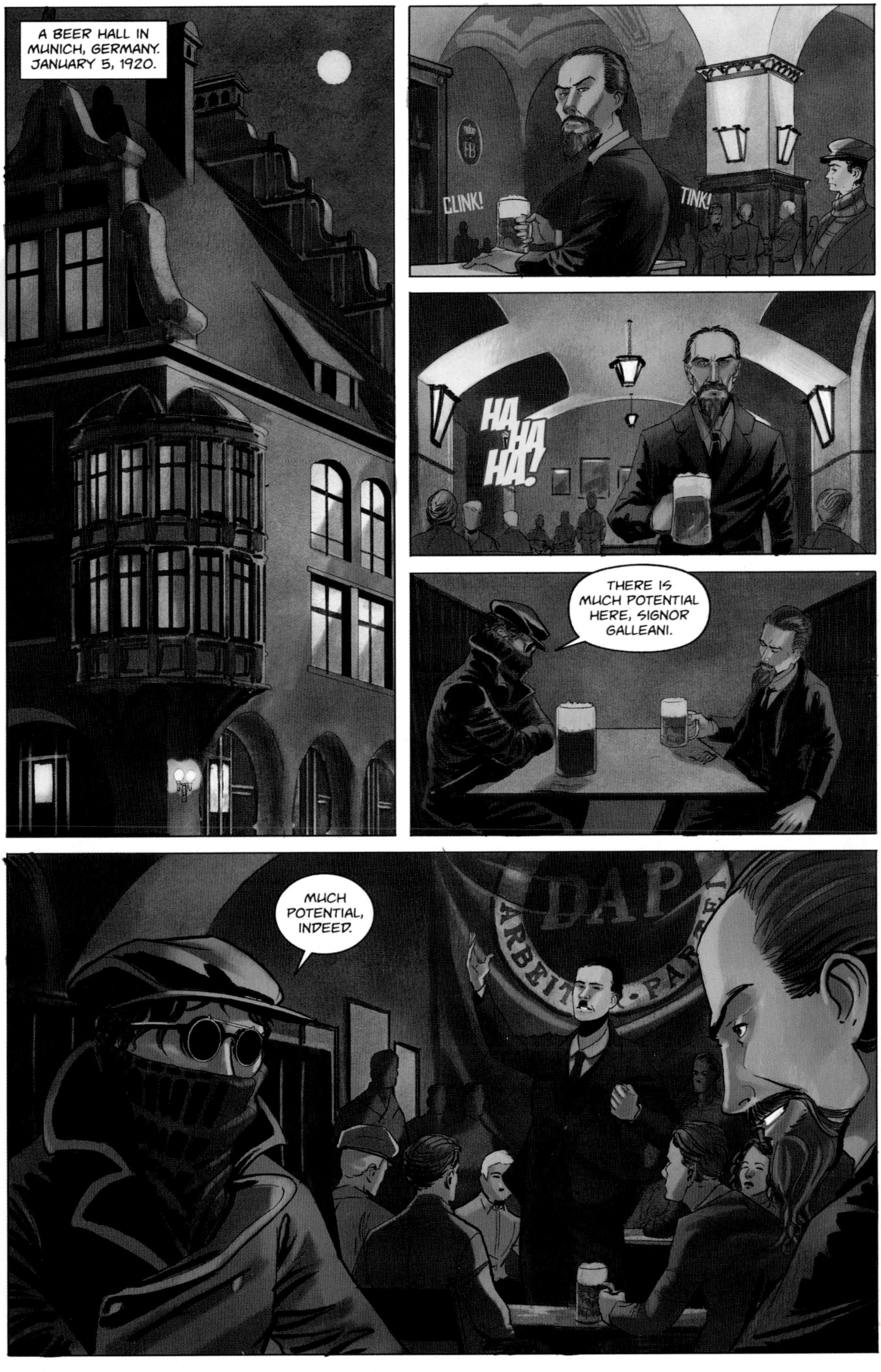

A BEER HALL IN MUNICH, GERMANY. JANUARY 5, 1920.
CLINK!
TINK!
HA HA HA!
THERE IS MUCH POTENTIAL HERE, SIGNOR GALLEANI.
MUCH POTENTIAL, INDEED.
DAP
ARBEIT

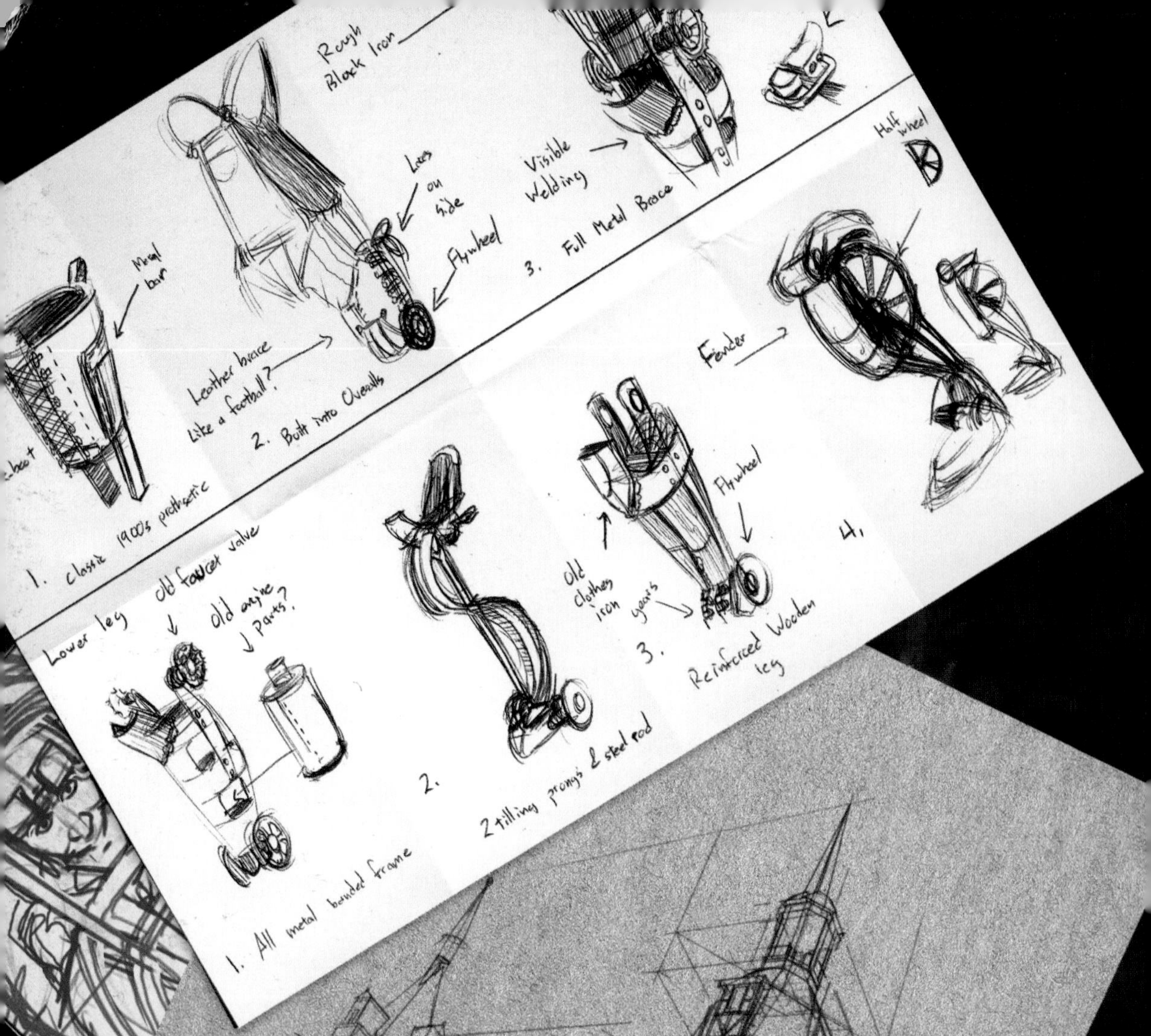
Rough Black Iron
Visible Welding
Full Metal Brace
Half wheel
Laces on side
Flywheel
Metal bar
Leather brace Like a football?
2. Built into Overalls
3.
1. classic 1900's prosthetic
Fender
4.
Lower leg
Old faucet valve
Old engine parts?
Old clothes iron
gears
Flywheel
3. Reinforced Wooden leg
2.
2 tilling prongs & steel rod
1. All metal banded frame

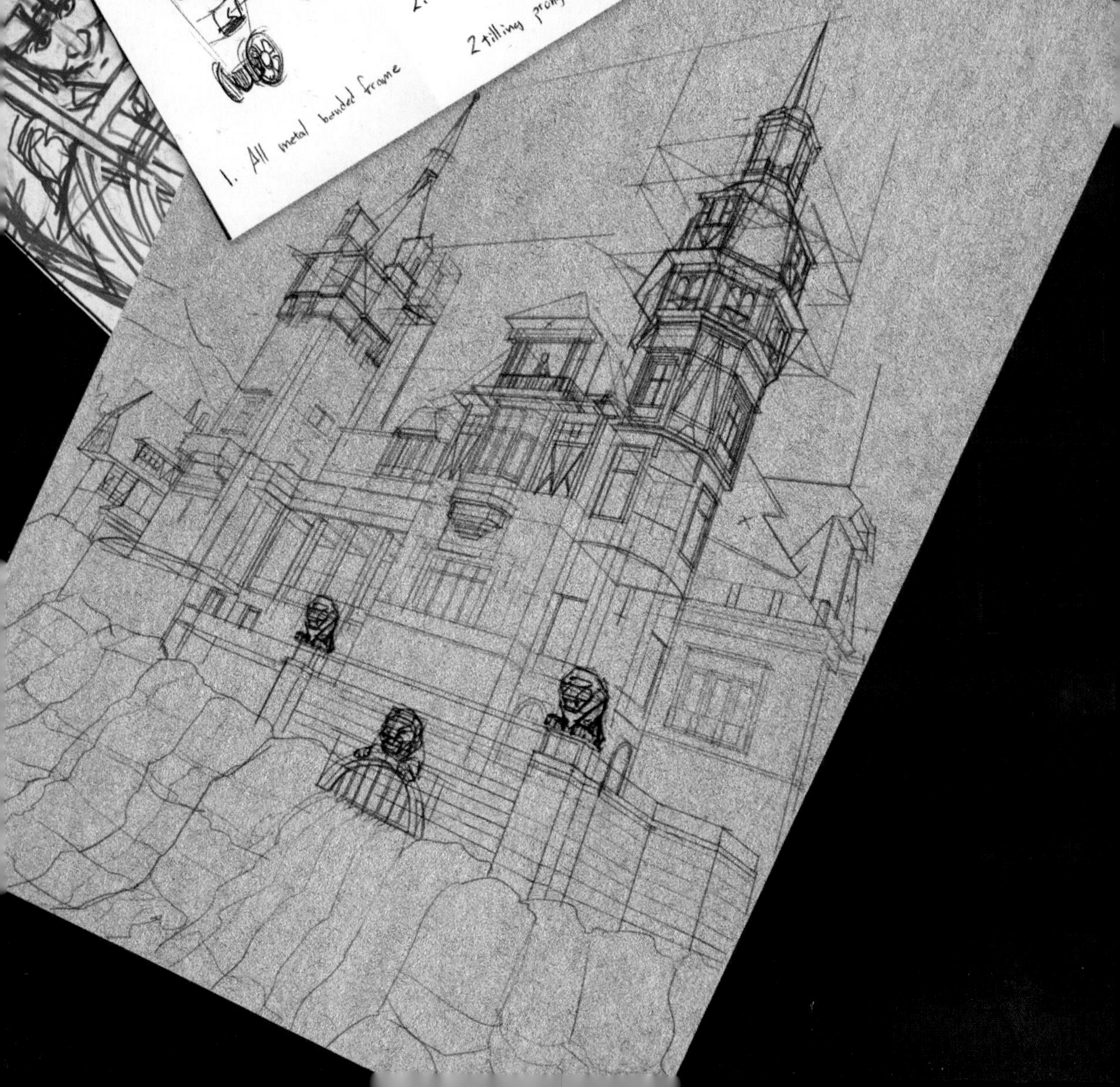

Kickstarter Acknowledgments:

To those that helped fund this project and encouraged us in our vision,
by giving at the highest levels:

Steve Gormally
Blacktop Creative
Thomas Crowell
Wayne and Robin Hoover
Brent Monroe
Michael & Lucinda Falkenberry
Sharon & Neil Gordon
Don Barden
Joel Leveille
Arthur Greeno
Garret Rutherford
Keith Kiser
Michael (a donor and friend of the project)
Paul Dennis
Don and Sandra Caswell
Steve Hester

Shani Godwin
Michael Nedvidek
Hannah Hardgrave
Dee Dee and Mark Walker
Jeannie Haralson
David (a donor and friend of the project)
Jay Morgan
Mark Miller
Phil Orazi
David Williams

Fred Reimer
Lisa Churchfield
In Memory of Dr. William Hardgrave

Meet the Creators

This project was dreamed up by the Lost Mountain Mechanicals:
three working grown-ups, all with families and all with careers, who just
decided to do something different—create a graphic novel series.

STEVE NEDVIDEK has worked in film, radio, and television and
received his Masters Degree in Theater from Wake Forest University,
where he completed his thesis in make-up design. He is an avid cartoonist,
model maker, writer, and movie watcher, and resides in the Atlanta suburbs
with his wife, three kids, and dog.

ED CROWELL holds advanced degrees in political science and
international affairs. He is an executive at a non-profit and a writer with
dozens of published articles. A lifelong fan of science fiction and fantasy,
he and his wife have two children who went off to college, but left Ed and
Cynthia with two cats, a fish, and a dog.

JACK LOWE is a student of film making and themed entertainment.
A passionate storyteller with a bent toward immersive, multi-sensory
experiences, Jack and his wife, three children, two dogs, and two cats live in
a 150-year-old farmhouse near Lost Mountain in Georgia.

J. MOSES NESTER is a graduate of the Savannah College of Art
and Design and now works as a freelance comic artist. His stories have
appeared in the *Horizon Anthology Vol. 1* and the *Game On* anthology.
Follow his work at partthewaters.tumblr.com.

S.J. MILLER is a graduate of the Savannah College of Art and Design and
is currently based out of Las Vegas, Nevada. Her favorite things include
science fiction, horror, and exploring exciting new ways to tell stories.
Follow her work at sjmillerart.com.

(From L to R) Ed Crowell, Steve Nedvidek, Jack Lowe

PHOTOGRAPH COURTESY OF ADAM LOWE.

J. Moses Nester

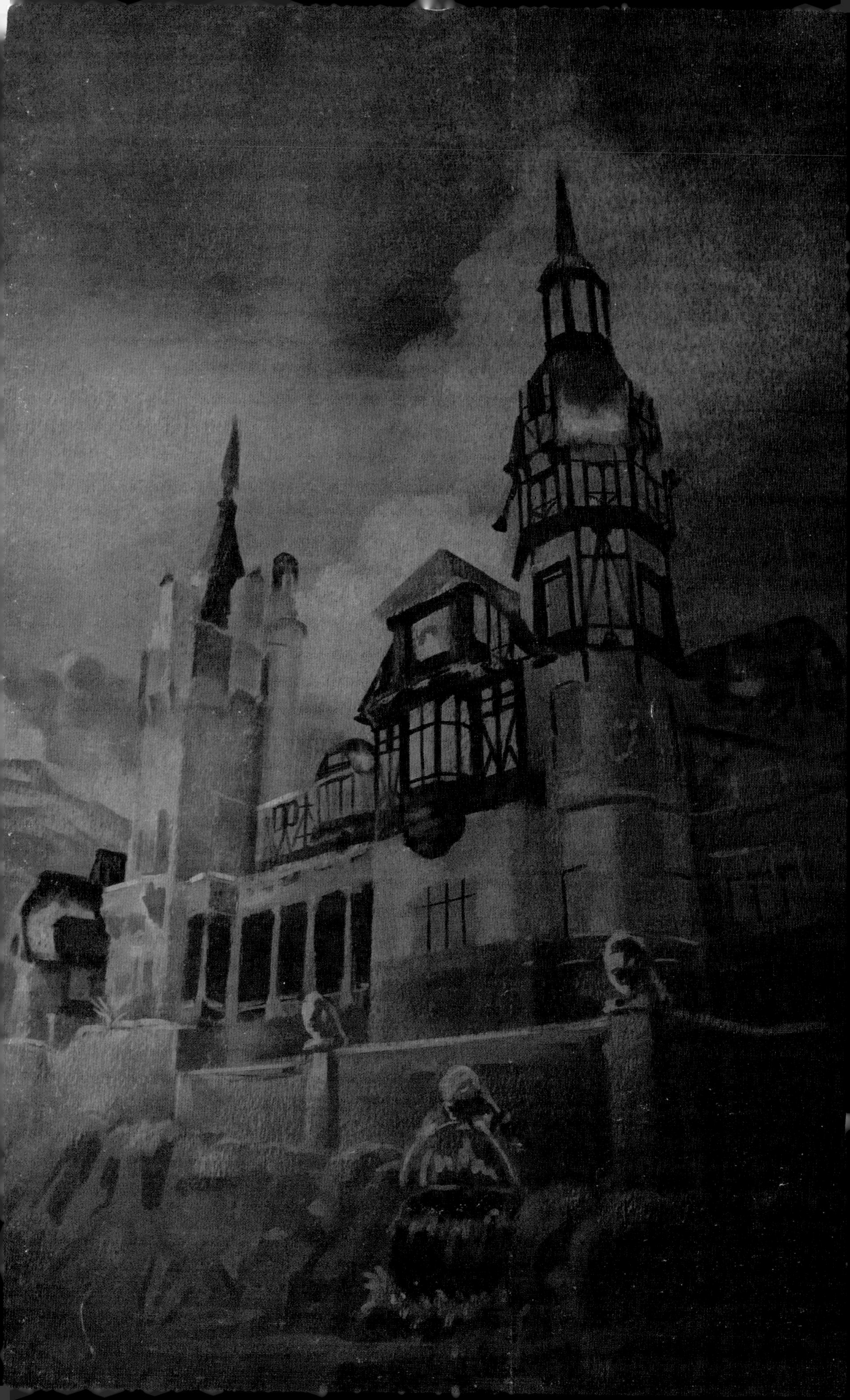